Lincoln

AND THE RADICALS

T. HARRY WILLIAMS

THE UNIVERSITY OF WISCONSIN PRESS

Published 1941
The University of Wisconsin Press
Box 1379, Madison, Wisconsin 53701
The University of Wisconsin Press, Ltd.
70 Great Russell Street, London

Printings 1941, 1960, 1965, 1972

Printed in the United States of America
ISBN 0-299-00274-8, LC 41-53088

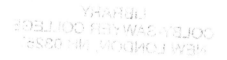

To my father

Introduction to the Third Printing

IT IS A STRANGE and stringent task for an author to evaluate one of his own books. In any case his reactions are likely to be mixed, but they are particularly confused if the book happens to be his first effort, written long years ago when he was just out of graduate school, and if, in addition, it presents a point of view which was prevalent then but has since been challenged, one, indeed, which he himself may have partially retreated from. The author of such a book will experience a variety of feelings—a surprised pride that his work still looks so good, a definite chagrin that he said certain things, a stubborn conviction that his thesis is basically sound, and, following immediately, a scholarly compulsion to admit that that thesis may need some modification.

Certainly I felt all of these emotions when I prepared to write an introduction for this printing of *Lincoln and the Radicals*. The book was originally published in 1941 and was written in the three preceding years. It was an extension and an enlargement of a doctoral dissertation on the Committee on the Conduct of the War completed at the University of Wisconsin under the direction of the late William B. Hesseltine. Although the book was drastically different from the dissertation, based on additional research and written anew, it displayed some qualities often found in a dissertation—and also in a first book. It did not hesitate to hand down judgments on people and events, and it did not boggle to state cases. Looking at these judgments now, I can see that a few of them are extreme and, looking at these cases, I can see that some of them are overstated. If I were saying it now, I would not change many of the opinions, but I would alter the emphasis in some of them, would soften or qualify the youthful certainty that marks some of them.

vii

These opinions, indeed the whole book, reflect the intellectual influences that played on all people who attended the graduate schools in the 1930's. Partly the product of the immediate environment, partly a continuation of previous philosophies, the intellectual thought of the time induced definite and peculiar thought patterns in the people exposed to it. Possibly because it was an era of social and economic division, students of history tended to see similar divisions in the past. For other reasons, all of them enshrined in current concepts of historical causation, they usually saw these conflicts in certain terms. Most of the differences that had appeared in American history, for example, were expressions of the clashing aspirations of economic groups, and sometimes of the desires of classes that were conscious of their identity. Even if Americans had not always been conscious of class, they had at least been aware of their material interests, and on frequent occasions they had been willing to act to better those interests. Economic motives, in fact, were the strongest force that moved men to mass action in historical situations.

One specific group had always been more conscious of its interests than all others, and more cohesive in its action and more calculating in its strategy. This was the business-banking faction, which rose to power during the Civil War and dominated the national scene in the years after Appomattox. The knowing historian of the 1930's was impressed, often overly so, with the machinations of the businessmen. He was likely to conclude that they controlled most political situations and most politicians. He was also likely to be suspicious of politicians, and other people too, who professed to act for motives other than economic ones, who, for instance, talked of moral or abstract principles. He would suspect that they might be masking something and would try to find out what it was.

The kind of history produced in the environment of the 1930's had undeniable virtues. It was a tough-minded kind of history, skeptical of any existing view, not afraid to advance a new view, even if that view questioned the most respectable historical opinions or personages. It had equally undeniable faults. It tended to exaggerate the importance of the economic element in human motivation and to overlook or subordinate other motives. As a result, it often presented a too simplistic picture of the past, and at its worst it offered a cynical, debunking portrait of the past. Today's historians, who are also products of a peculiar environment, are aware of the faults of the earlier school—some of them certainly call enough attention to these faults—but they do not always seem to realize that the earlier group had some virtues or that their own technique may have some shortcomings.

Today's historians think that they have a more sophisticated approach to the problem of human motivation than their predecessors, and there is much to justify the assumption. The findings of various allied disciplines, notably in the behavorial sciences, have opened up whole new avenues of analysis to the historian. Hardly any of us today would think to explain any episode of the past as the result of a single simple cause, economic or otherwise. And yet in the scamper to get away from the single-cause concept we may have lost something, some of that tough-minded skepticism that is a necessary attribute in the historian. Perhaps we now incline to underrate the significance of the economic factor. It just may be that we accept too easily the professions of actors in history as to their motivation—especially if the actors profess noble, moral principles which seem similar to certain principles fashionable in our own time.

We may have lost something else in the new approach. The history written in the last two decades plays down the notion that the divisions among Americans in the past have been very deep or very serious. The divisions that have occurred were few, we are told, and they were not over fundamentals. Americans have always agreed on principles and goals and have differed only as to the methods, which is not an important difference. It is a concept that has been called the history of consensus and consent. It has much to recommend it. Americans, the most pragmatic and practical people in the world, have exhibited an obvious moderation and unity in most of their controversies with one another. We can recognize this truth, and yet we should also recognize that there is a danger in the consensus concept. Carried to an extreme, it invests crucial episodes in our history with too much sweetness and love—great crises are made to seem like church festivals—and it leaves the record with its own brand of unreality. After all, we have had divisions among us, and some of them have been fairly divisive. One of them was so serious that it strains the best efforts of even the best adjusters to find consensus in it. It split the nation into wrangling sections and then threw it into civil war—and finally caused a bitter division among the supporters of the war in the majority section as to how that war should be conducted.

The reactions to *Lincoln and the Radicals* over the years have reflected the changing styles in historical interpretations. Reviewers of the original edition praised it as a pioneer work in Civil War politics and civil-military relations, and this evaluation stood for a satisfying period. But in recent years some historians, although admitting the factual accuracy of its story, have challenged some of the interpretations I drew from the facts. The book has become, in fact, something of a whipping boy for revisionist writers who, influenced by the ideals of their own time, cannot resist revising the picture of an earlier time to make it accord with their ideals. These critics have charged the book with certain faults, most of which can be wrapped up in one impeachment: it presents an analysis of Civil War politics that is too simple, too much written in clichés.

I would agree that some of the criticisms are in part justified. If I were rewriting the book, I would, as I have indicated, change the emphasis in some generalizations. For instance, the statement in the first chapter concerning the economic cohesiveness of Republicans and Radicals is exaggerated and needs modification. Not all Republicans and Radicals had the simple economic creed that I ascribe to them. But I would also contend that some of those who today talk of nothing but the economic diversity of Republican beliefs need themselves to do some more thinking about the subject. A great deal of investigation in the area of what might be called the Republican economic image will have to be done before any of us can generalize safely on this subject.

I would alter the emphasis in other parts of the book. Although I indicated the weaknesses of General McClellan, I would now focus more attention on those weaknesses; I would say that he failed because he was a poor soldier as well as because he aroused political opposition. While I was appraising leaders, I would upgrade the evaluation of President Lincoln, make the portrait of him more positive, and pay tribute to his superb political skills and his devotion to pragmatic reform. I would also make somewhat more positive the portrait of the Radicals, stressing that they were the firmest of nationalists, the men who would never give up the Union, and recognizing that they represented a powerful moral urge in American society. That urge was the antislavery movement and, although I conceded its force in the Republican party and in the country, I would now credit it with greater potency.

But the main thesis of the book I would not alter, at least not in a substantial way. It so happens that this is the thesis that has been most strongly challenged. The criticisms of it run as follows. It is a mistake to depict the political history of the Civil War as revolving around a controversy between President Lincoln and the Radical Republicans. True, there were differences in the Republican party, but these differences were only the normal ones that emerge in the ranks of any party in power. Most Republicans, Radicals and Conservatives alike, criticized Lincoln and on the same grounds, that he was a weak leader. The Radicals were not a cohesive, organized faction intent on driving a definite program to victory, and, above all, they were not a vindictive cabal determined to make war on Lincoln. In fact, the opposite to the last generalization is closer to the truth. The Radicals and Lincoln were in basic agreement on most issues and moved together to a common goal—and so even the Civil War

moves into the harmonious atmosphere of consensus history.
This presentation of rather intricate and delicate Republican rivalries I would have to reject. By my reading of the story, it is a strained and unrealistic interpretation. It is only fair to say, however, that all of us who argue the issue are caught up in problems of semantics. Just how specific or cohesive does a political group have to be to be labeled a faction? How definite a program does such a group have to have to be named a cabal? What degree of savagery or bitterness in its members justifies calling them vindictive? What measure of extremism in a political faction makes it deserving of the title radical? If we could agree on answers to these questions, which is probably impossible, we could advance to a clearer understanding of Civil War politics. As a first step, we would have to define who and what the Radicals were. To employ a sociological term, we would have to "structure" the Radicals.

In a longer essay elsewhere ("Lincoln and the Radicals," in Grady McWhiney, ed., *Grant, Lee, Lincoln and the Radicals,* Northwestern University Press, 1964, pp. 92–117), I have attempted to supply such a structure. Here I can only summarize the argument. The typical Radical—whether he be Charles Sumner, Thaddeus Stevens, or Benjamin F. Wade —was not a normal political type. The typical politician, although he may have his principles, is essentially pragmatic; he will compromise on the application of principle to achieve a settlement that everybody can live with. The Radicals were men of principle who, on the issue of slavery, would not compromise. They were men of morality who advocated an absolute solution. Before 1860 they were a singularly frustrated group. They saw a great evil, slavery, which they wanted to eradicate, but they could not lay hands on it. In their way stood the insuperable difficulty of the amending process. They would, very likely, have remained a frustrated, and a bitter, faction if the South had not seceded from the Union. The Southern action created a revolutionary situation. It brought to power in the national government the

Radicals, doctrinaires who if the South had not left would not have had power, political types who in American politics usually hover on the edge of power rather than being at its center.

In a revolutionary situation the Radicals reacted like true revolutionaries. Now they could put through their program; they could uproot the great evil. But obstacles still stood in their path. The greatest was Abraham Lincoln, the supreme American pragmatist. Lincoln was as antislavery as any Radical, but he would approach the problem in a different way, with the cautious empiricism of the politician rather than with the headlong rush of the theorist. Men as committed as were the Radicals had to oppose Lincoln, had to try to overrule him, even though he was the leader of their party. They did, it seems to me, make war on him in the political sense. Whether or not they were a cabal is a semantic irrelevancy. They were a definite faction and they knew what they were and they knew where they were going. Their greatest objection to Lincoln is the most revealing key to their nature. They were scornful of him, but not primarily because they regarded him as an inept leader or administrator. Rather, it was that he had no appreciation of doctrine, of moral theory. He was not a blueprint man. Men who did appreciate these things might unfortunately have to work with Lincoln—after all, he was President—but they would never cease their efforts to push and educate and remake him.

And so, I still believe, the concept of the conflict between Lincoln and the Radicals has validity, is of value in helping us to understand the Civil War. The mistake of the consensus historians, it seems to me, is in trying to fit the war into a normal American political pattern. The situation that created the war was not normal, the war itself was not normal, and the politics of the war could not have been normal.

Baton Rouge, Louisiana   T. HARRY WILLIAMS
March, 1965

Contents

LINCOLN AND THE RADICALS

1

A House Divided

ON A WARM JUNE NIGHT in 1862 an impassioned orator stood before a New York audience at Cooper Union, "the nation's forum." He was analyzing the radical and conservative factions in the Republican Party that were struggling for the mastery of the administration of Abraham Lincoln. Owen Lovejoy of Illinois belonged to the radical faith. Zealous, fiery, the Calvinist minister in politics, hating slavery since a mob had murdered his abolitionist brother twenty-five years before, he had prophesied in the House of Representatives long before the Civil War that the slaves would walk to emancipation as the children of Israel had journeyed to the Promised Land, "through the *Red* Sea." Now he faced his metropolitan listeners, a Jeremiah from the Western prairies, to denounce those moderate, conservative elements in the Republican organization whose influence prevented Lincoln from converting the war against the Southern Confederacy into a holy crusade for the destruction of slavery. "The President," cried Lovejoy, "is like a man driving a horse in the thills of a buggy, and leading another behind him by the halter-strap. The one in the shafts is a most superb animal—broad between the eyes, ears small, short around the throat, stifle full and hard, short coupled, and can clear ditch and hedge, high spirited and fast." This was the radical steed, eager to pull driver and buggy along the road of freedom, but it was held back by the conservative horse in the rear, a miserable, awkward, lagging beast. Lincoln contributed to the creeping progress of the vehicle by reining in the champing creature in front, because he too was slow and cautious. But, concluded Lovejoy, "If he does not drive as fast as I would, he is on the right road, and it is only a question of time."[1]

[1] *New York Tribune,* June 13, 1862, p. 1.

More than a year before, in Boston, another product of
Calvinism in politics, Wendell Phillips, the eloquent voice of
New England abolitionism, spoke in similar scornful terms of
the president he had supported in the election of 1860 and the
conservatives in the Republican Party. At Tremont Temple,
packed with his tumultuous followers, Phillips castigated Lincoln for his seeming intention to conduct the government without striking a vigorous blow at slavery, and predicted, "A pawn
on the political chessboard, his value is in his position; with
fair effort, we may soon change him for knight, bishop, or
queen, and sweep the board." The Republican Party had
timidly undertaken the solution of the slavery problem, he said,
but the drift of events and the pressure of the radicals would
force it to champion complete emancipation and political
equality for the liberated slaves. Phillips' forecast was amaz-
ingly accurate. Lincoln remained a harried figure on the chessboard, but the radicals captured all the pieces. Years later, near
the close of the war, Phillips exultingly referred to the victorious consummation of the radical program despite conservative opposition: "the administration has wished, many
times, but has been unable to resist the Revolution. It has
overborne them."[2]

☆

No polyglot army of an ancient emperor ever exhibited
more variety than did the Republican Party in 1860. Within
its diverse ranks were radicals and abolitionists who wanted to
destroy every vestige of slavery, moderates who would have
been content to restrict its expansion into the territories,
Whigs, Free-Soilers, and antislavery Democrats, Eastern manufacturers who hoped for a protective tariff and Western farmers
who favored free trade, hardened machine politicians and
visionary reformers. Two threads of unity bound this hetero-
geneous coalition into the semblance of a national organization. Each constituent part was opposed, although with varying

[2] *Speeches, Lectures, and Letters of Wendell Phillips* (Boston, 1881),
294, 305, 314; Phillips to George W. Julian, March 27, 1864, in the Joshua
Giddings-George W. Julian MSS. in the Library of Congress.

intensity, to the institution of Negro slavery. And the party broadly represented the social ideology of the "free," capitalistic society of the North, whose ruling middle class felt it must strike down the political power of the slavocracy in order to complete its economic control of the nation.

There was a right and a left wing in the party even before 1860. The moderates were typified by Lincoln, the courtly Orville H. Browning of Illinois, James R. Doolittle of Wisconsin, and Vermont's venerable Jacob Collamer. They advocated the gradual extinction of slavery, compensated emancipation, and colonization of the Negroes in another land. They detested slavery, and believed the institution could not survive the strain of a long civil war. But they also feared and distrusted the revolutionary ardor of the radicals and the spirit of fanaticism that was inherent in the abolitionists. They opposed the wartime abolition of slavery except as a final measure of military necessity to prevent the disruption of the Union.[3] Hence the conservatives fought from the beginning the hasty plans of the radicals to bring about immediate emancipation. Temperamentally they objected to the reforming zeal of the radicals. Furthermore, unlike the abolitionists, they had some appreciation of the practical difficulties that would follow the sudden liberation of several million slaves. The conservatives were reasonable, able men, but their very virtues rendered them incapable of coping with the determined radicals in a revolutionary period. In contrast to the radicals, the moderates were negative and vacillating, lacking a cohesive program of consistent action.

The radicals were the real driving power in the party. They were the men whom young John Hay, Lincoln's secretary, who had encountered their fierce prototypes of the French Revolution in his superficial reading, dubbed the Jacobins. Aggressive, vindictive, and narrowly sectional, the radicals hated slavery with a bitter personal feeling. But more than slavery they hated its political representatives, the proud cavaliers who had

[3] Speech of Senator James Dixon of Connecticut in the *Congressional Globe*, 37 Congress, 1 Session, 119; speech of Senator Browning, *ibid.*, 189.

dominated Congress in the fifties and who had scourged the sputtering radical minority with polished gibes. Unlike many of the moderates, the Jacobins welcomed the outbreak of civil war as the longed-for opportunity to destroy slavery and to drive the "slave traders" from the national temple. In 1861 they had opposed attempts at compromise which might have averted secession. Conciliation of the sections would have deprived the Republican Party of its excuse for being; would, thought Michigan's Zachariah Chandler, "rupture" the organization. Chandler worked vigorously against compromise, and calmly welcomed the holocaust: "Without a little bloodletting, this Union will not . . . be worth a rush!"⁴ The radicals stood for instant emancipation, the confiscation of "rebel" property, the use of colored soldiers, civil and, when it should become expedient, political equality for the Negro. They loved the Negro less for himself than as an instrument with which they might fasten Republican political and economic control upon the South. Closely associated with the Jacobins, but more sincerely radical, were the abolitionists. Fanatical and impractical, their motto was that of all revolutionaries, "Let there be justice even though the heavens crumble." The abolitionists, within yet beyond the party, often forced the radical politicos to adopt a more extreme position than the exigencies of the moment warranted.

The Jacobins were led by master politicians. In the House of Representatives, caustic, terrifying, clubfooted old Thaddeus Stevens ran the Republican machine, hurling his devastating taunts equally at Democrats, Republican laggards, the president, and "the vile ingredient called conservatism, which is worse than secessionism."⁵ In the Senate the radical leaders were Ohio's "Bluff Ben" Wade, endowed with a brutal wit, who had first won fame by offering to meet the Southern hotspurs upon the field of honor with squirrel rifles at thirty

⁴ Chandler to Governor Austin Blair, February 11, 1861, quoted on page 190 of the *Life of Zachariah Chandler*, by writers of the Detroit *Post and Tribune* (Detroit, 1880); *Detroit Free Press*, April 26, 1863.

⁵ Phrase used by Stevens in a letter of November 17, 1862, in the Thaddeus Stevens MSS. in the Library of Congress.

paces as the weapons; grim, furious Zack Chandler, "Xanthippe in pants," who bossed Michigan politics with an iron hand and a liberal supply of liquor; and Charles Sumner of Massachusetts, handsome, scholarly, and humorless, despised by many radicals for his cant, but valued as an impressive show-window display.

There were economic as well as political factions in the party, but the fissures of separation were narrower here. The Northern bourgeoisie sought through the Republican organization to complete "the industrial revolution" by wresting political power from the slavocracy, and for this class the party horoscope forecast fat rewards. To the owners of the spindles, the looms, and the iron furnaces of the Northeast, it promised a protective tariff. To business in general it offered a national banking system controlled by the financial interests, government subsidies for the construction of railroads, and free access to the rich resources of the public domain. To less fortunate members of the middle class and to the Northwestern farmers plagued by inadequate transportation facilities, it held forth the hope of free homesteads and federal aid for the improvement of rivers and harbors and for the building of railroads and canals. Eastern nabobs and Western agrarians might quarrel, as they did immediately after the war, over the tariff, but in 1860 they closed their ranks against a common foe, the planter aristocrats.[6]

No one better expressed the Republican ideal of a competitive capitalistic society, with freedom of economic opportunity for the middle class, disenthralled from the dominance of a feudal aristocracy, than did Abraham Lincoln as he analyzed

[6] The Republicans enacted most of their economic program into law during the war: the Morrill tariff, the Homestead Act, subsidies for the transcontinental railroads, and the establishment of the national bank system. Differences within the party grew out of disputes as to whether real or personal property should bear the burden of war taxation. Representative Sydney Edgerton of Ohio attacked one of Stevens' revenue bills because it bore heavily upon agriculture and favored "the great stockholders, the money lenders, and the merchant princes of Wall street, and all the great capitalists." *Congressional Globe,* 37 Congress, 1 Session, 282. See *ibid.,* 325–326, for similar remarks by Isaac N. Arnold of Illinois.

the issues of the war in his first message to Congress. "This is essentially a people's contest," he said. "On the side of the Union it is a struggle for maintaining in the world that form and substance of government whose leading object is to elevate the condition of men—to lift artificial weights from all shoulders; to clear the paths of laudable pursuit for all; to afford all an unfettered start, and a fair chance in the race of life."[7]

Senator John Sherman of industrial Ohio phrased the economic objectives of his party more bluntly: "We know very well that the great objects which those who elected Mr. Lincoln expect him to accomplish will be to secure to free labor its just right to the Territories of the United States; to protect, as far as practicable, by wise revenue laws, the labor of our people; to secure the public lands to actual settlers, instead of to nonresident speculators; to develop the internal resources of the country by opening new means of communication between the Atlantic and the Pacific."[8]

But the conquering bourgeoisie intended to do more than use their new-fledged political power to consolidate an already dominant economic position. They meant also to extend the new industrial order to the South and make that section an economic adjunct of the North. A "free" capitalistic Dixie would mean a richer market for Northern factories, untapped investment opportunities for Yankee entrepreneurs, and ideological re-enforcements for the protective tariff. These roseate anticipations could not be realized without first destroying slavery. John Sherman pictured for his Senate colleagues the tempting possibilities of an industrialized South unhampered by slave labor:

When I look upon those deep bays, those fertile fields, requiring only energetic labor to develop them, when I see those marts of commerce in the very center of our Atlantic coast, I wonder in amazement that a million of men are not now

[7] John G. Nicolay and John Hay, eds., *The Complete Works of Abraham Lincoln* (New York, 1905), 6:321.

[8] Rachael Sherman Thorndike, ed., *The Sherman Letters* (New York, 1894), 96.

crowded there, delving and striking and working with honest toil for an honest reward. . . . But, sir, there is no other cause [for this lack of development] except simply that labor . . . which has built up New York, New England, and the West, is there degraded by the presence of slaves.[9]

Representative J. K. Moorhead, a henchman of the Pennsylvania iron masters, declared that slavery hindered the material development of the South, that if Kentucky freed her slaves she could develop her iron resources and she would then join Pennsylvania in advocacy of the tariff. "We would have more labor for the laboring men of the country, and we would develop the resources of the country more fully than we have ever done."[10] The Republican plans for the economic renovation of the South envisioned a social revolution which would elevate the Negroes and poorer whites to the top of the political pile. Thus a Southern bourgeoisie would displace the ruling landed aristocracy, to make doubly sure that in the nation the Republican Party and the forces of industrial capitalism would retain the favored position they had won in 1860. Wendell Phillips frankly stated the Republican design for the new South when federal troops occupied Louisiana in 1863. "The whole social system of the Gulf states is to be taken to pieces; every bit of it."[11]

☆

Almost from the day when armed conflict began, the radical and conservative factions clashed over the purposes of the war. Lincoln and the moderates attempted to make the restoration of the Union the sole objective; and they would have restored it, if possible, without at the same time destroying slavery. Senator Browning, who often acted as Lincoln's spokesman, asserted in July, 1861: "For one, I should rejoice to see all the States in rebellion return to their allegiance; and if they return, if they lay down the arms of their rebellion

---

[9] *Congressional Globe,* 37 Congress, 2 Session, 1495.
[10] *Ibid.,* 37 Congress, 1 Session, 204.
[11] *New York Tribune,* January 24, 1863.

and come back to their duties and their obligations, they will be as fully protected, now and at all times hereafter, as they have ever been before, in all their rights, including the ownership, use, and management of slaves."[12]

In the president's mind, the preservation of the American experiment in government overshadowed all other questions. He regarded emancipation as incidental to this larger issue, to be resorted to as a last desperate measure, and then to be initiated by himself as an exercise of the war powers of the executive rather than by Congress. His intense conviction that secession must be crushed at all costs even impelled him to throw overboard considerations of party regularity. By inviting Northern Democrats and Border State slaveholders to accept prominent positions in the administration, he endeavored to enlarge the Republican organization into an all-inclusive Union party, a "popular front" whose one resolution was to end the war quickly and re-establish the nation.

Against this mild program the Jacobins inveighed, ranted, and sneered. Many of them felt that Lincoln was only a well-meaning incompetent who lacked the "inclination to put down this rebellion with the strong hand required."[13] The radicals were determined that the war must not end without the death of slavery. "We cannot afford to go over this ground more than once," wrote aristocratic Charles Francis Adams of Massachusetts. "The slave question must be settled this time once for all." Impetuous George W. Julian, leader of the Indiana radicals, exclaimed that the war would be "an empty mockery of our sufferings and sacrifices" if slavery were spared. "Bluff Ben" Wade declared that if the conflict "continues thirty years and bankrupts the whole nation, I hope to God there will be no peace until we can say there is not a slave in this land." The fervid outbursts of radicals like Julian and Wade against the president's policy were dictated by coolheaded considera-

[12] *Congressional Globe*, 37 Congress, 1 Session, 189.
[13] Grant Goodrich to Senator Lyman Trumbull, July 29, 1861, in the Trumbull MSS. in the Library of Congress. See also Trumbull to M. C. Lea, November 5, 1861, in Horace White, *Life of Lyman Trumbull* (Boston, 1913), 171–172.

tion of political expediency. If after a short war the Southern states returned to the Union with the institution of slavery still intact and the political control of the slaveholders unshaken, Republican influence in the government would be nullified and the economic revolution vexatiously delayed. A victory achieved upon Lincoln's plan, protested frank Martin Conway of Kansas, "must inevitably result in restoring the domination of the slaveholding class," and hence could "bring no lasting peace." "What!" cried a Western radical, "bring back the rebel States, into full fellowship as members of the union, with their full delegations in both Houses of Congress. They, with the pro-slavery conservatives of the Border States and the Democrats of the Northern states, will control Congress. Republicans and Republican principles will be in the minority and under law, and this latter state would be worse than the former—worse than war itself."[14]

In contrast to the administration's "sickly policy of an inoffensive war," as Julian termed it, the Jacobins demanded a line of action "suited to remorseless and revolutionary violence." The magnetic Senator Edward Baker, who was later to lose his life leading a rash charge at the battle of Ball's Bluff, proclaimed in 1861 a war of subjugation against the seceded states: "We may have to reduce them to the condition of Territories, and send from Massachusetts or from Illinois Governors to control them." Owen Lovejoy grimly predicted, "If there is no other way to quell this rebellion, we will make a solitude, and call it peace." Blunt John Hickman of Pennsylvania threatened that the conquest of the Confederacy would "leave the track of the chariot wheels of war so deep on the southern soil that a century may not obliterate it," and Zachariah Chandler, expressing the fierce, intolerant wartime spirit of the radicals, proclaimed, "A rebel has sacrificed all his rights. He

[14] Adams to J. M. Forbes, August 30, 1861, in Sarah Forbes Hughes, *Letters and Recollections of John Murray Forbes* (Boston, 1899), 1:234–235; *Select Speeches of George W. Julian* (Cincinnati, 1867), 7; *Congressional Globe*, 37 Congress, 2 Session, 82–87; 38 Congress, 2 Session, 162; J. H. Hood to Thaddeus Stevens, February 27, 1864, in the Stevens MSS.; J. H. Jordan to Lyman Trumbull, February 20, 1862, in the Trumbull MSS.

has no right to life, liberty, property, or the pursuit of happiness. Everything you give him, even life itself, is a boon which he has forfeited."[15]

Always a step before the foremost, Thaddeus Stevens was willing that the South "be laid waste, and made a desert," and "repeopled by a band of freemen." He told a Republican convention in Pennsylvania: "Abolition—yes! Abolish everything on the face of the earth but this Union; free every slave—slay every traitor—burn every rebel mansion, if these things be necessary to preserve this temple of freedom to the world and to our posterity." The sardonic old man observed to a young friend in the army, "I infer your duties lie at some distance from the rebels. It were a pity to hurt those that our Government treats so tenderly."[16]

If the Jacobins could not have their remorseless, revolutionary war, they were not sure that they wanted any at all. The vociferous John P. Hale of New Hampshire, shouting in the Senate at the beginning of hostilities, "This is the day; this is the hour; this is the time; this is the experiment," declared boldly, "If we cannot put down this rebellion, let them put us down." Even John Sherman, who was not an out-and-out radical, said, "For me, I am for a war that will either establish or overthrow the government. . . . We need such a war, and we have it now." Holding this uncompromising attitude, the radicals found it difficult, if not impossible, to support the administration's efforts to bring the war to a rapid conclusion without destroying slavery. They believed that if the struggle continued long enough, public opinion would force the government to resort to emancipation and the arming of the slaves.

[15] Julian, *Select Speeches*, 33; *Congressional Globe*, 37 Congress, 1 Session, 45, 75, 96; *ibid.*, 37 Congress, 3 Session, 1338.

[16] *Ibid.*, 37 Congress, 1 Session, 415; *New York Tribune*, September 11, 1862; Stevens in a letter of September 5, 1861, in the Stevens MSS. See also S. Fish to Lyman Trumbull, June 25, 1861, in the Trumbull MSS., advocating that the South be taught "a bloody lesson," which it would remember for "a thousand generations"; Trumbull to M. C. Lea, November 5, 1861, in White, *Trumbull*, 171–172, in which Senator Trumbull said, "War means desolation, and they who have brought it on must be made to feel all its horrors."

Hence they favored a policy that would prolong the war until they had sufficient control of the party to force the radical program upon the reluctant Lincoln. "And we don't want" the war "to be hurried," wrote Horace Greeley, the white-haired sage of the *New York Tribune*, "but to be earnestly carried on to a righteous conclusion."[17]

Their insistence upon the necessity of a long war placed the radicals in the embarrassing, and often sinister, position of regarding Union defeats on the battlefield as helpful to their cause. Congressman Charles Sedgwick of New York said, "We ought to be whipped into that humble frame of mind which will make us willing to get soldiers of any color, and enlist them without scruple even in the enemy's country." From Wendell Phillips came the prayer, "God grant us so many reverses that the government may learn its duty."[18] The Olympian Charles Sumner, so detached from individuals that he could ignore the fate of the common soldier in his zeal for radicalism, exclaimed:

I fear our victories more than our defeats. There must be more delay and more suffering,—yet another 'plague' before all will agree to 'let my people go'; and the war cannot, must not, end till then. . . . We are too victorious. . . . If the rebellion should suddenly collapse, Democrats, copperheads, and Seward would insist upon amnesty and the Union, and 'no question asked about slavery.' God save us from any such calamity! . . . Before this comes, I wish two hundred thousand negroes with muskets in their hands, and then I shall not fear compromise.[19]

[17] *Congressional Globe*, 37 Congress, 1 Session, 105; Thorndike, *Sherman Letters*, 113; Edward L. Pierce, *Memoir and Letters of Charles Sumner* (Boston, 1877–1893), 4:40; C. A. Preston to John Sherman, December 1, 1863, in the John Sherman MSS. in the Library of Congress; J. H. Walker to Thaddeus Stevens, February 27, 1864, in the Stevens MSS.; Greeley to Mrs. Margaret Allen, June 17, 1861, in the Horace Greeley MSS. in the Library of Congress.

[18] Hughes, *Forbes*, 2:96–97; *ibid.*, 1:321; *New York Tribune*, May 12, 1863. See also the New York *Independent*, July 30, 1863.

[19] Letters of July 21 and 29, 1863, in Pierce, *Sumner*, 4:142–143. See also J. H. Jordan to Lyman Trumbull, February 20, 1862, and A. B. Campbell to Trumbull, March 6, 1862, in the Trumbull MSS.

At the end of the war that ardent feminine radical L. Maria Child ascribed much of the success of the Jacobin program to the military disasters suffered by the federal armies:

If we had had thorough, conscientious rulers, in cabinet and field, the war would have been brought to a close so soon that we, in the pride of quick success, should have shoved aside the black man, as of no account in the settlement of our difficulties. Had it not been for reiterated calls upon our sons to fill the ranks of the army, popular opinion would never have sanctioned the arming of the negroes; and the present feeling in favor of emancipation is largely owing to the fact that *their* blood has been shed to spare *ours*.[20]

All this is not to say that the Jacobins conspired for the defeat of the military forces in order to further their political designs. It simply means that they felt no enthusiasm for a war that did not include as one of its inevitable results the destruction of slavery. Rather than see the South brought back into the Union with slavery still in existence, most radicals would have preferred that the nation remain permanently divided. But as they slowly compelled Lincoln to adopt the radical policies, the Jacobins became increasingly vigorous in their support of the war.

The Jacobins demanded of the administration not only that it prosecute the war to a righteous conclusion but that it commit the management of the conflict to unadulterated radicals. For this reason they bitterly resented Lincoln's attempt to convert the party organization into a broad-bottomed coalition of all the elements in the loyal states who would support a war for the Union, and his consequent bestowal of high civil and military offices upon Democrats and conservatives who supported his program. They feared that the inclusion of these extraneous groups in the government would smother their own influence and vitiate the party's opposition to slavery. Furthermore, if Democratic and conservative generals and politicians should prove to be the great heroes of the war, they would also inherit the lush political offices after the peace, thus dooming

[20] To George W. Julian, April 8, 1865, in the Giddings-Julian MSS.

the radicals to the cheerless existence of a frustrated minority. An alert Indiana editor, sensing Lincoln's intention of constructing an all-parties government even before he assumed the presidency, asked Julian, "Is there not a movement . . . to build up a 'union party' in the north which shall absorb Americans and Douglas men, and Conservative Republicans; done for the purpose of killing what they term the Abolition element in the Republican party, aimed at men of our Stamp. The movement cannot amount to anything unless it should be the disruption of the Republican party." John Sherman blamed Lincoln's procedure for the Republican losses in the elections of 1862: "The Republican organization was voluntarily abandoned by the president and his leading followers, and a no-party Union was formed." If the Republicans, advised Sherman, "have the wisdom to throw overboard the old débris that joined them in the Union movement, they will succeed. If not, they are doomed." Joshua R. Giddings, veteran foe of slavery and political godfather of Wade and Julian, thought that the president, by bringing into the party groups which could unite only upon a single issue, handicapped it with a platform that was too narrow to appeal to large numbers of voters, and condemned it to enter every campaign "without doctrines, principles or character." This, said Giddings, must inevitably result in the disintegration of the party.[21]

Upon the Democrats in Lincoln's popular front the angry radicals placed the onus for the administration's delay in taking an aggressive antislavery position. The president, wooing the support of the Democracy, appointed receptive members of that party to positions of power and influence: George B. McClellan, Don Carlos Buell, and Henry W. Halleck, in the army; and in the Cabinet, former Democrats Montgomery Blair and Gideon Welles. He braved the ire of the Republican spoilsmen, avid for the prizes of victory, by refusing to purge the government bureaus and departments of their Democratic incum-

[21] B. F. Diggs to George W. Julian, January 16, 1861, *ibid.;* John Sherman to General W. T. Sherman, November 16, 1862, in Thorndike, *Sherman Letters,* 167; Giddings to Julian, March 22, 1863, in the Giddings-Julian MSS.

bents, thus ignoring "the wholesome rule" that "no one who does not believe enthusiastically in the war should have a place." The Jacobins charged that the entire bureaucracy was shot through with Democratic treason, with the result, said John Sherman, that "there have been constant impediments thrown in the way of the organization of our military forces." Disgusted radicals like the pompous Salmon P. Chase thought that the misguided president was entrusting the direction of the war "almost exclusively to his political opponents." Democratic ascendancy, complained George W. Julian, was responsible for the administration's stand against emancipation and its policy of a milk-and-water war. "To this strange deference to slavery must be referred the fact that such swarms of disloyal men have been retained in the several departments of the government, and that the spirit and energy of the war have been paralyzed from the beginning."[22]

If Democratic prominence in the civil offices disturbed the Jacobins, Democratic domination of the army infuriated them. Partly because of Lincoln's patronage policy and more because of the previous convictions of most regular army men, Democratic officers controlled both the important and the subordinate commands in the early period of the war. Henry Wilson asserted in the Senate in 1861 that of the one hundred and ten brigadier generals in the army, eighty were Democrats. "Whenever there is a separate command," he deplored, "with but one solitary exception, that command is under the control of a general opposed to the present Administration." Julian estimated that four fifths of the major and brigadier generals were Democrats. The radicals suspected that the Democratic masters of the army nourished a sympathy for slavery that bordered on treason, and that the "infernal hold-back proslavery" philosophy of the military chieftains prevented a vigorous prosecution of the war. Martin Conway claimed that

[22] New York *Independent*, April 30, 1863, Washington correspondence; *Congressional Globe*, 37 Congress, 2 Session, 31; Jacob W. Schuckers, *Life and Public Services of Salmon Portland Chase* (New York, 1874), 458; George W. Julian, *Speeches on Political Questions, 1850–1868* (New York, 1872), 171; Julian, *Select Speeches*, 34.

there was not "more than one sincere abolitionist or emancipationist among the military authorities," and Joseph Medill of the *Chicago Tribune* sneered at the "scores of luke warm, half secession officers in command who cannot bear to strike a blow lest it hurt their rebel friends or jeopardize the precious protectors of slavery." In the place of conservative West Pointers the Jacobins demanded "generals with ideas," who on the battlefield would be "almost irresistible because swayed by the great invisible forces."[23]

So long as Democrats and conservatives occupied the positions of power in the government, the radicals believed that it was bootless for them to force the president to issue an emancipation edict. "Of what use would such a proclamation be," asked Wendell Phillips, "if conservatives or Democrats in the army and Cabinet enforced it? If the President should proclaim emancipation and Halleck and McClellan and Buell smother it under pretence of executing the measure, it will prove a failure." Consequently the implacable radicals insisted that all parties other than their own be expelled from the popular front. "We demand," said Phillips, "a proclamation of freedom, war on war principles to be conducted by such men as Sumner, Stevens, and Wade, and their friends in the Cabinet, and by Hunter, Sigel, and Fremont in the field. . . . No emancipation policy is of any value unless its earnest and downright friends are put at the head of affairs."[24]

Against Lincoln and his conservative program the Jacobins waged a winning battle. Both logic and time aided their cause. For Lincoln proposed the impossible—to conduct the war for

[23] *Congressional Globe,* 37 Congress, 2 Session, 83. 164; Julian, *Speeches on Political Questions,* 202–204; J. W. Shaffer to Lyman Trumbull, December 24, 1861, and S. Sawyer to Trumbull, December 18, 1861, in the Trumbull MSS. Medill to Edwin M. Stanton, January 21, 1862, in the Edwin M. Stanton MSS. in the Library of Congress; Harry Williams, "The Attack upon West Point during the Civil War," in the *Mississippi Valley Historical Review,* 25(1939):491–504; *New York Tribune,* October 29, 1862, Boston correspondence, p. 3; *ibid.,* July 23, 1862, p. 3.

[24] Quoted in Amos Kendall, *Letters Exposing the Mismanagement of Public Affairs by Abraham Lincoln* (Washington, 1864), 19.

the preservation of the status quo which had produced the war. The radicals, before the end of the struggle, had gutted his policies almost completely. They forced the adoption of emancipation as one of the objectives of the war. They pushed through measures providing for the employment of Negro soldiers and for the confiscation of the property of "rebels." They drove the Democratic generals from the army and weakened conservative influence in the Cabinet. They defeated Lincoln's attempt to control the process of reconstruction by refusing congressional recognition for his state governments in the South. At the close of the war the radicals, like Hamlet, looked at a political cemetery littered with dead but victorious issues, each the skull of a poor Yorick that once had been a live and burning contention.

The wily Lincoln surrendered to the conquering Jacobins in every controversy before they could publicly inflict upon him a damaging reverse. Like the fair Lucretia threatened with ravishment, he averted his fate by instant compliance. In 1865 L. Maria Child observed, perhaps ironically, "I think we have reason to thank God for Abraham Lincoln. With all his deficiencies," he had been a man "who was willing to grow."[25]

[25] Letter to G. W. Julian, April 8, 1865, in the Giddings-Julian MSS.

2
The Opening of the Duel

In 1860 the Republican Party, passing over its most prominent leaders, William H. Seward, Salmon P. Chase, and Simon Cameron, selected a dark horse candidate to bear its standard in the presidential election. The cleavage of the Democratic Party into a Southern and a Northern wing assured Republican victory, and Abraham Lincoln became president of a nation torn by sectional strife. Lincoln was known vaguely as a conservative, but the party bosses were confident that the inexperienced Illinois lawyer would permit his chosen advisers to mold his policies. Hence the composition of his Cabinet assumed double importance, and the factions scrambled to secure appointments. It was generally supposed that Lincoln would have to offer the first place to Seward and that the New Yorker's powerful machine would dominate the administration.

This probability dismayed the Jacobins, who profoundly distrusted Seward's sincerity. Although a veteran in the antislavery movement, Seward had never enjoyed the full confidence of the radicals. Small and unimpressive in appearance, delighting in cynical remarks which made him seem devoid of principle, he had a tolerant, compromising nature which unfitted him for association with the stern Jacobins. In the war years just ahead they were to sneer at him as "serpentine Seward," Lincoln's conservative father confessor, and even as early as 1861 they had a disquieting foretaste of his influence.

For in January, with Lincoln not yet in office and with the lower South in the throes of secession, Seward undertook to inform the Senate on the Republican position on the national crisis. He urged a conciliatory policy, the evacuation of federal forts in the South, and a strategy of inaction that would result in the ultimate return to the Union of the seceded states. These sentiments enraged the radicals, who were opposed to any adjustment of the sectional problem which would leave intact the political power of the slavocracy. They demanded a war to the hilt against slavery and slaveholders; but they preferred peaceful disunion to a compromise that would peril Republican supremacy. Consequently Stevens, Wade, Sumner, and Chandler bitterly condemned Seward's proposals. "If we follow such leadership," exclaimed the disgusted Wade, "we will be in the wilderness longer than the children of Israel under Moses."[1]

The Jacobins had prepared a slate of candidates for appointment to the Cabinet, but Lincoln largely ignored their recommendations. His selection of Seward for secretary of state was sullenly accepted by the radicals as inevitable. But their anger flared when they learned that the New York senator had manipulated Simon Cameron, the corrupt czar of Pennsylvania politics, into the post of secretary of war. They began to have nightmarish visions of a Cabinet composed of Seward and his tools.[2] Ascribing Machiavellian skill to Seward, they accused him of blocking the Cabinet designs of two radical aspirants, John C. Frémont and Cassius Clay. The Seward-Cameron alliance disturbed the latter's Pennsylvania rival, Thaddeus Stevens, who himself had Cabinet ambitions. From

[1] *Congressional Globe,* 36 Congress, 2 Session, 341–344; Congressman J. M. Ashley, "Calhoun, Seward, and Lincoln," in the *Magazine of Western History,* 13(1890):3–4; Hughes, *Forbes,* 1:186; Phillips, *Speeches,* 345–346. Conservatives applauded the speech, *New York Journal of Commerce,* January 14, 1861, quoted in William H. Hallock, *Life of Gerard Hallock* (New York, 1869), 99–100.

[2] James M. Ashley, "Abraham Lincoln," in the *Magazine of Western History,* 14(1891):28; Lyman Trumbull, letter of January 10, 1861, in White, *Trumbull,* 146–147; Horace White to Lyman Trumbull, January 10, 1861, and William H. Herndon to Trumbull, January 27, in the Trumbull MSS.; John T. Morse, Jr., ed., *Diary of Gideon Welles, Secretary of the Navy under Lincoln and Johnson* (Boston, 1911), 1:126–127. Lincoln's managers at the Republican convention had promised Cameron a Cabinet post if he would swing his delegates to Lincoln. Nevertheless, because of Cameron's record, Lincoln was extremely reluctant to fulfill the pledge. See James G. Randall, *The Civil War and Reconstruction* (Boston, 1937), 227; Clarence E. Macartney, *Lincoln and His Cabinet* (New York, 1931), 34–35.

his place in Congress, Stevens complained that none of his friends would be appointed. "There is considerable feeling, & some remonstrance." A Cabinet dominated by Seward as "Prime Minister" portended to the Jacobins an ignominious compromise with the South. Their misgivings on this score were intensified by a report from an Indiana leader who had visited Lincoln that the president-elect, "for fear of giving further umbrage to the South," was "unwilling" to appoint prominent radicals, but would offer two seats to the loyal slave states. The offended interviewer bewailed to Senator William P. Fessenden, "we may as well make a sacrifice of our principles as of our men."[3]

Lincoln's Cabinet appointments, his cautious speeches on his journey to Washington, in which he refused to lay down a policy, and his surreptitious entrance into the capital on February 23 to escape a rumored assassination plot, convinced the radicals that the president lacked the resolution and courage to crush the secession movement. They believed he had placed himself completely under the influence of Seward and the compromisers. Even such a moderate as Samuel Bowles of the *Springfield Republican* thought Lincoln a "simple Susan," and spoke scornfully of Seward's "Illinois attachment."[4]

In an attempt to frustrate Seward's power in the Cabinet, the Jacobins concentrated their forces to secure the treasury post for Salmon P. Chase, the radical and pretentious senator from Ohio. Horace Greeley, alarmed by rumors that the influence of the Seward forces was causing Lincoln to waver from his promise to appoint the Ohioan, temporarily abandoned his

[3] Cephas Brainerd to G. W. Julian, January 29, 1861, in the Giddings-Julian MSS.; Ruhl J. Bartlett, *John C. Frémont and the Republican Party* (*Ohio State University Studies*, Columbus, 1930), 70–71; Stevens, letters of February 4, 10, in the Stevens MSS.; Phillips, *Speeches*, 379; W. W. Gitt to William Pitt Fessenden, February 17, 1861, in the William Pitt Fessenden MSS. in the Library of Congress.

[4] George S. Merriam, *Life and Times of Samuel Bowles* (New York, 1885), 1:318; J. H. Harper to Congressman Schuyler Colfax, February 25, 1861, in the Schuyler Colfax MSS. in the Library of Congress; manuscript diary of General Samuel P. Heintzelman, February 17, in the Library of Congress.

New York Tribune and came to Washington to direct the campaign. After days of intrigue and backstairs politics Greeley wrote gloomily, "I think we have fought through the nomination of Chase for the Treasury, but I am not sure he will go in with much company." Seward and the advocates of compromise would have "full swing." "Old Abe," Greeley added, "is in the web of very cunning spiders and cannot break out if he would." Although Lincoln awarded the desired office to Chase, the Jacobins felt that one spokesman among the president's advisers could not modify the conservatism of the administration. Wade and Lovejoy stigmatized the Cabinet as "a disgraceful surrender to the South." The cabal of radical senators were deeply resentful because Lincoln had not come to Washington to consult them before selecting his official family.[5]

Radical criticism of Lincoln was not diminished by his mild and conciliatory inaugural address, in which he disclaimed any determination to invade the South or interfere with slavery. Apprehensive radicals exhorted their leaders to hasten the meeting of Congress so that the Jacobins could counteract Seward's influence over the president. Senator Lyman Trumbull was warned that because Seward and Cameron had shown "unmistakable symptoms of backing down," it was imperative that Lincoln have around him, to steel his uncertain will, men like "old Ben Wade and yourself." As March wore on and Lincoln took no action to recover the federal forts which the Confederate government had seized, or to relieve other strongholds like Sumter which were menaced by Southern forces, the Jacobins became increasingly bitter. The administration's "cringing & whining" attitude they ascribed to the malign sway of Seward.[6]

[5] Horace Greeley to B. Brockway, February 28, 1861, and also March 12, 1861, in the Greeley MSS.; Henry B. Stanton, *Random Recollections* (Johnstown, 1885), 70; Macartney, *Lincoln and His Cabinet*, 219; James G. Blaine, *Twenty Years of Congress, From Lincoln to Garfield* . . . (Norwich, 1884–1886), 1:285; Francis Fessenden, *Life and Public Services of William Pitt Fessenden* (Boston, 1907), 1:248.

[6] James D. Richardson, *A Compilation of the Messages and Papers of the Presidents, 1789–1897* (Washington, 1896–99), 6:5–12; Grant Goodrich to

While the radicals sniped furtively at Lincoln and the Cabinet, a rapidly mounting public opinion was demanding that the government send aid to the beleaguered forts, particularly to Sumter in Charleston harbor at the very fountainhead of secession. The tenseness of a situation that bordered on actual war had whipped the people of the North into a mental condition which needed only some dramatic incident to set off a great popular display of martial ardor. This was furnished when Lincoln at long last dispatched a relief expedition bearing food to Sumter, and the Confederacy, to prevent the landing of the ships, took the offensive and bombarded and reduced the fort. When the beaten garrison trailed out of their demolished walls on April 14, there arose from all over the North, from press and pulpit, a cry for revenge. The president was commanded to press an army of invasion into the South to wipe out the disgrace to the national honor. There was wild talk of superseding Lincoln with a stronger character and of forcing the resignation of the Cabinet.[7]

The news of Sumter and the swelling war spirit delighted the Jacobins. By accepting the Southern challenge to attempt no relief of the fort, Lincoln had made peaceful compromise impossible. The administration was committed to war, and war, exulted the radicals, meant the death of slavery. They were now eager to support the recently despised Lincoln; Wendell Phillips announced that at last he could stand with a clear conscience "under the flag." Quick to push the advantage of the situation, the Jacobins surrounded Lincoln with insistent demands for an advance of the army into Virginia, which had joined the Confederacy a few days after the fall of Sumter. "Wade and Chandler are here," wrote Senator

Lyman Trumbull, March 18, 1861, and William Butler to Trumbull, March 20, in the Trumbull MSS.; Daniel Baldwin to Trumbull, March 15, 1861, *ibid.*; D. D. Stewart to William P. Fessenden, March 30, 1861, in the Fessenden MSS.

[7] *New York Tribune*, April 3, 1861; *Springfield Republican*, April 11, 1861, quoted in Merriam, *Bowles*, 1:287–288; Heintzelman diary, April 14, 26, 1861; *Letters of John Hay and Extracts from His Diary* (privately printed, Washington, 1908), 1:28, diary entry of April 30; *New York Tribune*, April 26.

Morrill from Washington, "hot for war." Senator Henry Wilson and other New Englanders were also there, conferring with Lincoln, and "crowding on immediate & active campaigning." Against the clamor of the politicians, General Winfield Scott, "Old Fuss and Feathers," the hero of the Mexican War and now head of the army, insisted that the army existed mainly on paper and that no forward movement should be attempted until the raw volunteer levies were drilled into a fighting machine. Impatient Montgomery Blair, postmaster general and former Democrat, consorting strangely with the Jacobins at this time, was disgusted with the general's opposition to action. "This war will last forever," he declared, "if some thing does not happen to unseat old Scott."[8]

Although the Jacobins were shouting for aggressive action, they looked askance at Lincoln's bold use of the war powers, his establishment of a blockade of the Southern coast, and his proclamation increasing the regular army beyond the total set by previous law. These were functions, the radicals believed, that should be exercised by Congress. The concomitant of American wartime history, congressional jealousy of an executive suddenly endowed with immense powers, was beginning to operate. With Congress in adjournment and a distrusted "Prime Minister" dominating the government, the radicals were in no mood to approve the creation of a large army subject only to the president's will. Senator James W. Grimes denounced Lincoln's call for recruits to the regular army as "without any authority of law, and against law," and asked anxiously, "Will he be content with ten legions?" The Iowa solon wanted the army raised by authority of Congress; above all he wanted the party in Congress and not Lincoln to appoint the estimated nine hundred new officers. For if unrestrained the president would, the radicals feared, award most of the military patronage to conservatives and Democrats. In an effort to protect Lincoln from the machinations of Seward

<hr>

[8] Phillips, *Speeches*, 396–414; Lot M. Morrill to Fessenden, May, 1861, in Fessenden, *Fessenden*, 1:186; E. F. Jones to Benjamin F. Butler, May 2, 1861, and Montgomery Blair to B. F. Butler, June 8, 1861, in the Benjamin F. Butler MSS. in the Library of Congress.

at this critical point, Charles Sumner spent the entire latter half of May in Washington supplying him with gratuitous advice. He failed to impress Lincoln, however, and by early June he was back in Boston loudly damning the secretary of state.[9]

Control of the army patronage was of vital importance to the radicals. The success of their program of wartime emancipation depended upon commanding officers who sympathized with radical aims. For this reason they strongly objected to Lincoln's handing out commissions while Congress was not in session. They knew his propensity for enticing the opposition with appointive rewards, and they suspected both the principles and the loyalty of many of the regular army officers who were slated for promotion. The conciliatory attitude that several of the commanding generals adopted toward the slaveholders in their departments convinced the Jacobins that the cause of emancipation was hopeless until the personnel of the army was drastically changed. On June 3 General Robert Patterson told his troops that while it was their duty to suppress sedition, they should also protect the property of loyal slaveowners. Taking a backhanded slap at the Jacobins, Patterson reminded his men that the war was being waged "for the good of the whole country," and that they must, "should occasion offer, at once suppress servile insurrection." General George B. McClellan was just as reassuring and much more rhetorical in his proclamation to the people of western Virginia. His army did not come, he said, to interfere in any way with their slaves: "We will, on the contrary, with an iron hand, crush any attempt at insurrection on their part."[10] The radicals fumed with mounting rage at the policy followed by most generals of returning to their owners fugitive slaves who had drifted within the lines. They sneered at the offending offi-

[9] Grimes to W. P. Fessenden, May 12, June 6, 1861, in William Salter, *Life of James W. Grimes* (New York, 1876), 140–141; Pierce, *Sumner*, 4:36; Charles Francis Adams, Jr., *Richard Henry Dana* (Boston, 1890), 2:258–259.

[10] *War of the Rebellion: Official Records of the Union and Confederate Armies* (Washington, 1880–1901), series 1, 2:662, hereafter cited as *O. R.*; *ibid.*, 48–49. Radical comments on the action of Patterson and McClellan are given in the *New York Tribune*, August 22, 1862.

cers as "slave-catchers," but the administration did not rebuke the generals for the practice. The only crumb of comfort for the radicals was the refusal of General Benjamin F. Butler, at Fort Monroe, to surrender slaves in his camp. Butler, a Democratic politician from Massachusetts turned warrior and soon to turn radical, claimed that the Confederates were using slaves to construct fortifications, and that he too wás justified in employing them for that purpose. The Jacobins heartily applauded his action.[11]

While the radicals were chafing under Lincoln's refusal to move the armies and his failure to lay down an emancipation policy, Congress convened in special session, on July 4. The president's message did not mention slavery and stressed to the exclusion of all other topics the national obligation to maintain the Union; but it was immediately evident that the Jacobin leaders were determined to conduct the war on a partisan basis. On July 9 the House passed Owen Lovejoy's resolution, aimed at the "slave-catching" generals, that "it is no part of the duty of the soldiers of the United States to capture and return fugitive slaves." Lovejoy exultantly informed Sumner, "Our conservative people were timid and vexed, but they had to vote right at last."[12] In fire-breathing speeches the Jacobins threatened the South with subjugation and devastation and the extinction of slavery.[13] Congress broke out in a rash of confiscation bills. Four days after the opening of the session the House instructed its committee on the judiciary to prepare a bill confiscating the property of anyone holding office under the Confederacy or any seceded state.[14] Zachariah Chandler wanted to seize the property of governors of states, members of legislatures, judges, and officers above the rank of lieutenant who had taken up arms against the govern-

[11] *New York Tribune*, May 29, June 5, 1861; Simon Cameron to Butler, May 30, 1861, and Montgomery Blair to Butler, May 31, in the Butler MSS.; Benjamin F. Butler, *Butler's Book* (Boston, 1892), Chapter VI.

[12] Lincoln, *Works*, 6:297–325; *Congressional Globe*, 37 Congress, 1 Session, 32; Pierce, *Sumner*, 4:40, footnote.

[13] Speeches of Edward Baker, Owen Lovejoy, and John Hickman in the *Congressional Globe*, 37 Congress, 1 Session, 45, 75, 96.

[14] *Ibid.*, 23.

ment or aided "treason" in any manner. Sumner offered a simpler measure, to confiscate the holdings of all persons in rebellion. Most extreme was the bill of Senator Samuel C. Pomeroy of Kansas to put down "the slaveholders' rebellion." It provided for the abolition of slavery in the states in secession, and directed the president to issue a proclamation providing for "immediate and unconditional emancipation."[15] Out of all the proposed measures, the radical chieftains selected Senator Trumbull's as the one most likely to be accepted by Congress and by Lincoln. This bill, less drastic than the Jacobins would have wished, called for the confiscation of only that property used "in aid of the rebellion." It became law on August 6, to the accompaniment of a vindictive statement by Thaddeus Stevens that the South would be "laid waste, and made a desert," if this were necessary to preserve the Union.[16]

While the radicals were thus announcing that they intended to have a voice in the formulation of war policies, they took the first step in a program to bring the executive branch under congressional supervision. This took the form of an attack upon Seward's ally in the Cabinet, Secretary of War Cameron. His questionable record and suspected inefficiency made him a liability to the administration; many blamed him for the dilatory movements of the armies. The powerful New York financial interests wanted him removed. One of their number told Senator Fessenden: "The Government should know . . . that a feeling of great distrust and dissatisfaction exists . . . with the present Cabinet; it has not the confidence of the moneyied interests. . . . The *dissatisfaction* is *with Mr. Cameron.* . . . Public good requires another man in his place." Sensing in the popular disapproval of Cameron an opportunity to smear Seward, the House radicals secured the establishment of a committee to investigate the contracts let by any governmental department; and to determine whether the contracts had been advertised or awarded to the lowest bidder;

[15] Chandler's bill, *ibid.*, 11; Sumner's and Pomeroy's bills, 134. The wording of Pomeroy's bill is not given, but Senator John C. Breckinridge read it to the Senate. *Ibid.*, 142.

[16] *Ibid.*, 120, 218–219, 415, 430–431, 434, 454.

and whether anyone but the contractors had profited by the transactions. Ostensibly this famous "smelling committee" was charged with the responsibility of sniffing out scandal wherever it might exist, but the purpose back of its creation, explained Senator Grimes, was to investigate Cameron's alleged frauds.[17]

Before Congress met, the Jacobins' representative in the Cabinet, Salmon P. Chase, had induced Lincoln to appoint Irvin McDowell to the command of the troops gathering in front of Washington. McDowell, an Ohio graduate of West Point, had been a major in the regular army before Chase discovered him, and his rapid elevation to the rank of brigadier general stirred the jealousy of other officers, several of whom were to be his subordinates.[18] With a general of their own choice in command, the radicals again moved upon Lincoln with demands for aggressive action, urging that he order McDowell's army to invade Virginia. They were suspicious of the continued inactivity of the military forces, which they attributed to the Southern sympathies of the conservative generals. Mindful that General Scott was a Virginian, the radicals doubted whether he really intended or even desired to whip the rebels. They believed that an offensive movement, even if it ended in defeat, was necessary to sustain the war ardor of the people. "The idea of waiting until frost had set in, and merely defending our capitol was a preposterous one in a political point of view, and our struggle is not a purely military one," said one radical who had been in Washington advising the party leaders on military strategy. "A reverse . . . is better than inaction would have been."[19]

[17] J. G. Butterworth to W. P. Fessenden, July 3, 1861, in the Fessenden MSS.; *Congressional Globe*, 37 Congress, 1 Session, 23; Salter, *Grimes*, 154–155.

[18] Heintzelman diary, May 19, 22, 1861; Henry Villard, *Memoirs of Henry Villard* (Boston, 1904), 1:179; *Harper's Weekly*, January 17, 1863.

[19] Joseph Medill to Lyman Trumbull, July 13, 1861, in the Trumbull MSS.; *New York Tribune*, June 27, 28, 1861; Gustave Koerner to Lyman Trumbull, July 29, 1861, in the Trumbull MSS. Koerner was speaking of the Union defeat at Bull Run and the advantages that would result from the loss of the battle.

The radicals were aided in their efforts to force a battle by the Northern people's tremendous impatience for a quick, smashing victory in the early summer of 1861. A blithe optimism that the war would be ephemeral pervaded all classes. Men were knocked down on the streets for saying that the South would fight well; prognosticators asserted variously that the war would be ended before the second frost, the first snow, the next cotton crop, or the Christmas season.[20] This paranoiac cocksureness flared up into a demand for action when the news came that the Confederate Congress would hold its first meeting in Richmond on July 20. The spectacle of unashamed treason sitting down to deliberate so near the nation's capital excited popular indignation to the point of frenzy; Greeley's *New York Tribune* gave this emotion a slogan with its cry, "Forward to Richmond! Onward to Richmond!" The rebel Congress must not be allowed to meet there on July 20. By that date the place must be held by the national army.[21]

Both Scott and McDowell were opposed to any movement of their callow troops. McDowell later said that he had "begged" of Cameron and Chase, "who at that time was connected with the secretary of war in many of the plans and organizations going forward," that he should not be forced to "organize and discipline and march and fight all at the same time." Scott told Congressman William A. Richardson that he considered himself "the greatest coward in America" for not offering a last-ditch resistance to the demands of the politicians. "I deserve removal because I did not stand up, when my army was not in condition for fighting, and resist . . . to the last."[22] But the combined pressure of the Jacobins and

[20] *New York Journal of Commerce*, quoted in the *Detroit Free Press*, January 23, February 6, 1863; *New York Tribune*, May 1, 1861; Hughes, *Forbes*, 1:220; Adams, *Dana*, 2:259.

[21] This war cry ran every day in the *Tribune* from June 26 to July 6. It was written by Fitz-Henry Warren, the paper's Washington correspondent.

[22] *Reports of the Committee on the Conduct of the War*, 1863, 2:37; Villard, *Memoirs*, 1:179–180; Richardson's account of a meeting with Scott after the battle of Bull Run, in the *Congressional Globe*, 37 Congress, 1 Session, 246.

the public was too powerful to be withstood. Lincoln succumbed, and ordered McDowell to attack a Confederate army gathered near Manassas, or Bull Run.

Amid an enthusiastic display of popular rejoicing, McDowell's green civilians marched southward to crush the rebellion. "The interest now felt is intense," wrote a Washington editor, "but nobody here seems to doubt the results to follow this great military demonstration." Zachariah Chandler, excited by the prospects of a battle which he had done much to bring about, assured his wife that the Confederates would run until they reached Richmond.[23] Confident and curious congressmen, on horseback and in carriages, thronged the roads to Manassas on July 21 to witness the dispersing of the rebel hordes. Wade, Chandler, Trumbull, Grimes, Wilson, Albert G. Riddle, Elihu Washburne, and William Kellogg were among those who sought ringside seats for the encounter. Wade and Chandler's party, well supplied with food and liquor, intended to make a festive occasion of the beautiful Sabbath day. The men in Riddle's carriage had armed themselves with heavy revolvers, and Wade carried his famous squirrel rifle, with which he had bluffed the chivalry in the fifties, hoping at last to get a shot at a Southern gentleman. But the solons' pleasant anticipations of enjoying a picnic lunch while watching the overthrow of the Confederacy were suddenly and appallingly dispelled. McDowell's forces, after some initial success, fell back before the attacks of their foe in what quickly turned from an orderly retreat into a panic-stricken stampede. The congressional spectators were caught up in the rout, and several, including Henry Wilson, fled with the mass of fugitives to the safety of Washington. The old Roundheads Wade and Chandler, and the men with Riddle, were made of sterner stuff. Courageously they remained on the field, vainly attempting to rally the fleeing soldiers. In a last desperate effort they wheeled their carriages across a narrow road near Fairfax, completely blocking

---

[23] Washington *National Intelligencer*, July 17, 1861; Zachariah Chandler to Mrs. Chandler, July 16, 1861, in the Zachariah Chandler MSS. in the Library of Congress.

the passage. Then, with Wade shouting, "Boys, we'll stop this damned runaway," they placed themselves in the path of the onrushing mob, and checked it until relieved by fresh troops. The spectacle of Bull Run and their own dramatic participation in the battle was not calculated to impress the Jacobins present with a high regard for the competence of military men, or with any awe of military science as a sacrosanct subject immune from the interference of civilians.[24]

Manassas swung public opinion from joyous confidence to grim determination; stocks fell; and the circulation of the *Tribune* slipped. The people blamed Lincoln, Greeley, Scott, and the Cabinet, indiscriminately, for the disaster. Greeley at first tried to pin the defeat upon inefficient preparation by the administration, and demanded a fresh batch of generals and Cabinet members who would impart a much-needed vigor to the prosecution of the war. But a few days later, quailing before the whiplash of popular condemnation, he proffered repentance for his part in bringing on the premature battle, and barred all future criticisms of military movements from his columns. This reformation was ephemeral, but Greeley's mercurial nature had suffered a hard blow. He confided to a friend that for weeks after Bull Run he had been unable to sleep, tormented by fears of "a disastrous war and a disgraceful peace."[25]

If all did not agree with the troubled editor that the war would end in defeat for the government, everyone knew after Manassas that it would be no easy three months' affair. The situation called for a declaration of policy from Congress as to what the war was about. Furthermore, it was imperative that

[24] Albert G. Riddle, *Recollections of War Times, 1860–1865* (New York, 1895), 46–52; Washington *National Intelligencer,* July 30, 1861; Lyman Trumbull to Mrs. Trumbull, July 22, 1861, in White, *Trumbull,* 165–167; J. W. Grimes to Mrs. Grimes, July 22, in Salter, *Grimes,* 146–147; Nathaniel W. Stephenson, *Lincoln, An Account of His Personal Life* . . . (Indianapolis, 1924), 190–191. The suggestion as to the probable effect of Bull Run upon Wade and Chandler's opinion of military men is Professor Stephenson's.

[25] *New York Tribune,* July 23, 25, 1861; Greeley to B. Brockway, August 14, 1861, in the Greeley MSS.

the declaration be so broad and national that every faction in the loyal states could stand upon it in support of the war. Lincoln's conception of a war to preserve the Union was obviously the only catchall which could fulfill this need. On the day after the battle the venerable John J. Crittenden of Kentucky introduced in the House a resolution which had been blocked the previous Saturday by Thaddeus Stevens. The famous Crittenden resolution stated that "this war is not waged . . . in any spirit of oppression, or for any purpose of conquest or subjugation, or . . . of overthrowing or interfering with the rights or established institutions" of the seceded states, "but to defend and maintain the *supremacy* of the Constitution, and to preserve the Union with all the dignity, equality, and rights of the several States unimpaired; and that as soon as these objects are accomplished the war ought to cease."[26]

The House adopted the resolution immediately with only two dissenting votes; three days later the Senate accepted an almost identical measure. Presumably this resolution was a covenant that the destruction of slavery was not to be one of the ends of the war. Presumably it meant that as soon as victory was achieved, the government would restore the Union as it had been before 1860. Such a definition of the purposes of the conflict ran counter to every principle in the Jacobin creed. Yet in the critical days after Bull Run the radicals were afraid to oppose the Crittenden declaration. Only two Republicans in the House dared to vote against it, Albert G. Riddle, from rock-ribbed abolition territory in Ohio's Western Reserve, and John Fox Potter of Wisconsin, who had once offered to fight the Virginian Roger Pryor with bowie knives. Stevens and Lovejoy absented themselves during the roll call rather than record their approval of a policy to which they violently objected. The disgusted Stevens could not stomach the resolution because "it looked like an apology from us in saying what were the objects of the war, when we had no business to be asking questions." In the Senate only one Republican, Lyman

[26] *Congressional Globe,* 37 Congress, 1 Session, 222–223.

Trumbull, cast a contrary vote, and he merely because he disliked some of the phraseology; his suggested changes would not have altered the sense of the measure. The other Jacobins wryly swallowed the pill and voted aye. They agreed with Wade that to do anything else would fatally weaken and divide popular support of the war.[27] They were willing, temporarily, to subordinate their own convictions in order that the conflict might be continued. For they knew that war meant the death of slavery, and they were confident that the exigencies of the struggle would enable them to circumvent the Crittenden resolution.

Although Manassas constrained the Jacobins to efface themselves for the moment, they had not dropped their opposition to the administration. More doubtful than ever of Lincoln's "capacity or inclination" to organize ruthless victory, they renewed their demands for changes in the Cabinet and the army. In one direction the recent disaster had strengthened the antislavery case. The radicals now advanced the argument that since the Confederacy had demonstrated unconquerable military strength, the government could not hope to win the conflict unless it weakened the enemy by emancipating his slaves. Young Charles Francis Adams, observing the swirling capital intrigues, wrote his father that "this defeat tends more and more to throw the war into the hands of the radicals, and if it lasts a year, it will be a war of abolition." Two days after the battle Charles Sumner called upon Lincoln "to urge Emancipation" as a measure of military necessity, but the president rejected his proposal. With Sumner came a more formidable figure, Zachariah Chandler. The grim Michigan senator demanded that the government enlist Negro soldiers, including fugitive slaves, in the army. Chandler declared harshly that he would have no regrets if this incited a slave insurrection in the South. Again Lincoln refused. But the Jacobins were cheered by the passage of the confiscation bill providing for the seizure of property used by the rebels for military purposes. Sumner

[27] *Ibid.*, 257–265, 415; Albert G. Riddle, *Life of Benjamin F. Wade* (Cleveland, 1886), 243. Sumner did not vote either way.

religiously attributed the law to the chastening effects of Bull Run. "In the providence of God there are no accidents . . . ," he intoned, "and this seeming reverse helped to the greatest victory which can be won."[28]

On the day after Manassas Lincoln relieved McDowell from the command of his demoralized army and called George Brinton McClellan to Washington to take his place. The new commander, only thirty-four years old, possessed a precociously brilliant military and business record. A graduate of West Point, he had served as an officer in the Mexican War and an observer for the army in the Crimean War. He had been a successful executive of railroad companies. At the outbreak of the war he had returned to the army. Lincoln gave him the command of a small force in western Virginia, where he won several minor engagaments. Union victories were like hens' teeth in 1861, and McClellan's triumphs, well advertised by his florid proclamations, gripped the entire country. No small part of his prominence was owing to his impressive appearance. He looked the warrior. Short and stocky, handsome, magnetic, dignified, he reminded his admirers of the great Corsican. In fact, too many people called him "the Young Napoleon." He posed and talked and rode as he imagined Napoleon had. Later. his enemies pinned upon him the classic title "Mc-Napoleon." He was a cultured gentleman, conversant with good books, and an accomplished linguist. He could talk on a plane to which Lincoln rarely, and Wade or Chandler never, soared. He loved the punctilio and the ritual of the military hierarchy, and the flashing colors of parades and reviews and flags and drums and bugles, and the long straight lines of uniformed men down which a Young Napoleon galloped to thunderous huzzas. He was also an extreme egoist, and a good deal of a politician. He was connected with the Marcy machine

[28] Grant Goodrich to Lyman Trumbull, July 29, 1861, and Gustave Koerner to Trumbull, July 24, in the Trumbull MSS.; *Frank Leslie's Illustrated Newspaper,* August 10, 1861; Worthington C. Ford, ed., *A Cycle of Adams Letters, 1861–1865* (Boston, 1920), 1:23; Charles Sumner, *Complete Works of Charles Sumner* (Boston, 1875–1883), 6:31; *Life of Chandler,* 253; Pierce, *Sumner,* 4:40–41.

in New York, and before the war had been known as a Democrat.

When McClellan arrived in Washington, he found the city filled with drunken soldiers and quaking in its boots for fear the Confederates were about to sweep down Pennsylvania Avenue. This was the kind of situation that he was equipped to handle best. He was a superb organizer. Few officers equalled him in ability to whip raw troops into fighting men. Like many West Pointers, he was a skilled military engineer, marvelously proficient in constructing fortifications to defend a threatened city. He was one of the most widely read military scientists of his generation: indeed, his detailed knowledge of military history was his greatest handicap. He knew by rote all the maxims of the old masters; he could recite the lessons of Jomini and Vauban, and he tried to fight according to these classroom precepts. He fought by the rules, but sometimes to his confusion the Confederates cheated, and violated them. He knew what Napoleon would have done in every situation, but Napoleon had never seen Virginia mud. So the realities puzzled him and often paralyzed his decision. He knew what had been done in the past, but he was not always sure what George B. McClellan would do in the future. And yet he might—if the politicians had let him alone—he might have won the Civil War.

Despite McClellan's Democratic background, the Jacobins immediately took him under their wing. For some reason they thought that he was one of them. Chandler acted as though McClellan were his own discovery, and showed him around with a proprietary air. The impressionable young commander was dazzled by his reception in official Washington, which regarded him as a deliverer. "By some strange operation of magic," he wrote his wife, "I seem to have become the power of the land." His visit to the Senate charmed him; the eager members jostled one another to shake his hand. "They give me my way in everything, full swing and unbounded confidence." One of the admiring solons, James W. Grimes, assured his wife that the city was in no danger now that McClellan had taken over. "Would that we had the same confidence in some of the members of the cabinet!" he added. The radicals' sole anxiety was that the administration, "too much afraid of hurting somebody in the war," would not permit McClellan to go ahead and overthrow the Confederacy. But one shrewd observer in Washington predicted that the love feast between McClellan and the Jacobins would not last beyond the first course. Edwin M. Stanton, late of President Buchanan's cabinet, knew McClellan's political antecedents, and he believed no Democratic general could succeed in the war. Even if McClellan had "the ability of Caesar, Alexander, or Napoleon," asked Stanton, "what can he accomplish? Will not Scott's jealousy, Cabinet intrigues, and Republican interference thwart him at every step?"[29]

Delighted though they were with McClellan, the Jacobins continued to distrust the administration. Senator Fessenden complained of the "great want of wisdom among our rulers and leaders" which was numbing the conduct of the war. Ben Wade, in his customary cynical manner, exclaimed, "I do not wonder that people desert to Jeff Davis as he has brains; I may desert myself."[30] In August the Jacobins began to poke their heads above the parapet behind which they had ducked after Manassas. They judged that the temper of the people was once again favorable to the cause of emancipation. They resumed their attacks against the Cabinet, Lincoln's tenderness toward slavery in the Border States, and the slave-catching generals. They declared that the confiscation bill should be expanded to include the seizure of all the property of rebels,

[29] Zachariah Chandler to Mrs. Chandler, July 16, 1861, and Chandler to McClellan, August 16, 1861, in the Chandler MSS.; George B. McClellan, *McClellan's Own Story* (New York, 1887), 82–83; two letters of July 29 and August 4, 1861, in Salter, *Grimes*, 147; George Nourse to Lyman Trumbull, August 16, 1861, and Grant Goodrich to Trumbull, July 29, 1861, in the Trumbull MSS.; Edwin M. Stanton to James Buchanan, July 26, 1861, in Frank A. Flower, *Edwin McMasters Stanton* (Akron, 1905), 109; George C. Gorham, *Edwin M. Stanton* (Boston, 1899), 1:223–224.

[30] Fessenden, *Fessenden*, 1:189; Adam Gurowski, *Diary, March 4, 1861–November 2, 1862* (Boston, 1862), 90.

whether used for military purposes or not. They demanded an end of the "silk glove" policy in dealing with slavery.[31]

The radical offensive was concentrated against Simon Cameron, secretary of war. "His presence taints the reputation of the whole Cabinet," wrote William Cullen Bryant, poet-editor of the New York *Evening Post*, "and I think he should be ousted at once." The charges against Cameron were those of corruption and inefficiency. It was believed that he awarded all the war department's contracts to his Pennsylvania henchmen. Senator Grimes observed sarcastically that if the secretary "would call some Pennsylvanians into the field, instead of keeping them all at home to fill army contracts," business conditions generally would improve, and the army would have an oversupply of recruits.[32] But the Jacobins would have winked at Cameron's peculation if he had been right on the slavery question. They wanted an uncompromising radical in the war office, because its occupant held the key to military emancipation. He could make the army an instrument of freedom by staffing the important commands with officers who believed in the radical war aims. He could order the generals to receive fugitive slaves within their lines, thus destroying the institution by indirection. "We need a man in the War Department," declared John M. Forbes, a radical New England industrialist, "who, when the right time comes, will not hesitate a moment to assail the weakest point of the enemy."[33] The Jacobins growled at Cameron and his godfather, Seward, throughout August, but they could devise no scheme to get him out of the Cabinet. They also called vainly for the dismissal of Gideon Welles, the one-time Democrat who was secretary of the navy, and the substitution of an energetic radical. "If we

[31] Hughes, *Forbes*, 1:238, 241–242; *New York Tribune*, August 21, September 1, 1861; E. L. Pierce to B. F. Butler, August 10, in the Butler MSS.; Thaddeus Stevens, letter of September 5, in the Stevens MSS.

[32] Bryant to J. M. Forbes, August 27, 1861, in Hughes, *Forbes*, 1:242–243; Salter, *Grimes*, 152–153; Hughes, *Forbes*, 1:236–237; E. Peck to Lyman Trumbull, August 27, 1861, in the Trumbull MSS.

[33] J. M. Forbes to W. C. Bryant, August 24, 1861, in Hughes, *Forbes*, 1:241–242.

could get a good hurricane to help the tide," exclaimed Forbes, "it might sweep away some of the weaker materials in the Cabinet."[34]

Even as Forbes wrote, lowering clouds in the West portended a gathering storm. In the center of the swirling gusts stood the romantic figure of General John C. Frémont, commander of the Western Department.

Lincoln had invested Frémont with this important office in the early summer. The general, a dramatic figure to the public by reason of his explorations, journeyed to his headquarters at St. Louis amidst ringing applause from the whole North. From all sides came confident predictions that the dashing "Pathfinder" would give the country action and that Missouri would soon be cleared of Confederates. Powerful political elements had combined their forces to secure this substantial appointment for a man with scanty military training and experience. Horace Greeley pointed out the political advantages that the administration might win by bestowing high military office upon the Republican Party's first presidential candidate. Gustave Koerner, leader of the antislavery German population of the Mississippi Valley, assured Lincoln that the selection of Frémont, known to be opposed to slavery, would unite his countrymen in support of the war. Senator Trumbull emphasized the popular approval that would greet Frémont's appearance in the armed forces of the nation. Most important of all, the powerful Blair family—the father the unofficial adviser of the president, one son in the Cabinet, and another the chieftain of the Republican Party in Missouri—had chosen Frémont as their political cat's-paw and had thrown their influence behind his elevation to command.[35]

[34] *Ibid.*, 1:236-240; *New York Tribune*, September 3, 8, 1861; *Boston Transcript*, quoted in *Leslie's Newspaper*, August 31, 1861; *Leslie's Newspaper*, September 7.
[35] *New York Tribune*, May 15, 30, 1861, cited in Bartlett, *Frémont*, 71; Thomas J. McCormick, ed., *Memoirs of Gustave Koerner* (Cedar Rapids, 1909), 2:152; Koerner to Lyman Trumbull, May 31, 1861, in the Trumbull MSS.; Frémont to Trumbull, July 13, 1861, *ibid.*; William E. Smith, *The Francis Preston Blair Family in Politics* (New York, 1933), 2:55-59.

An acute observer could have predicted that Frémont would be a military failure. He owed his prominent public position to a vivid personality that invested his every action with drama, and to his marriage with the intrepid Jessie Benton, daughter of Senator Thomas H. Benton, political boss of Missouri and trusted friend of Andrew Jackson. He was impetuous, ambitious, and magnetic, and had the uncertain temperament of a prima donna.

The situation that confronted Frémont upon his arrival in St. Louis on July 26 (five days after Bull Run) would have taxed the abilities of an abler and more stable character. Missouri was rife with Confederate sympathizers, and only the determined efforts of General Nathaniel Lyon and Frank Blair had kept the state in the Union. Confederate troops menaced St. Louis. The poorly equipped federal forces were inadequate to hold the department against a strong attack. For a time Frémont wisely attempted no offensive operations, but devoted his efforts to strengthening the defenses of St. Louis and Cairo, and to organizing his resources. He constantly requisitioned the government for more men and supplies, which the overburdened authorities found it impossible to give him. Their inability to satisfy his many requests was, under the circumstances, natural enough. But the suspicious general concluded that someone wanted him to fail, and he voiced bitter criticism of the administration. He blamed the officers of the regular army for many of his difficulties. He believed them to be jealous of his rapid elevation and hostile toward him because he was a civilian. One of his supporters later charged that the regular officers opposed him because "he had not received with them the rite of infant baptism at West Point."[36]

Frémont's resentment toward the administration, coupled with his audacious nature, now impelled him to a rash move. His political activities had thrown him into close, confidential

[36] Frémont to Lyman Trumbull, July 13, 1861, in the Trumbull MSS.; Mrs. Frémont to Montgomery Blair, July 25, 1861, and to Mrs. Betty B. Lee, July 27, in Smith, *Blair Family*, 2:58, 59; Representative John P. C. Shanks, *Vindication of Major-General John C. Frémont . . .* (Washington, 1862), 5.

relations with the Jacobins. He was one with them on the slavery issue, and they buttered his ego with predictions that he would be the great hero of the war. On August 30 he suddenly intervened in the angry relations that existed between the radicals and Lincoln. He issued a military proclamation establishing martial law in Missouri, one section of which freed the slaves of all persons resisting the government, and ordered the confiscation of their property.[37]

The popular outburst indorsing this action was tremendous and instantaneous. Upon the radicals the antislavery principle of Frémont's proclamation fell like welcome manna from heaven; it suggested the method whereby slavery could be abolished. They loudly applauded the man who had dared to strike a real blow at the hated institution. Their press warned Lincoln not to revoke a measure that must eventually become a settled policy of the government. The administration's "hush-a-by-baby policy," rejoiced one Jacobin sheet, "is now necessarily about played out." Canny Simon Cameron, sensing the direction of the political winds, hastened to telegraph his congratulations to Frémont.[38]

But Lincoln knew that the proclamation, if permitted to stand, would alienate those Northern and Border State conservatives who would uphold a war to restore the Union but not an antislavery crusade. Their support was essential at this point. Accordingly Lincoln asked Frémont to modify the section of his proclamation dealing with slavery. When his request was refused, he issued an order countermanding that part of the edict.[39]

The president's repudiation of Frémont aroused a storm of radical criticism. Wade and Chandler were enraged. Only a

[37] *O. R.*, series 1, 3:467–468.

[38] New York *Sun,* September 3, 1861; New York *Tribune,* September 1, 2; *Leslie's Newspaper,* September 21; New York *Evening Post,* September 2; *National Intelligencer,* September 7; Allan Nevins, *Frémont, the West's Greatest Adventurer* (New York, 1928), 2:569.

[39] Lincoln to Frémont, September 2, 11, 1861, in John G. Nicolay and John Hay, *Abraham Lincoln, A History* (New York, 1890), 4:418, 420; for Frémont's refusal to modify his proclamation, see *O. R.,* series 1, 3:477–478.

person sprung from "poor white trash," Wade sneered, could have acted thus. "I shall expect to find in his annual message, a recommendation to Congress, to give each rebel who shall serve during the war a hundred and sixty acres of land." Grimes declared Frémont's proclamation "the only real noble and true thing done during this war." Sumner mourned, "We cannot conquer the rebels as the war is now conducted." Lincoln had seized dictatorial powers, he complained, "but how vain to have the power of a god and not to use it godlike!" "That nice young man" from Indiana, "Smiler" Colfax, predicted that Lincoln's policy would lose the party thousands of votes in the West. The preachers of New York and Boston, in a series of sermons, flayed Lincoln and upheld Frémont. Editors and party leaders spoke in similar strain, and many prophesied ominously that Frémont would supplant Lincoln as the Republican nominee in 1864.[40]

The Frémont affair brought into the open the long-smoldering hostility between the Jacobins and Lincoln. The radicals attempted to exploit the situation by making furious demands for changes in the Cabinet and army, but Lincoln defied them. The rapidly widening breach between the two factions of the party was fully apparent at the convention of the Massachusetts Republicans in Worcester on October 1. Here Sumner launched a bitter attack upon the administration. He demanded that the party go on record as favoring a policy that would compel the generals to free fugitive slaves. There was not, he insisted, "any sanction under the Constitution for

[40] Benjamin F. Wade to Zachariah Chandler, September 23, 1861, in the Chandler MSS.; *Life of Chandler*, 253-254; J. W. Grimes to W. P. Fessenden, September 19, 1861, in Salter, *Grimes*, 152-153; Sumner to Francis Lieber, September 17, 1861, in Pierce, *Sumner*, 4:42; South Bend *Register*, Colfax's organ, quoted in the *New York Tribune*, September 28, 1861; see also Joseph Medill to S. P. Chase, September 15, 1861, quoted in Bartlett, *Frémont*, 74-75; *New York Tribune*, September 16, 18, 1861; *ibid.*, September 30, quotations from fifteen pastors; Joshua Giddings to Mrs. G. W. Julian, September 17, in the Giddings-Julian MSS. John Jay to Joseph Holt, September 27, in the Joseph Holt MSS. in the Library of Congress; John Russell to Lyman Trumbull, December 17, in the Trumbull MSS.; *National Anti-Slavery Standard*, September 28.

turning a national camp into a slave-pen, or for turning military officers into slave-hunters." Inferentially he indorsed the arming of the slaves. The conservatives, led by Samuel Bowles of the *Springfield Republican,* opposed this "extreme doctrine," "his willingness to sacrifice . . . the Constitution," to attain emancipation, as more dangerous to the Union than "the bayonets of Beauregard." Their control of the convention was sufficient to defeat Sumner.[41]

While Lincoln was enduring the wrath and gibes of Frémont's supporters, the country began to murmur at the continued inactivity of the military forces. All eyes were on the banks of the Potomac, where McClellan drilled and paraded his magnificent army in the beautiful autumn weather. The press, its martial ardor temporarily repressed after Manassas, again shouted for an offensive movement. It dinned the old cry "Onward to Richmond" in the ears of its readers. Leading the clamor was the once-penitent Horace Greeley, who demanded that McClellan hurl his army at the foe before winter set in to prevent further operations. It was the radical press that called for action; the conservative and Democratic newspapers generally defended McClellan's insistence that more time was needed for preparation. The Young Napoleon, disturbed by the reappearance of the spirit that had caused the defeat of his predecessor, came to Lincoln with the plea, "Don't let them hurry me is all I ask." Lincoln assured him that there would be no advance because of political pressure.[42]

The Jacobin chieftains were as impatient for a battle as the

[41] *National Intelligencer,* September 20, 23, 1861; *New York Journal of Commerce,* quoted *ibid.,* September 20; New York *Commercial Advertiser, Boston Daily Advertiser,* quoted *ibid.,* September 26; Pierce, *Sumner,* 4:43–45; Heintzelman diary, November 11, 1861. General Heintzelman received from Sumner a copy of the speech in the form of a pamphlet, *Union and Peace. How shall they be restored?; Boston Post, Boston Daily Advertiser,* and *Boston Journal,* quoted in the *National Intelligencer,* October 5, 1861; *Springfield Republican,* October 2, 1861, quoted in Merriam, *Bowles,* 1:350–352.

[42] *New York Tribune,* October 18, 1861; *National Intelligencer,* September 25, October 22, 24, 1861; *Albany Evening Journal,* quoted *ibid.,* September 17; New York *World, ibid.,* September 25; *Boston Post, ibid.,* October 23; Hay, *Diary,* 1:42.

country was. Chandler had boasted during September that his friend McClellan would soon bag the Confederates, but by mid-October he began to lose faith in the young general who spent all his time at parades and champagne dinners. Ben Wade had given up completely on McClellan, and his disgust with the administration, "blundering, cowardly and inefficient," was greater than ever. He told Chandler that McClellan and Lincoln had no pride nor backbone, else they would not permit Washington to be besieged by an inferior force of Confederates. "So there they stay in perfect contentment behind their entrenchments from month to month, with more than two hundred thousand men around them, occasionally sending forth with great exultation a *bulletin* announcing that '*the capital is safe.*'" Not even "a galvanic battery," declared Wade, could inspire any action in Lincoln or the Cabinet. Troops had been drained from the Northwest to calm the fears of Lincoln for the safety of Washington and to enable Mrs. Lincoln to pursue "without interruption . . . her *French* and *dancing.*" McClellan's men would be hoary veterans before ever engaging in a battle. The general intended to go into winter quarters without striking a blow, concluded the angry Wade, and an outraged people would place the government in more competent hands.[43]

McClellan in the meantime was intriguing to bring about the downfall of General Scott. Although he possessed almost supreme power, he was technically the commander of only one army, the Eastern, now become the Army of the Potomac, whereas Scott was general in chief of the nation's entire military forces. Young and old Mars had quarreled from the beginning. McClellan complained of Scott's opposition to his plans for organizing the army: "He understands nothing, appreciates nothing. . . . I have to fight my way against him." Scott charged his subordinate with neglect of orders, arrogance, and lack of cooperation. Working with McClellan to unseat Scott was Montgomery Blair, who believed that "old granny

[43] Zachariah Chandler to Mrs. Chandler, September 17, October 12, 1861, in the Chandler MSS.; Wade to Chandler, October 3, 1861, *ibid.*

Scott" was paralyzing the whole government.[44] The agitation of the Jacobins for a battle aided McClellan's cause. Scott was an ideal scapegoat upon whom to unload the blame for the failure of the armies to move.

On October 25 Wade, Chandler, and Trumbull, the three musketeers of radicalism, suddenly appeared in Washington. Wade later explained the genesis of their visit: "Mr. Chandler and myself, feeling that the army was laboring under some serious defect somewhere, by reason of which no progress was made, went off to the army to satisfy ourselves, and if possible discover where the difficulty lay." They went immediately to McClellan. They found him at the home of Montgomery Blair, and for three hours that evening, until one o'clock the next morning, they pressed him to attack the foe, who was so close to the city that his "rattlesnake flag" could be seen from the Capitol. "We exhorted him," recounted Wade, "for God's sake, to at least push back the defiant traitors." Risk a battle, they cried. Defeat was preferable to delay. "Swarming recruits" would easily repair any losses suffered on the field. McClellan adeptly diverted their wrath to Scott. He told the senators that he was about ready to start a campaign, but Scott was obstructing his plans. He could do nothing until the ancient officer was retired.[45]

After the senators left, only half convinced by McClellan's excuses and openly derisive of his plea for more troops, the weary general sat down to write his wife. He felt elated; he believed he had finally got Scott out of the way. The senators were to see Lincoln. They would "make a desperate effort tomorrow to have General Scott retired at once."[46]

The Jacobin trio met Lincoln the next evening at the

[44] McClellan, *Own Story*, 84, 85, 86, 113, 136; Gurowski, *Diary*, 108; Scott to Simon Cameron, October 4, 1861, in the Stanton MSS.; *Cincinnati Commercial*, February 27, 1863; *New York Times*, October 24, 1861; Montgomery Blair to B. F. Butler, August 20, July 25, 1861, in Smith, *Blair Family*, 2:125–126.

[45] Benjamin F. Wade, *Facts for the People* (Cincinnati, 1864), 1–2, a pamphlet reproduction of a speech Wade made in Cincinnati. See also the *Cincinnati Gazette*, October 24, 1864; Chandler to Mrs. Chandler, October 27, 1861, in the Chandler MSS.; Hay, *Diary*, 1:48–49.

[46] McClellan, *Own Story*, 223–224.

White House. Young John Hay, the president's secretary, wrote in his diary, "This evening the Jacobin Club . . . came up to worry the administration into a battle." The conference was stormy. The senators demanded that Lincoln order McClellan to advance, and the president defended the general's "deliberateness." Chandler cried that if the armies retired to winter quarters, he was "in favor of sending for Jeff Davis at once." The solons could not budge Lincoln, and at midnight they departed in disgust.

Despite the lateness of the hour, the worried Lincoln immediately hastened to McClellan's headquarters to discuss his formidable callers with the general. He found McClellan fretting at the "popular impatience" for action, and disturbed by the visit of the senators. Lincoln calmed him, but said the spirit which the Jacobins represented was "a reality, and should be taken into the account." On the following evening Lincoln and Hay dropped around to Seward's house, where they found, to their great surprise, Wade and Chandler. "They had been talking to Seward to get up a battle," wrote the indignant Hay, "saying that one must be fought; saying that defeat was no worse than delay, and a great deal more trash."[47]

The Jacobin senators were dismayed by their flinty reception in administration circles. Chandler informed his wife, "We are not here a moment too soon, & for the reason apprehended. In fact I wish we had not left. Trumbull, Wade & myself have been busy night & day since our arrival, but whether our labor has been in vain or not, time alone must disclose. . . . If Wade & I fail in our mission, the end is at hand." Trumbull, equally discouraged, wrote, "If our army should go into winter quarters with the capital besieged, I very much fear the result would be a recognition of the Confederates by foreign governments, the demoralization of our own people, and of course an inability to raise either men or money another season. Such must not be. Action, action is what we want and must have."[48]

[47] Hay, *Diary*, 1:48–49; Chandler to Mrs. Chandler, October 27, 1861, in the Chandler MSS.; Wade, *Facts for the People*, 2.
[48] Chandler to Mrs. Chandler, October 27, 1861, in the Chandler MSS.; Trumbull to M. C. Lea, November 5, 1861, in White, *Trumbull*, 171–172.

The retirement of General Scott on November 1, one result of Wade and Chandler's visit, faintly cheered the few radicals who still had faith in McClellan. The Young Napoleon was now the supreme generalissimo of the federal armies. But by throwing Scott to the wolves, McClellan had prepared the way for his own destruction. Henceforth the Jacobins held him alone responsible for the determination of military policies. As they watched McClellan patiently drilling his soldiers, apparently frittering away the autumn with aimless reviews, their anger mounted. At one of his myriad-course dinners, elaborate affairs to which the envious Jacobin leaders were never invited, McClellan defended his cautious preparations, and was reported to have boasted that "there was no power on earth, neither that of the press nor of politicians, that should cause him to swerve a hair's breadth from the policy which he had adopted in relation to the present war." Such sentiments maddened the radicals. Grimes wailed to Fessenden, "The truth is, we are going to destruction as fast as imbecility, corruption, and the wheels of time, can carry us. . . . The army is in inextricable confusion, and is every day becoming worse and worse." Old Joshua Giddings charged that "our officers from the highest down to the lowest on the Potomac seem to have failed us." The energetic Chandler was attempting to persuade Cameron to detach the bulk of McClellan's army to the West, where it could be used for offensive operations by Frémont.[49]

The battle of Ball's Bluff was the final wedge which drove McClellan and the Jacobins apart. On October 21 a portion of General Charles P. Stone's division of the Army of the Potomac attacked a superior Confederate force, and was hurled back with large losses. The number of men engaged was small, and the affair was of minor importance. Nevertheless it aroused the Jacobins to savage anger. The commander of the decimated federal detachment had been Colonel Edward D. Baker, the former radical senator from Oregon, who a few months before

---

[49] *National Intelligencer*, November 8, 1861; Salter, *Grimes*, 156; Giddings to his daughter, October 27, 1861, in the Giddings-Julian MSS.; Chandler to Cameron, November 15, 1861, in *Life of Chandler*, 213–214.

had declared that the North might have to govern the South as conquered territory after the war. Baker was killed during the battle. Although Baker's own rashness was responsible for the disaster, the Jacobins cried that his superior officer, General Stone, had purposely sent the popular colonel to his death.

This amazing charge was a chimera of the suspicious radical mentality, warped by war hysteria. Stone was a West Pointer who stood high in the confidence of McClellan. Because his wife had relatives in the South, the Jacobins suspected his loyalty. He had been one of the conspicuous offenders in returning fugitive slaves. Whispered rumors insinuated that rebels bearing mysterious packages crossed and recrossed the river in his sector, that he was maintaining treasonable intercourse with the enemy. The radicals jumped to the conclusion that Stone had planned the slaughter of Baker's men. Representative Shanks declared that "the Ball's Bluff murder is but a part of this accursed tragedy, where treason and treasonable blunders murdered by the hands of slavery's maddening demons, a brave and loved officer and a thousand pure patriots." Giddings called the affair a disgrace, and Grimes spoke of it as "one of those resultless sacrifices of life of which we have had so many this year."[50]

After Ball's Bluff the radicals saw McClellan in a haze of suspicion. If Stone was a traitor, they reasoned, McClellan, his intimate and protector, must be of the same stripe. Suddenly they perceived a sinister motive in the commander's refusal to attack the enemy. He secretly sympathized with slavery, he did not wish to defeat the rebels, he was plotting to restore Southern control of the government! It was at this time that Chandler supposedly made his famous threat to break the young general.[51]

McClellan was now openly fraternizing with the Democracy. He received at his headquarters and visited such prominent

[50] Shanks, *General Frémont*, 9. Shanks' figures were highly exaggerated. Giddings to his daughter, October 27, 1861, in the Giddings-Julian MSS.; Grimes to Mrs. Grimes, November 10, 1861, in Salter, *Grimes*, 153–154; Thaddeus Stevens, letter of November 5, 1861, in the Stevens MSS.

[51] *Detroit Free Press*, January 10, 1863.

Democratic politicians as Edwin M. Stanton. The Marcy machine in New York was using all its powers of intrigue to advance his political and military fortunes. One of its members wrote to Stanton after learning of a squabble in the Cabinet between Cameron and Secretary of the Interior Caleb Smith, "I am glad to learn by the papers of to-day that there has been a collision of sentiment between Cameron and Smith. Such quarrels should be fostered in every proper way, though the General must, if possible, keep entirely free from them."[52]

While the gloomy Jacobins watched their control of the Eastern army slip away with the defection of McClellan, the radical cause received an even more stunning blow. Lincoln removed Frémont from the command in the West. After the repudiation of his proclamation the Pathfinder's position had become increasingly untenable. Large bodies of Confederate troops were at large in Missouri, and Frémont took no active measures to dislodge them. At the same time rumors became current that his relations with contractors and his purchase of war materials had an unsavory odor. Secretary of War Cameron, his own skirts none too clean, made a hurried trip to St. Louis and condemned the construction of defensive works around the city. Later the House committee on contracts appeared, to ferret out evidence of alleged corruption. Men with important business to transact complained that Frémont so surrounded himself with brilliantly attired foreign aides that they could not reach him. The general climaxed this list of complaints by embroiling himself in a bitter quarrel with his erstwhile sponsors and would-be directors, the Blairs. Frank Blair, a colonel of volunteers in Frémont's army, was the boss of the Republican Party in Missouri—until Frémont arrived. Then the radical faction, smarting under Blair's conservative leadership, went over to Frémont. Blair found his political power threatened. Soon the friendly relations between the two officers developed into open enmity. Blair criticized Frémont's awarding of contracts and opposed his emancipation proclama-

[52] McClellan, *Own Story*, 175–176; S. L. M. Barlow to Stanton, November 21, 1861, in Flower, *Stanton*, 122.

tion. Finally the irritated commander, charging Blair with insubordination, placed him under military arrest. In Washington the colonel's angered brother and father brought pressure on Lincoln to remove Frémont.[53]

In the face of this accumulated hostility Frémont's radical friends rallied to his support. Trumbull went to St. Louis and after a conference with the general wrote to Lincoln expostulating against the failure of the government to sustain its Western commander. When Cameron made his inspection of the department, Chandler was on hand to see that the general's interests were protected. Ben Wade assured the worried officer that the people had "unbounded confidence" in him, and encouraged him to "persevere in the course you have thus far pursued. No greater misfortune could befall the country than that you should retire at this period." Greeley declared his retention in command a military necessity, while Frémont's St. Louis organ threatened a revolt of the Western army if its dashing captain were removed.[54]

But the weary Lincoln, his vast fund of patience exhausted, had determined that the unruly commander of the Western department would have to go. On October 24 he issued an order removing him from command. The fatal document was delivered to Frémont while he was slowly following a Confederate army across the state, and General David Hunter immediately assumed control. The anger of the Jacobins at this final indignity to their cherished favorite was intense. Thaddeus Stevens spoke bitterly of "the hounds" who had "run down" Frémont. A Cincinnati editor claimed that Frémont's

[53] Smith, *Blair Family*, 2:66–68, 73–84; Bartlett, *Frémont*, 75–81; General J. M. Palmer to Lyman Trumbull, September 22, 1861, in the Trumbull MSS.; Gustave Koerner to Trumbull, November 15, *ibid.*; J. R. Shepley to W. P. Fessenden, September 17, in the Fessenden MSS.; *New York Tribune*, October 9, 1861, letters between Frémont and Blair; *National Intelligencer*, October 16, 17, 21, 1861.

[54] Trumbull to Lincoln, October 1, 1861, in the Trumbull MSS., copy; Chandler to Mrs. Chandler, October 12, 1861, in the Chandler MSS.; J. M. Palmer to Trumbull, October 13, in the Trumbull MSS.; Nevins, *Frémont*, 2:623; *New York Tribune*, October 29, 30, 31, 1861; *Missouri Democrat*, quoted in the *National Intelligencer*, November 6, 1861.

supporters in the West would flare out in revolution. Grimes asserted that the general's proclamation had been the cause of his removal. "That was the great sin for which he was punished. . . . a regular conspiracy was entered into to destroy his influence in the country and with the army, and finally to depose him." In a speech at St. Louis, the defiant general defended his record and announced that he was returning east "to answer all these charges more definitely." He went first to New York, where he was fêted by the antislavery forces of the metropolis, and heard Sumner and other prominent Jacobins laud his proclamation before a great meeting at Cooper Union.[55]

With the removal of Frémont, the Jacobins lost completely their grasp on the military machine. Democratic generals now commanded the two principal armies: McClellan in the East, and Henry W. Halleck, who succeeded Frémont, in the West. This meant that Democratic officers would also monopolize the subordinate positions. The radicals saw their hopes of military emancipation go a'glimmering. The new conservative dominance of the army came just at a time when the Jacobin chieftains had determined to launch a drive for emancipation as a necessary weapon of war. "It is to be presented strictly as a measure of military necessity," wrote Sumner, "and the argument is to be thus supported rather than on grounds of philanthropy."[56] This strategy was now futile. The radicals might as well have beat the air as attempted to destroy slavery through the medium of officers who were opposed to the dogmas of radicalism.

Halleck immediately gave the radicals a demonstration of the hopelessness of their cause as long as the Democrats controlled the army patronage. On November 20 he published an order

[55] Thaddeus Stevens, letter of November 5, 1861, in the Stevens MSS.; Richard Smith of the *Cincinnati Gazette* to Salmon P. Chase, November 7, 1861, in Nevins, *Frémont*, 2:624; Salter, *Grimes*, 154–155, quotation from two letters by Grimes; Gustave Koerner to Trumbull, November 18, 1861, in the Trumbull MSS.; *National Intelligencer*, November 16, 1861; Nevins, *Frémont*, 2:625.

[56] Sumner to John Jay, November 10, 1861, in Pierce, *Sumner*, 4:49.

concerning the treatment of fugitive slaves. He asserted that the Confederates were employing them as spies. Therefore he directed that all fugitives within his lines be ejected, and that none be admitted in the future. This action stung the Jacobins to cold fury. They charged that Halleck was protecting the interests of disloyal slaveholders. Some believed that Lincoln was behind Halleck, and denounced the "obnoxious order" as a part of the administration's policy of preserving slavery.[57]

The radicals were in a savage mood as autumn ended. The armies had failed to advance, Democratic officers filled the important commands, and the administration had refused to sanction a use of the war powers to abolish slavery. They knew that they must act quickly and drastically if they wished to control the war policies. Senator Grimes, arriving early in Washington for the December session of Congress, wrote to his wife: "I reached Washington last night, weary with the journey, and disgusted with what I heard from quite authentic sources of the course of the Administration. If the other Northwestern members feel as I do, there will be something more during the coming session than growling and showing our teeth. And, from what I hear, they do feel excited and incensed." The Jacobins realized now that they could never force the administration into an antislavery position with the inadequate weapon of private protest. A more vigorous line of attack was imperative. Grimes proposed the creation of a congressional investigative committee which could delve into the recesses of army secrets and guide the faction in the formulation of a program. He begged Fessenden to take the lead in setting up such an agency. "If you determine to probe the sore spots to the bottom, . . . we can inaugurate a new order of things, and the country can be saved," he urged. "But, if you rest quietly in your seat, we shall go on from one enormity to another, the evil of today will be urged as an apology for greater evil tomor-

---

[57] O. R., series 1, 8:370; John Russell to Trumbull, December 31, 1861, in the Trumbull MSS.; Joseph Medill to Trumbull, July 4, 1862, ibid.; New York Tribune, November 23, 1861; Salter, Grimes, 187–188; Pierce, Sumner, 4:39.

row, and the devil will be sure to get us in the end, and that right speedily."[58]

In this ominous pause, the Jacobins moved toward Washington and the opening session of Congress.

[58] J. W. Grimes to Mrs. Grimes, November 6, 1861, in Salter, *Grimes*, 153; Grimes to W. P. Fessenden, November 13, 1861, *ibid.*, 156–157.

3
The Ides of December

ONE OF LINCOLN'S ADVISERS, watching the angry Jacobins swarm into Washington and hearing the whispered gossip in Capitol corridors, wrote, "I can see that Lincoln is going to have trouble with the fiery element of his own party—Without violating confidence I think I may say that he is fully advised of it and will meet it bravely."[1]

The apprehensive conservatives knew that the radicals were ready to wage open warfare upon the administration. They foresaw a desperate Jacobin attempt to grasp control of the war policies. Fears of a bitter factional struggle that would disrupt party unity haunted them. They implored the radicals to keep the peace. From the *New York Times*, the journalistic fountainhead of conservative Republicanism, came the plea:

No greater disaster could happen to us than the destruction of that unanimity of public sentiment which has thus far been our strength in the struggle for the Constitution and the Union. . . . We cannot help hoping that Congress will . . . repress whatever rash attempts may be made, in the spirit of overzealous partisanship, to override and destroy it. *The time for the safe and successful treatment of the Slavery question, in its broadest aspects, has not yet come.*

Even William Cullen Bryant, whose New York *Evening Post* was strongly tinged with radicalism, sounded a note for party harmony:

Slavery has been the cause of enormous wrongs, but it must not therefore be stricken in passionate revenge. Let us not abandon any great and sacred principle of the Constitution in order to hurry its extinction. It is important to keep the war to its original object—the restoration of the Union and the preservation of the Constitution.[2]

[1] J. F. Speed to Joseph Holt, November 28, 1861, in the Holt MSS.
[2] *New York Times,* December 5, 1861; New York *Evening Post,* December 5, 1861.

The announced resolution of the Jacobins to force emancipation upon the government by congressional enactment as a war measure alarmed the moderates. It was not the function of Congress, insisted Lincoln's supporters, to define the purposes of the war. Senator Collamer, veteran Vermont Republican, summed up their views in an interview at Boston on his way to Washington: "War is not a business Congress can engineer. It is properly *executive business,* and the moment Congress passes beyond the line of providing for the wants of the government, and deciding the purposes of the war, to say how it shall be conducted, the whole thing will prove a failure."[3] A conservative Washington newspaper declared that McClellan and the officers of the army, not Congress, were the proper judges of the "military necessity" of emancipation:

. . . any attempt on the part of the legislative branch to direct or supervise the military movements of the administration would introduce confusion and perplexity into all the operations of the war at a time when most of all unity of will is necessary to their successful issue. There is danger of dissension . . . only upon a single topic—the disposition that shall be made of slavery in the conduct of the impending campaign.[4]

These appeals did not shake the Jacobins in their determination to call the administration to account for its conduct of the war. By December their accumulated grievances against the president had become too powerful to be shunted aside by any argument for party regularity. They were resolved that emancipation must be made the principal objective of the war. Greeley, who had been in a conciliatory mood for months, now thundered for the destruction of slavery as a measure of military necessity. "It is high time that we had either war or peace; and a contest in which we guard and protect our enemies on their most exposed and critical point is not war," he proclaimed. "It is at best but one of those sham fights so current of late on the Potomac." Grim old Thaddeus Stevens had

[3] *Boston Daily Advertiser,* quoted in the *National Intelligencer,* December 6, 1861.
[4] *National Intelligencer,* December 7, 1861.

decided that the radical machine must strike for complete emancipation; there was no other way to crush the Confederacy. But he feared that the conservative "cowards" could not stomach so drastic a measure. General David Hunter, an ambitious officer who had decided that the best way to advance his military career was to curry favor with the radicals, had impressed them with a scheme to organize an army of freed slaves. "It is time slavery had its quietus," he told Trumbull, "we have been trifling long enough." The radicals liked Hunter's proposal, but they knew Lincoln would never adopt it. They sneered at the president for considering the "lives, property, & slaves" of the rebels "more precious than the lives of our soldiers."[5]

The radicals were equally determined to force an advance of the armies. They believed that a forward movement was necessary to sustain popular support of the war. "A victory we want," cried Senator Jim Lane, "and a victory we must have."[6] Greeley was clamoring for a winter campaign. "The season is favorable for military operations in the South," he contended.[7] The Jacobins were convinced that aggressive military action would aid their emancipation program. So long as the armies remained snug in quarters and camp, they constituted no menace to slavery. But if they invaded rebel territory, large numbers of fugitive slaves would collect within the lines, and the problem of emancipation would be forced upon the administration. Gustave Koerner warned Trumbull that all agitation was dangerous until McClellan took the offensive. "If our armies were active and victorious, instead of *rotting* physically and mentally in winter quarters, which they do," he wrote, "we could indulge in a more stringent policy." The

[5] *New York Tribune*, December 10, 11, 23, 1861; Thaddeus Stevens to G. Smith, December 14, 1861, in the Stevens MSS.; David Hunter to Trumbull, December 9, 1861, in the Trumbull MSS.; G. A. Nourse to Trumbull, December 21, 1861, and C. H. Kettler to Trumbull, December 22, *ibid.*

[6] *Congressional Globe*, 37 Congress, 2 Session, 113; see also Senator Hale, quoted in the *New York Tribune*, December 13, 1861, Washington correspondence.

[7] *Ibid.*, December 16, 1861.

Jacobins blamed their one-time protégé McClellan for the failure of the armies to advance. They worked busily now to bring about his downfall. Greeley craftily suggested that his duties as general in chief and commander of the Eastern army were too heavy, that his authority should be divided among several officers. In Washington, Chandler was pulling strings to have McDowell made head of the Army of the Potomac.[8]

To the radicals the lethargy of the military forces portended a plot on the part of McClellan and his subordinates to prevent the subjugation of the Confederacy. This delusion of the Jacobin war mentality sprang from the conviction that the Democratic masters of the army were secretly in sympathy with the rebels. The radicals raged at the number of Democratic officers to whom Lincoln had given appointments. Julian and Wilson charged that four fifths of the general officers belonged to the opposition party. After the Ball's Bluff episode the radicals suspected these men of treason, or at least of having "no heart" in the war. "They want to save the Union in such manner as not to hurt its deadly assailants, its implacable foes," explained Greeley. "Hence they strike irresolutely, ineffectively. They wait to be assured that their blow will not reach too far, until the time for striking has passed." One of Stevens' friends begged, "For God's sake, and that of common humanity, do not permit that our loyal soldiers should any longer be compelled to grope in the dark with clogs upon their feet. Free them from imbecile and traitorous leaders." Representative Conway estimated in December that there was not "more than one sincere abolitionist or emancipationist among the military authorities."[9] This was a condition which the Jacobins meant to change. They knew they must shatter Demo-

[8] Koerner to Trumbull, December 12, 1861, in the Trumbull MSS.; *New York Tribune*, December 14, 1861; Robert B. Warden, *Account of the Private Life and Public Services of Salmon Portland Chase* (Cincinnati, 1874), 392.

[9] Julian, *Speeches on Political Questions*, 202–204; Henry Wilson in the Senate, December 23, 1861, in the *Congressional Globe*, 37 Congress, 2 Session, 164; J. W. Shaffer to Lyman Trumbull, December 24, 1861, and S. Sawyer to Trumbull, December 18, in the Trumbull MSS.; Joseph Medill

cratic control of the army before military emancipation could be effected.

During the late autumn the radicals had become obsessed with the fear that the Democratic army cabal would try to establish a military dictatorship. They had terrifying visions of McClellan and Halleck marching their armies on Washington, purging Congress of Republican members, and restoring the Union under Southern domination. An injudicious threat in the *New York Herald,* McClellan's principal journalistic champion, threw the radicals into an angry panic: "If the factious abolition leaders do not speedily draw in their horns, they may find in General McClellan such a tartar as the Long Parliament found in Cromwell, and the Council of Five Hundred found in Napoleon Bonaparte."[10]

The rumor spread that Lincoln was like putty in the generals' hands, that the military leaders dictated his every decision. They had threatened him with a military rebellion if Congress passed an emancipation bill; they would countenance no attack upon slavery. Nervous radicals exhorted their congressional leaders to curb the power-drunk military chieftains before they ran hog-wild. Trumbull had won general approval with his definition of the position in which Congress stood toward the army: "Our power is omnipotent over this Army; and they ought to have rules and regulations by which to be governed." His Illinois supporters cheered his audacity and encouraged him to stand firm against military despotism. "The representatives of the people should resist all dictation from army officers in settling the great controversy. . . . Army officers . . . are but the servants, & not the dictators of the people," wrote one. A friend of Stevens urged Congress not only to lay down whatever rules it saw fit for the control of the army, but to probe fearlessly "every act of treachery" com-

---

to Edwin M. Stanton, January 21, 1862, in the Stanton MSS.; Greeley in the New York *Independent,* April 9, 1863; L. C. Carter to Thaddeus Stevens, January 8, 1862, in the Stevens MSS.; Representative Conway in the *Congressional Globe,* 37 Congress, 2 Session, 83.

[10] *New York Herald,* December 11, 1861.

mitted by a traitorous officer. A congressional investigative committee, he declared, would keep the army in its place.[11]

In this grim and dangerous mood, the Jacobins took their seats on the opening day of Congress. Lincoln's message contained nothing to conciliate his opponents; rather it stung them to greater fury. His only reference to emancipation was a recommendation that the slaves freed by the confiscation act be colonized in another country. The rest of the message was an argument for the American system of government, and a clarion call for all factions to unite in restoring it. "In considering the policy to be adopted for suppressing the insurrection," he said, "I have been anxious and careful that the inevitable conflict for this purpose shall not degenerate into a violent and remorseless revolutionary struggle. . . . The Union must be preserved; and hence all indispensable means must be employed. We should not be in haste to determine that radical and extreme measures, which may reach the loyal as well as the disloyal, are indispensable."[12]

The message provoked only contempt in radical circles. Greeley disparaged the president's conservative position on the slavery issue, but hoped an open break between him and the Jacobins could be prevented. The abolition press attacked the document with unrestrained savagery. Wendell Phillips denounced as a shameless evasion Lincoln's failure to mention emancipation. "I demand of the government a policy," he cried. An Illinois radical said the message had "fallen stillborn." Charles H. Ray of the *Chicago Tribune* staff, writing to Senator Trumbull, assailed Lincoln for pandering to the border slave states. He added sweepingly, "when the time comes, we are ready to oppose Lincoln, the cabinet, McClellan or anybody else."[13]

[11] *Congressional Globe*, 37 Congress, 1 Session, 376; B. W. Reynolds to Lyman Trumbull, December 16, 1861, in the Trumbull MSS.; J. C. Conkling to Trumbull, December 16, and H. W. Blodgett to Trumbull, December 21, *ibid.*; L. C. Carter to Thaddeus Stevens, January 8, 1862, in the Stevens MSS.

[12] Lincoln, *Works*, 7:28–60.

[13] *New York Tribune*, December 4, 1861; *National Anti-Slavery Standard* (New York), December 14, 1861; Phillips, *Speeches*, 435; J. H. Bryant to

The radicals were still sputtering at the conservative tone of the message when a curious episode originating in the Cabinet added fuel to their wrath. Simon Cameron, who always kept his ear to the ground, had decided during the autumn that the country was with the radicals. Clever politician that he was, he had no intention of being caught on the losing side. So, deserting Seward, he set out to ingratiate himself with the Jacobins. On October 14 he instructed General Thomas Sherman, commanding an area occupied by federal troops at Port Royal, South Carolina, to accept and employ fugitive slaves in any capacity he saw fit, even to organizing them in "squads" and "companies." The astonished radicals were delighted with the secretary. "Indeed, he goes beyond Frémont," exclaimed Sumner. A month later Cameron, while visiting the regiment of General John Cochrane, advocated in a widely publicized speech the use of Negro soldiers.[14] The secretary was now riding high with the Jacobins, but he overestimated Lincoln's patience. In his annual report to Congress he inserted a recommendation for the creation of an army of freed slaves. He ventured this step at the secret instigation of Edwin M. Stanton, the Democrat, another wily observer who had concluded that the future lay with the radicals. Cameron hurried copies of his report to the newspapers without submitting it to Lincoln. The president, when he learned of the proposal to arm the slaves, ordered the report recalled, and compelled Cameron to delete this section.[15]

The Jacobins rushed to Cameron's defense, although many of them suspected the sincerity of his precipitate conversion to radicalism. They were angered by the rumor that McClellan

Lyman Trumbull, December 8, 1861, in the Trumbull MSS.; Grant Goodrich to Trumbull, December 5, and S. Ford to Trumbull, December 5, *ibid.;* C. H. Ray to Trumbull, December 6, 1861, *ibid.*

[14] *O. R.,* series 1, 6:176–177; Pierce, *Sumner,* 4:49; *New York Tribune,* October 29, 1861; *National Intelligencer,* November 14, 1861; John Cochrane, *The American Civil War* (New York, 1879), a pamphlet describing Cameron's visit and speech.

[15] Henry Wilson, "Jeremiah S. Black and Edwin M. Stanton," *Atlantic Monthly,* 26(1870):470; Pierce, *Sumner,* 4:46; Flower, *Stanton,* 122; Alexander Howard Meneely, "Three Manuscripts of Gideon Welles," *American Historical Review,* 31(1925–26):487.

had forced Lincoln's action. Stevens asserted that the general had threatened to resign unless the report was modified. Indignant radicals asked whether Congress was "so recreant as to submit to a military dictation."[16]

The temper of the radicals became evident immediately after Congress had organized. On December 5 Trumbull introduced in the Senate a new and drastic confiscation bill, which was championed by Wade and Chandler. Its purpose, explained one of Trumbull's supporters, was to "strike at the heart and life" of the Confederacy.[17] Thaddeus Stevens offered a resolution calling for emancipation as a military measure and directing the president to declare free all slaves who came into the federal lines. Representative Shellabarger brought up a resolution condemning the military authorities for returning fugitive slaves.[18] On December 4 came the tremendously significant action of the House—its refusal to readopt the Crittenden resolution defining the purposes of the war. This was a direct repudiation of Lincoln's message and his concept of the war as a struggle to preserve the Union.

The Jacobins followed these bold challenges to the administration with a bitter offensive against the generals who had made a practice of ejecting fugitive slaves from their camps. Sumner led off with a blast against Halleck's order of November 20. In the House, Lovejoy introduced a resolution branding the order "cruel and inhuman." Stevens and Julian joined the attack, Frank Blair acting as the general's lone defender. Julian charged that it was the policy of the administration to nurture officers who were opposed to emancipation.[19]

[16] *New York Tribune,* December 4, 1861, Washington correspondence, December 5, editorial; *National Anti-Slavery Standard,* December 14, 1861; *New York Tribune,* December 10, 1861, Washington correspondence; John Russell to Lyman Trumbull, December 17, 1861, in the Trumbull MSS.; J. H. Bryant to Trumbull, December 8, 1861, *ibid.*

[17] *Congressional Globe,* 37 Congress, 2 Session, 18–19; Blaine, *Twenty Years of Congress,* 1:374–375; J. H. Bryant to Lyman Trumbull, December 8, 1861, in the Trumbull MSS.

[18] *Congressional Globe,* 37 Congress, 2 Session, 6, 8, 15; *National Intelligencer,* December 3, 1861.

[19] *Congressional Globe,* 37 Congress, 2 Session, 33–34, 57–59; Pierce. *Sumner,* 4:66; Smith, *Blair Family,* 2:130; *National Intelligencer,* Decem-

The mounting aggressiveness of the radicals dismayed the conservatives. "I am fully persuaded that there is mischief brewing here," wrote Lincoln's friend J. F. Speed. "A large and powerful party of the ultra men is being formed to make war upon the President and his conservative policy." The alarmed conservatives of New York City discussed methods of protecting Lincoln from "the hostility of the abolition faction in Congress," who were trying "to turn the contest for our national preservation into an abolition crusade for its destruction."[20]

In the first week of the session the Senate and House met jointly to hear Sumner deliver a eulogy of the late Senator Baker, who the radicals believed had been sacrificed at Ball's Bluff by the traitorous Stone. Washington society turned out in force to be stirred by the brilliant orator. Lincoln sat in the crowded galleries. Sumner made the most of the impressive occasion. He attacked slavery as the cause of the rebellion, and called upon the administration to cease protecting the very institution and men that were responsible for the war. Dramatically he told the story of Baker's death. Then, looking straight at Lincoln, he charged that slavery had been "the murderer of our dead Senator." The correspondent of an abolitionist newspaper reported with satisfaction that as Sumner pronounced these words, the president started violently.[21]

Out of the welter of radical anger surrounding the Ball's Bluff disaster developed the Jacobins' most formidable challenge to Lincoln's conservative war policy. They believed that Stone was responsible for Baker's death, and that in some mysterious way McClellan had been back of the whole affair. They determined to probe the history of the battle in the hope

---

ber 12, 1861. The quotation was not in Lovejoy's original resolution, but in a substitute suggested by William E. Lansing of New York.

[20] J. F. Speed to Joseph Holt, December 8, 1861, in the Holt MSS.; N. J. Waterbury to Andrew Johnson, December 11, 1861, and Truman Smith to Johnson, December 14, in the Andrew Johnson MSS. in the Library of Congress.

[21] *Congressional Globe*, 37 Congress, 2 Session, 54–55; *National Anti-Slavery Standard*, December 21, 1861, Washington correspondence; Pierce, *Sumner*, 4:67.

of disgracing Stone. Tall, handsome Roscoe Conkling introduced a resolution in the House calling on the War Department to furnish all the information in its possession that would
explain the causes of the recent defeat.[22] Cameron, probably
acting under Lincoln's orders, refused the request.

Then the Senate radicals, seeing an opportunity to attack
McClellan through Stone, took a hand. On December 5
Chandler moved the creation of a committee to investigate the
causes of the Union disasters at Ball's Bluff and Bull Run.
Immediately several senators jumped to their feet with amendments to include other defeats. Lane demanded an inquiry into
the defeat at Wilson's Creek, for which Frémont had been
blamed because of failure to send needed re-enforcements. Lane
hinted that someone else, perhaps Lincoln himself, was the real
culprit. Grimes, who in November had argued to Fessenden
that Congress should thoroughly probe the sore spots of army
administration, now suggested a joint committee of both houses
with authority "to inquire into the causes of the disasters that
have attended the public arms." Because of the disagreement
among the radical leaders concerning the nature of the proposed agency, the Senate postponed action.[23]

Four days later the discussion was resumed. Grimes defended
his contention that the committee should have general powers
to investigate all lost battles; the inquiry would be barren of
results, he maintained, if restricted to a few specific defeats.
Grimes lauded Frémont's handling of affairs in the West, and
hoped the committee would dig up the inside story of his
removal, to determine whether Lincoln had committed an act
of injustice. Several Republican senators opposed a congressional investigation of the military activities of the executive
as a dangerous governmental innovation. Pomeroy feared it
would lead to the impeachment of high civil officials, possibly
of the president himself. The suave Lafayette S. Foster denounced the proposed inquiry as an unconstitutional invasion
of the president's powers as commander in chief of the military

[22] *Congressional Globe,* 37 Congress, 2 Session, 6.
[23] *Ibid.,* 16–17.

forces. He predicted that it would lead to confusion in the army. Were he a general, he observed, he would not want his subordinate officers running off to Washington at every opportunity to tattle his faults to some committee. "We cannot have men in the field fighting a battle, and have them here in our committee rooms testifying as to who was to blame for a disaster."

Foster's statement angered the always irritable William Pitt Fessenden, who was a cross between a statesman and a shrew, the shrew predominating. Fessenden cried that Congress had a more important function in the war than merely to pass appropriations:

I hold it to be our bounden duty, impressed upon us by our position here, to keep an anxious, watchful eye over all the executive agents who are carrying on the war at the direction of the people, whom we represent and whom we are bound to protect in relation to this matter. . . . [We] are not under the command of the military of this country. They are under ours as a Congress; and I stand here to maintain it.

As Fessenden concluded his outburst, John Sherman rose to offer a suggestion that changed entirely the character of the proposed committee. Why, he asked, engage in the futile exercise of investigating lost battles? They were past history. "To confine this inquiry to the disasters of the war would be to cripple and limit the proposed committee in all its operations. In my judgment, this ought to be a committee of inquiry into the general conduct of the war," past, present, and future—defeats, the orders of executive departments, the actions of generals in the field, and the question of war policies. Grimes immediately altered his amendment to fit this recommendation, and the bill as finally passed established a committee with spacious powers to investigate "the conduct of the present war." Henry Wilson was eminently satisfied with the change from the original measure. He predicted that the importance of the newly born agency would result not from its revelations of past mistakes but from its influence upon the future determination of military policy. He hoped the committee would light a fire under the generals who returned fugitive slaves and protected rebel property. "We should teach men in civil and in military authority that the people expect that they will not make mistakes, and that we shall not be easy with their errors. . . . I want military men to understand that they are not to stand upon technicalities for the preservation of the old Army or the getting up of a new one." The next day the House accepted the bill without debate.[24]

Thus was born the Committee on the Conduct of the War, the unnatural child of lustful radicalism and a confused conservatism. It played a dramatic and powerful rôle in the history of the next few years. Until the Committee was created the Jacobins were in the dark regarding the plans of the president and his military advisers; they knew almost nothing of the real condition of the military forces or of the secrets of army administration. The radicals could never have initiated and carried on their struggle against Lincoln without the vital information which the Committee furnished in its jaundiced reports. It became the spearhead of the radical drive against the administration. It investigated the principal military campaigns, worked to undermine Democratic and conservative officers, interfered boldly with the plans of commanders, and bullied Lincoln into accepting the radical program. It was the most potent weapon wielded by the Jacobin cabal in the successful campaign to make radicalism instead of moderation the political faith of the nation. Yet its creation caused not a ripple of attention. Many conservatives voted for the measure without realizing the significance of the agency they were helping to establish. The radicals blandly assured Lincoln that the Committee's only purpose was to promote the vigorous prosecution of the war; there was no intention of assailing the administration. But waspish old Adam Gurowski, the Polish refugee for whom Sumner had secured a job in the State Department and who worshipped the radical leaders, noted in his diary: "The Congress appointed a War Investigating Committee. There is hope that the committee will

<hr>

[24] *Ibid.*, 29–32, 40.

quickly find out what a terrible mistake this McClellan is, and warn the nation of him. But Lincoln, Seward, and the Blairs, will not give up their idol."[25]

The personnel of the Committee, named by the vice-president and the speaker after conferences with the Jacobin leaders, was preponderantly radical. Wade, the chairman, and Chandler were the leaders of the faction in the Senate. Three of the House members, George W. Julian, Daniel Gooch, and John Covode, were radicals. The Democratic Senate member was Andrew Johnson of Tennessee, a zealous supporter of the war and the leading "War Democrat" in the country. Moses F. Odell, representative from Brooklyn, belonged to the same faith. Wade, Chandler, Julian, Gooch, and Odell remained on the Committee for the entire period of its existence, thus investing its activities with a significant continuity of influence. Johnson, who at first took a prominent part in the Committee's work, resigned early in 1862 to become military governor of his state; his three Democratic successors were ignored by the Republican members and rarely attended a meeting. Covode left Congress in 1864, and Benjamin F. Loan, a Missouri radical, took his place.

The dominating figure of the Committee was its chairman, "Bluff Ben" Wade. "Around him all the other members . . . have revolved as around a central sun," wrote one contemporary critic. "He has furnished the brains and the momentum of the committee."[26] He had first entered politics as an anti-slavery Whig in Ohio, but had stayed clear of any formal affiliation with the emancipation movement until its political future was assured. He had captured a Senate seat in 1851 by an opportune denunciation of the Fugitive Slave Act in the Compromise of 1850. Almost overnight he became a hero to the opponents of slavery. This was the turbulent period when the fiery Southern congressmen intimidated Northern members in

[25] James M. Edmunds, "Zachariah Chandler," *Republic*, 4(1875):201; Gurowski, *Diary*, 136.

[26] New York *World*, August 12, 1864; *Detroit Free Press*, January 10, 1863.

debate with threats of physical violence; when Congressman Rust of Arkansas caned Horace Greeley on the streets of Washington; when Barksdale of Mississippi flashed his bowie knife during the House debates; when Dawson of Louisiana leveled a pistol at the "nigger-loving" Giddings; when Preston Brooks assaulted Sumner. The Southerners were always ready to settle verbal arguments in the halls of Congress with pistols for two. They challenged offending Northern members to duels, but the latter refused to fight, pleading that their moral scruples forbade the use of weapons. The scornful aristocrats stigmatized this attitude as cowardice. Wade, who possessed great physical courage, abruptly changed this situation. Soon after he took his seat a Southern senator, angered by something Wade had said in debate, sent him a challenge. All Washington gasped in astonishment when the old Western solon accepted. As the challenged party he had the privilege of choosing the weapons and the conditions of the duel. He named squirrel rifles at twenty paces, "with a white paper the size of a dollar pinned over the heart of each combatant."[27] The proud Southerner was horrified by this proposal. Wade was confusing the code duello with a frontier brawl! The indignant gentleman dropped the matter and the whole North rang with applause for Wade.

Having discovered the secret of bluffing the Southerners, Wade embarked on a savage vendetta against slavery and its representatives. He took particular delight in puncturing the solemn speeches of his opponents with shafts of crude and brutal wit that reduced their best effects to farce. His devastating sallies into the ranks of the cavaliers and his constant verbal readiness to use his squirrel gun in settling disputes gave him a vivid national reputation. In the Senate his striking figure commanded immediate attention. He was of average height, but square-built, heavy, and slightly stooped. His long white hair fell straight back from a good forehead. His complexion was clear and dark, his eyes small, jet black, staring. His jaw

[27] Linus P. Brockett, *Men of Our Day* (Philadelphia, 1868), 245–246; *Life of Chandler,* 146–147.

protruded aggressively and his upper lip doubled at the corners over the lower, giving his face a ferocious appearance. The antislavery leaders had distrusted him for a long time because of his opportunism and his willingness to sacrifice principle to party. But he was an oracle with the masses, and the business interests of Ohio cherished him because he could always be depended upon to support the protective tariff. Eventually he came to be regarded, even in his own party, as something of a dangerous crank. He championed too many new and radical ideas—the suffrage and legal equality for women; a national currency composed of greenbacks; and for a delirious and ill-judged moment, the redistribution of property and wealth. The leading Republican newspaper of Cincinnati once attacked Wade as "indigent in ideas and economic of practical suggestion, but rich in epithets and profligate in furious vituperation." James A. Garfield considered him "a man of violent passions, extreme opinions and narrow views . . . who is surrounded by the worst and most violent elements in the Republican party." In 1868 the *New York Herald*, describing Wade's iridescent career and his numerous switches on political issues, concluded, "There is nothing too radical or novel or grotesque to expect from 'old Ben Wade'; this old-line roundhead and abolitionist; this old hard-shell Baptist, backwoodsman, and western stump orator; this queer compound of the leading mental peculiarities of Parson Brownlow, John Brown, Joe Smith, Lucy Stone, 'old Thad Stevens,' Gerrit Smith, and Andy Johnson."[28]

Zachariah Chandler was the only member of the Committee who was not a lawyer. For this reason he had turned down suggestions that he be chairman, and took little part in the gathering of testimony and in the legal work of the Committee. But he was always at Wade's elbow with advice and counsel. Together he and Wade determined the policies the Committee

[28] Joshua R. Giddings to G. W. Julian, January 28, 1862, in the Giddings-Julian MSS.; *Cincinnati Commercial*, September 4, 1867; Theodore C. Smith, *Life and Letters of James Abram Garfield* (New Haven, 1925), 1:425–426; *New York Herald*, March 10, 1868.

followed. He was a consummate artist at manipulating votes in Congress, and to him was entrusted the task of rallying the Republican machine behind the Committee's lead.

Chandler had been a prosperous Detroit merchant before he entered politics. He captured control of the Republican Party in Michigan and in the fifties had himself elected to the Senate, where he joined Wade in opposition to the slavery interests. Lincoln placed the federal patronage in the state at his disposal, and this formed the basis of his political empire. His enemies charged that he habitually mellowed the legislature with whisky and then bribed it to do his bidding. At the time of his re-election in 1863 a Democratic newspaper reported, "Chandler is on the ground himself, and swears he can buy up all who will not come to his support of their own free will. It is the first time he has been here since his election, six years ago, and it is evident he has the same confidence in the power of money in the legislature that he had then." In 1861 he achieved notoriety for his share in wrecking the peace conference that was trying to work out a compromise to avert secession, and for his frank assertion that "a little blood-letting" would strengthen the Union. During the war Chandler assiduously courted the favor of the volunteer soldiers by sponsoring legislation to ease the rigors of military life. His activities earned him the title of "errand boy of every soldier's relative."[29] "Old Zack," with his spare, powerful figure and grim, monolithic face framed in an unruly mass of hair, was a familiar sight in Washington, buttonholing generals and congressmen on the streets, whispering political strategy in committee rooms and corridors, and boasting loudly of his victories in capital barrooms at night.

Roughhewn Andrew Johnson played a unique rôle in the history of the Committee. Only he of four Democratic members enjoyed the confidence of his radical colleagues and engaged actively in the Committee's investigations. He had been selected because of his record as an opponent of secession and

[29] *Detroit Free Press*, January 8, 1863; *Life of Chandler*, 190; Charles Moore, "Sullivan M. Cutcheon," *Michigan Historical Collections*, 30 (1905): 102.

a supporter of the war. He announced that during the nation's crisis he would forget previous party ties. Johnson welcomed his assignment to the Committee, for he hoped to use his position to prod the government into sending an army to expel the Confederate forces which had occupied his beloved East Tennessee. He worked closely with the radicals; his cooperation even extended to the point of asking Ohio Democrats, much to their perplexity, to support Wade for re-election. He joined the Committee in its war against McClellan, although the general was, like himself, a Democrat. He believed that McClellan was too friendly with the Peace Democrats, who were opposed to the war and whom Johnson considered little better than traitors. He also feared McClellan's political ambitions. Johnson, as one of the nation's leading Democrats, was a receptive candidate for his party's nomination for president in 1864. But if McClellan won the war, he would undoubtedly become the Democratic standard-bearer.[30] Johnson had no intention of being pushed aside by a man of McClellan's suspected principles.

The most able of the House members of the Committee was bespectacled, bearded Daniel Gooch of Massachusetts, whose benign, grandfatherly face seemed incongruous in that fierce company. A skilled lawyer, he conducted most of the cross-examination of witnesses and acted as the Committee's legal adviser. He had won the favor of the radicals in February, 1861, with a vigorous speech against any compromise with the seceding states. So highly did they regard his effort that they circulated it widely as a pamphlet. Although he posed as a conservative, Gooch stood very close to the Jacobins. He supported the use of Negro soldiers, emancipation, and, in 1864, the radical plan of reconstruction for the South. He was ready to wield against the hated rebels "all the power human ingenuity can devise or human agency can execute."[31]

[30] N. A. Gray to Johnson, March 1, 1862, F. J. Burrow to Johnson, March 3, 1862, F. W. Bradbury to Johnson, August 17, 1861, Benjamin Fuller to Johnson, August 17, 1861, and M. Warner to Johnson, February 4, 1862, in the Johnson MSS.

[31] Daniel W. Gooch, *Any Compromise a Surrender* (Washington, 1861);

The most radical figure on the Committee was George Washington Julian. Fiery, sincere, intellectual, a crusader for unpopular causes, he moved intimately in abolitionist circles. He was the trusted friend of William Lloyd Garrison, Wendell Phillips, and Lydia Maria Child. He acted as the political representative of the abolitionists, presenting their demands in Congress. For a long time he stood in the formidable shadow of Joshua R. Giddings, dean of the emancipation movement, whose daughter he had married. His stern father-in-law guided his actions and inspired him to greater exertions for the cause of radicalism. Julian cared little for political expediency and usually took a more advanced stand on controversial issues than his more circumspect colleagues. He hated slavery with a burning, consuming emotion. On the Committee he interested himself in pushing projects to arm the slaves and to establish them in colonies on confiscated plantations. He believed McClellan to be a traitor, and welcomed appointment to the Committee as an opportunity to prove his suspicions.[32]

The Democratic House member, smooth-shaven, stocky Moses Odell, came from a Brooklyn district. Next to Gooch and Wade, he was the most diligent worker on the Committee. He had held various appointive offices under Democratic presidents and in 1860, with the backing of the city merchants, he won a seat in Congress. When the Southern states seceded, he denounced their action. He told a soldier audience in Brooklyn that his only loyalty was to the government, and that he would support the administration in its efforts to subdue the rebellion. This speech led the radicals to place him on the Committee. He was fiercely hostile to McClellan because the general consorted daily at his headquarters with the leaders of the Peace Democracy. These gatherings, charged Odell, were a "continuing caucus for the consideration of plans of resistance to all measures which proposed to strengthen the army or the navy

Pierce, *Sumner*, 4:13; Daniel W. Gooch, *Secession and Reconstruction* (Washington, 1864), 5, a pamphlet.

[32] Grace Julian Clarke, *George W. Julian* (Indianapolis, 1923), 224; George W. Julian, *Political Recollections, 1840–1872* (Chicago, 1884), 200–201.

. . . and to devise means of embarrassing the government by constitutional quibbles and legal subtleties." When Odell signed the Committee's 1863 report which branded McClellan as a treasonable incompetent, the indignant Brooklyn Democrats read him out of the party.[33]

John Covode, the Pennsylvania radical who completed the Committee's roster, possessed an exaggerated reputation as a congressional sleuth. He had been the chairman of a House committee which probed alleged frauds in the administration of Lincoln's Democratic predecessor, James Buchanan. After his retirement from Congress, in 1864, he became an investigator for the War Department. Although his work on the Committee was of small moment, he regarded himself with immense seriousness. When presented with a sword at a public ceremony, he gravely asked whether the gift were a reward "for services as a member of the War Committee."[34]

☆

The Committee on the Conduct of the War was an important experiment in the history of American government and in the relations between the civil and military authorities of a democracy at war. It represented a full-throated attempt on the part of Congress to control the executive's prosecution of the war. In another and more realistic sense, the Committee was the implemented agency by which the radical faction hoped to direct the military struggle for the attainment of its own partisan ends. The bold and skillful machine politicians of the Committee were determined that it should be more than a mere fact-finding body. Wade announced that its function was to secure for Congress, and the radicals, a dominating voice in the conduct of the war and the formulation of war policies. The Committee, he asserted, would supply Congress with information concerning the causes of the failure of the army and the administration to achieve victory, so that Congress could

[33] *Harper's Weekly*, June 14, 1862; William D. Kelley, *Lincoln and Stanton* (New York, 1885), 6; *New York Times*, April 10, 1863.
[34] *Albany Argus*, February 4, 1863, quoted in the *Detroit Free Press*, February 7, 1863.

"apply any remedy that may be necessary."[35] "We have gone forth in the spirit of the resolution that created us a committee," said the chairman, "to inquire into the manner in which this war has been conducted; to ascertain . . . wherein there was anything in which we could aid the administration in the prosecution of this war, and wherever there was a delinquency that we might ferret it out, apprise the administration of it, and demand a remedy."[36]

Not a single member possessed either military experience or military education, but the Committee did not consider that this defect need deter it from investigating army operations or rendering judgments on the abilities of military men. Wade and Chandler contemptuously rejected the claim that military science was a specialized, technical subject, mysterious except to "the favored few" educated at West Point. The confident Wade declared that the average American could easily master the existing body of military knowledge in a few weeks.[37] Such being their temper, the members never hesitated to overrule the generals or impose their concepts of correct military strategy upon the army. Chandler and Wade had dogmatic ideas on the proper conduct of operations, and continually urged their plans upon the commanding generals. They believed that wars were won by fighting; their notion of strategy was perpetual attack. "In military movements delay is generally bad—indecision is almost always fatal," was the Committee's maxim.[38]

Most of the witnesses who testified before the Committee were officers of the army. Many of them, products of West Point and the regular army, viewed the Committee as a meddlesome civilian agency and objected to supplying it with military

[35] Wade's statement during the Bull Run inquiry, in *Reports of the Committee on the Conduct of the War*, 1863, 2:78, hereafter cited as *C.C.W.*

[36] Benjamin F. Wade, *Traitors and Their Sympathizers* (Washington, 1862), 2, a pamphlet reproduction of a speech by Wade in the Senate, April 21, 1862.

[37] *Congressional Globe*, 37 Congress, 2 Session, 164–165; *ibid.*, 38 Congress, 2 Session, 826; Harry Williams, "The Attack upon West Point during the Civil War," *Mississippi Valley Historical Review*, 25(1939):491–504.

[38] *C.C.W.*, 1863, 1:62–63.

information. Their attitude was most defiant when the Committee, seeking to lift the veil of military secrecy, asked generals to disclose their plans for the future. The army, Wade insisted angrily, had no right to withhold vital information from Congress. When the investigators failed to get the desired replies from commanding generals, they turned to subordinate officers. Here too they often met with stony refusals. Not only did the soldier regard it as dangerous to reveal proposed movements to a large number of persons, but his hierarchical philosophy made him unwilling to discuss the plans of his superior with a civilian body. The Committee encountered the same reaction when it asked military witnesses to discuss and criticize the actions and decisions of other officers. It seemed perfectly natural to the civilians of the Committee that in probing the details of army administration they should collect the opinions of all officers regardless of rank. Consequently they encouraged subordinates to speak freely of the actions of their superiors, to give opinions about battles they had not seen, to say what they would have done had they been present on a certain field. For a subordinate to criticize his superior was heresy to the military creed and dangerous for the subordinate, hence many refused to answer. Such an attitude profoundly disgusted the investigators, who could not see that "an independent opinion" was destructive of military discipline.[39]

The officers who insisted on such scrupulous adherence to the punctilio of military etiquette were members of McClellan's circle; even after his departure from the army they remained united as a group. They were young men who owed their high place in the army to McClellan's favor. Democrats or conservatives in politics, they were opposed to emancipation. But there was another faction of regular army officers, the "radical" group, composed of men who believed resentfully that McClellan and his conservative successors had slighted them in the matter of promotions. These officers adopted the radical philosophy to gain the Committee's support and to advance

[39] *Ibid.*, 1863, 1:129–130, 179; *ibid.*, 1863, 2:275, "Ball's Bluff."

their military fortunes with its powerful aid. In their testimony and in confidential letters to members of the Committee, they supplied military gossip, pungent criticisms, and violent denunciations of their superiors. Because of its power over promotions the Committee possessed a compelling weapon with which to force the kind of testimony it wanted, and shrewd witnesses played up to its radicalism. The members maintained an unceasing watch over the political utterances of military men; officers who had rashly spoken out against emancipation or who had proved recalcitrant witnesses found the formidable influence of Wade and Chandler holding back Senate confirmation of an advanced commission.[40]

The Committee's incessant efforts to purge the army of conservative officers, the violent partisanship with which it conducted its inquiries, and certain peculiar features in its methods of procedure caused contemporary critics to stigmatize it as a military Inquisition or a Court of Star Chamber. At its first meeting the Committee decided to conduct all its hearings in secret, and the members swore not to reveal any information given by witnesses.[41] This restriction was designed primarily to prevent military plans and intelligence from reaching the enemy through public channels. The bosses of the Committee, however, played fast and loose with their own rule whenever a political advantage was to be gained. They divulged their confidential information to the radical machine. At times they even inspired propaganda campaigns in the radical press with secret reports from the Committee's archives. In another ruling adopted at an early meeting the Committee determined that for the purpose of taking testimony a quorum was not necessary. This enabled one or two Republican members to examine witnesses at any time. Officers appearing in answer to a summons would find to their surprise only Wade

[40] *New York Tribune,* December 24, 1862, January 26, 1863, Army of the Potomac correspondence; Colonel W. B. Hazen to John Sherman, December 10, 1862, in the John Sherman MSS. in the Library of Congress; *Detroit Free Press,* April 7, 1863.

[41] *C.C.IV.,* 1863, 1:68. It was expected that the witness would maintain the same silence. The Committee reserved the right to lay vital information before the president and the Cabinet.

and Chandler present. The Republican members followed a general practice of ignoring their Democratic colleagues. They held sessions of which the Democrats were not apprised, at which important questions of policy were decided. Johnson's successors, realizing the impotence of their position, rarely troubled to attend any of the Committee's meetings.[42]

The secret hearings invested the Committee with powers unlike those of other similar investigative bodies, and gave color to the charge that its sessions savored of Star Chamber methods. When the Committee set out to accomplish the downfall of a conservative general, its first step was to call a parade of witnesses who were known enemies of the suspected officer and who supplied a mass of hostile if inaccurate evidence. Finally the Committee summoned the general himself. He appeared alone before the Committee's bar, without benefit of legal counsel. He was not given an opportunity to examine the previous testimony; he might guess but could not know that grave charges had been made against his character and loyalty. He knew nothing of the specific nature of these charges, unless the Committee chose to give him a vague explanation. Thus Wade once told General Stone, suspected by the radicals of treason, that the Committee had evidence which impugned his loyalty. But the chairman refused to acquaint Stone with the exact nature of the indictments against him. As a result the agonized and innocent officer was forced to present an inadequate, general defense. On another occasion the Committee collected evidence to prove that General George G. Meade should not be credited for the Union victory at Gettysburg. But when Meade came to testify, he was not informed that his generalship had been criticized. Wade merely observed that the Committee was compiling a history of the war and wanted his contribution.[43]

The Committee, despite the secret sessions and the sinister

[42] See Wade to C. F. Dana of the *New York Tribune*, February 3, 1862, in the Charles A. Dana MSS. in the Library of Congress; *C.C.W.*, 1863, 1:71; in general Odell had the confidence of his radical colleagues and was taken into their deliberations.

[43] *C.C.W.*, 1863, 2:426–433, "Ball's Bluff"; George Meade, *Life and Letters of George Gordon Meade* (New York, 1913), 2:169.

epithets of its enemies, was not in any legal sense a court. It possessed no judicial powers and could pass no sentence. Rather it was a grand jury which reported to the president officers it believed guilty of incompetence and treason. The Committee, explained Wade, rendered no final judgments on military men: "We only state what, in our opinion tends to impeach them . . . and then leave it to better judges to determine." This was not quite an accurate statement, as the Committee always attempted to bully the judge, Lincoln, into making the right decision. The members would descend upon Lincoln like swarming bees with demands that a particular general be removed from command. They insisted that their evidence showed how unfit the accused was to hold a position of trust. If the president resisted, they threatened to arouse Congress and public opinion against him by publishing their testimony "with such comments," as Wade said ominously on one occasion, "as the circumstances of the case seemed to require."[44] When the Committee's pressure failed to move Lincoln, as was sometimes the case, the members turned to intrigue to weaken the position of their victim and waited for the publication of their report to blast his reputation. The same procedure, with certain necessary variations, was followed when the Committee was attempting to secure the advancement or prevent the removal of an officer who believed in the radical war aims.[45]

In December, 1861, the Committee began to play its great rôle in the drama of the war. When it advanced from the wings, the brilliant young George Brinton McClellan, with sash and sword, strutted in the center of the stage. Shakespeare would have seen Iago approaching Othello. Mrs. Harriet Beecher Stowe would have said that Simon Legree was about to take a hand with Little Eva.

[44] *C.C.W.*, 1863, 2:426–433, "Ball's Bluff"; *ibid.*, 1865, 1:xix.

[45] For a more complete treatment of the Committee's methods, see Harry Williams, "The Committee on the Conduct of the War," *Journal of the American Military History Institute*, 3(1939):139–156.

4

Seven Against McClellan

On december 19 the Washington correspondent of Greeley's *New York Tribune* reported with elation that the Committee was about to begin its investigation into the causes of military inefficiency and that Republicans could look for "thorough work." A few days later he wrote that McClellan's subordinates had refused to answer some of the Committee's questions, but he assured his readers, "Military resistance will not stifle its labors. Several officers have already been examined, and though the day for the telling of truth has not fully arrived, the profitable gathering of facts is successfully begun."[1]

The Committee held its first meeting on the morning of December 20 in the room of the Senate Committee on Territories, of which Wade was also chairman, and decided to probe the causes of the Bull Run disaster. Their determination to restore Frémont's reputation was evident in a communication to the War Department demanding all the available information bearing on the general's career at St. Louis.[2] But the Committee's chief interest was in McClellan and the Army of the Potomac, and why the commander did not hurl his magnificent host upon the foe. Accordingly Wade asked McClellan to appear for an interview before any witnesses were examined. The Young Napoleon, however, was lying upon a sickbed, stricken, the rumor ran, with typhoid fever, and he could not come. But the Committee believed that the military crisis was so pressing and urgent that delay was dangerous. Wade summoned McClellan's officers to appear for questioning.[3]

At the time that the Committee began its investigation, the

---

[1] *New York Tribune*, December 20, 23, 1861.
[2] *C.C.W.*, 1863, 1:67–68.
[3] *Ibid.*, 1863, 1:5.

Jacobin camp teemed with charges of McClellan's disloyalty. The radicals were ready to accept any fantastic tale of his villainy. They believed that he was privy to a plot hatched at his headquarters to involve the government in a war with Great Britain and thus prevent the conquest of the Confederacy. His father-in-law and chief of staff, General Randolph Marcy, was supposed to be in secret sympathy with the rebellion. It was asserted that McClellan was "playing politics, not war"; that he could have captured Richmond in November, but had let the chance slip by because he hoped to negotiate a peace between the sections and get himself elected president with the aid of Southern votes. Later the Jacobins were to embrace the grotesque fiction that he sneaked into the enemy camp before every important battle to give the Confederate generals his plan of operations. War had so destroyed their critical faculties that they pointed to his ban on the singing of abolition songs in camp as evidence of treason.[4] The radicals had some slight basis for their suspicions because of the foolish actions of the general's political allies. Samuel Barlow, who had appointed himself McClellan's manager, wrote an injudicious letter proposing a scheme to bring about peace on terms extremely advantageous for the South. The recipient of the letter turned it over to Edwin M. Stanton, Cameron's successor in the war office, with the scornful comment, "It is from our friend Barlow, the particular friend of Genl. M'Clellan."[5]

The Committee swallowed all the lurid accusations against McClellan. Julian later confessed that the members "became morbidly sensitive" where the general was concerned, and "were practically incapable of doing . . . [him] justice." Wade rapidly came to the conclusion that McClellan was deliberately magnifying the number of the enemy and deceiving the president in order to palliate the army's do-nothing policy. It was McNapoleon's plan, charged Wade, to prolong the war until

[4] Kelley, *Lincoln and Stanton*, 6–7; C. H. Howland to Lyman Trumbull, January 9, 1862, in the Trumbull MSS.; N. B. Judd to Trumbull, September 28, 1862, *ibid.*; Edgar Conckling to Joseph Holt, November 8, 1864, in the Holt MSS.; *New York Tribune*, June 19, 1862.

[5] The letter was written to Edwards Pierrepont, who gave it to Stanton, January 28, 1862. Stanton MSS.

the North and South, wearied with the struggle, would recall the Democratic Party to power to make a peace.[6]

In answer to the Committee's summons, the officers of the Eastern army appeared for examination. The Committee bluntly told these men that Congress wanted the army to strike a blow at the rebels before winter set in. Wade lectured the generals on the political necessity for an offensive movement: "We must run some risk; we cannot keep such an army as this without doing something; we must get money for the army, and to get that we must do something, and do it as soon as it can be done; we must run a little hazard. . . . There are great political reasons why we should make a demonstration as soon as it can be done prudently."[7]

The Committee had learned from private inquiries, before it examined any witnesses, that McClellan had discussed his plans for future operations only with his small coterie of intimates and had held no councils of war. Disgruntled generals, irritated because McClellan had not admitted them to his confidence, corroborated this point in their testimony. McClellan's secrecy of counsel shocked and alarmed the Committee. Ready to see treason in anything he did, they pounced upon this information as further proof of his sinister plot to prevent the conquest of the Confederacy. The Committee gave McClellan's satellites a thorough grilling in a futile attempt to make them reveal the nature of the movements he proposed against the enemy. But these men refused to answer such questions on the ground that army regulations prohibited a subordinate from criticizing his superior. Angered by these displays of West Point obtuseness, Wade burst out at one officer, "[How] can this nation abide the secret counsels that one man carries in his head, when we have no evidence that he is the wisest man in the world?"[8] Every witness, when he left the committee room, knew that the inquisitors disapproved of his chief's concepts of strategy and direction of the army. The Committee had sown seeds of dissension in the Army of the

[6] Julian, *Recollections*, 203–204; Wade, *Facts for the People*, 2, 6.
[7] *C.C.W.*, 1863, 1:128, 159. The quotation is from both citations.
[8] *Ibid.*, 1863, 1:129–130. See also *ibid.*, 171–172.

Potomac which were to sprout into jealousies and intrigues that would curse that army for the balance of the war.

One of the witnesses who criticized McClellan was General Samuel P. Heintzelman, who described in his diary the Committee's technique in getting the kind of testimony it wanted. On December 14 Heintzelman came to Washington on business and learned from a friend that Zack Chandler was looking for him. He made an appointment to see the senator at five-thirty that afternoon in a room at Willard's Hotel. "I went & found him alone," wrote Heintzelman of the meeting. "He locked the door & we had a talk of two hours on the affairs of the army. . . . He asked me if McClellan had ever called a council of war. I told him I believe not. At all events he had never consulted me on any military subject. That I had proposed several theories since the war commenced, but McClellan had not noticed those I left for him with the Chief of Staff, Marcy. I also told him that if my advice had been taken the Potomac would not have been Blockaded & I doubt whether we would have sustained the defeat at Manassas. . . . I also told him my views about carrying on this war & the mistakes I thought had been made. He dont want me to speak of our interview."[9]

Chandler was satisfied that Heintzelman was an enemy of McClellan and arranged for the resentful officer to appear before the Committee. After a little prodding from Wade, Heintzelman spoke out freely against his superior in his testimony. From this time on his references to McClellan in his diary became increasingly bitter. Whenever Heintzelman was in Washington he hunted up Chandler for a confabulation, and the shrewd senator always dangled before him the bait of an independent command to be secured through the Committee's influence.[10]

While the Committee was tutoring the army officers on the necessity for an advance, the Jacobin machine started a savage offensive against the administration. The radical press broke

[9] Heintzelman diary, December 16, 1861.
[10] Ibid., December 24, 1861, January 6, 13, 1862; C.C.W., 1863, 1:117–122.

The Small Politicians in Congress Cackling at General McClellan.

out with demands for "an active war" and drastic measures against slavery; Jacobin leaders denounced the "sorry, rotten" Cabinet, the proslavery generals who were paralyzing the army, and the poor incapable president. The old cry for an invasion of the South was raised. Republicans implored their congressional leaders to have the Committee spur the army on to action. "We want the army to kill somebody," plaintively began one appeal to Senator Fessenden. From conservative Republican newspapers came words of defense for "slow and sure" McClellan, and intimations that he was about to crush the rebellion. *Harper's Weekly* ran the above cartoon of the Young Napoleon: "THE SMALL POLITICIANS IN CONGRESS CACKLING AT GENERAL MC CLELLAN."[11]

[11] *Chicago Tribune,* January 13, 1862; *New York Tribune,* January 13, 1862; letters to Lyman Trumbull from Gustave Koerner, January 2, 1862, S. S. Enos, January 7, Colonel R. C. Hawkins, January 9, in the Trumbull MSS.; G. S. Ward to W. P. Fessenden, January 23, 1862, in the Fessenden MSS.; *Harper's Weekly,* January 18, 1862, and January 25, for the cartoon; *New York Times,* January 15.

In truth the radical politicos were roaring, and at both McClellan and Lincoln. Declaring that nothing had been done and "there are no symptoms that anything will be done," Senator Fessenden charged that "Favoritism has officered the army with incapables." He added savagely, "If the President had his wife's *will* and would use it rightly, our affairs would look much better." In the House, Owen Lovejoy voiced an eloquent demand for military action, with the cry that the people "have furnished the men and the money; and why does not the Army move?" Thaddeus Stevens in a brilliant speech challenged Lincoln's contention that in war the president must become a temporary dictator. The acidulous old boss of the House admitted that one branch of the government should assume complete control of the direction of the war, but he insisted that Congress rather than the executive should be the dictator.[12] Stevens' speech was a manifesto—if the Jacobins could dominate Congress they would run the war to fit their own notions, even if they had to ride roughshod over Lincoln.

Not all the members of the Jacobin cabal devoted their efforts to public denunciation of the administration. Some turned their talents to private intrigue in the inviting turmoil of army politics. Charles Sumner asked officers with the right political opinions to give him an inside picture of the military situation. From General James S. Wadsworth, an ambitious New York politician serving his army apprenticeship, came the satisfactory reply, "I tell you confidentially but advisedly, that the army has lost confidence in its commander. . . . Our only hope now is in the legislative branch. If you are competent to the crisis you may save the country; but you must do it soon or be too late." That perennial puller of strings, Zachariah Chandler, was busy with a scheme to put the radical favorite McDowell into McClellan's place.[13] Chandler intended to

[12] Fessenden, letter to his family, January 14, 1862, in Fessenden, *Fessenden*, 1:259–260; Lovejoy's speech in the *Congressional Globe*, 37 Congress, 2 Session, 194; Stevens' speech, *ibid.*, 37 Congress, 2 Session, 440.

[13] Wadsworth to Sumner, January 10, 1862, in Henry G. Pearson, *James S. Wadsworth of Geneseo* (New York, 1913), 102–103; MS. diary and letterbook of Salmon P. Chase, quoted in Alexander Howard Meneely, *The War*

accomplish this change through the machinery of the Committee.

The directing spirits of the Committee decided in the first week of January that they had collected enough evidence of McClellan's incompetence to take an appeal to Lincoln. Further, having failed to make the commander's intimates reveal his future plans, Wade wanted to know whether Lincoln had any information on the subject. Accordingly the Committee asked for an interview with Lincoln and the Cabinet. The president, probably with a feeling of dread, agreed to a conference at the White House at seven-thirty in the evening on January 6.[14]

Wade and his grim cohorts came to the executive mansion that winter night determined to have a showdown with Lincoln. They demanded that he order McClellan to advance. They told him that according to their testimony the army was in splendid condition, the weather and roads ideal for an invasion of Virginia, and the number of the enemy inferior. Wade also asked the president what he knew about McClellan's proposed movements.

Lincoln replied that he had no knowledge of McClellan's plans or his reasons for not attempting a forward movement. This was McClellan's business as commander, he said, and he had no intention of interfering. Seward defended McClellan's deliberate policy, and Chase was the only Cabinet member who spoke out in support of the Committee. "The spectacle seemed to us very disheartening," recalled Julian later. Several members informed Lincoln that the testimony of witnesses indicated McClellan's unfitness to command. Wade bluntly and savagely "arraigned General McClellan for the unaccountable tardiness of his movements, and urged upon the administration, in the most undiplomatic plainness of speech, an immediate and radical change in the policy of the war."[15]

Lincoln rejected Wade's angry demands. He told the Com-

Department, 1861 (Columbia University Studies in History, Economics, and Public Law, no. 300, New York, 1928), 359.

[14] C.C.W., 1863, 1:72–73.

[15] Julian, Recollections, 201–203; Life of Chandler, 226; Chandler's

mittee he would not interfere with his general. Nevertheless, although he had thus proclaimed his trust in McClellan, the president was secretly troubled by the commander's reticence as to his movements. Conservative Cabinet members like Edward Bates, the attorney general, implored Lincoln to take real command of the army and force McClellan to reveal his intentions. Sharp-eyed capital observers noted that the Committee's attack had weakened McClellan with the president, and they predicted more formidable attempts in the future. Wily Edwin M. Stanton, who was snuggling up to the radicals in the hope of securing Cameron's job with their aid while at the same time holding hands with his Democratic friends, warned Barlow of the dangers besetting McClellan. "Your anticipation that he would be assailed by certain parties, I think, is well founded," he wrote on the day after the Committee met Lincoln. "No direct assault upon him has yet been made but there have been several indirect lunges, the object whereof cannot be mistaken." Frémont had come into town to testify before the Committee, and Stanton hinted that the Jacobins might try to elevate him to McClellan's place.[16]

Lunges against McClellan now became the order of the day. For three weeks he had not stirred from his house, where he was confined to a sickbed, and the radicals spread the report that he was at the point of death. They told Lincoln that if McClellan died with his future plans unrevealed, the whole military machine would be thrown into chaos. Their stories frightened the gullible president into the belief that a crisis threatened the nation. He desperately needed advice, but he was not sure where to go. On January 10 he came to the office of Quartermaster General Montgomery C. Meigs. In a despairing mood he said, "General, what shall I do? The people are impatient; Chase has no money and he tells me he can raise no more; the General of the Army has typhoid fever. The

account of the conference in the *Congressional Globe*, 37 Congress, 2 Session, 3390. The last two accounts are inaccurate in important details.

[16] Howard Beale, ed., *The Diary of Edward Bates, 1859–1866 (Annual Report of the American Historical Association, 1930, vol. 4, Washington, 1933)*, 220; Stanton to Barlow, January 7, 1862, in Flower, *Stanton*, 123.

bottom is out of the tub. What shall I do?" Meigs, who seemingly was not above playing the game of army politics, said that
McClellan would be incapacitated for weeks, during which time
the enemy might attack. He advised Lincoln to consult with
those generals who were next in rank to McClellan. "Perhaps,"
he hinted to the president, "you may select the responsible
commander for such an event."[17]

Lincoln grasped at this suggestion like a drowning man at
the proverbial straw. He asked McDowell and General William
B. Franklin, one of McClellan's young men, to meet him at
eight that evening. Seward, Chase, and Assistant Secretary of
War Tom Scott were present to represent the Cabinet. The
worried president spoke regretfully of the clamor of the Jacobins for an advance of the armies, a clamor which might become loud enough to force his hand. He expressed his dismay
at the possible consequences of McClellan's illness and the
prospect of a leaderless army. Obviously he wanted the generals
to tell him what course to take. McDowell, with the approving
eye of his mentor Chase upon him, denounced McClellan's
reported plan to attack Richmond from the east by way of the
Peninsula between the York and James rivers. He played upon
Lincoln's fears by asserting that this would leave Washington
open to capture, and recommended instead a land advance
south from the capital. Franklin warmly defended his commander. Confused by this dissension between the military
experts, Lincoln made no decision; but two days later he called
the same group together, with Meigs and Montgomery Blair
also in attendance. The president was jubilant. He had heard
from McClellan that morning: the general had recovered and
would come to a council the next day.[18] Several of the conspirators must have metaphorically gnashed their teeth at this
thunderclap.

[17] "General M. C. Meigs on the Conduct of the Civil War," documents
in the *American Historical Review*, 26(1921):292.

[18] McDowell's memorandum of the meeting, in Henry J. Raymond, *Life
and Public Services of Abraham Lincoln* (New York, 1865), 772–774; "Meigs
on the Conduct of the War," *loc. cit.*, 292; McDowell's memorandum, in
Raymond, *Lincoln*, 776; Warden, *Chase*, 400; Meneely, *War Department*,
360–362.

McClellan's dramatic decision to leave his sickbed and con-
front his enemies was the work of the oleaginous Stanton.
Getting wind of the secret conferences at the White House,
Stanton went to McClellan with the warning, "They are counting on your death, and are already dividing among themselves
your military goods and chattels." Stanton's actions at this time
as always were fantastically tortuous. He was angling for radical support to get into the Cabinet as secretary of war, with
juicy diatribes against McClellan as the bait. At the same time
he posed to the commander as a faithful friend. It was chronic
with Stanton to play both ends against the middle. Moreover,
there was calculating astuteness in his apparently devious wind-
ings. He could not secure the war office without McClellan's
indorsement and had to keep the general's favor until the
appointment was in his pocket. "His purpose," charged Mc-
Clellan later, "was to endeavor to climb upon my shoulders
and then throw me down." Hence Stanton risked his mission
to the sick officer, hoping the radicals would never know he
had peddled information which damaged their cause.

McClellan strode into the conference on the thirteenth, enraged against McDowell whom he considered to be at the
bottom of the plot against him. During the somewhat embarrassing meeting, McDowell repeated his proposal for a direct
movement upon the enemy, using Washington as a base. Then
the pompous Chase, McDowell's champion, demanded that
McClellan disclose his plan of operations. This the commander
refused to do, adding sarcastically that everything he said would
be in the newspapers the next day if divulged to so large
a group. He offered to explain things to Lincoln and the secretary of war, but he would not discuss his plans with the
assembled group unless the president ordered him to do so in
writing. He eased Lincoln's fears by saying that he had fixed
upon a time for a forward movement, the outlines of which he
sketched in a general manner. This satisfied the president, who
broke up the council without pressing the commander
further.[19]

[19] McClellan, *Own Story*, 151–159. McClellan offered the plausible sug-

Two days later McClellan provided a regrettable example of the manner in which the entire conduct of the war was shot through with politics. His foremost journalistic supporter was James Gordon Bennett's *New York Herald*. The paper's Washington correspondent, Malcolm Ives, told Stanton that Bennett could present a much stronger defense of McClellan if he knew something of the general's plans. Ives wanted to talk with McClellan, and the tireless Stanton arranged an interview. McClellan, who had refused to discuss his movements with the president's advisers and who had sneered that these men would reveal his secrets to the press, opened his heart to Ives. He talked enough to give the reporter a good idea of what would happen when the campaign started. Ives swore not to publish any of the details, but the episode demonstrated McClellan's willingness to play the political game.[20]

McClellan's recovery temporarily balked the schemes of his enemies, but he still had to face down the deep-seated hostility of the Committee. Now that he was up and around, the inquisitors wanted to have their long-delayed interview with him. Their conviction that something was rotten in his administration of the army had been strengthened by the testimony of General Ben Butler, the breezy, noisy, likable Massachusetts politician who had delighted the radicals with his definition of fugitive slaves as contraband of war. In a jaunty, cocksure manner, Butler assured the Committee that the Confederate force opposed to McClellan's great army could not number more than seventy thousand. Butler's estimate was too low, but Wade and Chandler accepted it as gospel. Why did not McClellan sweep this insignificant enemy into the Potomac, asked their suspicious minds.[21]

On the fifteenth the Committee finally met McClellan. Tech-

---

gestion that Stanton was opposed to McDowell's getting the command because McDowell was under the domination of Chase and hence could not be controlled by Stanton. See also "Meigs on the Conduct of the War," *loc. cit.*, 292–293; Raymond, *Lincoln*, 776–777.

[20] Malcolm Ives to J. G. Bennett, January 15, 1862, in "Federal Generals and a Good Press," excerpts from the James Gordon Bennett Papers, *American Historical Review*, 39(1933–34):286–287.

[21] *C.C.W.*, 1863, 3:285–287; Wade, *Facts for the People*, 2.

nically he did not appear as a witness, hence no record of the proceedings was taken down. The Committee's journal merely observed that "some time was passed in a full and free conference." According to newspaper reports the conference lasted from ten in the morning until four in the afternoon, the Committee demanding that McClellan reveal his plans and his reasons for not advancing, and the general doggedly refusing. In the biography of Chandler, written by Detroit newspapermen who had access to the senator and his papers, a more dramatic account is given. Chandler bluntly asked McClellan why he did not attack. The commander replied that he could make no forward movement until more bridges had been built over the Potomac, bridges which would enable the army to retreat safely in case of a reverse. Chandler burst in, "General McClellan, if I understand you correctly, before you strike at the rebels you want to be sure of plenty of room so that you can run in case they strike back!" Wade added sarcastically, "Or in case you get scared." McClellan attempted to explain the necessity for adequate lines of retreat, but Wade brushed aside his homily on military science with the curt announcement that the people expected "a short and decisive campaign." After the badgered general had left, Wade said, "Chandler, what do you think of the science of generalship?" The disgusted solon snapped, "I don't know much about war, but it seems to me that this is infernal, unmitigated cowardice."[22]

☆

Edwin M. Stanton received his reward, the reward of untiring industry and polished equivocation. On January 11 Simon Cameron resigned as secretary of war, and two days later Lincoln appointed Stanton to the office. Cameron had been a liability to the administration and the party from the beginning of the war. He executed the work of his department in a blundering, inefficient manner, and his handling of financial matters smelled to high heaven. The Eastern banking interests, upon whom the government depended for loans, cried

[22] *C.C.W.*, 1863, 1:75; *Harper's Weekly*, February 1, 1862; *Detroit Free Press*, January 10, 1863; *Life of Chandler*, 225–226.

out for his removal. It was charged that he manipulated the awarding of contracts by his department to pay off old political debts and gave the juiciest plums to his Pennsylvania henchmen. He was one of the owners of the Northern Central railroad, which secured a lion's share of government business, although its rates were higher than those of competing lines. After an investigation, the House committee on contracts produced evidence which indicated wholesale corruption in the fiscal transactions of his bureaus. The Republican leaders in Congress denounced Cameron unsparingly. Roscoe Conkling declared that a set of "harpies were preying on the government." Henry Dawes told how the secretary had won over his enemies with fat contracts at meetings "where the hatchet of political animosity was buried in the grave of public confidence and the national credit was crucified between malefactors." As the storm of denunciations mounted in volume, Lincoln seized the opportunity to rid himself of a political incubus. He asked Cameron to resign, and eased the way by offering to make him ambassador to Russia.[23] The czar of Pennsylvania politics departed for the Russian court unwept and unsung. Lincoln, remembering Cameron's advocacy of a slave army and his shift to radicalism, was glad to see him go. The Jacobins made no move to save him, for they wanted a man of iron will in the war office, and Stanton measured up to their bill of particulars.

Stanton had sold the Jacobin chieftains the idea that he was the man for the job, and the radical directory threw its full strength into a drive to place him at the head of the War Department. Wade, Chandler, Sumner, and Wilson were behind his candidacy; they accepted him as an unflinching radical, and they expected him to make McClellan fight or get out. Salmon P. Chase took the lead in lining up support for Stanton among the Republican senators. He sent Stanton to talk

[23] House of Representatives *Reports of Committees,* 37 Congress, 2 Session, vol. 1, no. 2, report of the committee on contracts; *Congressional Globe,* 37 Congress, 2 Session, 203–204, 298–299, 300, 302; Washington *National Intelligencer,* December 10, 1861; G. S. Ward to W. P. Fessenden, January 23, 1862, in the Fessenden MSS.; *Frank Leslie's Newspaper,* October 31, 1862; Alexander K. McClure, *Lincoln and Men of War Times* (Philadelphia, 1892), 146–147; Smith, *Blair Family,* 2:231.

with Fessenden, who was delighted with the prospective secretary's opinions. "He is just the man we want," wrote the Maine senator. "We agree on every point: the duties of the Secretary of War, the conduct of the war, the negro question, and everything else." On the day before he was appointed, Stanton met the bosses of the radical machine at a dinner given by Cameron, who had resigned himself quickly to the prospect of being kicked upstairs. Stanton and Chandler discussed the military situation during the meeting, and both, recalled General John Cochrane, who was present, were "harmonious in censure of General McClellan's dilatory conduct of the war." The extent to which Stanton had ingratiated himself with the radicals, causing them to forget his former affiliation with the Democrats, was shown by Senator Trumbull's quick indorsement of his accession to the war office. Trumbull hardly knew Stanton, but he welcomed his presence in the Cabinet because "our earnest men here who have conversed with him, say he is fully up to all they could ask. . . . I feel very much encouraged by the change." Everywhere radicals hailed Stanton as a secretary who would put the West Point clique in its place, kick out the proslavery generals, and make the armies move. Here was a man, shouted the *Tribune,* who would take no dictation from McClellan.[24]

But Stanton would not have been Stanton if he had not manipulated in support of his candidacy every party, faction, and individual with influence. If the Jacobins thought Stanton was their man, the conservative Republicans, the Democrats, and the Border State unionists were just as convinced that the secretary belonged to them. Stanton never exhibited more bril-

[24] Henry Wilson, "Jeremiah S. Black and Edwin M. Stanton," *Atlantic Monthly,* 26 (1870):463–475; Pierce, *Sumner,* 4:63; Warden, *Chase,* 400–401, Chase diary, January 12, 1862; Fessenden, *Fessenden,* 1:230–231; John Cochrane, *War for the Union* (New York, 1875), 19; Lyman Trumbull to J. W. Fell, February 1, 1862, in "Trumbull Correspondence," *Mississippi Valley Historical Review,* 1(1914):103; *New York Tribune,* January 21, 1862; St. Louis *Missouri Democrat,* January 23, in Smith, *Blair Family,* 2:141; John Russell to Lyman Trumbull, February 4, in the Trumbull MSS.; Gurowski, *Diary,* 145; *Life of Chandler,* 187; Riddle, *Wade,* 316; Riddle, *Recollections,* 296.

liantly his gift for being all things to all people than when he rode into the War Department with the backing of a number of discordant groups, each of which believed that it had put a representative in the Cabinet. As he negotiated with the leaders of the separate factions, Stanton changed his political color with the rapidity of a chameleon, now glowing a radical pink and in the next instant fading to a conservative brown. He must at times have seemed to flash like a prism with all the colors in the spectrum.

The conservatives in the Cabinet, Seward, Welles, and Blair, pushed Stanton's cause with Lincoln because they thought they were getting an ally to take the place of Cameron, who had deserted to the radicals. For the same reason, moderate Republicans like Senator Doolittle and the editors of *Harper's Weekly* backed Stanton. The leaders of the Border State unionists, men who represented slaveholding communities and who would have fought any measures directed against slavery, were delighted that such a doughty foe of abolitionism had replaced the detestable Cameron. They looked to Stanton to save the president from the assaults of the Jacobins.[25] In the same fools' paradise were the Democrats, enraptured at the prospect of a champion in the Cabinet. Stanton had won Bennett and the *Herald* by promising that his policy as secretary would be identical with McClellan's. Loyal Democrats deluged Stanton with congratulatory letters which in a few months would have an ironic and fatuous ring. Judge A. G. W. Carter of Ohio exclaimed, "The great democracy of the West feel especially grateful that the administration has at last called into its councils so thorough and pure a Democrat as Edwin M. Stanton." Finally Stanton had the powerful support of McClellan, who believed the new secretary to be his truest friend. The rela-

[25] A. H. Meneely, "Three Manuscripts of Gideon Welles," *American Historical Review*, 31(1926):491–493; Welles, *Diary*, 1:127; John Bigelow, *Retrospections of an Active Life* (New York, 1909), 1:542–543; James R. Doolittle to Mrs. Doolittle, January 24, 1862, in the Doolittle MSS. in the Library of the State Historical Society of Wisconsin; *Harper's Weekly*, January 25, 1862; letters to Joseph Holt, the Border State leader, from J. F. Speed, February 4, 1862, Sam Haycroft, January 19, T. P. Trott, January 27, in the Holt MSS.

tions between the two men had been close since McClellan came to Washington. The general frequently went to Stanton's house to get advice or to "dodge enemies in the shape of browsing Presidents"; he remembered gratefully Stanton's service at the time of the secret conferences of the Cabinet. At McClellan's quarters his staff officers received with joy the news of the appointment. Stanton himself told McClellan that his only reason for taking the job was to help the general crush the rebellion. And in the White House Lincoln thought that he had picked a secretary who would cooperate with Mc-Clellan.[26]

Stanton went into the war office amid ringing predictions from the press and the public that this iron secretary would make the generals fight. "The country looks to you with longing heart to infuse vigor, system, honesty & *fight* into the service," wrote Joseph Medill of the *Chicago Tribune*. He voiced the thoughts of the average American civilian, impatient at the seemingly needless delay and procrastination of the military forces. The people looked to Stanton, gruff, energetic, and explosive, to cut the red tape of West Point traditionalism that bound the armies inactive in winter quarters. The Eastern army would now move, declared one editor ambiguously, even if it went to the devil. Stanton's overpowering personality and tremendous driving power gripped the popular imagination. Short, thick-bodied, with long black hair and expressive eyes, he looked like a bearded gnome. He exuded physical and mental energy and ran his department with an autocratic hand. This, together with his proficiency in verbalization and self-advertising, caused contemporaries to praise him as a great war secretary, an American Carnot, "the organizer of victory." More recent critics have questioned his abilities as a military administrator, but he had the boldness to make decisions and

[26] Malcolm Ives to J. G. Bennett, January 15, 1862, in "Federal Generals and a Good Press," *American Historical Review*, 39(1933–34):285; A. G. W. Carter to Stanton, January 17, 1862, in the Stanton MSS. See also letters to Stanton from Judge Leavitt, January 16, F. Ball, January 16, G. W. Woodward, January 14, *ibid.*; McClellan, *Own Story*, 153, 161; Cochrane, *War for the Union*, 19.

he kept the department free of corruption. Like many civilians of the day, he believed that a military education or training had nothing to do with making a man a successful general, and he was violently prejudiced against West Pointers. "There are fundamental defects in the mental processes of many of our generals . . . ," he said. "They seem unable to realize that this is a Republic, in which the people are above generals, instead of generals above the people."[27]

The new secretary immediately disclosed his tie-up with the Jacobin machine. The entire Committee met with Stanton soon after he took office, and the secretary said to Wade, "We must strike hands, and uniting our strength and thought, double the power of the government to suppress its enemies and restore its integrity." This rhetorical statement masked the beginning of an astute political alliance between Stanton and the Committee which continued until the end of the war. The secretary swung departmental patronage to the members and aided them in their electoral contests. The Committee reciprocated by investigating charges of fraud against the War Department and exposing their falsity. The members instructed Wade to offer Stanton the services of the Committee "either individually or as a body, in any way that he may desire their assistance." Each member had a card admitting him to Stanton's office "at all times." Gideon Welles, who hated Stanton, thought that the "Black Terrier" dominated the Committee, but in reality the Committee was the preponderant force in the partnership.[28]

In Stanton's accession to power the Committee saw new hope for victory in its war against McClellan. The despondency of

[27] Medill to Stanton, January 20, 1862, in the Stanton MSS.; *Cleveland Plain Dealer,* quoted in Smith, *Blair Family,* 2:141; Flower, *Stanton,* 358; William E. Doster, *Lincoln and Episodes of the Civil War* (New York, 1915), 116.

[28] Flower, *Stanton,* 119; *C.C.W.,* 1863, 1:83; W. B. Kernan to Stanton, January 28, 1862, in the Stanton MSS., concerning Stanton's indorsement of Wade's senatorial candidacy; Zachariah Chandler to P. C. Watson, assistant secretary of war, September 10, 1862, *ibid.;* James F. Joy, "The Committee on the Conduct of the War," *Detroit Free Press,* January 10, 1863. For the Committee's investigation of charges against Stanton, see *C.C.W.,* 1863, 1:80, 81.

the members over their failure to unseat him gave way to elation after they had talked to Stanton. "He agreed with us fully," said Julian, "in our estimate of General McClellan, and as to the necessity of an early forward movement. We were delighted with him."[29] The Committee and Stanton went into a series of conferences, at which Wade revealed the evidence gathered in the last few weeks. They wanted to strike at McClellan but they knew that for the moment he was too strong with Lincoln. But if the commander could not be attacked, his subordinates were vulnerable. The Committee turned its wrath upon General Stone, of Ball's Bluff notoriety, who possessed the qualities necessary for a sacrificial victim. Stone became the innocent principal of the American Dreyfus case.

Since the minor battle at which Baker met his death, the Jacobins had raged in private against Stone. They believed that he was a traitor and had planned the massacre of Baker's troops; they hinted broadly that in some mysterious way McClellan was back of the whole affair. They had no evidence to back up their suspicions, but the leaders expected the Committee to dig up the damning facts. In the House, Roscoe Conkling shook his handsome, curly head as he roared a denunciation of "the most atrocious military murder ever committed in our history as a people." He cried the Committee on to investigate the disaster. "Let mismanagement and drowsiness tremble and wake up. Ball's Bluff cries aloud for scrutiny, and I hope the war committee will think so, and probe it thoroughly, unrestrained by any statement that the public interest does not require it, come from what quarter it may."[30]

There were other counts in the radical score against Stone. Ugly stories floating through the suspicion-charged air of Washington accused him of carrying on a treasonable intercourse with the enemy. Rebel spies, these rumors whispered, passed and repassed through his lines with no interference; Stone wrote and sent letters to the Confederates and received

[29] Julian, *Recollections*, 204.

[30] Alfred R. Conkling, *Life and Letters of Roscoe Conkling* (New York, 1889), 140, 147. The quotation is from both citations.

mysterious packages in return. Gossip asserted that he and his wife, who had Southern connections, associated on intimate social terms with the slaveholders in his district, and that the Stones were dazzled by the attentions of the aristocrats. It was charged that he assigned generals to protect the property of notorious rebels, and used his soldiers as "slave-catchers" for owners seeking the return of fugitives.

The situation was loaded for an explosion, and John A. Andrew, Massachusetts' forthright, radical governor, pulled the trigger that set it off. Andrew heard that volunteer officers from the Bay State in Stone's regiment had returned runaway slaves at the general's orders. The impulsive governor sat down to compose a letter to one of the officers concerned, in which he denounced the employment of any Massachusetts man for the nefarious business of slave-catching. To Stone this was impudent civilian interference in army affairs, and he protested bitterly. An acrimonious correspondence followed. Finally Andrew turned the letters over to Sumner, who flayed Stone in a Senate speech. The general replied to Sumner with an angry letter which was a virtual invitation to a duel. Then the Committee stepped into the squabble.[31]

When the inquisitors started their secret examination of witnesses from the Army of the Potomac, they endeavored to persuade some of the officers to fix the responsibility for the disaster at Ball's Bluff. Stone himself, appearing as a routine witness on January 5, was questioned in a general fashion about the battle and his policy concerning fugitives. He placed the blame for the defeat upon Baker's bungling generalship and asserted that he returned slaves only when asked to do so by the proper civilian authorities.[32] As he walked from the committee rooms, Stone probably had no inkling that the Jacobins were whetting an ax for him.

[31] Henry G. Pearson, *Life of John A. Andrew* (Boston, 1904), 1:312–315; Flower, *Stanton*, 135–137; R. B. Irwin, "Ball's Bluff and the Arrest of General Stone," in Robert U. Johnson and Clarence C. Buel, eds., *Battles and Leaders of the Civil War* (New York, 1887), 2:132–133; Pierce, *Sumner*, 4:67–68.
[32] *C.C.W.*, 1863, 2:267–272, 279–281.

Now followed a long parade of witnesses consisting of volunteer officers in Stone's command and civilian residents from his district. The great majority of these men nourished bitter grievances against Stone because of the iron, West Point discipline which he enforced and his supposed prejudice against civilian soldiers. They regaled the Committee with fantastic tales of his alleged treason. Culled from campfire gossip, their evidence asserted that Stone had been guilty of criminal negligence at Ball's Bluff; his troops distrusted his loyalty; secessionists applauded him "above all other men"; he had permitted the enemy to erect fortifications near his lines; he carried on a mysterious and probably treasonable intercourse with the Confederates across the river; and once he had actually engaged in a conference with rebel officers under a flag of truce![33] The inquisitors snatched hungrily at these juicy morsels. They were eager to be convinced that Stone was a clever and sinister plotter manipulating a gigantic conspiracy against his country. Their excited and emotional minds did not see the absurdity of the picture which they accepted—of a Machiavellian Stone conducting his traitorous activities in the open sight of two armies with no attempt at concealment.

Perhaps they did not want to see. Wade and Chandler ran the entire investigation with flagrant unfairness. They asked leading questions designed to produce criticisms of Stone, and they bullied witnesses into giving the right answers. Nearly every officer was asked a question of this nature: "So far as you know, is not there such a general suspicion of General Stone among officers and men that they would be unwilling to go into battle under him?"[34] To one witness who attempted to defend Stone's course at Ball's Bluff, Wade shouted, "Now, if it was not the object to take Leesburg, what, in God's name, was this fragment of a force sent over on these miserable scows for?" On one occasion the stern chairman asked an officer why Stone had not destroyed a certain flour mill near his lines. The officer professed ignorance. With the air of one re-

---

[33] See *ibid.*, 283–289, 294–297, 297–301, 301–306, 383–388, for examples.
[34] *Ibid.*, 328, 338, 341.

vealing a great secret, Wade said, "He did not tell you why he had not battered it down, as it was supplying the rebel army with flour?" When another witness condemned Stone's laxity in permitting Confederate sympathizers to pass through his lines. Wade observed approvingly, "Then it is no mystery to you that the secessionists should have accounts of everything going on on this side?"[35]

Thus the Committee dragooned and cajoled the evidence it was after. Then the members marched triumphantly to the war office to present their findings to Cameron. But the Pennsylvanian was already packing his bags for Russia and did not act. At this point Stanton took over. He and the Committee radicals immediately went into the first of those secret conferences at which they condemned the sins of McClellan and discussed methods of effecting a change in commanders. The Committee opened its testimony to Stanton, including the material which "seemed to impeach both the military capacity and the loyalty of General Stone."[36] The conspirators were in a surly mood because McClellan was riding high with Lincoln, but in the Stone evidence Stanton saw an opportunity to strike at the commander by pulling down one of his favorites. On January 28 the secretary issued an order for Stone's arrest and gave it to McClellan to execute.

Formally the Committee always denied that it was the instigating force behind Stanton's action. In the official report of the case, Wade insisted that the Committee had merely submitted its evidence to the secretary with no recommendation except that Stone be required to give an explanation. Of the members' reactions when they heard of Stone's detention, Wade added coyly, "They were satisfied that the information which they had furnished . . . had in all probability furnished some of the grounds upon which his arrest had been made." But McClellan told a different story. He quoted Stanton as saying the order for Stone's arrest was issued "at the solicitation of the congressional committee on the conduct of the war, and based

[35] *Ibid.*, 313, 316, 347.
[36] *Ibid.*, 17, 74.

upon evidence taken by them." McClellan also asserted that when he asked Stanton to give Stone a military trial, the secretary refused with the excuse that the Committee was still gathering evidence and was not ready to frame charges against the accused.[37] Later, in the Senate, Stone's friends tried to smoke Wade out on the Committee's rôle in the affair. Wade was adequately evasive; he would not say the Committee had forced the arrest of Stone, but he admitted it had done something. In thinly veiled phrases he implied that the general was a traitor, and called Ball's Bluff "that great, terrible blunder and catastrophe. . . . Your soldiers had been slaughtered by hundreds, like cattle taken to the shambles, apparently under circumstances deeply impeaching somebody that had the command." In a dangerous war crisis, cried the grim chairman, the government could not afford to wait for "technical" proof of the guilt of a suspected soldier. It must act immediately. "There was, and is, probable cause for the arrest of General Stone," he concluded.[38]

McClellan shrank from carrying out the order to arrest his friend and supporter. He knew the falsity of the charges and the motive behind them. When Stanton refused to give Stone a military hearing, McClellan, seeking desperately for a way out, asked that the accused officer be granted the opportunity to state his case to the Committee. Stanton was willing, and on January 31 Stone again confronted his vindictive and now triumphant foes.[39]

At this fatal interview Stone was obviously a crushed and frantic man. He spoke with great emotion and in broken tones. His loyalty to McClellan and his faith that the commander would protect him from threatened disgrace was intense, and this handicapped him in presenting an adequate defense. Previously he had remained quiet under the stinging attacks made by Conkling and others after Ball's Bluff, in obedience to Mc-

[37] *Ibid.,* 17–18. 501, 504–505, 509–510. The Committee denied flatly to McClellan that it had ever intended to prepare formal charges against Stone.
[38] *Congressional Globe,* 37 Congress, 2 Session, 1666–1668, 1735–1737; Wade, *Traitors and Their Sympathizers,* 2–5.
[39] *C.C.W.,* 1863, 1:79.

Clellan's instructions and because of assurances that the commander had given a true picture of the battle to Lincoln. He did not tell the Committee until a year later of this or of the mysterious orders he received that morning at McClellan's headquarters. Then he revealed an episode which demonstrated McClellan's willingness to sacrifice a trusting subordinate to save his own position:

The morning that I came before the committee I was instructed, at General McClellan's headquarters, that it was the desire of the general that officers giving testimony before the committee should not state, without his authority, anything regarding his plans, his orders for the movements of troops, or his orders concerning the position of troops.[40]

The injunction applied to past orders, and it placed a tremendous burden upon Stone when he tried to repel the accusations against his generalship at Ball's Bluff. It also kept McClellan pretty well out of the discussions.

Addressing himself to Wade, the agonized officer said Stanton had told him that the Committee was in possession of testimony which impugned his loyalty. He was present to explain his innocence. Bluntly the old Jacobin senator replied, "In the course of our investigations here there has come out in evidence matters which may be said to impeach you." Wade refused to let Stone examine the testimony; neither would he reveal the names of the witnesses on the grounds that as subordinates they might be made victims of Stone's wrath. His procedure left Stone wholly in the dark as to the specific nature of the charges against him. However the chairman did vouchsafe to inform Stone that there were four general indictments of his conduct: he had ordered Baker's men to cross the river without adequate means of transportation; he had failed to re-enforce Baker during the battle; he had held "undue intercourse with the enemy, both by letter and by personal intercourse with their officers"; and he had permitted the rebels to erect batteries and fortifications which he could have battered down with his guns.

[40] Stone's statement to the Committee in 1863, *ibid.*, 2:489, 492.

Wade's refusal to present a bill of particulars forced Stone to reply with a general and somewhat vague defense. He had to guess at what hostile witnesses had said. Nevertheless he was able to demonstrate that he had given Baker wide discretionary power at Ball's Bluff and that the latter's repulse was the result of his own rashness. Stone offered to take the members over the battleground so that they could see for themselves the physical difficulties involved in sending re-enforcements to Baker. Wade declined the invitation in a remarkable statement considering that the Committee had already condemned Stone on this point. They were not military men, he said airily, and hence would not understand the technical problem in dispute. Stone made a detailed answer to the charge of his intercourse with the enemy. All communication, he asserted, dealt with such routine matters as supplies for prisoners and the exchange of mail. He had watched carefully to insure that no letters or newspapers containing military information went through to the South, while in similar documents coming north he often found valuable knowledge. The Confederate batteries near his lines, the general said, were in reality too far distant to be bombarded. He asked whether the witnesses who had criticized him on this score were artillery officers and hence capable of judging the facts. Wade's reply showed the offhand manner in which the Committee had condemned Stone: "I do not know about that"—they were military men and that was enough.[41]

The accusation of treason inherent in all the Committee's indictments crumpled Stone. "That is one humiliation I had hoped I never should be subjected to. I thought there was one calumny that could not be brought against me. . . . That one I should have supposed that you, personally, Mr. Chairman, would have rejected at once," he cried as he recalled his services in organizing the defenses of Washington in "the seven dark days" at the beginning of the war. "I have, so help me Heaven, but one object in all this, and that is to see the United States successful . . . ," ended the tortured officer. "I have

[41]*Ibid.*, 17–18, 426–433.

been as faithful as I can be. And I am exceedingly sore at this outrageous charge."[42]

Stone's testimony and his impassioned plea did not change the situation one iota. The Committee turned the new evidence over to Stanton, and the secretary increased his pressure upon McClellan to execute the order for the arrest. The commander was as certain as ever of Stone's innocence. He later told a group of officers at a dinner how he kept Stanton's order in his pocket for days because he believed the Committee's evidence was flimsy and based upon hearsay. But in the face of the Jacobin attack, McClellan was becoming alarmed for the safety of his own position. He had no intention of bringing down the Committee's wrath upon his own head by shielding Stone. If the radicals wanted blood, McClellan preferred to see somebody else laid on the altar. Attorney General Bates recorded in his diary a conversation between an army officer and McClellan about Stone and the Committee. McClellan said, "They want a victim." The officer replied, "Yes—and when they have once tasted blood, got one victim, no one can tell who will be the next." The shot struck home. "Thereupon," noted Bates, "the Genl. colored up, and the conversation ceased."[43]

McClellan soon found an opportunity to get out from under. On February 8 a Negro refugee came in from Leesburg with a hazy story about Stone's friendly relations with the secessionists of the neighborhood. This fanciful tale was of a piece with the Committee's evidence which McClellan had denounced, but it gave him a plausible excuse to abandon his friend. He transmitted the information to Stanton and consented to arrest Stone. At midnight of the same day Stone was placed in military custody and taken a prisoner to grim Fort Lafayette in New York harbor.[44] A few hours before his arrest he had talked to Stanton at the war office, and begged for a court of inquiry or

[42] *Ibid.*, 427, 429. The quotation is from both citations.
[43] Heintzelman diary, July 23, 1862; Bates, *Diary*, 229.
[44] *C.C.W.*, 1863, 2:499, 509–510; Irwin, "Ball's Bluff and the Arrest of General Stone," in *Battles and Leaders*, 2:133–134. For accounts of the case favorable to Stone see Blaine, *Twenty Years of Congress*, 1:378–395; New York *World*, April 13, 1863; *New York Journal of Commerce*, quoted in

an investigation of his case by the secretary. With consummate hypocrisy Stanton replied, "There is no occasion for your inquiry; go back to your command."[45]

In Jacobin circles there was open jubilation at the news of Stone's disgrace. Old Count Gurowski rejoiced to his diary that a "conceited regular" who "admired slavery" and who would have saved the Union in his "own peculiar way" had received fitting retribution. "I wish he may speak, as in all probability he was not alone," wrote the Count. A Pittsburgh radical, writing to congratulate Stanton upon the arrest of the traitor, added the encouraging words, "By the help of God I hope you may be able to lay your hands on a few more such." Among administration supporters the arrest had something of the effect of a bombshell. Lincoln, apparently willing to let the Jacobins have their way in the affair, said and did nothing. But Bates probably voiced the sentiments of the conservatives when he recorded his fear that the Stone case would establish "a precedent for Congressional interference with the command of the army, which might lead to the terrible results seen in France, in the days of the revolution."[46]

Meanwhile behind the walls of Fort Lafayette, prison officials acting under orders from the War Department placed General Stone in solitary confinement in a small room. At the end of fifty days his doctor protested that this harsh treatment was undermining the general's health. Then Stanton ordered the prisoner transferred to Fort Hamilton, where he was permitted to exercise under guard. Stone remained in prison for a total period of one hundred and eighty-nine days. During this time he made repeated and pathetic requests to the government for a military trial, or, if there were no charges against him, for permission to return to the army. A stony silence was his only

the *Detroit Free Press*, January 1, 1863; *Detroit Free Press*, April 10, 1863, Washington correspondence. A burning defense of Baker and an attack upon Stone is found in John D. Baltz, *Edward D. Baker* (Lancaster, Pennsylvania, 1888), *passim*.

[45] Statement of Senator McDougall, in the *Congressional Globe*, 37 Congress. 2 Session, 1662–1663.

[46] Gurowski, *Diary*, 153; S. B. W. Gill to Edwin M. Stanton, February 11, 1862, in the Stanton MSS.; Bates, *Diary*, 229.

answer. Stanton's refusal to grant Stone a hearing was a direct violation of the articles of war, which specified that an arrested officer was entitled to a prompt trial. Finally Stone's friends in the Senate, against the fierce opposition of Wade and Chandler, forced the adoption of a resolution requesting the president to transmit all information at hand which bore on the case. The author of the resolution, California's James A. McDougall, whose brilliant talents were unfortunately obscured by chronic drunkenness, flayed Stanton and the Committee in a biting speech. He demanded a court-martial for Stone, and accused the secretary of surrounding the whole case with a veil of official secrecy which kept the real facts from the public. He denounced the Committee as an Inquisition characterized by an intolerant partisan spirit, the exercise of despotic power, and a flagrant disregard of every rule of evidence or law of inquiry. It was deplorable, cried McDougall, that senators "should convert themselves into organized systems of police service, with committees traversing the land and bringing in *ex parte* witnesses, and ascertaining from persons favorable to the conclusion they sought that there was probable cause of crime." McDougall's attempt to force the case into the open failed. Lincoln would not antagonize the Jacobins on this issue. He now assumed full responsibility for Stone's arrest, and refused the Senate's request in a message which James G. Blaine thought Stanton wrote at the war office. Not until August 16 did Stanton, acceding to continued protests, decree Stone's release, accompanied by the weak excuse that the "necessities of the service" did not permit a trial "within the time required by law."[47]

Stone was a free man. His release was an indirect admission by the government that it had done him an injustice. But he had received no official vindication and no promise that he would be restored to command. For months he waited for an order to go back to the army. Then he came to Washington to ask for an active assignment and to take steps to clear his name.

[47] *Congressional Globe,* 37 Congress, 2 Session, 1624, 1662–1668, 1679, 1732–1736; *C.C.W.,* 1863, 2:500.

He saw Lincoln, Stanton, and General Halleck, now chief of the Union armies. Vainly he requested a court of inquiry. Everyone sympathized with him and denounced the perpetrators of his arrest—and threw the blame on someone else. Stanton said it was McClellan, and McClellan said it was Stanton. The kindly Lincoln told Stone that while the arrest "was done under his general authority he did not do it."[48] The most that Stone could wring from the authorities was permission to go before the Committee for a re-examination of his case.

On February 27, 1863, Stone met the inquisitors for the third time. His final appearance was a triumphant acquittal. He had now seen a copy of the testimony and the charges against him, and could answer each accusation specifically. He easily demolished the Committee's previous jaundiced indictment. Wade, in seeming astonishment, asked, "Why did you not give us these explanations when you were here before?" Stone replied, "Because . . . the committee did not state to me the particular cases. . . . I gave general answers to general allegations." By this time Stone was inclined to blame McClellan for his disgrace. If the former commander had recommended the arrest, Stone exclaimed bitterly, he "had written down his own condemnation."[49]

This was as close as Stone ever came to any official exoneration. He was never able to secure the formal trial to which he was entitled. Finally Stanton with extreme reluctance ordered him into service in Louisiana. Later he returned to the East as an officer in the Army of the Potomac in which his career had begun so brightly. But his usefulness and opportunity for advancement were gone. Malicious gossip and ruthless persecution pursued him to make his position unbearable. In 1864 he resigned his commission.

☆

In this first tense phase of its existence the Committee did not confine its attentions to McClellan and the Eastern army. While it was engineering the decapitation of Stone, it started

[48] Stone's statement to the Committee, *ibid.*, 500–501.
[49] *Ibid.*, 486–502.

another intrigue leading in an opposite direction. This was an attempt to refurbish the somewhat tarnished reputation of General Frémont, upon whom rested the radical hopes for military emancipation, and to restore him to a position of influence in the army. At their first meeting the members had resolved to take up Frémont's cause, and Wade had addressed a communication to the War Department requesting the transmission of all available information relative to Frémont's administration in the West. When Cameron tried to dodge the demand with a vague reply that his office had nothing on the Frémont case, the Committee decided to establish the facts through an investigation of its own. Frémont was summoned to appear in Washington on January 6.[50]

Fresh from social triumphs in New York, he and his intrepid wife arrived in town to find themselves the darlings of capital society and the center of excited political gossip. It was whispered by those in the know that Frémont's allies on the Committee would use him as a weapon with which to displace McClellan.[51] Hailed as a martyr to the cause of freedom, the general was the hero of the Jacobin leaders. They seized the occasion of a White House ball to administer a chilling snub to Lincoln. Although the Frémonts accepted an invitation to attend, many of the radicals declined. Over eighty notes of regret came to Mrs. Lincoln. Ben Wade returned his invitation card with a brutal comment: "Are the President and Mrs. Lincoln aware that there is a civil war? If they are not, Mr. and Mrs. Wade are, and for that reason decline to participate in feasting and dancing." The ball was a painful affair. Lincoln seemed more preoccupied and socially awkward than usual. The guests almost ignored the president to mill admiringly around the magnetic Frémont and his wife. Mrs. Frémont later recalled the scene with a pardonable touch of elation: "So many criticized the conduct of the war and regretted that the effort of four years before had not been successful; and there

[50] *Ibid.*, 1:68–69.
[51] E. M. Stanton to Samuel Barlow, January 7, 1862, in Flower, *Stanton*, 123.

was so much feeling of sorrow that General Frémont's policy of emancipation was not to be carried out, that it became embarrassing, and we left."[52]

Frémont met the Committee on January 10 for an abbreviated session. He came loaded with documents and eager to recount the story of his persecution at the hands of the administration. Wade, however, advised him to prepare a written statement of his case and submit it to the Committee. Seven days later the general again appeared in the committee rooms and read a long defense of his Western activities. He stressed the wide powers of discretion granted him by the administration so that he could achieve his military objectives, and denied that he had been extravagant in his construction of forts and handling of contracts. Lyon's defeat, he explained, was due to that officer's own impetuosity and not to any failure of his commander to send re-enforcements. He had judged that before Missouri could be cleared of rebels, Cairo and St. Louis must be made safe; and having accomplished this task, he was on the point of crushing the enemy when he was removed.[53]

After hearing this document read, the Committee instructed Gooch to study it and prepare to cross-examine Frémont at a future date. On January 30 the general made a third appearance. The mild examination to which he was subjected was a marked contrast to the wringer through which Stone had been drawn. Gooch, assisted by other members, asked a number of friendly questions designed to aid the general's defense. Many were merely repetitions of charges against the administration in Frémont's written statement. In this complete and happy accord, the witness and his amicable inquisitors talked at length of the accusations flung at him by hostile critics. Although Frémont defended all his financial transactions, he conceded that he had permitted subordinates to draw up the details of contracts which he signed without close scrutiny. But he contended that the government's failure to furnish him with adequate

---

[52] Nevins, *Frémont*, 2:631–632; Heintzelman diary, February 6, 1862.
[53] *C.C.W.*, 1863, 3:32, 33–43.

support and supplies had forced him to resort to hasty action. The Committee was especially eager to hear about the ill-fated proclamation of emancipation, and Frémont obliged with a full description. He justified his procedure with the argument of military necessity. "Our means there were all the time very inadequate, and I thought that the time had come when it was necessary to strike some decided blow against the enemy, and I judged that the measures proposed by the proclamation were such as would give us a great and important advantage over our enemy." The proclamation, he said in reply to a question by Wade, "operated admirably," and the results of its modification were "injurious." But his policy of freedom had lost him the confidence of the administration.[54]

Frémont's vigorous defense delighted the Committee. Later Wade was to record the Committee's official opinion that "the administration of General Frémont was eminently characterized by earnestness, ability, and the most unquestionable loyalty." Rumors of the members' exultation seeped out from the ostensible secrecy of the committee chambers to the public. Frémont had "staggered" them by the ease with which he disproved accusations; they were convinced that Generals Buell and Halleck, who succeeded him in the West, had merely copied his plans of operation. Washington was thrilled by a report that the Committee would force Lincoln to elevate Frémont to McClellan's place as chieftain of the armies. Spurred by these cheering stories, the general's partisans started a vigorous campaign to get their favorite restored to active service. Charles A. Dana, chief editorial writer of Greeley's *Tribune,* led the fight, and from Secretary Stanton Dana exacted the emphatic assurance: "If Gen. Fremont has any fight in him he shall (so far as I am concerned) have a chance to show it, and I have told him so."[55]

[54] *Ibid.,* 43–77.
[55] *Ibid.,* 6; Heintzelman diary, February 14, 1862; John R. Howard, *Remembrance of Things Past* (New York, 1925), 173; William Brotherhead, *General Frémont* (Philadelphia, 1862), 9; Edwin M. Stanton to C. A. Dana, February 1, 1862, in the Dana MSS.

The Committee was eager to throw its powerful influence behind Frémont's cause. Wade was bitterly convinced that the general had been the innocent victim of a wicked plot. In a letter to Dana which violated the Committee's secrecy rule, the chairman scathingly assailed Lincoln as the author of a supreme injustice:

The character of so many persons and the deep and excited feelings of the community are so involved in Fremont's case that it may be long before the committee can complete their investigations especially as the witnesses are so remote and widely scattered and it is a settled rule of the committee to keep everything secret until the final publication. But in strict privacy I will say this to you, that the investigation had proceeded far enough to convince me beyond a doubt, that no public man since Admiral Byng was sacrificed by a weak and wicked administration, to appease the wrath of an indignant people has suffered so unjustly as Genl Fremont. This persecution will prove the darkest page in our history and while it is impossible for me to say anything in public at present, about his case, I intend privately to make a full statement of the case to the Secy of War and if possible prevail upon him to restore the Genl to some active and useful command. I know the Secy to be a lover of justice and he has some confidence in me. You may be assured that whatever influence I have, will be exerted with him, in favor of the Genl.

I should have done this before, but have only just reached a point in the investigation, enabling me to know with certainty that I am right.[56]

Although Wade was already persuaded of the righteousness of Frémont's case, he continued the investigation. The Blair brothers appeared as witnesses to excoriate their one-time friend for his conduct of operations in Missouri. Officers from the Western army came to defend Frémont against charges of military inefficiency. General Hunter, the Pathfinder's successor, encountered a rough and sarcastic reception and a volley of hostile questions. The contractor who had built the much-

[56] Benjamin F. Wade to C. A. Dana, February 3, 1862, *ibid.*

criticized forts received the same treatment when he implied that Frémont had been guilty of oversight.[57]

Armed with the results of their inquiries, the members descended upon Lincoln with threatening demands that he again place Frémont in active service. The radical machine in Congress went into action at the same time. Representative J. P. C. Shanks, in a speech lauding Frémont's military career, shouted that the people had appointed him to the army out of a "wish to distinguish one of themselves," then had seen their favorite struck down by jealous professional soldiers educated with the people's money. In burning words meant for McClellan, Shanks denounced "the military bigot, who sees West Point first, and after it the country." When Frank Blair dared to attack Frémont in the House, the Jacobins wheeled up their heaviest guns in the form of Stevens and Colfax to reply and to thunder for a new command for the general.[58]

The harassed president yielded to the pressure. On March 11 he issued an order creating the Mountain Department in western Virginia and placing Frémont in command. The Jacobins exulted; Frémont, they cried, knew how to wage grim war against slaveholders. In a speech before the American Anti-Slavery Society, Wendell Phillips called the general "the real President of the American mind."[59]

In order to give Frémont an independent command, Lincoln had to take troops away from McClellan, and the commander protested bitterly. He was ready at last to fight and wanted every available man for the effort.

[57] *C.C.W.*, 1863, 3:154–163, 186–210, 225–227, 234–235, 270–279.

[58] Shanks, *General Frémont*, 5–6; *New York Tribune*, March 4, 1862; *Congressional Globe*, 37 Congress, 2 Session, 1118–1124; *Speeches of Messrs. Colfax of Indiana and Thaddeus Stevens of Pennsylvania, in Reply to Messrs. Diven and Blair's Attacks on General Frémont* (Washington, 1862), a pamphlet; John C. Frémont to Thaddeus Stevens, April 28, 1862, in the Stevens MSS.

[59] *O. R.*, series 1, 5:54; Wheeling *Intelligencer*, in the *New York Tribune*, May 7, 1862; Wendell Phillips' speech, in the *New York Tribune*, May 7, p. 8; David Davis to Joseph Holt, March 27, April 28, 1862, in the Holt MSS.; New York *World*, January 29, 1863.

5
Making McClellan Fight

IN THE MIDDLE of January Stanton and the Committee closeted themselves day after day in conferences that sometimes lasted for six hours. The members were going over all their evidence with the secretary, and Wade was denouncing McClellan for his long period of inactivity. Julian later recalled Stanton's gratifying reactions: "He agreed with us fully in our estimate of General McClellan, and as to the necessity of an early forward movement." Stanton was eager to join the Committee in a concerted drive to make McClellan fight. In an explosive letter to Charles A. Dana, the secretary promised a new policy in the conduct of the war: "As soon as I can get the machinery of the office working, the rats cleared out, and the rat-holes stopped, we shall *move. This army has got to fight or run away; and while men are striving nobly in the West, the champagne and oysters on the Potomac must be stopped.*"[1]

Radical opinion gathered behind Stanton and the Committee. The Jacobins continued to press the charge that McClellan held the armies in quarters because he secretly sympathized with the Southern cause. "I doubt his capacity," proclaimed the postmaster of Chicago, "and I doubt also whether his whole heart is enlisted in the work that has been assigned him."[2] A Massachusetts radical, writing to Johnson of the Committee to urge the adoption of emancipation as a military measure, asked whether McClellan was trying to prolong the war until he could get himself elected president. If this was the case, said the suspicious correspondent, he was "no man to have control of the men who desire to fight rebels and traitors."[3] In Wash-

[1] Julian, *Recollections,* 204; *C.C.W.,* 1863, 1:75; Edwin M. Stanton to C. A. Dana, January 24, 1862, in the Dana MSS.; Flower, *Stanton,* 125.

[2] J. L. Scripps to Lyman Trumbull, February 1, 1862, in the Trumbull MSS.; Governor Richard Yates of Illinois to Trumbull, February 14, *ibid.*

[3] Matthew Warner to Andrew Johnson, February 4, 1862, in the Johnson MSS.

ington the rising Jacobin demand for aggressive action beat around Lincoln. Fessenden was in such a savage mood toward the administration for its support of McClellan that he declared he was ready to "cut everybody's throat." He despondently feared that nothing could move the military forces, but Zachariah Chandler was confident of the results of a little political pressure. Chandler announced the manifesto of the radical machine in the Senate: "The time has arrived when the order 'forward' will close this rebellion. . . . There has not been a day since the 1st day of November when we could not have closed the war in sixty days."[4]

Stanton and Wade brought the radical case directly to the president, and insisted that he order McClellan to strike a blow. The country wanted real war, they urged, and further delay would be disastrous to the party. They did not neglect to remind Lincoln that the Republicans had lost heavily in the fall elections and they ascribed the reverses to the inactivity of the army. The president yielded. He later admitted to Henry J. Raymond of the *New York Times* and to Ulysses S. Grant that the pressure of the politicians and the public had forced his hand. It is probable that in addition Lincoln was weary at last of McClellan's arrogance. John Hay remarked that at this time the president began to interfere more actively in the commander's plans. "He stopped going to McClellan's, and sent for the General to come to him."[5]

On January 27 the president issued an order "for a general movement of the land and naval forces" on February 22. Although his critics jeered at the notion of informing the Confederates that they could expect an attack on Washington's Birthday, Lincoln went ahead vigorously. Four days later he handed out another order directing McClellan to provide for the safety of Washington and then to move his army southward to seize the railroad supplying the Southern forces at Manassas. In the radical camp there was exultation at the president's

---

[4] Fessenden, *Fessenden*, 1:260; *Congressional Globe*, 37 Congress, 2 Session, 774. The order of the sentences has been reversed.

[5] Raymond, *Lincoln*, 265; Ulysses S. Grant, *Personal Memoirs of Ulysses S. Grant* (New York, 1885–1886), 2:122; Hay, *Diary*, 1:153.

action. The Jacobins credited Stanton with having opened Lincoln's eyes to McClellan's incompetence. Indeed, most contemporaries supposed the secretary had drafted the two orders. Actually Stanton was thrown into a tremendous state of excitement when the instructions came to the department. He sent Wade a note marked "most confidential" describing the nature of the president's mandate. He advised the chairman to be ready to invoke Congress in executive session for any emergency. "It is no less important that Congress should at once *place itself in fighting condition* by the rule for Executive Session in both houses. Any hour the necessity may be upon you unprepared. Please communicate confidentially with the loyal and honest members of both houses and have action—immediate action."[6]

Stanton and the Committee were counting their chickens too soon. If they had been devotees of Robert Burns, they might have remembered the warning about what often happens to the schemes of mice and men. McClellan had no intention of carrying out a movement against the enemy according to the plan ordered by the president. From the beginning the commander had planned to take Richmond from the east, approaching up the Peninsula and using some river like the James as a line of supply, with naval units guarding the rear.[7] Lincoln the layman had always feared this plan. What would happen to Washington, he asked, while the main Union army was down in the Peninsula? He felt that McClellan should move south from the capital, keeping his army between the Confederates and the city. McClellan had calmed his misgivings and secured a reluctant indorsement of the Peninsula proposal. But in late January the president's objections to the water route revived, fanned by supporting words from Stanton and the Committee. The order of January 31 marked a return to Lincoln's original position.

⁶ *O. R.*, series 1, 5:41; Welles, *Diary*, 1:95–98; Flower, *Stanton*, 138–139; Gorham, *Stanton*, 1:333–334; Washington *National Republican*, in the *New York Tribune*, September 17, 1862; Edwin M. Stanton to Benjamin F. Wade, January 27, 1862, in the Stanton MSS.

⁷ McClellan, *Own Story*, 203.

McClellan, confident of his ability to handle the president, asked for permission to submit his objections to the two orders in writing. Lincoln already regretted his hasty action in yielding to the radicals, and he readily agreed. He wrote to the commander asking for "satisfactory answers" to a number of questions: Would McClellan's plan require the expenditure of more time and money than the president's own? Would it make victory more certain and valuable? Would it enable the army to retreat safely in case of disaster? McClellan replied in a long letter. He explained the dangers of an advance from Manassas, which would necessitate frontal assaults upon entrenched positions and a constantly lengthening line of supply and which promised no opportunity of decisively smashing the enemy. The Peninsula plan on the other hand offered the shortest possible land route to Richmond over a terrain favorable to military operations. The lines of retreat were safe with the fleet protecting the flanks. There need be no fear of an attack upon Washington while the campaign was in progress because the rebels, with their own capital threatened, would have to withdraw every available man for its defense. And with Richmond captured, added the commander as a clincher, the Confederacy was smashed, the war over.[8] So said McClellan, and Lincoln believed. The president never formally revoked his January orders but he did not require McClellan to execute them. The Young Napoleon went ahead with his original design.

Lincoln's switch of opinion left the Jacobins boiling. Their newly found hope that he had emancipated himself from McClellan's influence was gone, and they were in a more dangerous mood than ever. Their anger vented itself in savage assaults upon the conservatives in the Cabinet. The frightened Bates wrote in his diary: "If we fail to do something effectual in the next thirty days, the administration will be shaken to pieces, the Cabinet will be remodelled, and several of its members must retire." A Western radical who had come to Washington

[8] Lincoln to McClellan, February 3, 1862, in *O. R.*, series 1, 5:41–42; McClellan to Stanton, February 3, *ibid.*, 42–45.

to advance the interests of General Hunter noted how the atmosphere was charged with hostility toward the administration. In a letter to Trumbull he described the powerful position which the Committee held in the picture. "I am satisfied the only way anything can be done is through Wade's committee. I am confident that Mr. Lincoln and Genl. McClelland [sic] are both afraid of it," he wrote.[9]

Although Stanton was disappointed by the collapse of his promising intrigue, he did not drop his efforts to make McClellan fight or get out. He was a master of propaganda and he turned to this weapon to weaken McClellan in the opinion of the public. General Grant, appearing out of obscurity, had just achieved the capture of two Confederate forts in Tennessee, and the country, hungry for a military success, was hailing the new general. Stanton seized the chance to add his voice to the chorus and at the same time to administer a slap to McClellan. On February 19 the secretary dispatched a letter to the *Tribune*, ostensibly to announce the recent victories and to extend the nation's gratitude to Grant. Actually the communication was a superb piece of innuendo. It contrasted, by implication, action and success in the West with inactivity and emptiness in the East. "Patriotic spirit with resolute courage in officers and men is a military combination that never failed," said Stanton with a side look at McClellan. "We may well rejoice at the recent victories, for they teach us that battles are to be won now, and by us, in the same and only manner that they were ever won by any people, since the days of Joshua,— by boldly pursuing and striking the foe." Stanton sent a similar letter to General F. W. Lander, who had won a minor battle on the upper Potomac. He praised Lander for striking the foe in bad weather and over muddy roads, conditions which McClellan was always using as an excuse for not moving, and for scorning "to waste life in camp when the enemies of their country are within reach." The Jacobins applauded these telling sallies. Greeley charged that McClellan wanted to prevent de-

[9] Bates, *Diary*, 227–228; J. W. Shaffer to Lyman Trumbull, January 31, 1862, in the Trumbull MSS.

(*Scene.*—*A Private Lunatic Asylum.*)

KEEPER. "Yes, Sir; one of our incurables. Dangerous, you ask? No, not at all   Lately he has been rather *rabid*, but we keep him in check, as you see.   Take Food? Yes, Sir, but sparingly: he has Strange Notions on that point, and no doubt has injured his brain by Eccentric Feeding.   Noisy? Oh, very! sometimes makes such a Row that he disturbs all the other Patients.   What are his Delusions, you say?   Why, he has so many it's hard to remember 'em.   Sometimes he fancies he's a General, and sometimes he thinks he's a Nigger; but oftenest he gets it into his head that he's a Newspaper Editor, which is the drollest of all—ha! ha! ha!"
GEN. McC——N. "Ah! indeed! Poor GREELEY! I heartily pity him!"

Horace Greeley's opposition to McClellan's war policies. From Harper's Weekly, *March 29, 1862.*

cisive military action in order to bring about a peace that would preserve slavery and then have himself elected president with Southern support. The conservatives, recognizing Stanton's letters for what they were, replied with a warm defense of the commander.[10]

While Stanton was trying his hand at molding public opinion, the Committee prepared for another drive against McClellan. In a meeting on February 18 Odell told the members that McNapoleon had permitted the rebels to erect batteries on

[10] *New York Tribune,* February 20, 1862; Stanton's letter, February 19, in the Stanton MSS.; Gorham, *Stanton,* 1:285–286; William H. Hurlbert, *General McClellan and the Conduct of the War* (New York, 1864), 164; Edwin M. Stanton to F. W. Lander, February 17, 1862, in the Stanton MSS.; *New York Tribune,* February 22, 1862; *Harper's Weekly,* March 8, 1862.

the Potomac, thus blockading the river to Union forces. He bitterly condemned the general, and he and Chandler urged that the Committee go to Stanton with a protest and together with the secretary compel McClellan to open the river. Wade objected that this might be interpreted as a reflection upon Stanton, and it was finally decided that the Committee would meet the secretary to discuss the matter but for the pretended purpose of congratulating him upon the "recent victories" achieved in the West under his administration. Wade and Johnson representing the Committee called at the War Department the next day. The chairman said they had come to press "the importance and necessity of at once wiping out that disgrace to the nation—the blockade of the Potomac and the siege of our capital." Stanton caught the cue readily. He replied that he felt as deeply on the subject as did the Committee, "that he did not go to his bed at night without his cheek burning with shame at this disgrace upon the nation." It was McClellan's job to destroy the batteries, agreed the secretary, but the general had refused to act. Then Stanton, undoubtedly with great relish, said McClellan was in the building and offered to have him brought over to explain the situation to the Committee.

McClellan must have noticed the hostility with which the air of the room was charged as he entered. Wade repeated his arguments for the general's benefit and demanded immediate action. The commander replied with the familiar argument, now becoming maddening to the Committee, that his preparations were not yet complete and his lines of retreat not adequate. Wade lost his temper completely. He shouted that an army the size of McClellan's did not need any avenues of retreat if it was given a chance to fight. Let McClellan take his soldiers over the Potomac and keep them there until they had whipped the rebels. If they could not win a victory, "let them come back in their coffins." The interview ended on an embarrassed note.[11]

Johnson wrote the report of the meeting for the Committee's journal. He recorded that "the interview with the Secretary

[11] *C.C.W.*, 1863, 1:83–85; Benjamin F. Wade to E. M. Stanton, February 19, 1862, in the Stanton MSS.; *Life of Chandler*, 227–228.

had been a very satisfactory one; that the Secretary listened attentively to all that the chairman said, and although the chairman sometimes made his statements to General McClellan in pretty strong and emphatic language, the Secretary indorsed every sentiment he uttered. The Secretary feels as strongly upon this subject as this committee does."

Stanton and the Committee held another conference at the secretary's home on the evening of the twentieth to discuss the Potomac business again. They realized that in the rebel blockade they had something that would alarm Lincoln, for the president had told McClellan the river must be free before the army departed to the Peninsula. Finally, after more secret conclaves, Stanton and the Committee brought their demands to the White House. Lincoln must force McClellan to fight or remove him. Wade threatened to raise a revolt in Congress by offering a resolution directing the president to order McClellan to advance. The disturbed Lincoln listened gravely. He dreaded an open break in the party and once more he was beginning to have cankering doubts about his commander. He promised to see McClellan.[12]

While these busy intrigues were maturing in Washington, McClellan had been absent in the field. Toward the end of February he returned to town. Many of his preparations for the campaign were now complete, and he invited the division commanders to a council at his headquarters on March 7. Then suddenly the president "at a very early hour on the morning" of that day summoned him to an interview. To the general's dismayed surprise he found Lincoln again opposed to the Peninsula plan. The President repeated his conviction that McClellan's movement would leave Washington open to capture, and he demanded that the Confederates be driven from Manassas before anything else was attempted. He also said he had been told some ugly things about McClellan—that the general wanted to strip the capital of defenses so the rebels could seize it.[13] Undoubtedly Lincoln had received this information from

---

[12] *C.C.W.*, 1863, 1:85–86; *Life of Chandler*, 228.
[13] McClellan's report, in *O. R.*, series 1, 5:49–50; McClellan, *Own Story*,

the Committee and Stanton. It is possible that he heard it corroborated by some of the officers, who may have been brought to him by the Committee as supporting witnesses. McDowell, who hated McClellan, may have been one of these. He constantly flitted around the War Department and the Capitol picking up gossip, and a short time before had informed Heintzelman that in official circles there was a great deal of dissatisfaction with McClellan's proposed operations and that Lincoln might call a meeting of officers to consider the plans.[14]

Lincoln's unexpected opposition and his apparent acceptance of the tales of McClellan's enemies stunned the commander. As the president spoke, McClellan saw the threatened collapse of his careful preparations and possibly his dismissal as head of the armies. He pleaded that even then his officers were at headquarters to consider the details of the coming campaign. Lincoln, hesitant about overriding McClellan on his own authority and always hungry for the advice of a body of military experts, snapped at this information as a chance to shift an unwelcome responsibility. He suggested that the two rival plans, his and McClellan's, be submitted to the generals for a decision, and he promised to accept the opinion of the majority. McClellan was saved.

If Lincoln had known the secrets of army politics, he might have realized he was handing the victory to McClellan. Stanton knew and protested, too late. Personal jealousies and partisan differences had split the twelve division commanders of the Army of the Potomac into two savagely hostile factions. In one group were McDowell, Heintzelman, E. V. Sumner, John G. Barnard, and E. D. Keyes. They were the senior generals, who had been in the service for years; several of them were older in years than McClellan and they resented his rapid rise to power

---

195–196; James F. Joy, "The Committee on the Conduct of the War," *Detroit Free Press*, January 10, 1863. McClellan states in his report, written at a later date, that his conference with Lincoln took place on March 8. However, other evidence indicates that it occurred the previous day.

[14] Joy, *Detroit Free Press*, January 10, 1863. Joy of course was intensely hostile to the Committee, and some of his statements must be discounted. Heintzelman diary, February 17, 1862.

which they felt should have been theirs. In particular they detested the officers in the other faction: Fitz John Porter, Andrew Porter, William B. Franklin, W. F. Smith, James F. Negley, Louis Blenker, and George McCall. These were the young men whom McClellan had brought into the army, whose fortunes he pushed, and whose advice he asked in preference to that of the older officers. The two cliques also held diametrical political opinions. The elder generals were Republicans and believed with the Committee that emancipation should be made an end of the war. They fraternized intimately with the Jacobin politicos, perhaps in the hope of thus satisfying their ambitions for advancement, for they felt, in the bitter words of Keyes, that McClellan would "disfavor Republican officers."[15] McClellan's "pets," as Stanton scornfully called the younger officers, were conservatives and agreed with the commander that politics, at least of the radical variety, had no place in the conduct of the war. They opposed emancipation and were given to cynical remarks, which enraged the Jacobins, to the effect that there were no great moral issues in the conflict. This was the council which now considered Lincoln's and McClellan's disputed plans.

The decision was foreordained. By an eight to four vote the council decided for McClellan. Only McDowell, Sumner, Heintzelman, and Barnard supported the president; Keyes unexpectedly sided with the McClellan faction. Then the generals adjourned to report their verdict to Lincoln. While McClellan was giving the president the news, Stanton walked in. The secretary was apparently unaware of the meeting at McClellan's quarters, and he now objected vigorously to its acceptance of McClellan's plan. But Lincoln kept his bargain and told McClellan to go ahead with the movement to the Peninsula.[16] The president kept one ace up his sleeve. On the follow-

[15] Warden, *Chase*, 498–499; E. D. Keyes to Edwin M. Stanton, October 27, 1862, May 13, 1863, in the Stanton MSS.; New York *Independent*, May 26, 1864; Cochrane, *War for the Union*, 46; testimony of Governor William Sprague of Rhode Island, in *C.C.W.*, 1863, 1:566.

[16] Heintzelman diary, March 8, 1862; McClellan's report, in *O. R.*, series 1, 5:49–50; Flower, *Stanton*, 138–139; Gorham, *Stanton*, 1:347–348.

ing day, without consulting McClellan, he issued an order that
the army was not to change its base without leaving an adequate force to defend Washington and that not more than half
of the army should be taken to the Peninsula unless the rebel
batteries on the Potomac were silenced. And knowing McClellan, Lincoln decreed that the movement must begin on the
eighteenth.[17]

The Jacobins were frantic with rage at the way in which
McClellan had again foiled them. Stanton sneered at the eight
generals who were "afraid to fight" and vainly urged Lincoln
to disregard the council's decision. In a grim mood, the secretary told Senator Browning he meant to try one commander
after another until he got a good one. Wade thought the majority of the division generals were as traitorous as McClellan.
The Young Napoleon was terribly aware of the dangerous
attack which he had luckily weathered. Marcy, his chief of
staff, confessed to Heintzelman that if the council had decided
against McClellan, the armies would have had a new commander in the person of Frémont or Halleck.[18]

The Committee, its hands deep in army politics, knew long
before the March council temporarily saved McClellan that
the commander dominated the division generals and discussed
his plans only with the two Porters and Franklin. The Committee had tried to remedy this situation. Its plan was to have
the twelve divisions of the Army of the Potomac consolidated
into four or five corps on the European model. The new commands would naturally go to the generals with senior commissions—the Republican faction. McClellan would be forced
to consult them about future operations because of the importance of their positions, and in a council they could always

Heintzelman gives the date of the council as March 7. For accounts of
the meeting by participants, see the following pages in C.C.W., 1863,
vol. 1: Sumner, 360; Barnard, 387; McDowell, 270; Franklin, 681; Keyes, 598.
    [17] O. R., series 1, 5:50.
    [18] Hay, Diary, 1:53–54; Flower, Stanton, 139; Theodore C. Pease and
James G. Randall, eds., Diary of Orville Hickman Browning (Collections of
the Illinois State Historical Library, vol. 20, Lincoln Series, no. 2, Spring
field, 1927), 533; Wade, Facts for the People, 3; Heintzelman diary
March 8, 1862.

dictate the decision. It was a clever scheme to weaken McClellan's authority, and Stanton liked it. The secretary talked about the corps proposal with Heintzelman in the latter part of February. "He wishes to divide the Army into 'corps de armies' & I am to have one," wrote the gratified Heintzelman in his diary. "The Sec. wishes me to see the President & give him my views. I think that the Sec. will carry out his views in spite of Gen. McClellan. He is quite surprised . . . that there has been no council of war in this Army. I told him that I had never had a word of conversation with Gen. McClellan on any military subject. . . . He is determined that something shall be done here & that shortly."[19]

Both Stanton and the Committee were determined, and they paid Lincoln several visits to press the merits of corps upon him. They argued that larger military units would result in increased efficiency in battle. Lincoln liked the idea but said McClellan was opposed. The commander, just as aware of the politics in the situation as the Committee and quite as ready to mislead Lincoln with specious reasons, advised delay until the campaign demonstrated which generals were competent to head corps.[20] To the Committee's disgust, Lincoln agreed with McClellan. Then the March council in which the general's "pets" controlled the decision jarred the president's easy good nature. Suddenly he saw the light. On March 8 he ordered the army organized into corps and designated the generals to command them—Sumner, McDowell, Keyes, Heintzelman, and Nathaniel P. Banks, a Republican politician from Massachusetts. McClellan was not consulted.[21] On the eve of the campaign the commander had lost an important trick to the radicals. He was in the painful position of having to work with five subordinates who distrusted him and who did not believe in his

[19] *Ibid.*, February 21, 1862. At the same time Heintzelman talked with McDowell, who knew all about the movement for the organization of the army into corps.

[20] *C.C.W.*, 1863, 1:86–88; Julian, *Recollections*, 204–205; McClellan's report, in *O. R.*, series 1, 5:50.

[21] *Ibid.*, 18; McClellan, *Own Story*, 222; Heintzelman diary, March 8, 1862.

plan of operations. He knew they would watch him like hawks for any mistake and report it immediately to the Committee or Stanton.

The Washington scene was tense in that blustery March of 1862. Plots and counterplots boiled beneath the troubled surface; Stanton hatched innumerable schemes to destroy his enemies; McClellan twisted and turned as the radicals struck; the Jacobins and the conservatives struggled feverishly to control the hesitant Lincoln who wanted so much to do the right thing. And behind all was the implacable Committee. Then comedy of a sort intervened, but it was comedy that turned jeering laughter at McClellan. As the commander began to move his troops, the Confederates evacuated Manassas and Centreville to take up new lines of defense for the coming attack. They had held these sites near Washington since the previous fall. McClellan had refused to attack them, although the Committee demanded and Lincoln urged that he do so. Large bodies of rebels garrisoned the places, claimed the general, and bristling guns guarded strong fortifications; besides, nothing important would result from a victory here. But when the news came that the Confederates were leaving, McClellan decided to occupy the forts. He said he wanted the soldiers to "gain some experience on the march," and to force them to get rid of "the superfluous baggage and other *'impedimenta'* " which had accumulated around the camp.[22] So he paraded the army out to Manassas, solemnly took possession of the deserted ramparts, and marched back looking foolish, having permitted the enemy to get away "without the loss of a man or a meal of victuals."[23] This was bad enough but it was not all. Others, including the Committee, came to view the celebrated strongholds which had held McClellan at bay so long. They discovered evidence that the forts had been occupied by a small force. They found piles of dirt thrown up as entrenchments. And peering out from the earthworks were the guns McClellan had dreaded—logs painted black! Laughter, sardonic and scorn-

[22] *O. R.*, series 1, 5:51.
[23] Mark Skinner to Edwin M. Stanton, March 20, 1862, in the Stanton MSS.

ful laughter, shook the country. "People said a great deal about
it, and thought a great deal more," said Hay. Even the conservatives began to doubt McClellan now.[24]

The Jacobins could not be surprised by any stupidity he
committed, but they were disgusted beyond measure by his
Manassas adventure. Their impatience with Lincoln for sustaining such a commander in power became intense. Fessenden
exploded in a letter to his family, who were rapidly becoming
accustomed to angry communications. "You will have heard of
the wooden guns at Centreville?" he asked. "It is all true, and
we are smarting under the disgrace which this discovery has
brought upon us. We shall be the scorn of the world. It is no
longer doubtful that General McClellan is utterly unfit for
his position. . . . And yet the President will keep him in command, and leave our destiny in his hands. . . . Well it cannot
be helped. We went in for a railsplitter, and we have got one."
Stanton was in a fine frenzy. Bluntly he told the president and
the Cabinet that drastic action was imperative "to relieve the
other armies and the country of the Potomac incubus"; he
recommended wholesale dismissal of the "traitors" among the
division generals. As the storm of denunciation broke upon
McClellan, the Committee saw another opportunity to pull
him down. The members came to Lincoln with demands for his
removal. If he had not known about the wooden cannon he was
incompetent, they argued; if he had known, he was disloyal.
Whichever the case, he should go.[25]

The president's faith in McClellan was strained dangerously
by the Manassas fiasco. He thought the commander had missed
a chance to end the war at one blow. And he could not with-
stand the pressure of the Committee and Stanton and the
Jacobin machine for the dismissal of McClellan. In characteris-
tic fashion he yielded halfway. On March 11 he gave out an
order which "relieved" McClellan of his position as general
in chief, but retained him as commander of the Army of the

[24] Hay, *Diary*, 1:54; *Harper's Weekly*, March 29, 1862, The Lounger's
Column.
[25] Fessenden, *Fessenden*, 1:261; Flower, *Stanton*, 140; Julian, *Recollections*, 205, 208–210; C.C.W., 1863, 1:249, 254–255.

Potomac. Halleck was placed in control of Western operations, and the Mountain Department was created for Frémont. All generals of departments were instructed to report directly to Stanton, which meant that for all practical purposes the secretary was to exercise the powers hitherto wielded by McClellan. With a brutality that was rare in him, Lincoln immediately sent copies of the order to the press, and it was in a Washington newspaper that McClellan first learned of his disgrace.[26]

The Committee was "surprised and delighted" by Lincoln's hasty action. So was Stanton, who congratulated the president at a Cabinet meeting and treated those present to a denunciation of "the imbecility which had characterized the General's operations on the upper Potomac."[27] But the Jacobins were not entirely satisfied with Lincoln. Why had he kept McClellan in command of the Army of the Potomac? Why had he not ejected the traitor from the service altogether? McClellan still controlled the most important army in the country and was still, in their estimation, a force for evil. The Committee, full of "passionate impatience for decisive measures," resolved to keep a watchful eye on him.[28]

The country was also watching McClellan as he completed his slow and laborious preparations to transport his army to the Peninsula, and later as he began a snail-like advance toward Richmond. From radical circles emanated a steady flow of savage criticism of the general. He was not moving fast enough, he was afraid to fight, he would not attack the rebels when they were in entrenched positions. Perhaps, sneered the Jacobins, he feared some more wooden guns.[29] The general's friends advised him to continue his cautious strategy and not to be swayed by the clamor of his enemies, "the carpet knights" in Washington; McClellan replied that he "would not allow these treacherous

[26] *O. R.*, series 1, 5:54; McClellan, *Own Story*, 225.
[27] Julian, *Recollections*, 205; Hay, *Diary*, 1:55.
[28] Julian, *Recollections*, 208–209; Bates, *Diary*, 240.
[29] *Chicago Tribune*, March 21, 1862; Mark Skinner to Edwin M. Stanton, March 20, in the Stanton MSS.; J. Gardiner to Lyman Trumbull, April 10, and G. D. Pond to Trumbull, April 14, in the Trumbull MSS. For a defense of McClellan from these attacks, see the letter dated March 24, in *War Letters of William Thompson Lusk* (New York, 1911), 129–130.

hounds" to drive him from his course. Stanton sent reassuring words to the harassed general through Barnard—McClellan was not to move until he was "fully ready," the general had "no firmer friend" than the secretary.[30]

This was sheer Stantonish hypocrisy. Already the secretary was hatching more schemes to destroy McClellan. He had summoned to Washington General Ethan Allen Hitchcock, an ancient officer rounding out his days in honorable obscurity. Hitchcock understood he was to act as a military adviser to the War Department, but upon his arrival he found to his intense amazement that Stanton wanted to make him commander of the Army of the Potomac. He refused the offer, although Stanton argued that there was tremendous pressure being brought upon Lincoln to remove McClellan. Hitchcock did however consent to become a consulting expert in Stanton's office, and the secretary appointed him chairman of a new agency, the Army Board, composed of the heads of bureaus in the War Department. Another council to supervise McClellan had sprung into existence. Stanton soon let Hitchcock know where McClellan stood. The secretary came to the general's office and, wrote Hitchcock in his diary, "shutting the door behind him, stated to me the most astounding facts, all going to show the astonishing incompetency of General McClellan. I cannot recite them; but the Secretary stated fact after fact, until I felt positively sick."[31] After this Stanton could depend upon Hitchcock.

On March 24 Stanton asked the Committee to come to his office for a conference. The secretary was in a downcast mood. He told the members that Lincoln still had confidence in McClellan and would not, despite the general's blunders, remove him. What else was said and done at this meeting the records do not reveal. But it seems certain, in the light of the astonish-

[30] Frank Blair, Sr., to McClellan, April 12, 1862, and McClellan to Mrs. McClellan, April 21, in McClellan, *Own Story*, 281, 313; Barnard to McClellan, March 19, 1862, *ibid.*, 246.

[31] William A. Croffut, ed., *Fifty Years in Camp and Field; the Diary of Major-General Ethan Allen Hitchcock, U.S.A.* (New York, 1909), 437–439, 440, hereafter cited as Hitchcock, *Diary*.

ing events that followed soon after, that the inquisitors and Stanton here worked out a scheme to make McClellan fail in his campaign. A short time later Senator Browning saw Stanton at an evening gathering of Republican politicians, again aggressive and confident and seemingly bursting with important secrets. During the conversation Stanton denounced McClellan fiercely, and afterwards he took Browning home in his carriage. "As we rode down the avenue," wrote the senator in his diary, "he expressed the opinion that McClelland [sic] ought to have been removed long ago, and a fear that he was not in earnest, and said that he did not think he could emancipate himself from the influence of Jeff Davis, and feared he was not willing to damage the cause of secession." At the same time John Hay's delicate nose sensed intrigues in the air. Hay heard whispers of intensive backstairs activity and he guessed against whom it was being directed. "McClellan is in danger, not in front but in rear," Hay observed.[32]

The first blow devised by the Committee and Stanton for McClellan fell immediately. While the general was absent superintending the removal of his troops to the Peninsula, Wade and Chandler haunted the office of the president, pouring into his ears their suspicions of McClellan's motives and harping on the old charge that the commander wanted to lay the capital open to capture. McClellan was leaving only a few thousand men to defend the city, they cried, and a much larger force was necessary. Why did not the president take Blenker's division away from McClellan and add it to Frémont's army which was guarding the approaches through the Valley? Lincoln, his fears for the safety of Washington easily aroused, was impressed. When he went out to Alexandria to bid McClellan Godspeed, he told the general of the pressure being exerted for Blenker's withdrawal, but he added assurances that he was opposed to weakening the Potomac army in any way. Back in the frenzied atmosphere of Washington, however, with the Committee and Stanton storming at him, Lincoln's resolu-

[32] C.C.W., 1863, 1:91; Julian, *Recollections*, 210; Browning, *Diary*, 538–539; Hay, *Diary*, 1:56.

tion wavered. Stanton wanted to send Blenker's and another division to Frémont, telling Lincoln that even without these troops McClellan would have "the largest and best army ever led to battle." Finally Lincoln caved. He ordered Blenker to join Frémont. But writing to inform McClellan of his decision, the president tried to soften the blow: "This morning I felt constrained to order Blenker's division to Fremont, and I write this to assure you that I did so with great pain, understanding that you would wish it otherwise. If you could know the full pressure of the case I am confident you would justify it."[33]

McClellan was thus mulcted of 10,000 men whom he had counted upon using in his campaign. But the plan conceived by the Committee and Stanton—to cripple McClellan's army so badly that he could not succeed—was just getting under way. It unfolded rapidly as events followed one upon the other with a clocklike and suspicious precision. Before he departed for the Peninsula, McClellan had prepared a list of the troops he was leaving behind for the defense of Washington: 20,000 men in the forts guarding the city and at least 45,000 in the Shenandoah Valley, up which any enemy assault would have to pass. McClellan sent his chief of staff over to the war office with the report to get the approval of Hitchcock. According to McClellan, "General Hitchcock, after glancing his eye over the list, observed that he was not the judge of what was required for defending the capital; that General McClellan's position was such as to enable him to understand the subject much better than he did, and he presumed that if the force designated was in his judgment sufficient, nothing more would be required."[34] McClellan went to Virginia secure in the belief that his arrangements for the protection of Washington in compliance with Lincoln's orders had received official sanction.

Presumably all this was known to General James S. Wads-

[33] Joy, "Committee on the Conduct of the War," *Detroit Free Press*, February 15, 1863; McClellan, *Own Story*, 164–165; Edwin M. Stanton to Abraham Lincoln, March 30, 1862, in the Stanton MSS., copy of original; Lincoln to McClellan, March 31, 1862, in *O. R.*, series 1, 5:58.
[34] *O. R.*, series 1, 5:63.

worth, commander of the capital defenses. Wadsworth was a Republican political leader from New York and a known and bitter enemy of McClellan. He had said some sharp things about the wooden guns and he stood in high favor with Sumner and the radical chiefs. When Lincoln had proposed Wadsworth's name for the Washington command, McClellan had protested vigorously; but the president had made the appointment as a concession to the Jacobins.[35] Now on April 2, the day after McClellan joined his army in the field, Wadsworth suddenly appeared at the war office. To Stanton he handed a report —an analysis of the forces at his disposal for the defense of the city. It was an amazing document. In it Wadsworth contended that his troops were green and undisciplined and too few in number to repel a rebel attack, "entirely inadequate to and unfit for" the duty assigned them. As for his artillery, it was in worse condition than the garrison. Washington was in danger, cried Wadsworth, because of McClellan's negligence.[36]

Wadsworth's report threw the War Department into an uproar of action. Immediately Stanton, following what seems a preconcerted plan, sent copies of it to the Army Board and the Committee. From Hitchcock the secretary requested an opinion as to whether McClellan had obeyed the president's orders to provide adequate defenses for the city. In a few hours back came the reply from the chairman of the Army Board, who just a short time before had refused to criticize McClellan's arrangements: the general had not followed Lincoln's instructions and the capital was not properly protected.[37] Wadsworth and Stanton took their story to Lincoln and the Cabinet at a tense midnight interview, according to one report, at which they scared the president and his advisers "almost out of their sense."[38] On

[35] Pearson, *Wadsworth*, 108; McClellan, *Own Story*, 226; Doster, *Lincoln*, 52–53.

[36] *O. R.*, series 1, vol. 11, part 3, pp. 60–61; Pearson, *Wadsworth*, 118–120. For Democratic attacks against Wadsworth's report and claims that he falsified the figures, see the New York *World*, April 20, 1863; *Boston Advertiser*, quoted *ibid.*, May 9, 1863; *Detroit Free Press*, January 20, 1863. A Republican version is presented in the *New York Tribune*, July 17, 1863.

[37] Stanton to Hitchcock, in *O. R.*, series 1, vol. 11, part 3, p. 57; Hitchcock to Stanton, *ibid.*, 61–62.

[38] New York *World*, January 19, 1863.

the following day Wadsworth met the Committee. He repeated the charges in his report and delighted the members with a biting excoriation of McClellan and all his works. Then the Committee and Stanton and Wadsworth all swarmed at Lincoln crying that Washington lay helpless before the rebels and something must be done. They demanded that he order one of McClellan's corps then embarking for the Peninsula to remain in front of the city. The president was in a whirlpool of doubt and indecision. He had always believed McClellan's plan would endanger Washington, and now all the people who ought to know, his secretary of war, the Committee, and the respectable Hitchcock, were confirming his fears. The pressure was too strong, and he gave way immediately. On April 3 he authorized Stanton to detain either McDowell's or Sumner's corps.[39] For his own good reasons Stanton chose McDowell, who was instructed to report directly to the secretary.

A few days later Lincoln wrote to McClellan soundly berating him for violating the order of March 8, that the capital "be left entirely secure" before any offensive movement be attempted. The letter reveals the terrific compulsion the radicals had brought to bear on the president to force the withdrawal of Blenker and McDowell. It also discloses Lincoln's total misunderstanding of the arrangements which McClellan had made for the defense of Washington. The president assumed that the 20,000 men under Wadsworth constituted the only force available to meet a Confederate attack, and seemingly did not consider the Union armies in the Valley which the enemy would have to smash before thrusting at Washington. It was a misunderstanding which Wade and Stanton did nothing to dispel. "And allow me to ask," said Lincoln in his letter, "do you really think I should permit the line from Richmond via Manassas Junction to this city to be entirely open except what resistance could be presented by less than 20,000 unorganized troops? This is a question which the country will not allow me to evade." In a more kindly vein Lincoln advised McClellan to speed up his movements, for the public was

[39] C.C.W., 1863, 1:251–253; O. R., series 1, vol. 11, part 3. pp. 65–66; McClellan, *Own Story*, 261.

growling for action and victory. "And once more let me tell you it is indispensable to you that you strike a blow. I am powerless to help this. . . . The country will not fail to note, is now noting, that the present hesitation to move upon an intrenched enemy is but the story of Manassas repeated."[40]

It was hardly just for anyone to expect McClellan to strike much of a blow. With McDowell's corps of 30,000 men and Blenker's division taken from him, McClellan had lost approximately one third of his army on the eve of a crucial campaign. He had planned his operations in the certainty that these units would be a part of his host. And although McClellan was appallingly cautious and always too prone to exaggerate the size of the enemy, he really needed a numerically superior force to carry forward his advance against the Confederates, who had the advantage of fighting from behind strong defensive positions. When he finally locked with Lee in the decisive battle for Richmond, McClellan fought with an army which was no larger than the one he opposed.

The decimation of McClellan's army which the Committee and Stanton had contrived touched off a storm which wrecked Lincoln's hopes for a coalition government, undefiled by partisan motives, to prosecute the war. For this was politics, and the Democrats recognized it. Never again would they trust Lincoln. Their press screamed then and for the duration of the war that the Committee had deliberately sabotaged McClellan because the radicals did not want a Democratic general to win the war, that Stanton wanted to be president and McDowell commander in chief, and that Lincoln had acted as the tool of the Jacobin plotters.[41] Even the conservative Republicans were shocked by what the Committee had done. "It is impossible to exaggerate the mischief which has been done by division of counsels and civilian interference with military movements,"

[40] Lincoln to McClellan, April 9, 1862, in *O. R.*, series 1, vol. 11, part 1, p. 15; McClellan, *Own Story*, 276–278.

[41] New York *World*, May 3, 1862, April 6, 1863; *New York Herald*, April 22, 27, 1862, February 25, 1863; *Detroit Free Press*, January 10, February 1, June 1, 1863; New York *Commercial Advertiser*, April 15, 17, 1862, quoted in Gorham, *Stanton*, 1:415–416, 417–418.

said *Harper's Weekly* solemnly. General Heintzelman, no friend to McClellan, found the recall of McDowell too much to swallow and condemned it as "a great outrage." Gideon Welles thought the whole affair was a clever scheme to make McClellan throw up his command, which would then go to one of the radical generals.[42] If this was what the Jacobins hoped for, McClellan disappointed them. He hung on, but the iron had been driven into his soul. He never forgave Lincoln and Stanton.[43] And as he struggled up the Peninsula the sickening realization gnawed at his mind that lying in wait in Washington were powerful and ruthless enemies who hoped to destroy him. From this moment McClellan was a beaten man.

The Jacobins who engineered the intrigue to cripple the Army of the Potomac wanted McClellan to fail. They were determined to make the destruction of slavery the great goal of the war. They believed that a peace on any other terms would be a mockery. In the spring of 1862 they saw little hope of forcing Lincoln to espouse emancipation and less chance to force a drastic confiscation bill through Congress. What if McClellan defeated the rebels and ended the war? Their plans for a Carthaginian peace would be smashed. Furthermore, the radicals sincerely believed that McClellan was a traitor. They were continually plagued by the fear that he might turn his army upon the government and establish a military dictatorship with Southern men as his advisers. Even if McClellan meant to whip the rebels, the radicals envisioned a gloomy future for their cause. For then McClellan, that scheming politician, would become president, and the Democrats and the South would rule for years to come. McDowell let this cat out of the bag in a conversation with Franklin, who relayed the information to McClellan. According to Franklin, "McDowell told me that it was intended as a blow at you. That Stanton had said you intended to work by strategy and not

[42] *Harper's Weekly*, August 9, 1862; *New York Times*, April 7, 1862; Heintzelman diary, April 3, 1862; Welles, *Diary*, 1:349.
[43] McClellan to Mrs. McClellan, April 6, 11, 1862, in McClellan, *Own Story*, 308, 310.

by fighting; that all of the opponents of the policy of the administration centered around you—in other words, that you had political aspirations."[44]

The Committee and Stanton had an urgent immediate motive for removing McDowell from McClellan's control and placing him in a position where he could act independently. If Richmond were to be captured, far better to have the job accomplished by a radical general like McDowell, who as a war hero would reap the political rewards that came after victory. The Jacobin chiefs fondly hoped that while McClellan engaged the main body of the rebel host in the Peninsula, McDowell could march his army triumphantly into the rebel capital. Certainly the radicals did not believe the stories with which they scared Lincoln—that Washington was in dire danger. Even later when Stonewall Jackson was terrifying the president with deceptive thrusts up the Valley, the radicals were serenely confident of the city's safety. "There has never been any danger here," wrote Senator Grimes, and Salmon P. Chase voiced the same sentiments. Assistant Secretary of War P. C. Watson repeatedly assured Stanton that the rebel troops in the Valley were "designed for menace merely and not for attack. . . . I cannot see any cause for alarm, but I can see that the policy of the Rebels will be to make extravagant demonstrations."[45]

The Jacobins expected McDowell to march directly upon Richmond. "It has been one of my prime objects of desire," Secretary Chase wrote him, "that you should advance toward and *to* Richmond." Stanton "thought the whole force of McDowell should be kept together and sent forward by land, on the shortest route to Richmond." General Herman Haupt later told the Committee of a conference attended by Lincoln, Stanton, Chase, and McDowell, at which they discussed plans for building a railroad to facilitate McDowell's movement. "By forced marches," Haupt related, "the whole of the corps of

[44] Franklin to McClellan, April 7, 1862, *ibid.*, 151.
[45] Salter, *Grimes*, 197; Schuckers, *Chase*, 434; Watson to Edwin M. Stanton, May 8, 9, 1862, in the Stanton MSS. The quotation is from both letters.

General McDowell was to be taken to Richmond, where he would be able to act in concert with General McClellan."[46]

The "culmination of a long cherished plan"[47] of the radicals to secure an independent command for McDowell proved a barren victory. McDowell indeed started for Richmond several times, but on each occasion Lincoln, who was really frightened, called him back to meet an illusory Confederate attack. Finally McDowell was ordered to remain in the Valley to cover Washington. He protested vigorously but in vain to the president that a golden opportunity to take Richmond was being tossed away. "I shall gain nothing for you there," he wrote bitterly to Lincoln.[48] He was tragically right. While the opposing armies battled fiercely in the Peninsula, victory swaying from one to the other, the corps that might have swung the balance to the Union stood impotent at Washington.

Despite the loss of a substantial portion of his army, Mc-Clellan decided to proceed with his original plan of operations. In April and May he moved toward Richmond, slowly and cautiously. At times it seemed to the exasperated country that the army must be crawling to the rebel capital on its hands and knees. McClellan risked no direct assaults. When he found the enemy entrenched, he dug himself in and went through the long procedure of a siege. Continually he wailed to the government that he needed re-enforcements. But he did force the Confederates to fall back steadily, and his advance troops were at one time within five miles of Richmond. The readers of the radical press, however, received no such impression of Mc-Clellan's successes. The Jacobin journals played down his victories or credited them to the radical officers, who, according to colored dispatches, constantly whipped the rebels in brave

[46] Chase to McDowell, May 14, 1862, in Schuckers, *Chase*, 435; Edwin M. Stanton to Herman Dyer, May 18, 1862, in the Stanton MSS.; *C.C.W.*, 1863, 3:428.

[47] *New York Times*, April 7, 1862.

[48] McDowell to Stanton, May 9, 1862, in the Stanton MSS.; Stanton's orders to McDowell, May 17, in *O. R.*, series 1, vol. 11, part 1, p. 28; Stanton to McClellan, May 18, in McClellan, *Own Story*, 345–346; Mc-Dowell to Lincoln, May 24, 1862, in *C.C.W.*, 1863, 1:274–275.

attacks which McClellan knew nothing about. Why did he not know? Because during every battle he was miles behind the lines, safe. A young admirer of McClellan in the army described the journalistic program truthfully when he indignantly exclaimed that a "pack of vagabonds" in the shape of reporters was trying to tear the general down.[49] Greeley's correspondent with the army, Samuel Wilkinson, confided to Heintzelman that he made it a consistent policy in his dispatches to disparage and belittle McClellan. David Davis, an old Illinois friend of Lincoln's and a conservative, charged that "the abolitionist papers wanted the Generals who do not think with them to prove failures." Against the savage blasts of the radicals, the voices of moderate papers like *Harper's,* who defended McClellan as "the Quaker General" winning victories without a costly loss of life, went unheard.[50]

And in Washington the Jacobin cabal, led by the Committee, continued to snipe at McClellan and cry the radical press on to renewed attacks. They jeered at the general's slow movements and said he could not bear to hurt his rebel friends. The *Tribune's* capital correspondent reported that Stanton and the Committee were working for the removal of McClellan but could not budge Lincoln. As McClellan's stock fell the radicals became louder in their demands that the Potomac command be assigned to Frémont, a fighting general, they asserted, who, given the army, would have marched it into Richmond by now.[51] All around official Washington the busy radicals circulated the charge of McClellan's disloyalty. According to Fessenden, McClellan was "either totally unfit for his position or worse, and this opinion prevails in high quarters." McClellan had made the rebels retreat, he conceded, but every time they stopped he would stop and "squat" down for a siege. Bates, attending a conclave of politicians at Wade's house one

[49] Captain Lusk, letter written in May, 1862, in *Lusk Letters,* 146.
[50] Heintzelman diary, April 21, May 13, 1862; David Davis to Joseph Holt, April 28, 1862, in the Holt MSS. Davis spoke specifically of attacks against McClellan in the *Chicago Tribune. Harper's Weekly,* May 24, 1862.
[51] *New York Tribune,* April 23, 1862, Washington correspondence; *Harper's Weekly,* April 12, 1862.

evening, heard Congressman John A. Gurley denounce McClellan and affirm that the general had said the South was right and he would never fight against her. In his diary Bates recorded, "Wade is more guarded in his talk, but evidently approves Gurley's opinions."[52]

In May, in another dog-fight between the radical and the McClellan generals, the old issue of army politics flared up to stir the Committee to wrath. When the inquisitors had persuaded Lincoln to order the corps organization they settled back buoyantly confident that now the radical faction would be able to dominate the Eastern army. But after the campaign got under way, disturbing reports filtered back to Washington that McClellan was making a dead letter of the corps order. Governor William Sprague of Rhode Island, who had been accompanying his state's regiments in the army and regularly tattling McClellan's sins to Stanton, complained that the general ignored the senior officers and continued to counsel with his pets—had, in short, "wholly nullified" the president's instructions. In his bitter diary Heintzelman grumbled that McClellan never asked him for advice and that young Fitz John Porter commanded as many men as a corps general. Heintzelman thought his part in the capture of Yorktown had been deliberately slighted in McClellan's report, and he prepared a written description of the battle for future use. He was "confident that Ben Wade will call for it in due time."[53]

Finally McClellan came out openly against the corps arrangement. Alleging that some of the corps commanders were incompetent, he asked Lincoln for authority either to appoint new ones or to revert to the division organization. McClellan's request excited the frantic protest of the Committee, which saw its work about to go for nothing if the president yielded. Lincoln was disposed to give McClellan his way, but he reproved the general for his stubborn opposition to the corps plan: "I now think it indispensable for you to know how your struggle

[52] Letters of May 17, 24, 1862, in Fessenden, *Fessenden*, 1:260–261, 262–263; Bates, *Diary*, 253.

[53] Sprague to Edwin M. Stanton, May 3, 1862, in the Stanton MSS.; Heintzelman diary, April 28, May 16, May 19, 1862.

against it is received in quarters which we cannot entirely disregard. It is looked upon as merely an effort to pamper one or two pets and to persecute and degrade their supposed rivals." And with his usual shrewd sense of the realities Lincoln added, "Are you strong enough—are you strong enough, even with my help—to set your foot upon the necks of Sumner, Heintzelman, and Keyes all at once?" Then to the Jacobins' intense disgust the president instructed Stanton to let McClellan temporarily suspend the corps organization.[54] The Committee raged because McClellan had snatched its previous victory from them, and regarded Lincoln with increased distrust. But at this point the anger of the entire Jacobin machine turned against the president on a more important issue. Again he had dared to revoke an emancipation proclamation issued by a commanding general. The newest officer to attempt the passage of the radical political program by military action was David Hunter.

Apparently Hunter decided after his unpleasant experience with the Committee during the Frémont investigation that the future lay with the radicals. Immediately he began to cultivate intimate relations with the Jacobin leaders and to let them know that he favored military emancipation. He became especially cordial with Stanton, whose bidding he was always ready to do. For the rest of the war he was, in the words of one critic, a "hanger-on at Washington, doing dirty jobs for the War department."[55] In January he begged Stanton for an independent command with the promise that he would strike a blow for radicalism: "Please let me have my own way on the subject of slavery. The administration will not be responsible. I alone will bear the blame; you can censure me, arrest me, dismiss me, hang me if you will, but permit me to make my mark in such a way as to be remembered by friend and foe."[56] Soon after this the secretary assigned Hunter to the command

---

[54] McClellan to Stanton, May 9, 1862, in *O. R.*, series 1, vol. 11, part 3, pp. 153–154; Lincoln to McClellan, May 9, 1862, *ibid.*, 154–155; Stanton to McClellan, May 9, *ibid.*, 154.

[55] *Utica Telegraph*, in the *Detroit Free Press*, January 30, 1863.

[56] David Hunter to Edwin M. Stanton, January 29, 1862, in the Stanton MSS.

of the Department of the South, comprising South Carolina, Georgia, and Florida. The imposing title of Hunter's department was hardly deserved, as the Union forces controlled only a few points on the coast like Port Royal. But since it was an area in which large numbers of fugitive slaves were expected to flock to the army camps, it offered a fruitful ground for an experiment in emancipation. Perhaps that was why Hunter was sent there.

Stanton must have told the general he could have a free hand with the slavery question. On May 9 Hunter issued a proclamation which declared the slaves in his department "forever free," and directed that they be enrolled for military service. He based his authority to order emancipation upon martial law and he justified his action as a measure of military necessity. In a letter to Fessenden, whose son was an aide on his staff and drilled a colored regiment, Hunter explained his position and asked for support. The Union armies, he asserted, could not continue to serve "as a police force for the protection of the property" of rebels. "Liberate the slaves by proclamation," he urged, "and the props of the Southern Confederacy are knocked away."[57] Hunter did not have to implore radical favor. His bold edict, going beyond Frémont, stirred the Jacobins to vociferous applause. Governor Andrew said it would encourage recruiting in New England; he pledged that if the government upheld Hunter the roads would swarm with soldiers. The radical chiefs headed by Stanton and Chase rushed to Lincoln with demands that the proclamation be allowed to stand. It was approved, Chase told him, by more than nine tenths of the Republicans. The radicals were apprehensive about the president's reactions, and one pessimistic congressman correctly predicted that Lincoln would sacrifice Hunter to the Border State slaveholders.[58]

Lincoln did not have the slightest intention of permitting

[57] *O. R.*, series 1, 14:341; Fessenden, *Fessenden*, 1:255–256.

[58] Andrew's letter of May 19 to Stanton, in the *New York Tribune*, May 24, 1862; *ibid.*, May 17, Washington correspondence; Warden, *Chase*, 434; Fessenden, *Fessenden*, 1:262; Charles B. Sedgwick to John M. Forbes, May 18, in Hughes, *Forbes*, 1:308–309.

the proclamation to go into operation. He was not ready to risk losing the support of the conservatives, the War Democrats, or the Border States by embracing radicalism. Unhesitatingly he overruled Hunter on May 19 and revoked the edict. The right to free the slaves by military action, he asserted, was reserved to him as commander of the nation's armed forces and could not be exercised by individual generals. Lincoln left the door ajar to the Jacobins by saying that he alone would determine when emancipation was necessary, which hinted that at some future date he might decide it was. But this was scant comfort to the disappointed radicals, who saw Lincoln still enmeshed in the net of conservatism. Greeley angrily demanded that the administration get itself a policy and quit appeasing the Democrats. Among the sullen Jacobins only Senator Grimes took a philosophical view of the episode. He professed no indignation because he had expected Lincoln to nullify the proclamation. Why rail? asked Grimes. Emancipation would come in the end, "protracted by the obstinacy and stupidity of rulers it may be, but come it will nevertheless."[59]

When the storm over the Hunter affair raged itself out, the radicals again turned their attention to McClellan and his army in the Peninsula. The general was still going forward but at an even slower pace now, for he was meeting more stubborn opposition. The Jacobins continued to hurl bombs after him. One of Stanton's agents accused him of paying the Democratic press to attack the War Department, and asked what business "that Peacock with 49 tails" had commanding an army. Other radicals condemned the administration for permitting "West Point pro-slavery" generals to prosecute the war, while worthy men of the right stamp like Frémont and Banks wasted in obscurity.[60] In the middle of June Wade took a flying trip to the army. He visited the radical generals and told them that Mc-

[59] O. R., series 3, 2:42–43; New York Tribune, May 20, 1862; Salmon P. Chase to Horace Greeley, May 21, in Bartlett, Frémont, 87–88; Ellis P. Oberholtzer, Jay Cooke, Financier of the Civil War (Philadelphia, 1907), 1:196–197; Salter, Grimes, 196–197.
[60] Jesse Hoyt to John Tucker, assistant secretary of war, June 20, 1862, in the Stanton MSS.; Grant Goodrich to Lyman Trumbull, June 30, 1862, in the Trumbull MSS.

Clellan was not advancing fast enough, that the people demanded action. He also spoke out freely and vigorously against McClellan's mild treatment of Southern civilians. "He is for taking everything from the rebels," wrote Heintzelman.[61] There must be an end to the policy followed by McClellan of placing guards around the property of known rebels, Wade announced to the generals, because "this was not the way in which the people desired the war to be conducted, and . . . generals were trying the patience of the country too far."[62]

While the Jacobins growled at McClellan, one of his bitter critics experienced a change of heart and repudiated his previous attacks. This was Samuel Wilkinson, the *Tribune* correspondent who had written so many dispatches with the purpose of undermining the general. For some reason Wilkinson now came over to McClellan's side. He sent a story to his paper censuring the administration and the radical politicians for crippling McClellan's army and charging that somebody wanted to make the commander fail. The pained Greeley printed the dispatch but editorially disavowed Wilkinson's opinions.[63] It could not be said that Lincoln shared Wilkinson's new-found confidence in McClellan. The president believed McClellan was hopelessly stalled before Richmond, and his hopes that the general could win the war were about played out. With the Jacobins yelling for McClellan's scalp, Lincoln was in an agony of indecision. In desperation he made a furtive journey to West Point, where General Scott was living in retirement, to seek the old warrior's counsel.[64] Whatever Lincoln learned from Scott was to prove of small moment, for rapidly moving events in Virginia wrenched the initiative from his hand—and toppled the Young Napoleon.

On June 1, while the Army of the Potomac sweated and swore through the marshes of the Peninsula, Robert E. Lee assumed command of the Confederate forces defending Richmond. McClellan now faced a master tactician, one of the

[61] Heintzelman diary, June 15, 1862.
[62] *New York Tribune*, June 18, 1862, Washington correspondence.
[63] Wilkinson's dispatch of June 28, *ibid.*, July 3, p. 1.
[64] *Ibid.*, June 25, 1862; *New York Herald*, June 25.

greatest in military history. Audacity was Lee's keynote, and he conceived an audacious plan to crush McClellan. Briefly stated, it called for Jackson to return rapidly from the Valley, so rapidly and secretly that Washington would not know he had disappeared, and join Lee before Richmond. Then the combined armies would fall upon McClellan and crumple him. In late June Lee carried through the concentration of his forces and on the twenty-sixth he attacked McClellan. Then followed the great Battle of the Seven Days, in which McClellan fell back, inflicting heavy losses on the Confederates; shifted his base to the James for better protection; repulsed Lee at Malvern Hill; and then retreated again to Harrison's Landing, where he stopped to lick his wounds. He managed the withdrawal with skill. It was an orderly retreat, not the rout which Lee had intended. He brought back an army, not a rabble. Nevertheless he had failed, and knew it, and in this bitter moment he lost his head. He sent a telegram to Stanton which did him no good with Lincoln: "If I save this army now, I tell you plainly that I owe no thanks to you or to any other persons in Washington. You have done your best to sacrifice this army."[65]

The Fourth of July in Washington was a beautiful day. Fleecy clouds flecked a blue sky and a bright sun gleamed on the Capitol and the White House and the city.[66] But in the president's office, in Congress, wherever men gathered, there was gloom and consternation; and tension gripped the whispered conversations of the politicians. The news had arrived from the Peninsula that McClellan was falling back, that he was smashed, defeated.

The Committee sprang into action. This was the moment for which it had been waiting. The king was dead, long live the heir! And Wade and Chandler had an heir. They had prepared him for the succession and anointed him with the radical oil. Now they led him out for Lincoln to see. It was General John Pope, just lately come out of the West.

[65] O. R., series 1, vol. 11, part 1, p. 61.
[66] New York Independent, December 3, 1863, Washington correspondence.

6
Tax, Fight, and Emancipate

IF JOHN POPE had possessed a coat of arms, it would have been bombast rampant upon an expansive field of incompetence. His military abilities were meager, but like other Civil War generals he was skillful in the art of self-advertising and he talked himself into positions of power for which he had few qualifications. When the war started he secured a command in the Western army and he participated in Halleck's successful campaign in the early months of 1862 which resulted in the occupation of Corinth, Mississippi.

The victory-starved Northern public was well accustomed to seeing the name of Pope prominently displayed in the press accounts of Halleck's exploits. Pope saw to that. He knew how to write official reports that were sparkling and quotable, and that rendered proper credit to John Pope. According to one army correspondent, Henry Villard, Pope deliberately magnified his own rôle at Corinth, reporting that he had captured ten thousand prisoners when actually he had taken only one tenth that number. From the beginning Pope courted the favor of the Jacobins, writing adulatory letters to Senator Trumbull and proclaiming his support of the radical war aims. Soon the Jacobin chiefs began to sit up and take notice of this fighting general from the West who understood so well the causes and the nature of the war. The Committee, constantly on the lookout for a general with the right political ideas whom it could push into McClellan's place, saw in Pope a chance to accomplish its design. The members pelted Lincoln with praise of the new military luminary and urged that he should have an important command in the East.[1] Lincoln too was impressed with Pope and in June called the general to Washington.

[1] Villard, *Memoirs*, 1:279–280; John Pope to Lyman Trumbull, May 8, December 31, 1861, in the Trumbull MSS.; *Boston Traveller*, quoted in the *New York Tribune*, May 31, 1862, p. 1; Wade, *Facts for the People*, 5–6.

Pope dazzled the capital. He was a commanding figure, with piercing eyes, long hair combed back, and an immense beard. But his forte was his conversation. He talked incessantly and he talked well. He exuded self-confidence and he boasted loudly that if given an army he would thrash the rebels in one battle. His monologues were larded with criticisms of McClellan. Soon after arriving he came over to Congress to meet the members on the floor. He treated the admiring legislators to a lecture on how the administration should conduct the war and delighted the radicals with some vicious thrusts at McClellan. Greeley's Washington correspondent concluded that Pope would do. He told his readers: "General Pope is one of the stirring sort of men, and will not be likely to stand on the bank of the Potomac until all the water has run down before crossing, nor plan regular sieges where the same end may be gained by a bold dash with sword and bayonet."[2]

When he was not fraternizing with the radical politicos, Pope stayed at Lincoln's elbow proffering advice on military questions. The president came to rely upon the positive general who always knew what ought to be done, and decided to make greater use of his talents. On June 26 Lincoln ordered the creation of a new army, the Army of Virginia, and placed Pope in command.[3] This aggregation with the optimistic title was called into being by the simple process of combining the forces around Washington—the troops of McDowell, Frémont, and Banks. The Jacobins hailed Lincoln's action as evidence that at long last he was willing to advance the fortunes of a radical general. Almost unnoticed in the chorus of approval was the departure of a tragic figure from the military scene—John C. Frémont, once proclaimed by the radicals as the coming hero of the war but now forgotten in the rush to Pope. Frémont's rôle in the recent Valley campaign had been far from glorious. When he took over the Mountain Department the radical press shouted that the nation could look for great victories, that Frémont's name alone was a terror to the rebels. But to

[2] *New York Tribune*, June 26, 27, 1862, Washington correspondence.
[3] *O. R.*, series 1, vol. 12, part 3, p. 435.

the disgust of his partisans the general failed in everything. Supposed to intercept Stonewall Jackson, he let his fast-moving opponent get away; and when he finally caught up with the Confederates, Frémont suffered a sound whipping. As usual the general was disposed to blame someone else for his own inefficiency, and again he picked the administration as the butt of his wrath. He was in a surly mood when Lincoln transferred him to Pope's new army. Frémont's commission bore an earlier date than Pope's, hence technically he was superior in rank to Pope. Therefore Frémont decided that the president wanted to humiliate him by making him serve under a junior officer. Rather than submit to this indignity, he asked to be relieved of duty, and Lincoln thankfully granted the request. So passed Frémont from the army. The radicals wrote off the episode as another indictment against Lincoln, but their machine made no move to save Frémont.[4] The leaders were too busy planning a rosy future for Pope.

Although the Jacobins exulted at Pope's sudden rise to favor and power, they were determined that their new favorite should advance to a still higher place. The Committee meant to make him commander of the Eastern army. But barring the way to this ambitious project was the figure of McClellan, pushing his soldiers toward Richmond. As long as McClellan had a chance to win, Pope's cause was hopeless. Then came July and the collapse of McClellan's campaign, when even the conservatives abandoned the general. The failure in the Peninsula was the signal for a concerted and savage attack upon the administration by the radicals, who cried aloud for a ruthless antislavery policy and the removal of the traitorous general who had betrayed the nation's trust. Governor Israel Washburn of Maine bluntly told Seward "that unless there is a thorough change in the manner of carrying on the war," the Republican Party would be repudiated by the people. From Illinois Trumbull's radical supporters wrote to denounce the proslavery clique dominating the army and to

[4] *New York Tribune*, June 4, 27, 1862; *O. R.*, series 1, vol. 12, part 3, pp. 437–438.

demand appointments for loyal Republican generals.[5] In Washington the Jacobin cabal wheeled up its heaviest guns to train on McClellan. Fessenden was beside himself with wrath and bursting with epithets: McClellan was "utterly unfit for his position and more than suspected of being a coward—morally and physically," and his career had been "a succession of blunders"; "Seward's vanity and folly and Lincoln's weakness and obstinacy" were ruining the country. Salmon P. Chase used even more bitter words—McClellan was "the cruellest imposition ever forced upon a nation" and had "cost us fifty thousand of our best young lives." Chase took his anger to Stanton and found the war secretary in a like mood and eager to act against McClellan. The two Cabinet members decided that the command of the army must go to another general—"some more active officer," said Chase. They knew the man they wanted. Together they descended upon Lincoln and proposed that he order Pope to the James to take over McClellan's troops. At the same moment Stanton was sending a letter to McClellan: "No man had ever a truer friend than I have been to you and shall continue to be. You are seldom absent from my thoughts."[6]

The Committee beheld with immense satisfaction the tempest of abuse beating around McClellan. This time the members were sure they could unhorse their hated enemy, and they were determined to hoist Pope into the vacated saddle. But they wanted Pope to make an official appearance before the full Committee. Then they could place their authoritative stamp of approval upon him and champion his cause more effectively with Lincoln. Accordingly the handsome officer met the inquisitors on July 8 in a cordial interview. He gave them

[5] *Wilkes' Spirit of the Times* quoted in the *New York Tribune*, July 5, 1862; Israel Washburn to William H. Seward, July 2, 1862, in the Stanton MSS.; D. L. Phillips to Lyman Trumbull, July 5, 1862, and L. L. Enos to Trumbull, July 14, in the Trumbull MSS.

[6] Fessenden in a letter to his family, July 6, in Fessenden, *Fessenden*, 1:263–264; H. C. Fahnestock to Jay Cooke, July 7, quoting conversation with Chase, in Oberholtzer, *Cooke*, 1:197–198; extracts from Chase's diary, in Schuckers *Chase*, 447; Stanton to McClellan, July 5, 1862, in McClellan, *Own Story*, 476–477.

what they wanted. He believed in fighting and not in strategy, in attack instead of delay. The Peninsula movement had been a ghastly mistake; the Union forces should have advanced directly south from the capital upon Richmond. He urged that McClellan's men in the Peninsula be brought back to Aquia Creek and combined with his own troops. Then on to Richmond! With such an army, Pope told the thrilled Committee, he would march to New Orleans. Most important of all, the general enchanted the members with the correctness of his political views. He indorsed the radical war aims and advocated military emancipation and harsh treatment for rebels. The Committee was more than satisfied with Pope. Wade haled a few more witnesses, such as Assistant Secretary of War John Tucker and General Meigs, before the bar for the purpose of getting some ammunition to use against McClellan,[7] but the Committee had already decided to back Pope. It was ready to move heaven and earth to get him McClellan's army.

Lincoln now became the somewhat puzzled center of a tug of war between the radicals and McClellan. On the one side were the Committee and Stanton, pulling at him to transfer McClellan's army to Pope so the latter could make a land advance upon Richmond, or at the very least to send Pope to the Peninsula to supersede the Young Napoleon. McClellan, however, wanted to stay where he was. He was strongly entrenched at his new base, able to defy any attack, and his army was in fine condition. Send him re-enforcements, he begged the president, and he would start another offensive. In a quandary Lincoln made a trip down to McClellan's camp to look over the situation personally. He spent two days talking with McClellan and the generals. To his surprise the officers, even McClellan's enemies, were almost unanimous in insisting that the army was secure and should stay and fight.[8]

This was evidence Lincoln could not disregard, but neither could he ignore the fierce demands of the Jacobins for McClellan's dismissal. At this critical point, when the president's

[7] *C.C.W.*, 1863, 1:276–282, 294–297.
[8] Heintzelman diary, July 8, 9, 1862.

mind was still undecided, McClellan did a rash thing which practically sealed his own doom. He wrote a letter to Lincoln in which he presumed to give his superior officer advice on how to conduct the political affairs of the government as they related to the war. McClellan admitted that his views on partisan issues did not "strictly relate to the situation of this army or strictly come within the scope of my official duties." But they amounted to convictions, and it was his duty to speak out, even though he felt himself to be "on the brink of eternity." The administration must adopt a policy as to the purposes of the war, said the general, and that policy should be conservative. Lincoln should proclaim that the conflict was not being waged for the subjugation of the people of the South. "Neither confiscation of property . . . or forcible abolition of slavery should be contemplated for a moment." Then came a sentence which must have startled Lincoln to the marrow—apparently a veiled threat of that military dictatorship which the radicals had feared. "A declaration of radical views, especially upon slavery, will rapidly disintegrate our present armies." Finally, if Lincoln resolved to carry out the policy McClellan suggested, McClellan was ready to act as his general in chief.[9]

The famous Harrison's Landing letter, as it came to be known, created an angry furore in the radical camp. The voice was that of a general supposedly untouched by politics, but the words might have come from Clement Vallandigham, the New York *World*, or any Democratic source. Lincoln, much perturbed, showed the document to the Cabinet. Stanton and Chase cried that the sentiments expressed were in themselves justification for the removal of the author. Chase's motives were frankly political. "I did not regard Genl. McClellan as loyal to the Administration," he said, "although I did not question his general loyalty to the country." In the opinion of Welles, McClellan had now made his downfall certain.[10]

The Committee, aware that McClellan was rapidly losing

[9] *O. R.*, series 1, vol. 11, part 1, pp. 73–74; McClellan, *Own Story*, 487–488. McClellan handed the letter to Lincoln when the latter visited his camp. It was dated July 7, 1862.
[10] Warden, *Chase*, 440; *Diary and Correspondence of Salmon P. Chase*

Lincoln's support, redoubled its efforts for Pope. That effervescent general continued to advance from one triumph to another with the radicals. On July 14 he issued to the Army of Virginia an address crammed with purple passages and bad rhetoric. It was a covert assault upon McClellan's idea of working by strategy, and an open promise to the Jacobins that Pope, if he had the command, would fight with smashing attacks. Pope had a knack for writing proclamations, but this one was drafted by a greater propagandist than he—Edwin M. Stanton, who dictated it to the general at the war office.[11] The secretary had Pope say to his soldiers:

I have come to you from the West, where we have always seen the backs of our enemies; from an army whose business it has been to seek the adversary and to beat him when he was found; whose policy has been attack and not defense. . . . I presume that I have been called here to pursue the same system and to lead you against the enemy. . . . The strongest position a soldier should desire to occupy is one from which he can most easily advance against the enemy. Let us study the probable lines of retreat of our opponents, and leave our own to take care of themselves. Let us look before us, and not behind. Success and glory are in the advance, disaster and shame lurk in the rear.[12]

To the soldiers of Banks and McDowell, who had so recently braved the sword of Stonewall Jackson in the Valley, these words were a slap in the face.

The Jacobins applauded this fighting proclamation which promised the kind of war they wanted. A few days later Pope gave them more to cheer about. He issued a barrage of orders outlining the manner in which he would deal with civilian rebels. The army was to "subsist upon the country" in which it operated, paying for its supplies in vouchers redeemable at the end of the war, provided the holders could prove their loyalty.

(*Annual Report of the American Historical Association*, 1902, Washington, 1903), 2:47–48; Gideon Welles, *Lincoln and Seward* (New York, 1874), 191.

[11] Jacob D. Cox, *Military Reminiscences* (New York, 1900), 1:222. Cox got this information from Pope.

[12] *O. R.*, series 1, vol. 12, part 3, pp. 473–474.

All disloyal males were to be arrested. Any civilians caught sniping at the troops would be shot without trial. These orders stirred the radicals to extravagant peals of approval. Pope, they thought, was forcing the administration to adopt the radical policies of a remorseless war. One of Trumbull's friends encouraged the senator to bring into the army more generals like Pope who were "not afraid to fight outside of entrenchments" and predicted that if the government would "let the blacks do all the spading, drudgery & teaming," the Union cause might yet triumph.[13] Pope was in high feather at the wide popular acclaim he had aroused. On July 21 he dined with Chase; over the meal Pope vented his conviction that slavery must perish by military emancipation, and said he would like to use slaves in some capacity in the army. Jubilantly Pope told Chase that Lincoln had called Halleck from the West to assume command of all the Union armies. He was sure his old chief would oust McClellan.[14]

The president, tortured by uncertainty as to the proper disposition of McClellan and his army, had finally decided that a military expert must cut the puzzling knot. As the Committee and McClellan dinned their clashing arguments at him, Lincoln became convinced that he should have at his side a permanent adviser to guide him through such controversies. He wanted some successful general, and his thoughts turned to Halleck, the victor of the recent Western campaign, whose reputation was greater then than it ever was afterward. Pope, Stanton, and Chase urged him to bring Halleck to Washington—Pope because he thought his former superior would push the fortunes of an old friend, and the secretaries because they hoped to use Halleck to junk McClellan. On July 11 the president ordered Halleck to report at the capital and appointed him general in chief of the armies, the position which had once

[13] *Ibid.*, part 2, pp. 50–52; *New York Tribune*, July 19, 1862, Washington correspondence; Schuckers, *Chase*, 448; T. O. Washburn to Lyman Trumbull, July 22, 1862, in the Trumbull MSS.

[14] Chase diary, July 21, in *Report of American Historical Association, 1902*, 2:46–47.

belonged to McClellan.[15] Halleck accepted the position with reluctance and trepidation, he wrote to McClellan. He did not want to mix "in the politico-military affairs of Washington," and he feared the Republican press would "cry down any one who attempted to serve the country instead of party," as it had McClellan.[16]

To most radicals Lincoln's selection of Halleck for such an important post was a disagreeable shock and another proof of the president's mania for favoring Democratic officers. The Jacobins remembered the general as the author of the notorious order of the previous year which excluded fugitive slaves from his lines and they knew him as a leader of the conservative faction in the army. Halleck, however, busied himself to remedy their impressions. Soon he was being quoted in Greeley's *Tribune* as saying that military authorities must make every possible use of the slaves against the enemy. A little later the radical General Keyes could write to Stanton that Halleck's views on the nature of the war "are now the same as mine have always been."[17] But try as he might Halleck never secured the full trust of the radical leaders.

Henry Wager Halleck held on to his post for the rest of the war, and at times he exercised some small influence upon the conduct of operations and the formulation of military policy. His was one of the most difficult jobs ever given to any warrior: he was a desk general, "the home director of military operations in the field," and as such he received no credit for anything he did. When the generals in the field won a battle, they took the praise; when they lost, the blame was hurled at Halleck.[18] Most of the commanders treated him in a rude cavalier fashion, frequently taking appeals over his head to Lincoln or Stanton. The secretary was guilty on the same count. With

[15] Welles, *Diary*, 1:108–109; Welles, *Lincoln and Seward*, 192; Nicolay and Hay, *Lincoln*, 6:2; O. R., series 1, vol. 11, part 3, p. 314.

[16] *Ibid.*, 343.

[17] *New York Tribune*, July 26, 1862, editorial; *ibid.*, August 2, 1862, Washington correspondence; E. D. Keyes to Edwin M. Stanton, May 13, 1863, in the Stanton MSS.

[18] Doster, *Lincoln*, 179.

his gruff manner, he apparently frightened Halleck, who never dared to proffer at the war office anything but timid suggestions, most of which were rejected.[19] John Hay quoted Lincoln as saying that Halleck persistently and successfully evaded all responsibility, and was little more than "a first-rate clerk." Many and barbed were the sneers flung at the inactive general hunched over his desk in Washington. In the last months of the war, when the collapse of the Confederacy was assured, a rumor spread that at last Halleck was going to take the field. A New York journal of radical persuasion observed tauntingly: "The public, which has appreciated the dashing and soldierly qualities of Halleck, will look to his new career with an interest not unmixed with a generous apprehension that his notorious daring may lose him to the country."[20]

He is a touching and pathetic figure, this general whose knowledge of the theory of military science led some irreverent critic to pin upon him the nickname "Old Brains." Perhaps he failed to impress his generation because he lacked the grand appearance of so many of his brother officers—which to the unsophisticated America of the sixties seemed an essential attribute of the warrior. A large head carried forward on a small, spare figure, heavy features and bulging eyes of "a dim, uncertain gray," and a dark olive complexion—this was the picture of Halleck carried away by men who knew the glories of a McClellan or a Pope.[21] "I was greatly disappointed in his appearance," wrote Captain Lusk. "Small and farmer-like, he gives a rude shock to one's preconceived notion of a great soldier." Nor did Halleck practice the solemn mannerisms and the martial pose with which other generals attempted to awe subordinates and civilians. Simple, dull, and unorthodox, he irritated many people. Gideon Welles once became so enraged that he snarled in his diary that Halleck could do nothing "but scold and smoke and scratch his elbows."[22] Critics poked fun

[19] Washington *National Intelligencer*, February 26, 1863.
[20] Hay, *Diary*, 1:187; *Wilkes' Spirit of the Times*, May 6, 1865.
[21] *Boston Traveler*, army correspondence, quoted in the *New York Tribune*, May 31, 1862, p. 1.
[22] Letter of July 28, 1862, in *Lusk Letters*, 170; Welles, *Diary*, 1:373.

too at his profound military scholarship and the myriad trea-
tises he wrote on the art of war. "He is wise in military history,"
said one editor. "If old battles were to be fought over again,
probably Halleck would be our best general. It is his memory
and not his invention that is strong."[23]

Halleck spent much time translating the works of foreign
military authorities into English, and this excited derisive
laughter in a boisterous young nation which scoffed at the
value of specialized training for any trade, especially the military. That brash civilian officer, Ben Butler, expressed better
than anyone the common opinion of Halleck: "At a moment
when every true man is laboring to his utmost, when the days
ought to be forty hours long, General Halleck is translating
French books at nine cents a page; and, sir, if you should put
those nine cents in a box and shake them up, you would form
a clear idea of General Halleck's soul." Perhaps Wade uttered
the final estimate of "Old Brains," as far as the radicals were
concerned. "Put Halleck in the command of twenty thousand
men," snorted the senator, "and he will not scare three setting
geese from their nests."[24]

When Halleck took over his duties, Lincoln stepped aside
from the raging controversy between the partisans of Pope and
of McClellan, leaving to the general the hard task of making a
decision. McClellan interpreted the appointment of a new general in chief as an attempt by his enemies to replace him with a
superior authority, for the ultimate purpose of removing him
from the Potomac command. Ominous rumors from the James
sifted back to Washington to frighten the administration and
damage McClellan—the army would resist if Lincoln tried to
dismiss its idolized "Little Mac"; scores had said they would
resign their commissions rather than serve under Pope.[25] Mc-

[23] New York *Independent,* April 30, 1863.
[24] Colonel Theodore Lyman to Mrs. Lyman, July 20, 1864, quoting
Butler, in George R. Agassiz, ed., *Meade's Headquarters, 1863–1865, the
Letters of Theodore Lyman* (Boston, 1922), 192–193; Adam Gurowski, *Diary,
1863–1865* (Washington, 1866), 297.
[25] McClellan, *Own Story,* 450–451; *Harper's Weekly,* July 26, 1862; General Alfred Pleasanton to Joseph Holt, July 14, 1862, in the Holt MSS.

Clellan's real danger, however, was not from Halleck but from the Committee. The inquisitors, realizing that the crucial moment had arrived, now struck McClellan openly.

Zachariah Chandler planned the strategy and led the attack. He had flown into a rage at the news of the Peninsula defeat, even though he had expected failure with the traitor McClellan in command. But he fiercely resolved that McClellan must never have another opportunity to lead an army into a trap. McClellan must be destroyed, and Chandler himself would do it. He determined to assail the general publicly in the Senate. "I shall open up on the traitorous cuss this week in my usually mild & conservative way. I can hold my tongue no longer & *will not try*."[26] Chandler also wanted an opportunity to answer those Democratic newspapers which were charging that the Committee and Stanton had caused McClellan's defeat by securing the withdrawal of McDowell's corps. He spoke twice in the first days of July, bitterly denouncing McClellan and asking the War Department to prepare a report of the Peninsula campaign. If the modest Stanton would not comply, cried Chandler, he himself would give the country the damning facts about McClellan.[27]

This was but the prelude to a more sensational onslaught by the Committee. Evidently the members decided that an official account of McClellan's blunders would be more devastating if delivered by a representative of the Committee than by Stanton. The Committee had ready at hand in its files ample information with which to blast McClellan, but any public presentation of it was prevented by the existence of the secrecy rule. Chandler contemptuously kicked aside this stumbling block. On July 15 the Committee met briefly, and Chandler moved that the secrecy regulation be abolished. The inquisitors voted to let any member use the testimony in speeches in Congress. Significantly enough Wade and Chandler did not trouble

[26] Zachariah Chandler to Mrs. Chandler, July 6, 1862, in the Chandler MSS.

[27] *Congressional Globe*, 37 Congress, 2 Session, 3149–3150, 3219, 3220–3221; *New York Tribune*, July 11, 1862; Chandler to Mrs. Chandler, July 11, 1862, in the Chandler MSS. Chandler spoke on July 7 and 11.

to tell Democratic Senator Wright, Johnson's successor and a McClellan supporter, that there was to be a meeting.[28]

Chandler now had at his disposal all the vast resources of the Committee's investigations and he could attack McClellan with the official sanction of the Committee. On the next day he arose in the Senate to present the radical manifesto—McClellan, the author of the nation's disaster, must go. Trembling with anger and shaking his shaggy locks, Chandler told the history of the Army of the Potomac from the day McClellan became its commander, through the long autumn and winter of inaction and the Peninsula campaign, until beaten by Lee it retreated to Harrison's Landing. Dramatically and methodically, with judicious mendacity, the senator castigated McClellan. He raked up the Ball's Bluff affair and cried, "Let the men who executed and planned this horrible slaughter answer to God and an outraged country." He described McClellan's refusal to attack in the autumn and his holing up for the winter, the blockade of the Potomac, the general's strange delay after spring came, and the wooden guns at Manassas. After recounting each episode he asked, why was no movement made, "Why was this disgrace so long submitted to?" He answered his own questions: "No man knows, nor is any reason assigned." McClellan had lied, charged Chandler, about the smallness of the army he took to the Peninsula. Even after the loss of McDowell, he had 158,000 "of the best troops that ever stood on God's footstool."[29] With this army McClellan could easily have captured Richmond, but for some mysterious reason he refused to grasp the rich prize set so invitingly before him. Instead he "sat down in a malarious swamp" and started a siege. It was siege, siege all the way up the Peninsula, Chandler complained, when a bold assault would have carried the army into the rebel capital. On several occasions the corps generals, unknown to McClellan, won victories by smashing tactics, and the road to Richmond was open. They wanted to take it, but McClellan

[28] *C.C.W.*, 1863, 1:102; *Congressional Globe*, 37 Congress, 2 Session, 3390, Wright's statement.

[29] Chandler's figures were wrong. McClellan never had more than 95,000 men actually at his disposal.

always said no. What did he do after each of these glorious opportunities? "We found another big swamp, and we sat down in the center of it, and went to digging." Running between the lines of Chandler's whole philippic was censure of Lincoln, who had brought McClellan to power and sustained him in spite of every blunder, who even now permitted the recreant to retain command of the army. Chandler closed with a ringing denunciation of McClellan's Democratic supporters, "the northern traitors, who under the guise of patriotism, are stabbing their country in the back."[30]

No one, least of all Lincoln, could doubt after this where the Jacobin machine stood and what it demanded of the administration. Chandler's bold speech, played up in the radical press and circulated widely as a pamphlet, inflamed the radicals to a fighting pitch. The Committee had ripped the mask from McClellan, they thought, and exposed his treason and incompetence. What hallucination then possessed the president to keep him in command? The Jacobin newspapers, charging that all of McClellan's favorites were infected with the virus of disloyalty, clamored for a wholesale flushing of the army's Augean stables. Greeley's Boston correspondent wrote: "It is very much to be questioned if pro-slavery generals, however great their abilities as organizers, strategists, and fighters, can wage this war of ideas successfully. Heart is quite as important as head or hand in such a contest."[31]

Slowly the Jacobins were closing the circle around McClellan, and Lincoln, even had he willed, could not have stopped them. The pressure was too strong, and was steadily increasing. Jay Cooke, the Philadelphia financial tycoon who handled the government's war loans, went to Lincoln with the story that subscriptions were falling off at an alarming rate be-

[30] *Congressional Globe,* 37 Congress, 2 Session, 3386–3392; *Life of Chandler* 228–238; Zachariah Chandler, *Conduct of the War* (Washington, 1862), a pamphlet.

[31] David Prince to Lyman Trumbull, July 30, in the Trumbull MSS.; Caleb Smith to Edwin M. Stanton, July 29, in the Stanton MSS.; *New York Tribune,* July 17, editorial, Washington correspondence; *ibid.,* July 23, p. 3, Boston correspondence; *Chicago Tribune,* July 28, 30, 1862.

cause the people were dissatisfied with the dilatory conduct of the war. He begged the president to appoint a "more pushing, active and bold warrior in McClellan's place." All the while Stanton and Chase pounded at Halleck, demanding that he transfer McClellan's army to Pope. Chase was worrying about a disturbing possibility with which Pope had startled him. Evidently driven to the point of frenzy by the long weeks of uncertainty, Pope conceived the fear that McClellan was about to make a sudden dash upon thinly guarded Richmond, and if successful would walk off with the final honors of the war. He rushed to the secretary with his misgivings, crying that McClellan meant to cheat him out of the spoils of victory. Such an eventuality alarmed Chase; he thought it "would only restore undeserved confidence and prepare future calamities."[32] While sudden dashes were not McClellan's specialty, his army was a menace to Richmond, and so long as it remained in its present position the Confederates dared not undertake an offensive. But Halleck, already under the thorough domination of Stanton, now proceeded to choke off any possibility of an aggressive movement by the Young Napoleon.

"Old Brains" went down to the camp on the James on July 25 and talked with McClellan. He found the general eager to try another advance upon Richmond, if the government would provide sufficient re-enforcements. Halleck agreed to supply a certain number but not as many as McClellan wanted. He then presented an ultimatum to McClellan—attack with his army slightly augmented by new troops or withdraw and join Pope. Stanton and Chase were highly pleased with Halleck when he reported to them his interview with McClellan. Observers like Heintzelman recognized in this the beginning of the end. "It looks as if the Govt. was determined to force McClellan to resign," wrote Heintzelman.[33] In a few days Halleck ordered McClellan to remove all his sick and wounded, and

[32] Cooke's manuscript account of his interview with Lincoln, in Oberholtzer, *Cooke*, 1:199–201; Chase diary, July 26, 1862, in Warden, *Chase*, 441–442.

[33] Halleck to Edwin M. Stanton, July 27, 1862, in the Stanton MSS.; Heintzelman diary, July 26, July 29, 1862; Schuckers, *Chase*, 448.

on August 3 the final blow fell. McClellan was directed to transport the army to Pope at Aquia Creek, and to carry out the movement with the utmost secrecy, the destination "concealed even from your own officers." The Committee and Stanton had triumphed. But the odor of politics that smelled up the entire episode did not go unnoticed. Welles denounced the withdrawal as a scheme by Stanton to oust McClellan, and Heintzelman wrote sadly in his diary, "They mean to get rid of McClellan & dont dare to go at it openly. This splendid army has to be broken up to get rid of him."[34]

Slowly and with much delay, as he did everything, McClellan complied with Halleck's order. He sent the troops forward to Pope, although with bitter reluctance. His young officers went cursing the man under whom they had to serve.[35] But John Pope was wildly jubilant. As he marshaled his army for action, he poured forth orders and proclamations with luxurious abandon. For Lee's soldiers he had no respect. He was going to "bag the whole crowd" at one swoop. His headquarters would be "in the saddle," he announced, and he was marching southward to crush the Confederacy "at the very earliest blush of dawn."[36]

☆

The Jacobins had forced Lincoln to take the general they wanted—a man who would fight and who believed in the radical war aims. Visions of greater victories haunted their minds. They dreamed of filling all the commands with radical officers, and of proclamations of emancipation issuing on every hand. And at the same time they scored another resounding triumph over the administration by pushing through Congress measures directed at the destruction of slavery. Steadily the Jacobin machine was seizing the control of the Republican Party, and Lincoln's hopes of a nonpartisan coalition faded

[34] O. R., series 1, vol. 11, part 1, pp. 80–81; McClellan, *Own Story*, 466; Welles, *Diary*, 1:83; Heintzelman diary, August 11, 1862.

[35] See McClellan, *Own Story*, 508–533, for McClellan's correspondence on the subject with Halleck and Mrs. McClellan.

[36] O. R., series 1, vol. 12, part 2, p. 72.

rapidly. The weeks of July were spacious days for radicalism. An obscure Republican congressman from Maine furnished the Jacobins with a slogan to inscribe on their banner as they drove to conquest. Speaking in the House in February, Frederick A. Pike shouted: "Our duty to-day is to tax and fight. Twin brothers of great power; to them in good time shall be added a third; and whether he shall be of executive parentage, or generated in Congress, or spring, like Minerva, full-grown from the head of our Army, I care not. Come he will, and his name shall be Emancipation. And these three—Tax, Fight, and Emancipate—shall be the Trinity of our salvation. In this sign we shall conquer."[37]

Unfortunately for the radicals, Pike's enunciation of the dogma of the Jacobin faith did not move Lincoln. Not only did he refuse to be converted and repent of his sins, but he stubbornly denied the third part of the Trinity. To the disgust of the radicals he still persisted in worshipping a false god—his policy of a conservative coalition party with but one purpose, the restoration of the Union. He did take one step toward the radical altar, but it was a timid one; and the Jacobins, who demanded an enthusiastic convert or none, repulsed him. Lincoln had always been an advocate of gradual, compensated emancipation, to be accomplished by the only method he considered constitutional—through voluntary action by the states in which slavery existed. Now on March 6 he proposed such a scheme to Congress, largely for the purpose of conciliating the rising antislavery spirit which the radicals were whipping up in the country. Stressing that gradual emancipation was "better for all," he recommended that the government cooperate with any state wishing to free its slaves by providing "pecuniary aid"—in other words, compensation.[38]

Congress passed a bill embodying Lincoln's ideas. But the measure failed to achieve any practical results, primarily because the loyal Border States in which Lincoln hoped to start the process were opposed to any federal interference with their

[37] *Congressional Globe*, 37 Congress, 2 Session, 658.
[38] Richardson, *Messages of the Presidents*, 6:68–69.

domestic institutions. Nor did the president win over the Jacobins; they were bitterly contemptuous of his scheme. Stevens dismissed it as "about the most diluted, milk and water gruel proposition that was ever given to the American nation." John Hickman thought Lincoln was in reality trying to protect slavery and was offering "a compensation to the North for disappointed hopes." The fiery Pennsylvanian denounced Lincoln's plan as "rather a palliative and caution than an open and avowed policy; it is rather an excuse for non-action than an avowed determination to act. . . . Neither the message nor the resolution is manly and open. They are both covert and insidious."[39]

This was in the spring, when McClellan was moving his army to the Peninsula and Lincoln and the country expected him to make a triumphal entry into Richmond in a few short weeks. Faced by the possibility that the war might soon be ended, the radicals were despondent about forcing any effective antislavery policy upon the administration. "In the present stage of the negro question, you cannot for months to come get the emancipation of all rebel slaves," wrote one radical to Sumner, advising support of half-loaf measures until then. But the conservative Senator Doolittle arrived at the gloomy conclusion that the Jacobins would soon dominate the party. If the war continued for any time, he predicted, they would assert their control and kick out moderates like himself.[40] His analysis was correct. As the months wore on and McClellan slowly muddled through the Virginia swamps, the radicals became increasingly bold and insistent in their demands for a drastic abolition policy. The Committee and the leaders of the radical machine held a conference at Stanton's office in April to discuss the strategy of their campaign. Stevens denounced the Cabinet and McClellan, and asserted that Congress should pass measures which would strip the rebels of all property and rights and give them reconstruction on terms that would end treason for-

[39] Stevens' speech, in the *Congressional Globe,* 37 Congress, 2 Session, 1154; Hickman's, *ibid.,* 1175–1176.

[40] J. M. Forbes to Charles Sumner, April, 1862, in Hughes, *Forbes,* 1:301–302; James R. Doolittle to Mrs. Doolittle, March 7, 1862, in the Doolittle MSS. in the possession of the Wisconsin State Historical Society.

ever. In the Senate Grimes demanded that the administration take a radical stand on the purposes of the war. Horace Greeley feared that Lincoln's conservatism and his tenderness for the Border States would insure military failure. "We shuffle and trifle on, and let the Union go to ruin," he complained. Fessenden was so furious at the president that he announced himself ready to "kick out at all hazards" in Congress, because further "silence would be criminal."[41] It was in June, with McClellan definitely bogged down before Richmond and the antislavery feeling in the country increasing by leaps and bounds, that the Jacobins at last sensed victory. Heartened by the knowledge that public opinion was swelling behind them, they brought their attack into the open. They realized that military reverses and the possibility of defeat were aiding their cause. "It is strange when a rattlesnake is attacking us that we should be so delicate about the stick we hit him with," observed a prominent New England radical hopefully.[42]

Before the hot days of summer brought new hope to the Jacobins, they had started to whittle away at slavery where it was most vulnerable, chipping off those parts of the institution that lay nearest to hand. In April they piloted through Congress a bill abolishing slavery in the District of Columbia, with compensation for owners, and the speeches of the radicals bristled with threats to the South and to Lincoln of worse to come. New Jersey's John T. Nixon proclaimed in the House that before the people of the North accepted defeat "they will arm every slave against his rebel master; will drive the whole white population beyond the borders; and hold the once proud states . . . as Territories for the home of the enfranchised negro." Albert G. Riddle from Ohio's Western Reserve, the

[41] Julian, *Recollections*, 212–213; Salter, *Grimes*, 194; Greeley to Congressman William P. Cutler, April 28, 1862, in Julia P. Cutler, *Life and Times of Ephraim Cutler with Biographical Sketches of Jervis Cutler and William Parker Cutler* (Cincinnati, 1890), 294; Fessenden, *Fessenden*, 1:262–263.

[42] J. M. Forbes to C. M. Sedgwick, June 2, 7, 1862, in Hughes, *Forbes*, 1:315–316; Forbes to Charles Sumner, *ibid.*, 317–318; Sedgwick to Forbes, June 29, *ibid.*, 321; James A. Garfield to Harmon Austin, June 25, in Smith, *Garfield*, 1:225; J. M. Forbes to Parke Godwin, June 23, in Hughes, *Forbes*, 1:314–315.

most violent antislavery section in the country, prophesied grimly that this bill was but the entering wedge to complete emancipation, that the war would go forward "without compromise or cessation" until that great end was achieved. In the turgid rhetoric of which he was a master, Riddle exclaimed, "Think of slaves tilling the valley of Bull Run or the fire-girt field where Baker fell; of their turning up and grinning at the bones of the young heroes of the North around Donelson. Fancy the taskmaster lashing his bondmen to toil on the nameless plains of the far-off Tennessee, gorged with the red, rich, free, proud, bounding blood of the Northwest. . . . *Do gentlemen expect to see slaves hoeing corn there?*"[43] In the Senate Sumner and Wilson carried the debate for the radicals. Sumner lauded the proposed measure as "the first installment of that great debt which we all owe to an enslaved race . . . the first practical triumph of freedom." Slavery was the power behind the rebellion, he cried, and it "must be suppressed at every cost, and if its suppression here endangers slavery elsewhere, there will be a new motive for determined action."[44]

Quickly the radical machine followed this victory with another bill, debated in May and passed in June, abolishing slavery in the national territories.[45] But their drive struck a snag when they tried to dictate that all fugitive slaves escaping to the Union lines should be held under the government's protection. The Jacobins had always raged at generals who returned fugitives to their owners, sneering that such officers compelled the soldiers to act as errand boys for the rebels. They wanted the refugees kept in the camps and put to work digging trenches and performing other labor of a military nature. If this policy could be forced upon the government, the radicals saw a chance to bring about a measure of practical emancipation; for obviously Negroes who had aided the nation's war effort could not be sent back into servitude. With these thoughts in mind the Jacobin leaders put through Con-

[43] *Congressional Globe,* 37 Congress, 2 Session, 1526, 1629–1631, 1640–1642, 1648–1649.
[44] *Ibid.,* 1446–1451.
[45] *Ibid.,* 2041–2048, 2066–2069, 2618, 2769, 2845.

gress on March 13 a law in the form of an article of war, prohibiting the employment of the military power "for the purpose of returning fugitives from service or labor." Any officer found guilty by a court-martial of violating this article was to be dismissed from the service.[46]

But on April 10 the Committee to its intense anger learned from General Daniel Sickles that Lincoln had never officially communicated the new article to the army and that generals were still acting as slave-catchers. Wade evidently turned the information over to the radical chieftains, because four days later Grimes arose in the Senate to denounce the conservative clique in the army and by implication the president for sustaining them. He charged that certain generals were returning slaves into bondage, "not in aid of any judicial process, but in obedience to their own unbridled will." Did the military imagine itself to be the supreme power in the land, he cried, that it could ignore a law of Congress? He warned the guilty generals that they had "disgraced themselves, . . . dishonored the country, and injured the public service, by the promulgation of their ridiculous orders about slaves." Instead of chasing down refugees, the military authorities should enlist them as soldiers. Grimes' speech was but the opening gun of a barrage that followed, as the Jacobins fought to stop slave-catching and to force the employment of fugitives in the army. Sumner made a fierce attack upon Halleck and Buell, denouncing them as mere lackeys eager to do the bidding of rebel owners of human property, and contrasted their conduct with that of McDowell, a general who welcomed the fleeing slaves to his camp. Wilson, taking a shot at McClellan, observed that some commanders "seem to be more anxious to catch negroes than to catch rebels." Greeley joined the assault, demanding that the government guarantee freedom to those slaves who would desert their masters and agree to perform military service.[47] Finally on June 9 George W. Julian proposed in the House

[46] Richardson, *Messages of the Presidents*, 6:97.

[47] *C.C.W.*, 1863, 3:640; Salter, *Grimes*, 184–193; Sumner's speech in the *Congressional Globe*, 37 Congress, 2 Session, 1893–1894; Wilson's, *ibid.*, 1956; *New York Tribune*, May 12, 1862.

a bill to repeal the Fugitive Slave Acts of 1793 and 1850, which
furnished the legal basis for the rendition of escaped bondsmen
by the civil and military authorities. This would have given the
Jacobins all they wanted and more, but at this stage of the
game they could not manage the passage of Julian's measure.
The laws which Julian wished to destroy remained on the
books until 1864, an anomaly in the midst of antislavery legislation soon to come. Julian was disgusted because the administration failed to support him. In a Committee meeting he
snorted that the Union armies, perambulating around the
country to guard the property of rebels, appeared to be "organized peace societies" instead of instruments to hurt the
enemy.[48]

Although the Jacobins were pleased to hack away the secon-
dary appendages of slavery, such victories only magnified their
great fundamental purpose—to bring about the emancipation
of all the slaves in the Southern states. In July, when McClellan
had stumbled back from Richmond and the nation was momentarily appalled by his defeat, the radical chiefs thought
they saw a chance to accomplish their objective under the guise
of military necessity. Sumner went to Lincoln immediately,
urging a proclamation of emancipation on the Fourth of
July to "make the day more sacred and historic than ever."
Seward noted apprehensively, in a letter to Charles Francis
Adams in London, that the radicals were "demanding an edict
of universal emancipation" as a war measure. Hamilton Fish
of New York, later to be a great secretary of state under Grant,
complained to Fessenden that the government was "being
destroyed by War, without making War"; if the administration would not adopt an antislavery policy, Fish was for peace
terms rather than that the country should "spend more treasure
and more blood" in a war without a purpose. Enthusiastically
Horace Greeley cried in the *Tribune* that emancipation by
weakening the Confederacy would insure a speedy, overwhelming triumph for the Union. But Lincoln turned his usual irri-
tating deaf ear to the eager radicals. He told Sumner that an

[48] *Congressional Globe*, 37 Congress, 2 Session, 2623; Julian, *Recollections*,
218; *C.C.W.*, 1863, 3:352.

edict of freedom would drive three more border slave states to secede, and stir up such dissatisfaction in the army "that half the officers would fling down their arms." General Wadsworth, after talking to the president, gloomily reported to Greeley's capital correspondent, Adams S. Hill, that conservatism still dominated the White House. "He says that the President is not with us; has no Anti-slavery instincts," the correspondent informed the home office. "W. believes that if emancipation comes at all it will be from the rebels, or in consequence of their protracting the war."[49]

But the bosses of the Jacobin machine were of no mind to wait on the future. With public opinion ready to accept emancipation, they were determined to jam it down the administration's throat if necessary. Ready at hand they possessed the weapon to accomplish their design—Trumbull's confiscation bill, introduced in the previous December and hanging fire ever since. In briefest essence, this was a measure which would free the slaves of every person in rebellion against the government and of any person who aided or abetted the rebellion. Its provisions were sweeping enough to satisfy the most advanced Jacobin, and it brought emancipation in the form desired by the radical leaders—by action of Congress instead of the president. From the beginning Jacobins like Stevens had contended that according to the Constitution Congress alone and not the executive could assume dictatorial war powers. It was for Congress to say how the war should be conducted and for what purpose. The radicals wanted emancipation to come from Congress because this would establish a precedent for legislative supremacy over the whole prosecution of the war. Only when they felt uncertain about their control of Congress did the radicals urge emancipation by presidential edict. In July they judged they had the necessary control.

The Confiscation Act was debated at great and sometimes

[49] Pierce, *Sumner*, 4:82–83; William H. Seward to C. F. Adams, July 5, 1862, in White, *Trumbull*, 210; Hamilton Fish to William P. Fessenden, July 10, in the Fessenden MSS.; *New York Tribune*, July 17, 19, 1862; Adams S. Hill to S. H. Gay, July, 1862, quoted in James Ford Rhodes, *History of the United States from the Compromise of 1850 . . . to 1877* (New York, 1893–1906), 4:64, footnote.

boring length from March until its final passage on July 17. The radical faction backed it solidly, but it met stern opposition from many of the conservative Republicans who condemned the more extreme provisions as unconstitutional. Wade, speaking with authority as chairman of the War Committee, championed the bill, although he did not consider it stringent enough. "I would make it stronger if I could," he shouted. "When I have brought a traitor who is seeking my life and my property to terms, and when I become bankrupt in my endeavors to put him down . . . , I have no scruples about the property of his that shall be taken to indemnify me." The Jacobins frankly proclaimed a determination to scourge the South among their reasons for supporting confiscation. Michigan's Jacob Howard said in the Senate that one of the objects of the bill as "punishment, punishment of the most wanton crime ever committed since he who took the thirty pieces of silver betrayed his Lord and Master." Henry Wilson declared that the Republican Party had a solemn duty "to lay low in the dust under our feet, so that iron heels will rest upon it, this great rebel, this giant criminal, this guilty murderer, that is warring upon the existence of the country."[50] When the conservatives tried to maintain that emancipation was a matter for Lincoln to decide, Wade arose with an angry outburst: "The President cannot lay down and fix the principles upon which a war shall be conducted. . . . It is for Congress to lay down the rules and regulations by which the Executive shall be governed in conducting a war."[51]

By the middle of July it was apparent to all observers of capital politics that the Jacobin machine, despite conservatives and Democrats, would force the Confiscation Act through to passage. Then Lincoln, who had kept out of the fight to this point, quietly let it be known that he would veto the measure in its present form. This information, noised around Congress by administration lieutenants, threw the radicals into sput-

[50] Wade's speech in the *Congressional Globe*, 37 Congress, 2 Session, 1918. See *ibid.*, 3006, for a similar declaration from Chandler. Howard's speech, *ibid.*, 1720; Wilson's, *ibid.*, 1896.
[51] *Ibid.*, 1917.

tering and impotent rage. With Congress ready to adjourn there was no time to pass the measure over a veto. Just as they were about to taste the heady brew of victory, Lincoln threatened to dash the cup away. "If he does there will be an end of him," grimly wrote Henry Cooke, whose Washington office of the great banking house was a favorite rendezvous for the Jacobin politicos. At this critical point Fessenden, entirely on his own initiative, took it upon himself to go to Lincoln to find out the president's objections to the bill. He found Lincoln far from enthusiastic about the entire measure, but willing to accept it if two clauses were eliminated: one which would confiscate the slave property of persons who had committed treason before the passage of the act, and another which would work a forfeiture of the real estate of the offender beyond his natural life.[52] To the Jacobins the retroactive provision and permanent forfeiture were the soul of the act, and they were wild with anger at the president's obduracy.

In particular they were infuriated because Lincoln had dared to threaten Congress with a veto before final passage of the bill. This was executive usurpation of the rights of Congress, they cried. The president was trying to bully the representatives of the people; he was a dictator! Wade blasted Fessenden for "mousing around" the executive office to find out the presidential will. Perhaps senators were willing to abdicate the powers of Congress, he exclaimed, and crawl before the White House throne:

. . . [We] ought to have a committee on vetoes; we ought to have a committee to wait on the President whenever we send him a bill, to know what his royal pleasure is in regard to it; and whether it contains anything he would like to modify. . . . I am astonished that men should come in here, creeping in at the back door, with vetoes.

And the old Jacobin finished with a sneer that only a few favored senators could secure an audience with the royal presence. "Others, when they go to see the President, find that they

---

[52] Henry Cooke to Jay Cooke, July 16, 1862, in Oberholtzer, *Cooke*, 1:199; Fessenden, *Fessenden*, 1:272–275.

are debarred all access to him. Nobody can see him, it seems, except some privileged gentlemen who are charged with his constitutional conscience!"[53]

The Jacobins might rage but they had to surrender if they wanted their bill. So on July 17, when the measure came up for final approval, they reluctantly and sullenly attached to it an explanatory resolution removing the clauses to which Lincoln had objected.[54] With this change the president signed the act. Then he did something which left the Jacobins momentarily speechless with cold fury. He sent to Congress the veto message he would have sent had they refused to modify the bill. After their abject capitulation, this seemed to the radicals the cruellest kind of mockery. Many of them walked out when the message was read, and in the Senate no one offered the usual resolution to print it. Hysterical gloom ruled the Jacobin ranks as Congress adjourned. Julian said that "it was the belief of many that our last session of Congress had been held in Washington. Mr. Wade said the country was going to Hell, and that the scenes witnessed in the French Revolution were nothing in comparison with what we should see here."[55]

The despair that enveloped the radicals was not justified by the facts of the situation. In the Confiscation Act, even after it was modified, they had scored a substantial triumph and had taken a long step toward emancipation. Going into effect as soon as it was passed, the bill declared free the slaves of every person found guilty of treason after its passage, and of all persons who in any way aided or supported the rebellion. If this provision could have been enforced, it would have struck the shackles from practically every slave in the South. On paper the act set free more slaves than did Lincoln's later emancipation proclamation, which was also a paper edict so far as immediate concrete results were concerned. Other clauses secured objectives for which the Jacobins had fought long and hard.

[53] *Congressional Globe*, 37 Congress, 2 Session, 3375. See *ibid.*, 3382, for another speech of the same tenor.
[54] *Ibid.*, 412–413, appendix; Richardson, *Messages of the Presidents*, 6:96.
[55] *Ibid.*, 85–87; *New York Tribune*, July 17, 18, 1862, Washington correspondence; Julian, *Recollections*, 220.

One provided that the slaves of active rebels or of any owner abetting the Southern cause should be free after entering the Union lines, and prohibited the military authorities from returning slaves to disloyal masters. Another directed the seizure of the estates of high Confederate officials.[56] Greeley thought the bill excellent, while the exultant Sumner called it "a practical measure of emancipation." One cankering fear plagued the radicals—that Lincoln and the conservative generals would make the law a cipher by refusing to cooperate in its enforcement. Trumbull wanted Lincoln to bring all the generals to Washington to hear the bill explained, so there could be no excuses of misunderstanding later. The *Tribune* calculated that half of the officers sympathized with the rebellion or with slavery, and that nothing but a stern war order from the president could force them to execute the will of Congress.[57]

From section eleven of the Confiscation Act the Jacobins drew particular comfort. They looked upon it as big with bright possibilities for the future. This clause authorized the president "to employ as many persons of African descent as he may deem necessary and proper for the suppression of this rebellion, and for this purpose he may organize and use them in such manner as he may judge best for the public welfare." Although the execution of the provision was not obligatory upon Lincoln, the radicals regarded the section as a congressional mandate to use slaves as laborers in the army and even to enroll them as soldiers. In forcing the administration to adopt such a policy, radicals like Grimes foresaw more important gains for emancipation than in confiscation itself. The government would never dare put back the chains on men who had helped defend the nation. This of course was not the reason advanced by the radicals in public debate. Then they talked about the military necessity of employing slaves to strengthen the army and weaken the Confederacy.[58] Their argument

[56] The bill is given in the *Congressional Globe*, 37 Congress, 2 Session, 412–413; Richardson, *Messages of the Presidents*, 6:93–96.

[57] *New York Tribune*, July 19, 21, 28, 30, 1862; Pierce, *Sumner*, 4:82–83; James W. Grimes to Salmon P. Chase, July 29, in Salter, *Grimes*, 215–216.

[58] Senator Grimes to Mrs. Grimes, May 4, 1862, in Salter, *Grimes*, 196;

aroused widespread popular applause. From all over the North complaints were rising that the Union armies had to fight rebels and dig ditches at the same time. Why did not the government put fugitive slaves to building fortifications or laboring in the malaria swamps of the South, people asked, instead of forcing "our own overworked and overtasked men" to do such drudgery. The Congregationalists of Michigan indorsed a resolution declaring: "That it is cruel to our soldiers to compel them to labor in the heats of the South from which they can be spared, and that therefore all possible aid should be drawn from the 'contrabands' to relieve them from such labors."[59] The Jacobins capitalized the grumbling dissatisfaction among the people. While the Confiscation Act was under discussion, the Committee collected evidence from military witnesses to show that escaped slaves furnished important information about the enemy, were excellent laborers, and would make good soldiers; later Chandler and Wade employed this material tellingly when they spoke for the measure. The importance which the Jacobins attached to section eleven became evident on July 15, two days before the act passed Congress. Then the leaders of the faction issued an "address to the people" in which they demanded that slaves be employed in a military capacity. The document bore the names of such prominent radical lights as Wade, Chandler, Wilson, Hale, Julian, Lovejoy, and Stevens.[60]

☆

Abraham Lincoln caught the significance of events in those hot July days when the spirit of radicalism burgeoned in the nation and the Jacobins in Congress wrenched from him the control of the Republican Party. He knew at last that the radicals represented an implacable force which he could not

---

Fessenden, *Fessenden*, 1:257–258; W. H. Stokes to Lyman Trumbull, March 17, 1862, in the Trumbull MSS.

[59] D. L. Phillips to Lyman Trumbull, July 5, 1862, and G. Nichols to Trumbull, July 15, in the Trumbull MSS.; *The Congregational Churches of Michigan for the First Fifty Years* (printed by order of the Association, 1892), 186.

[60] *C.C.W.*, 1863, 3:328–330, 344, 351–352; the radical address, in the *New York Tribune*, July 19, 1862, p. 4.

ignore and to which perhaps he must yield. On July 10, while driving to the funeral of Stanton's infant son, he confided to Seward and Welles, who were in the carriage with him, that he had decided to issue a proclamation of freedom. And on the twenty-second he startled the other members of the Cabinet by reading to them the draft of an edict freeing the slaves in the rebellious states. He would have given it to the country immediately, had not Seward argued that the moment was not propitious. Wait for a military victory, he urged, otherwise the proclamation would impress the world as a shriek of despair from an expiring government.[61] Lincoln saw the wisdom of this advice. He put the document aside and looked about for a general who could win him a triumph. At this moment John Pope was shouting that if he had the Army of the Potomac he would march into Richmond.

Other reasons than fear of the Jacobins helped mold Lincoln's decision to free the slaves by executive action. Undoubtedly he had in mind the critical foreign situation: certain European countries were on the verge of extending diplomatic recognition to the Confederacy. In England and France the liberal parties favored the Union cause; they believed the North was fighting the battle of democracy against aristocracy. But they found it difficult to justify their position when the government of the United States proclaimed again and again that its only purpose in waging war was to restore the Union. Lincoln knew that a bold declaration of an antislavery policy would rally the European liberals and inspire them to oppose any friendly gestures by their governments toward the Confederacy. But bulking larger in Lincoln's thoughts than the uncertainties of diplomatic developments were the grave issues of domestic politics. The strongest cornerstone of his program had been the all-parties coalition of Republicans, Democrats, and loyal slaveholders, to fight the war to a conclusion. To hold this discordant conglomeration together it was imperative that he be able to repress the abolitionist instincts of his own

[61] Welles, *Diary*, 1:70; Welles, *Lincoln and Seward*, 210; Nicolay and Hay, *Lincoln*, 6:128.

party. This Lincoln could not do. Every time the Republicans, the dominant and most numerous element in the combination, moved toward radicalism, the other factions took fright and drew away. And in the summer of 1862 the Republican Party was rapidly going radical. The Confiscation Act, repudiating the purposes of the war as defined in the Crittenden Resolution, smashed Lincoln's plan beyond repair. He had lost the Border States and many of the conservatives. There remained only the Republicans. And while he had hoped to build an inclusive political alliance to sustain his efforts to restore the Union, it was important above all else that he have the support of his own ardent followers. Without their aid he could not preserve the American experiment in government. Nor was he blind to the mounting Jacobinism among the people whose tribune he always considered himself to be. If they demanded that the Union be saved through emancipation, Abraham Lincoln would save it that way.

7
From Pope to McClellan to Burnside

WENDELL PHILLIPS made a speech on August 1. The fiery abolitionist had not changed his opinion of Lincoln and the
Republican conservatives. "I do not think that anything which
we can call the *government* has any *purpose* to get rid of
slavery," he cried. "On the contrary, I think the present purpose of the government . . . is to end the war and save slavery." Only a staggering military reverse, "a baptism of blood,"
he said, would shock the administration from its lethargy and
drive it to radicalism.

Phillips spoke the sentiments of the extremist wing of the
Republican Party, but in August the Jacobins were not far behind him in hurling bitter indictments at the administration.
The angry flames kindled by the fight over the Confiscation
Act still burned, and the radicals had no inkling of Lincoln's
decision to embrace emancipation. Greeley filled the *Tribune's*
columns with demands for an antislavery policy and the dismissal of the proslavery generals who controlled the armies. A
proclamation of emancipation by Lincoln, predicted the editor, would "lift the nation right off its feet, and surprise it into
one unanimous yell of enthusiasm."[1] Privately Greeley asserted
that he would not abate his efforts "till the Government toes
the mark on the Slavery question." Chase thought the president was slowly coming around to the radical position, but
most Jacobins did not share this cheerful view. They believed
that conservative influences still dominated Lincoln's thinking. He was not enforcing the emancipation provisions of the
confiscation measure, they charged, or enlisting Negro soldiers
under the authorization granted on July 17. Nevertheless they

[1] Phillips, *Speeches*, 448–449, 458; *New York Tribune*, August 2, 6, 8, 11,
15, 21, 1862. The quotation is from the issue of August 8.

were more determined than ever to force the radical war program upon him.[2]

The Jacobin leaders saw hope for their cause if they could effect a reform of the Cabinet. They looked upon Lincoln as a well-intentioned, amiable puppet who merely reproduced the ideas of his closest advisers, in this case Seward and Blair. The radicals wanted to increase their representation in the Cabinet, so they could put the words into the puppet's mouth and make it talk their way. A story circulating in the newspapers drove them to wild expressions of anger. According to this account Lincoln, a few weeks previously, had laid before the Cabinet an emancipation proclamation which he proposed to issue, but Seward and Blair had talked him into tearing it up. Wendell Phillips told a slightly different version. He asserted that the president had written an edict freeing the slaves but McClellan "bullied him out of it." Then Lincoln decided to remove McClellan but Kentucky bullied him out of that. "The man who has been beaten to that pulp in sixteen months, what hope can we have of him?" asked Phillips scornfully. The same gloomy thoughts possessed Thaddeus Stevens. "It seems to me we are just as far from the true course as ever," wrote the grim dictator of the House. "A change of Cabinet is our only hope; but I do not hope for that."[3]

In the closing days of August, Greeley brought the angry mutterings of the radicals into the open. He published in the *Tribune* an open letter to Lincoln condemning the administration's conservative policy and demanding emancipation. Confidently arrogating to himself the function of speaking for the Northern people, Greeley headed his communication "The

---

[2] Horace Greeley to Mrs. R. M. Whipple, August 6, 1862, in the Greeley MSS.; Salmon P. Chase to Charles Sumner, August 12, 1862, in Pierce, *Sumner*, 4:65; Israel Holmes to James R. Doolittle, August 6, in the Doolittle MSS. in the Library of Congress; Senator Jacob Howard to Lyman Trumbull, August 16, in the Trumbull MSS.; John Sherman to William T. Sherman, August 24, in Thorndike, *Sherman Letters*, 157.

[3] *New York Tribune*, August 22, 1862, Washington correspondence; *Chicago Tribune*, August 23; Phillips, *Speeches*, 454; Thaddeus Stevens, letter of August 10, 1862, in the Stevens MSS.; Charles Sumner to John Bright, August 5, in Pierce, *Sumner*, 4:82–83.

Prayer of Twenty Million." It detailed the grievances of the Jacobins in a series of hard-hitting sentences, each of which began dramatically "We complain"—"We complain that the Confiscation Act which you approved is habitually disregarded by your generals, and that no word of rebuke for them has yet reached the public ear. . . . We complain that a large proportion of our regular army officers with many of the volunteers evince far more solicitude to uphold slavery than to put down rebellion."[4]

Lincoln replied to Greeley through the newspapers. He wanted the nation to hear his views. He was holding back the emancipation edict until after a victory, but he confidently expected Pope to smash the rebels in the next few days. So he tried to give the Jacobins a hint that a new policy was in the offing. His only purpose, he told Greeley, was now as always to preserve the Union. "My paramount object in this struggle is to save the Union, and it is not either to save or destroy slavery." Then came the intimation of things to come. "I shall do less whenever I shall believe that what I am doing hurts the cause, and I shall do more whenever I shall believe doing more will help the cause." To most radicals this announcement demonstrated a cynical indifference to the great moral issues of the war, but Greeley thought the president was moving in the right direction. "As to old Abe's letter, I consider it a sign of progress," he wrote to a friend. "I have no doubt the Nation will get on the right ground at last. . . . It is time to fight with both hands *now*."[5]

☆

The scene shifts to Pope, marching in the "blush of dawn" to bag the Confederate army. The voluble general so confident of his glorious destiny came upon Lee at Manassas, the scene of two previous Union humiliations. Here in the last days of August was fought one of the most tragic battles of the war.

[4] *New York Tribune,* August 20, 1862; New York *Evening Post,* August 25.

[5] Lincoln, *Works,* 8:15–16; Horace Greeley to G. M. Wright, August 27, 1862, in the Greeley MSS.

Against the brilliant tactics of Lee and Jackson, Pope was helplessly incompetent. At no time during the long engagement did he know definitely where the enemy was, and he would not let anybody tell him. On one occasion when Jackson fell back to draw him into a trap, Pope hurried off a message to Washington boasting that the rebels were in headlong retreat and that he was about to start the pursuit. Finally, beaten and sore, his army withdrew from the field and crossed the Potomac in a night of driving rain, making for the safety of the forts guarding Washington. Once over the river the troops stumbled ahead without order and with stragglers strung out along the entire line of march. True to his earlier instructions Pope had left his lines of retreat to take care of themselves. The wet and angry soldiers streamed into the capital cursing Pope and McDowell, whose blunderings they blamed for the disaster, and crying for "Little Mac."[6] In the city panic reigned as the government prepared to arm clerks and citizens to repel the Confederates.

The grim tidings from Manassas exploded with the violence of a bombshell among the Jacobins. At once they saw the looming danger in the situation—the probable dismissal of Pope, the restoration of McClellan, and the end of radical control of the Eastern army. This they were determined to prevent at any hazard. But to save Pope they must convince Lincoln and the country that their general was not the failure he seemed. There was but one way, and that was to shift the odium of the Manassas disaster from Pope to McClellan. Strangely enough, they had unknowingly already prepared themselves to accomplish this feat. All during August ugly rumors had circulated through the radical camp that McClellan, in disobedience of the president's orders, was delaying the transfer of his troops to the Army of Virginia, with the purpose of bringing about Pope's defeat. Stanton seized on these stories and ordered Halleck to substantiate them with

⁶ *New York Tribune*, September 5, 1862, army correspondence; Doster, *Lincoln*, 155–156. See also the Heintzelman diary, August 30, 1862, for evidence that the army lost faith in Pope during the battle.

official evidence. On August 30, the very day Pope retreated, Stanton told Hay "that nothing but foul play could lose us this battle, and that it rested with McClellan and his friends."[7]

No sooner was the beaten army safe in Washington than the Jacobins rose valiantly to Pope's defense. They screamed treachery and treason at McClellan, and charged that he and his pets had deliberately stabbed Pope in the back. Not only from the politicians did these startling accusations emanate; the officers in the radical faction believed and asserted that the "pro-slavery cliques" had refused to cooperate with Pope, wishing to see the enemy win at Manassas rather than a Republican general.[8] It was difficult for the Jacobins to pin the onus of the defeat directly upon McClellan, who during the battle was sitting quietly at Alexandria miles away. But his young generals had been present, commanding large segments of Pope's army. They were the men who betrayed Pope, cried the radicals, and they had done so at the order of their master or at least with his approving knowledge. Triumphantly the radicals pounced upon Fitz John Porter, McClellan's most trusted intimate, and held him up as the villain of the piece and the scapegoat for Pope's tragic blunders. Young Fitz John, who up to now had cut a glamorous, dashing figure in the war, was bewildered to find himself playing this new and unhappy rôle. But it was inevitable that the Jacobins should cast him for the part. He had talked too much and too foolishly; and at Manassas he had made the supreme mistake of being smarter than Pope.

Of all the officers in McClellan's circle, Porter had been the most outspoken in denouncing the breakup of the Potomac army and its transfer to Pope. Ordered to serve under Pope, he was bitterly resentful, and during the campaign he said and wrote a great many harsh things about his superior officer.

[7] Stanton to Halleck, August 28, 1862, in *O. R.*, series 1, vol. 12, part 3, p. 706; Halleck to Stanton, August 30, *ibid.*, 739–741; Warden, *Chase*, 456; Hay, *Diary*, 1:62.

[8] *Wilkes' Spirit of the Times*, September 6, 1862; Villard, *Memoirs*, 1:336; Henry Cooke to Jay Cooke, September 2, in Oberholtzer, *Cooke*, 1:202–203; *C.C.W.*, 1865, 1:311, testimony of General Abner Doubleday.

Some of them leaked out to the wrong people. Describing Pope's movements in a letter to General Ambrose Burnside, another McClellan favorite, he sneered, "The strategy is magnificent, and tactics in the inverse proportion. . . . [The Confederates] have a contempt for this Army of Virginia. I wish myself away from it, with all our old Army of the Potomac, and so do our companions." Porter with his corps was at Manassas, arriving on the scene after a forced march, but he did not participate directly in the fighting. He received a vague order from Pope to attack what the latter thought was a small, isolated body of the enemy. Actually, as Porter realized, it was one of the principal sections of the Confederate army under General James Longstreet moving up to join Lee. Wisely Porter did not attack, but by skillful handling of his troops he kept Longstreet immobilized and prevented him from falling upon Pope. He accomplished more than if he had plunged into the battle, and Pope expressed his satisfaction. But back in the excited atmosphere of Washington after the retreat, Pope, with disgrace confronting him, saw the situation in a new light. Suddenly he perceived that Fitz John had maliciously knifed him and caused his defeat. Zachariah Chandler convinced Pope of Porter's treachery. To the depressed general Chandler exclaimed, "I consider that your campaign has been one of the most brilliant that has been fought up to this time." The senator had only one fault to find, "That you ever allowed Fitz John Porter to leave the battle-field alive!"[9] Later Pope was to bring charges against Porter which resulted in a court-martial and the railroading of Porter out of the army.

During the very days that Manassas was being fought and lost, Stanton and Chase were busily at work concocting an intrigue to force McClellan from the military service. At the moment the Young Napoleon's star had sunk to its nadir. Technically he was still commander of the Army of the Potomac, but after being stripped of his troops to aid Pope, he

[9] Fitz John Porter to Ambrose Burnside, August 27, 1862, in *O. R.*, series 1, vol. 12, part 3, p. 700; *Life of Chandler*, 240–243; Heintzelman diary, September 5, 1862.

presented the saddest of spectacles, a general without an army. Stanton decided that a golden opportunity was at hand to destroy permanently the archenemy of radicalism. But by the time the secretaries got their scheme in motion, the situation had abruptly changed. Pope's defeated army was staggering into Washington, its commander faced the threat of removal, and there were cries for the restoration of McClellan. Stanton and Chase had to switch their tactics hurriedly, and what started as a plan to kill off McClellan became a part of the radical drive to save Pope from decapitation.

The project which the secretaries hatched with fond hopes had originated in the rumors which filled the air in late August, to the effect that McClellan was out to hamstring Pope. Stanton ordered Halleck to present a report stating whether McClellan was withholding men and cooperation from the Army of Virginia. "Old Brains" obliged with the kind of reply the secretary wanted: McClellan was. Armed with this report, Stanton and Chase composed a manifesto, to be signed by the Cabinet and presented to Lincoln, demanding that he remove McClellan. The general had disobeyed the president's instructions to re-enforce Pope, charged the secretaries, and had thereby placed the latter's army in a dangerous situation where it faced attack from a numerically superior foe. To continue McClellan in a position of power, asserted the document, could only result in "the waste of national resources, the protraction of the war, the destruction of our armies, and the imperiling of the Union."[10]

Stanton and Chase put their names to the manifesto, and easily persuaded Caleb Smith of the Interior Department to add his. Then they ran into an unexpected snag. On August 30, the day Pope retreated, Chase took the protest to Welles, but the crusty old naval secretary, who had no use for Stanton, refused to sign. His indorsement was necessary to the success of the scheme, as other conservatives in the Cabinet would probably follow his lead. Stanton himself worked on Welles in

[10] *O. R.*, series 1, vol. 12, part 3, pp. 706, 739–741; Flower, *Stanton*, 176–177.

the evening and for hours detailed McClellan's crimes, but he could not budge "Old Neptune." Attorney General Bates also objected to the document, thinking its tone too extreme. He was willing, however, to approve a milder statement to the effect that the Cabinet believed McClellan incompetent to hold an important command. Bates drew up such a paper, and Stanton, Chase, and Smith signed it. Then Chase came around to see Welles again on September 1, now bearing the Bates composition and arguing that unless McClellan were removed the administration would fall to pieces. "Stanton . . . is mad . . . and determined to destroy McClellan," wrote Welles in his diary.[11] But Stanton was too late. The moment had passed. Lincoln had seen Pope's beaten and demoralized army crouching before Washington, and had decided to restore McClellan to command.

The president knew that McClellan, with all his faults of delay and indecision, was a superb organizer who could whip the disorganized troops into shape faster than any other officer. And with Lee threatening to invade the North it was imperative that the army be in condition to take the field within a few weeks. On September 2 Lincoln walked into a solemn Cabinet meeting and startled the members by announcing that he had ordered McClellan to take command of Pope's army. It was a bitter moment for Stanton and Chase. They protested angrily, but Lincoln had made up his mind. The crushed Chase went home to record in his diary "that I could not but feel that giving command to him [McClellan] was equivalent to giving Washington to the rebels."[12] Stanton, according to reports, was so disgusted that he wrote out his resignation and would have given it to Lincoln but for the fervent pleadings of Sumner to spare the radical cause a further calamity.[13]

[11] Welles, *Diary*, 1:93–98, 100–102; Welles, *Lincoln and Seward*, 193–194; excerpts from the Chase diary, in Warden, *Chase*, 456–458; Chase diary in the *Report of the American Historical Association*, 1902, 2:62–63; Flower, *Stanton*, 177. The Bates paper is in the Stanton MSS.

[12] Warden, *Chase*, 459; Chase diary in the *Report of the American Historical Association*, 1902, 2:63–65; Welles, *Diary*, 1:104–105; Welles, *Lincoln and Seward*, 194.

[13] S. H. Gay, managing editor of the *New York Tribune*, to A. S. Hill.

Particularly galling to the Jacobins was a story gossiped around the capital that Lincoln had appointed McClellan not because he wanted to, but because the conservative generals bullied him into it with the threat of a military dictatorship. Indignantly Henry Cooke repeated this tale to his brother Jay. The nation was being "sacrificed to the damnable ambition of petty generals," declared Henry, who liked to mouth the opinions uttered by Chase; he added that there would be no fighting done by McClellan "unless we are driven like a cornered and cowardly rat to repel the attack of our enemy. Jay, this is truth." Sourest of all the radicals was John Pope. "Is it that I am to be deprived of my command because of the treachery of McClellan and his tools?" he wailed to Stanton.[14] His brief period in the spotlight was closed. The government shipped him back West to fight Indians in Minnesota.

To the Jacobin politicos the sight of McNapoleon again in the saddle was the next to the last straw, the sickening crash of their hard-won gains, and the end of their hopes for a radical war. Zachariah Chandler revealed his despair in a long letter to Trumbull: "It is treason, rank treason, call it by what name you will, which has caused our late disasters. . . . Your president is unstable as water, if he has as I suspect been bullied by those traitor generals. How long will it be before he will by them be set aside & a military dictatorship set up. . . . For God & country's sake, send someone to stay with the President who will controll [sic] & hold him. I do not despair, but my only hope is in the Lord." While waiting for divine aid to manifest itself, Chandler was ready to try a desperate expedi-

September, 1862, in Rhodes, *History of the United States*, 4:137, footnote; A. W. Stevens to George W. Julian, February 2, 1899, in the Giddings-Julian MSS.; Montgomery Blair to McClellan, April 22, 1870, in McClellan, *Own Story*, 545; Henry Cooke to Jay Cooke, September 3, 1862, in Oberholtzer, *Cooke*, 1:203–204. General Ambrose Burnside later told Henry Raymond of the *New York Times* that McClellan insisted, before accepting the command, upon the removal of Stanton and Halleck. Burnside claimed he persuaded McClellan to abandon the idea. "Excerpts from the Journal of Henry J. Raymond," *Scribner's Monthly*, 19(1880):423.

[14] Two letters from Henry Cooke to Jay Cooke, September 3, 4, 1862, in Oberholtzer, *Cooke*, 1:203–205; John Pope to Edwin M. Stanton, September 5, 1862, in the Stanton MSS.

ent to recoup the radical fortunes. He proposed to organize the Republican governors as a powerful pressure group which would force the adoption of the Jacobin war program upon Lincoln. "I fear nothing will now save us but a demand of the loyal governors *backed by a threat,*—that a change of policy & men shall instantly be made," he told Trumbull. The action he wanted to take was clearly a violation of the Constitution, but the Jacobins never let the Constitution stand in their way. On the same day that he wrote to Trumbull, Chandler fired a peppery letter at the War Department to let Stanton know the Committee was watching the drift of events. "Is there any hope for the future?" asked the senator. "Are imbecility and *treason* to be sustained and promoted to the end of the chapter?"[15]

Thaddeus Stevens viewed the military and political scene after Pope's removal with resigned pessimism. He thought that Lincoln's pandering to the conservatives as evidenced in the McClellan case meant that the president was "preparing the people to receive an ignominious surrender to the South." Stevens saw no hope for radicalism as long as Lincoln and the present Cabinet held the reins: "Whether we shall find anybody with a sufficient grasp of mind and sufficient moral courage, to treat this as a radical revolution, and remodel our institutions, I doubt. It would involve the desolation of the South as well as emancipation; and a repeopling of half the continent. This ought to be done but it startles most men." Other Jacobins re-echoed the angry sentiments of Chandler and Stevens. From Chase's correspondents in New York came excited letters describing the opposition to McClellan's appointment as so great that a popular uprising might break forth, and asserting that the people demanded Lincoln's resignation because he was "fickle, careless, and totally unqualified."[16]

[15] Zachariah Chandler to Lyman Trumbull, September 10, 1862, in the Trumbull MSS.; Chandler to P. C. Watson, assistant secretary of war, September 10, 1862, in the Stanton MSS.

[16] Thaddeus Stevens, letter of September 5, 1862, in the Stevens MSS.; Stevens' speech to the Republican convention which renominated him for Congress, in the *New York Tribune,* September 11, 1862; H. C. Bowen to Salmon P. Chase, September 13, and John Jay to Chase, September 27, in

While the Jacobins raged to each other, McClellan was drilling and reorganizing the army which had been shattered at Manassas. He had need to act fast, for Lee had struck into Maryland and was moving north, and the country was nervous as the threat of a rebel invasion loomed. McClellan marched to bar Lee's path, and the two armies met at Antietam Creek. For three days the contending forces surged furiously together in one of the bloodiest encounters of the war. At the end neither could claim an advantage, and both held their original positions. But Lee, with a smaller army, had suffered greater proportionate losses, and he could not continue the offensive. Too weakened to attack and unable to decoy McClellan into an assault, Lee did the only thing possible; he retreated across the Potomac into Virginia. McClellan might have made his dubious triumph more certain by smashing vigorously at the Confederates as they crossed the river, but his exaggerated caution held him inert until Lee was safe.

Lincoln was vastly disappointed when he heard that McClellan had let the Confederates get away. Still obsessed with the notion that one great victory would end the war, the president had hoped McClellan would bag Lee's entire army. Nevertheless Antietam, despite the indecisive results, was a Union triumph—the first rebel thrust into Northern territory had been turned back and contrary to the customary practice a Confederate general had retreated after a battle. It was the moment for which Lincoln had waited since July, the victory which Seward said must come before the president told the country and the radicals about his proclamation of emancipation. Ironically Antietam, McClellan's sole important military success, gave Lincoln an opportunity to proclaim a policy to which McClellan was bitterly opposed. On September 22 the president officially announced his intention of freeing the slaves by exercise of the war powers vested in him as supreme commander of the military forces. His proposed edict was only

Bartlett, *Frémont*, 84–85; Governor John A. Andrew to J. M. Forbes, September 13, in Hughes, *Forbes*, 1:331–332; Eleutheros Cooke to Jay Cooke, September 4, in Oberholtzer, *Cooke*, 1:205.

a pale likeness of the sweeping measure demanded by the Jacobins. It threatened the rebellious states with emancipation if they did not cease their resistance to the government by the first day of the next year. On that date, warned Lincoln, he would declare free the slaves in any state still in rebellion. Presumably if all the states in the Confederacy laid down their arms before that date, slavery within their borders would remain intact. Lincoln threw in plenty of comforting assurances for the conservatives. He reiterated his belief in compensated emancipation, and promised that he would again ask Congress to provide financial assistance to any loyal slave state willing to abolish the institution. Puzzling to radicals and conservatives alike was his ambiguous statement that his proclamation had not changed the character of the war. It was still a war to restore the Union. But the verb *restore* had mysteriously acquired a modifier. The president would now be satisfied with "practically restoring" the Union.[17]

The Jacobins greeted Lincoln's announcement of a new policy with guarded expressions of chilly approval. They viewed it as a move in the right direction but they wondered why he had not moved sooner and why he moved so haltingly now. For his proclamation, with its mild tone and the mere threat to emancipate at a future date, did not measure up to radical standards. Neither could the Jacobins see anything but barren failure for the president's plan as long as the enforcement of it was left in the unsympathetic hands of the Democratic generals and the conservatives in the Cabinet. The McClellans, the Buells, the Sewards, and their like, would smother any attempt to destroy slavery, warned the radicals. Let Lincoln purge the administration of such and install in their places men who believed in emancipation. Then the nation with freedom as its watchword would go forward to victory.[18]

To secure control of the Cabinet and the army now became

[17] Richardson, *Messages of the Presidents*, 6:96–98.
[18] *New York Tribune*, September 23, 24, 1862, editorials and Washington correspondence; New York *Independent*, September 25; *Chicago Tribune*, September 24.

the supreme objective of the Jacobins. They wanted more men like Stanton and Chase among the president's advisers and radical generals in all the important commands. Only then, they were convinced, could they be certain of forcing Lincoln to proclaim the promised emancipation and of compelling him to enforce it vigorously. Fear as well as self-interest spurred the radicals to action. They believed the leaders of the Democratic party would never permit the administration to adopt an antislavery policy, and were plotting with McClellan to overthrow the government by force if Lincoln tried to issue his proclamation. The general, the Jacobins charged, had agreed to lead a revolt by the Eastern army and to set up a military dictatorship. "A change must be had," cried one radical editor apprehensively. "There are evil omens in the air, signs of portent, premonishing anarchy, and the violent overthrow of Constitutional authority." Senator Grimes advised Trumbull that it was imperative to get a Republican general at the head of the loyal Western army. This general could march his troops against McClellan if the latter attempted a *coup d'état.* But Grimes doubted whether McClellan had "genius enough to make himself a dictator. . . . [A] man of ours in the Cabinet would make him crawl in a minute. There is where our trouble is. We must bind up our 'tow-string' of a President with strong, sturdy rods in the shape of Cabinet ministers."[19] General John M. Palmer, a prominent figure among the Illinois Republicans, gave Trumbull the same counsel. The president's policy of building up a coalition party by appointing Democrats to powerful civil and military offices had failed, Palmer claimed, because the very men thus placed in power were now planning to wreck the administration. Lincoln had created a Frankenstein which would destroy him. "Did such a thing ever happen before," asked the disgusted Palmer, "that a President had no friends amongst his own appointees or did any party before the Republicans

[19] *Frank Leslie's Newspaper,* September 27, 1862. See also the *Philadelphia Inquirer,* quoted *ibid.,* September 27; James W. Grimes to Lyman Trumbull, October 6, 1862, in the Trumbull MSS.

voluntarily throw away the whole patronage of the Government and allow its open assailants to entirely supersede it in the control of affairs . . . ?"[20] The Jacobins believed that it was of greater immediate importance to cleanse the army of McClellan and his satellites than to reform the Cabinet, because Lincoln accepted and followed the opinions of military men in preference to those of civilians. The president "is almost a child in the hands of his generals," wrote young James A. Garfield of Ohio, who was in Washington to see his friend Chase. Senator John Sherman informed his brother, General William T. Sherman, that the Jacobins were determined to get all the commands in the army transferred to officers like Frémont, Hunter, and Banks, who "show a sympathy with the Radical faction."[21] As a first long stride toward this goal, the radical machine prepared for a final battle to destroy McClellan.

The Young Napoleon, momentarily a hero after Antietam, was back in his familiar rôle of the general who would not fight. He hugged the safe side of the Potomac, he refused to take the offensive, and he nagged Lincoln for re-enforcements.[22] As the weeks wore on and McClellan made no move to follow up his victory, the country began to chafe under the continued inactivity, and the press clamored for action. The Jacobins seized on the popular impatience to point out that the general who had let Lee slip away in safety at Antietam and who now insisted that his army was not strong enough to invade Virginia was the same McClellan who in the previous spring had missed

[20] John M. Palmer to Lyman Trumbull, October 3 or 4, 1862, *ibid.* The first page of this letter is missing, and no year date appears on the other pages. The Library of Congress has placed the letter among the Trumbull papers for 1863. This is an error, as the substance of the letter shows it was written in 1862. Palmer discusses events which had just occurred in the fall of 1862, and talks about the plot of the Democrats to prevent Lincoln from issuing the emancipation proclamation.

[21] Smith, *Garfield*, 1:240–241; John Sherman to William T. Sherman, September 23, 1862, in Thorndike, *Sherman Letters*, 164–165.

[22] For McClellan's reasons for delaying action, see McClellan, *Own Story*, 619–620, 623, 627–628.

an opportunity to capture Richmond by the same tactics
of delay and procrastination. Greeley's managing editor sneeringly predicted that "the two armies will watch each other for
nobody knows how many weeks, and we shall have the poetry
of war with pickets drinking from the same stream, holding
friendly converse and sending newspapers across by various
ingenious contrivances." Fantastic stories of McClellan's treasonable conduct during the fighting at Antietam were circulated by the Jacobins, who were almost paranoiac where the
general was concerned. They charged that he had sneaked into
Lee's camp at night to find out how the rebel commander
wanted the battle managed and later had received and obeyed
orders from Lee to stall the Union forces until the Confederates could retreat.[23]

The angry growling of the radicals apparently made no impression upon Lincoln, who seemed resolved to stand pat on
McClellan and the Cabinet. In the latter part of September
the Northern governors met at Altoona, Pennsylvania, to discuss ways of aiding the government to prosecute the war.
Startling rumors came out of Altoona to cheer the Jacobins.
According to press reports the governors believed McClellan
a failure and were considering serving the administration with
a united demand that he be removed and a Republican general
put in his place. The *New York Herald* screamed that the
meeting was a Republican plot to kill off the general. Later a
committee of the governors, headed by the redoubtable Andrew, called on Lincoln to give him their views about the war
and to tell him that they wanted more Republican influence in
the Cabinet. They got no further than the opening salutations.
The wily president sensed their purpose and shut them off
by doing all the talking himself during the entire interview.
He ushered the frustrated and somewhat dazed visitors out of

[23] *New York Tribune*, September 22, October 3, 1862; Welles, *Diary*,
1:142; S. H. Gay to A. S. Hill, September 25, 1862, quoted in Rhodes,
History of the United States, 4:184–185; Edgar Conckling to Joseph Holt,
November 8, 1864, in the Holt MSS.; *Wilkes' Spirit of the Times*, April 29,
1865.

the room without giving them an opportunity to present their complaints.[24]

Lincoln's refusal to kick out McClellan and the Democratic generals—his "criminal vacillation," as Garfield indignantly exclaimed—drove the radicals to despairing anger. "I have ceased to write or talk about the generals and the Administration," the disgusted Grimes told Fessenden. "The men of brains are still overslaughed and ignored, and it would seem that they are to continue to be." Old Thad Stevens wailed bitterly, "Nothing seems to go right. I am almost despairing. Without a new Cabinet, there is no hope." Greeley's Boston correspondent begged the administration to oust the West Point clique and give the commands to "generals with ideas," men like Frémont, who were "almost irresistible because swayed by the great invisible forces."[25] The radicals' gloomy conviction that the president was infatuated with McClellan and wedded to him for the rest of the war was far wide of the mark. Actually Lincoln was profoundly disgusted with the general's protracted inactivity after Antietam and his repetitious excuses for not moving. Once again, and this time finally, Lincoln decided McClellan would not do. Wearily he realized that he must gamble with a new commander. The radicals sensed his hardening attitude in the closing weeks of October, and their hopes bounded. Sumner optimistically predicted that the president was about to throw overboard his all-parties policy and embrace the Jacobin program. James A. Garfield, haunting Chase's house and picking up scraps of information from the conversations of his host and Stanton, reported the same conclusion. Lincoln, having failed to buy up the Democrats by kindness, had concluded he "had better not drive away all his friends by neglect," Garfield wrote. He was con-

[24] *New York Tribune,* September 25, 29, 1862, Washington correspondence; *New York Herald,* September 27; Nicolay and Hay, *Lincoln,* 6:164–166; Charles H. Ambler, *Francis H. Pierpont* (Chapel Hill, 1937), 156–157.

[25] James A. Garfield to Mrs. Garfield, October 3, 1862, in Smith, *Garfield,* 1:245–246; James W. Grimes to William P. Fessenden, October 12, 1862, in Salter, *Grimes,* 217; Thaddeus Stevens, letter of October 17, 1862, in the Stevens MSS.; *New York Tribune,* October 29, 1862, p. 3.

vinced that the president meant to remove McClellan and was only waiting for the approaching fall elections to be over, for fear of giving the Democrats an issue.[26]

Presenting the Democrats with an issue would have been carrying owls to Athens. They did not need the martyrdom of McClellan to aid their cause in the gloomy autumn of 1862. They reveled in a cornucopia of issues: popular dissatisfaction with the administration because of its repeated military failures, the anger aroused by the policy of arbitrary arrests to which the government had resorted, the looming possibility of conscription, and the resentment of the conservatives at Lincoln's threat to proclaim emancipation. The Republicans went into the campaign disunited and listless, split by the bitter fight between the two factions. Lincoln's emancipation edict had repelled the conservatives without being drastic enough to draw the radicals to him. Neither could the radicals forget that the president still sustained McClellan and his pets in command of the armies. Halfheartedly Jacobins like Trumbull took the stump for the administration only because they considered it a slightly lesser evil than the Democrats.[27] By triumphant majorities, the Democrats swept the elections. They carried seven important states, including New York, Pennsylvania, Ohio, and Lincoln's own Illinois. They shaved the Republican control of the House of Representatives to a dangerously narrow margin.

Momentarily the enormity of the Democratic victory stunned the Jacobins. "It would not have been so great a calamity if the Army of the Potomac had been driven in, bloody and broken, to the defences of Washington," lamented Garfield. But they were quick to see how the situation could be turned to profit for radicalism if they could make Lincoln think that the party's reverses were due to his conservative program and his practice of lavishing appointments upon Democrats. "If

[26] Charles Sumner to John Bright, October 28, 1862, in Pierce, *Sumner*, 4:106–107; James A. Garfield to Mrs. Garfield, October 12, November 5, 1862, in Smith, *Garfield*, 1:250–251, 253–254.

[27] Lyman Trumbull to Zachariah Chandler, November 9, 1862, in the Chandler MSS.

the disastrous elections shall act as a spur to the President to give him some motion," wrote Garfield a few days after his first gloomy analysis, "I shall welcome them as messengers of mercy." The radicals labored vigorously to convert Lincoln. Greeley shouted in the *Tribune* that the administration had lost the confidence of the people because it had failed to support a drastic antislavery policy and because it had placed in command of the armies disloyal officers who would not fight against the Confederacy. Bryant in the *Evening Post* called in stentorian tones for a Republican war conducted by Republicans. The country, the poet-editor declared, wanted no more "rose-water statesmanship, or generals who are afraid to fight the enemy; or a policy which drifts with events like a piece of cork upon a stream." Carl Schurz, the German-American political leader who had tried being a general with notable inefficiency, urged Lincoln to remove all the Democratic officers on the grounds that being Southern sympathizers they were bound to be incompetent. The administration had lost the elections, argued Schurz, because it had admitted "its professed opponents to its counsels. It placed the army, now a great power in the Republic, into the hands of its enemies. . . . Let us be commanded by generals whose heart is in the war and only by such." With special bitterness the Jacobins cried out that Lincoln's attempt to create a coalition Union party was the cause of the election debacle. His one-plank platform, the restoration of the Union, was too narrow in its appeal, complained Joshua R. Giddings, and he had forced the Republicans to go into the elections "without an issue, without principles." John Sherman grimly predicted that unless the Republicans had the courage "to throw overboard the old debris" in the form of Democrats and conservatives whom Lincoln had brought into the party, "they are doomed." Joseph Medill, the editor of the influential *Chicago Tribune*, denounced the president in an angry letter to Trumbull: "It is enough to make the strongest men weep tears of blood. The President has allowed the Democratic party to shape the policy of the war and furnish the Generals to conduct it, while the Republicans have furnished the men and the money."[28]

In the person of McClellan the Jacobins saw incarnate all the forces which had brought about the Democratic triumph in the elections—the armies' long periods of inactivity and the repeated military disasters, the stranglehold of the Democrats upon the military patronage, and Lincoln's tender, "rosewater" policy toward slavery. Would the president dare to continue in power the man who had almost ruined the party? they cried angrily. One editor thought he would, and exclaimed bitterly, "But everything is to be sacrificed, even the lives of the living and the sweet memories of the dead, to support a leader who is keeping our armies in the sleep of death, and to glorify a soldier whose very nature is in a trance and who has never won a battle or even been under fire."[29] Lincoln, however, realized that he would be tempting the rupture of his already sorely strained party if he ignored the demands of the furious radicals; besides he was convinced that McClellan was too slow and cautious to carry through an offensive that would end the war. It was rumored that Wade, Chase, Stevens, and Sumner, speaking for the radical machine, had frightened the president with the threat that unless McClellan were removed, they would lead an open revolt when Congress met in December and withhold appropriations to prosecute the war. Stanton buzzed around Lincoln's office with reports from Halleck claiming that McClellan's army was in excellent condition and should move against the enemy, but its commander refused to obey orders to attack. Fervently Stanton implored the president

[28] James A. Garfield to Mrs. Garfield, November 5, 1862, in Smith, *Garfield*, 1:253; Garfield to J. H. Rhodes, November 10, 1862, *ibid.*, 254; *New York Tribune*, October 22, November 5, 1862; New York *Evening Post*, November 5, 1862; Carl Schurz to Abraham Lincoln, November 8, 1862, in Frederic Bancroft, ed., *Speeches, Correspondence, and Political Papers of Carl Schurz* (New York, 1913), 1:209-210; Joshua R. Giddings, letter of November 2 to his daughter, in the Giddings-Julian MSS.; John Sherman to William T. Sherman, November 16, 1862, in Thorndike, *Sherman Letters*, 167; Joseph Medill to Lyman Trumbull, November 14, 1862, in the Trumbull MSS. See also J. M. Forbes to William P. Fessenden, November 15, in Hughes, *Forbes*, 1:338.

[29] *Wilkes' Spirit of the Times*, November 1, 1862.

to dismiss McClellan.[30] Finally on November 5, the day after New York voted in the last of the fall elections, Lincoln acted. He removed McClellan from the command of the Eastern army. The decapitation struck consternation into the conservative camp. Old Frank Blair, the father of Frank, Jr., and Montgomery, rushed to Lincoln to beg another chance for the general. He argued eloquently, but the president was adamant: he was through trying to "bore with an augur too dull to take hold." At the conclusion of the interview, Lincoln got up, stretched, and remarked, "I said I would remove him if he let Lee's army get away from him, and I must do so. He has got the 'slows,' Mr. Blair." The Democrats, indignant and alarmed at the fall of their idol, roared that politics had dictated Lincoln's action and accused the administration of plotting the downfall of every general who was not a Republican.[31]

The Jacobins hailed the disgrace of McClellan as the arrival of justice long delayed and a harbinger of Lincoln's complete conversion to radicalism. "God will save us yet," Greeley exclaimed piously, as he gave the president dubious commendation for acting "at the last hour—too late to save his friends, but not too late, we trust, to save the country." Fessenden hoped that the departure of McClellan presaged the death of the all-parties policy. "Fear of offending the Democracy has been at the bottom of all our disasters," the senator wrote. "I am not clear that the result of the elections is not fortunate for the country, for it has taught the President that he has nothing

[30] *New York Herald,* November 17, 1862, Washington correspondence; Cochrane, *War for the Union,* 26–28; Flower, *Stanton,* 192–194; Henry W. Halleck to Edwin M. Stanton, October 28, 1862, in the Stanton MSS. On October 27 the secretary asked Halleck to present a report about the readiness of McClellan's army to move, and whether it could not advance because of a lack of supplies, as McClellan claimed. Halleck replied that the army was excellently supplied. McClellan had said that his men did not have shoes. On the back of Halleck's letter Stanton wrote, "Having waited 3 weeks after receiving peremptory orders to move, it is strange that he [McClellan] should have just now discovered that his army wanted shoes & could not move till supplied."

[31] *O. R.,* series 1, vol. 19, part 2, p. 545; Frank Blair, Sr., to Montgomery Blair, November 7, 1862, in Smith, *Blair Family,* 2:144–145; Rochester *Union,* quoted in the *Detroit Free Press,* February 20, 1863; Kendall, *Letters Exposing Abraham Lincoln,* 38–39.

to look for in that quarter." The same bright augury cheered Sumner, who rejoiced to his English friends over the removal of "the general who has been our military incubus," and thanked providence for the military disasters which had compelled Lincoln to espouse emancipation. The Jacobin press, exploiting the situation to the full, thundered for domination of the armies by radical generals and for important commands for officers like Frémont and Wadsworth. Washington observers expected Lincoln to go the whole way with the radicals. The British ambassador reported to his government after the overthrow of McClellan: "His dismissal was taken as a sign that the President had thrown himself entirely into the arms of the extreme Radical party, and that the attempt to carry out the policy of that party would be persisted in."[32]

In radical circles it was hoped that the elimination of McClellan from the military scene meant the end of West Point influence in the army and the repudiation of West Point ideas of winning the war with strategy. A Republican journalist, composing what was intended to be an epitaph for McClellan and all graduates of the military academy, expressed a fervent wish that volunteer officers who believed in fighting would now be given a chance. McClellan's greatest fault, declared the editor, was his insistence upon too much preparation and drill: "The primary dogma of West Point is the theory of adequate preparations; and the nation in this war, the first ever waged under West Point influences, is paying dearly for its whistle in the enormous outlay of money for material of war, and the astonishing levies and waste of human life. . . . He was taught never to commence an enterprise before he was thoroughly prepared, and in his mind, and in that of all the young West Pointers of this war, preparation was the giant

[32] *New York Tribune*, November 10, 14, 1862; *Chicago Tribune*, November 10, 12; William P. Fessenden to J. M. Forbes, November 13, 1862, in Hughes, *Forbes*, 1:336–337; J. M. Forbes to Joshua Bates, November 11, *ibid.*, 339; Charles Sumner to the Duchess of Argyll, November 12, 17, 1862, in Pierce, *Sumner*, 4:107, 108; James A. Garfield to J. H. Rhodes, November 10, in Smith, *Garfield*, 1:254–255; New York *Evening Post*, November 14; Lord Lyons to Lord John Russell, November 17, 1862, in Nicolay and Hay, *Lincoln*, 6:194–195.

solely competent for the task of subduing this revolt."[33] Mc-Clellan gave the radicals a scare before he retired to private life. The soldiers idolized "little Mac," and there were angry mutterings in the army when he was removed, ominous rumors of a mutiny, and wholesale resignations threatened by the general officers. The Jacobins reflected uneasily that McClellan's spell over the army might linger, even with the general gone.[34]

McClellan was not the only Democratic giant in the military forest whom Lincoln crashed to earth at this time. A few days before he removed the Young Napoleon, the president dismissed Don Carlos Buell, commander of the Department of the Ohio and of the largest army in the West. Buell—handsome, austere, bearded, unpopular with the volunteers because of his rigid discipline—was a West Pointer and a devoted member of McClellan's circle. He owed his important position to the latter's friendship. In the opinion of the radicals, his influence in the conservative clique was second only to McClellan's; they recognized his importance in their sneers at the "McClellan-Buell gang." Buell had faced the suspicion and enmity of the Jacobins from the beginning. He was a brother-in-law of the Confederate General David E. Twiggs, and this alone caused them to suspect his loyalty.[35] In addition he was known as a Democrat and a partisan of slavery. He maddened the radicals by saying that he did not know what the war was about or which party was right and which one wrong. Volunteer officers in his army complained to their senators that he was "pro-slavery to the core."[36] The Committee put him down

[33] Philadelphia *North American,* quoted in the *New York Tribune,* November 12, 1862.

[34] *Detroit Free Press,* January 22, 1863; John M. Palmer to Lyman Trumbull, November 15, 1862, in the Trumbull MSS.; *Philadelphia Inquirer,* quoted in the *New York Tribune,* December 1, 1862; Villard, *Memoirs,* 1:337.

[35] T. S. Bell to Joseph Holt, August 28, 1864, in the Holt MSS.; *Chicago Tribune,* quoted in *Leslie's Newspaper,* September 27, 1862; *Ohio State Journal* (Columbus), quoted in the *New York Tribune,* October 13, 1862.

[36] *New York Tribune,* October 24, 1862; *Boston Traveller,* quoted *ibid.,* May 31, 1862, p. 1; M. Warner to Andrew Johnson, February 4, 1862, in

in its list of officers to be destroyed when he expressed his opposition to the Confiscation Act and declared that such measures "robbed our cause of its sanctity."[37]

As a general, Buell had the same faults and virtues as McClellan. He was a good organizer, but he had the "slows." He made excellent plans but he did not win any battles. When the Confederates under Braxton Bragg invaded Kentucky, he stopped them; but like McClellan after Antietam, he stopped also. Stigmatizing Buell's "atrocious conduct" of operations, a radical editor exclaimed, "Truly a West Point diploma can cover more sins than even charity itself."[38] The Jacobins charged that he was more interested in protecting the property of notorious Kentucky rebels than in defeating the enemy.[39] The governors of the Western states, Andrew Johnson of Tennessee, Oliver P. Morton of Indiana, and Richard Yates of Illinois, became convinced that Buell was incompetent and deluged the government with demands for his removal.[40] But the most tragic blow which fate dealt the general was that his army became demoralized and lost its confidence in him. The American volunteer soldier remained a citizen after he enlisted. He read the newspapers, discussed political issues, and thought he could still criticize the acts of any officer of the government, including his commanding general. This demo-

the Johnson MSS. See also A. Denny to John Sherman, November 28, 1862, in the Sherman MSS.; *Chicago Tribune,* army correspondence, quoted in the *New York Tribune,* August 4, 1862; Mark Skinner to Edwin M. Stanton, October 20, 1862, in the Stanton MSS.; Colonel Thomas Allen to Lyman Trumbull, February 20, 1863, in the Trumbull MSS.; Colonel F. R. Stanley to John Sherman, November 24, 1862, in the Sherman MSS.

[37] New York *World,* August 12, 1864.

[38] *Pittsburgh Gazette,* quoted in the *New York Tribune,* October 6, 1862. See also General John M. Palmer to Lyman Trumbull, November 15, 1862, in the Trumbull MSS.

[39] *Cleveland Herald* and *Cincinnati Gazette,* quoted in the *New York Tribune,* August 8, 1862; A. H. Stokes to Lyman Trumbull, November 17, 1862, in the Trumbull MSS.

[40] Andrew Johnson to Edwin M. Stanton, March 29, 1862, in Robert W. Winston, *Andrew Johnson* (New York, 1928), 235; Philadelphia *Press,* quoted in the *New York Tribune,* November 18, 1862; Villard, *Memoirs,* 1:307–308; Oliver P. Morton to Abraham Lincoln, October 21, 1862, in *O. R.,* series 1, vol. 16, part 2, p. 634.

cratic philosophy took an extreme turn in Buell's army. The soldiers objected to his dilatory conduct, and they found their resentment supported by their home newspapers, which blasted the general's concept of strategy and his lenient treatment of rebels. Buell's policy became the subject of bitter campfire debate, and generals and colonels made speeches to privates in which they violently denounced their superior officer. One officer later recalled a major of an Indiana regiment in a diatribe to his men "in which he questioned the loyal purposes of General Buell and censured his course of conduct." There was wild talk among the officers of arresting Buell, and the general charged that the *Indianapolis Journal,* Morton's organ, tried to incite the soldiers to shoot him. Finally the officers held a secret meeting in a house near Lebanon, Kentucky, to canvass ways of getting Buell ousted. The ringleader was General Albin Schoepf, who previously had spoken suspiciously of the high esteem in which the secessionists of the state held the commander; now he declared flatly, "If they admire him so much he must sympathize with them some at any rate. . . . I would not like to trust him a great deal, and I have not the utmost confidence in him anyhow." As a result of the meeting the conspirators sent a petition to Lincoln, asking that Buell be dismissed."[41]

The news that Buell had lost control of his officers excited the radicals to hope and labor for his overthrow. Zachariah Chandler came West to do some personal snooping, and reported to the War Department that the army would be all right if it were given a new commander. "Buell's course has simply exasperated, not demoralized the army of the West," he wrote.[42] Halleck, watching the forces gathering against Buell, was convinced that the general was doomed. "The Gov-

[41] *O. R.,* series 1, vol. 16, part 1, p. 641, testimony of Colonel Marcellus Mundy in the court of inquiry which Buell later demanded. See also *ibid.,* 639–640, Mundy's testimony; 107, General A. McD. McCook's; 541, 546, General T. L. Crittenden's; 148–149, Colonel A. D. Streight's; 231, General S. S. Fry's; 642, Buell's; 135–138, General J. B. Steedman's.

[42] Zachariah Chandler to P. C. Watson, September 10, 1862, in the Stanton MSS. See also the *New York Tribune,* September 25, Washington correspondence; James A. Garfield to Mrs. Garfield, October 3, 1862, in Smith, *Garfield,* 1:246.

ernment seems determined to apply the guillotine to all unsuccessful generals," he informed a friend. "It seems rather
hard to do this where the general is not in fault, but perhaps
with us now, as in the French Revolution, some harsh measures
are required." Lincoln's patience with his sluggish Western
commander was rapidly wearing thin and he was ready to heed
the complaints of the Jacobins. When they charged that Buell's
malingering had cost the Republicans the elections in Ohio
and Indiana, the president acted. On October 24 he removed
Buell and appointed in his place William S. Rosecrans, a general whom the radicals had long favored for the position.[43]

The radicals were delighted with Lincoln. They praised him
for realizing at long last that the war must be fought by Republican generals whose hearts were in the cause. The elated
Greeley cried, "Be patient a very little while, and all the
'augurs that won't bore' will be served as Buell has been."[44]

With McClellan and Buell gone, the Jacobins breathed more
easily. The two generals had commanded the largest armies in
the nation, and nightmares in which they marched their troops
upon Washington to establish a Democratic dictatorship had
plagued the radical mind. Later a Republican congressman
recalled in his diary the perilous times "when McClellan and
Buell held the East and West in their hands."[45] The fall of
the Castor and Pollux of the conservative clique caused the
radicals to glow with optimism about Lincoln's future disposal of the military patronage. A Western colonel of radical
beliefs told Trumbull that the entire country now knew the
danger of employing Democratic generals. Their instincts
might be good, the colonel said mysteriously, but they "cannot
resist the sinister influences of secession and secessionists—
particularly if wrapped up in crinoline."[46]

[43] Henry W. Halleck to General Horatio C. Wright, August 25, 1862, in
O. R., series 1, vol. 16, part 2, p. 421; *New York Tribune*, Washington correspondence, October 23, 1862; *O. R.*, series 1, vol. 16, part 2. p. 642.

[44] *New York Tribune*, October 25, 1862, editorial and Washington correspondence.

[45] Diary of William P. Cutler, January 17, 1863, in J. P. Cutler, *Life
of the Cutlers*, 298.

[46] Colonel G. T. Allen to Lyman Trumbull, November 12, 1862, in the
Trumbull MSS.

Lincoln dashed the galloping hopes of the Jacobins. He gave the command of the Army of the Potomac to Ambrose Burnside, a shining light in the McClellan circle and the author of affectionate letters to the departed commander which were filled with references to "dear Mac."

8

Fredericksburg
and the Reign of Terror

TODAY AMBROSE BURNSIDE is remembered because he gave his
name to a hirsute facial adornment for men. In his own time
he was something of a figure, until fate forced him to accept a
responsibility he was never meant to carry. Then he stood
cruelly revealed as an amiable, uncertain little man of mediocre
ability who shifted his friendships and his principles with the
prevailing political winds. A graduate of West Point, he had
engaged in various business enterprises before the war, finally
through his friendship with McClellan catching on with the
Illinois Central railroad. Between business ventures he took a
flier at politics, running unsuccessfully as a Democratic candidate for the House of Representatives from Rhode Island.
When hostilities broke out he re-entered the army. He became
a trusted member of the McClellan clique, and the commander
pushed his fortunes vigorously. He was a good corps or division officer, where he could carry out decisions someone else
had made, but he was unfit to hold an independent command.
Most people liked him at first sight, and his soldiers idolized
him. He had the grand manner, and his admirers called him
the "Chevalier Bayard" of the army. It was felt in conservative
circles that his accession to the command of the Army of the
Potomac was peculiarly fitting—that as a Democrat he was Mc-
Clellan's legitimate successor.[1] To the radicals it seemed that
only a change of names had been effected and that McNapoleon's malign influence would continue to rule through
Burnside.

The Jacobins were in a snarling mood when they returned

[1] *Lusk Letters,* 170; William Swinton, *Campaigns of the Army of the
Potomac* (New York, 1882), 231.

to Washington for the opening session of Congress in December of 1862. Their momentary elation over the decapitation of McClellan and Buell had failed with the appointment of Burnside, and they feared Lincoln was trying to resuscitate his all-parties coalition. Julian found his comrades ready to attack the president openly if he resumed amorous relations with the Democrats, and Fessenden, disgusted beyond measure with the dominating conservative influence in the Cabinet, predicted "an outbreak in Congress" unless Lincoln changed his advisers. Greeley's capital correspondent reported that the radical bosses were hopeful about the future only because they could not afford to be otherwise and because the future could not possibly be as bad as the past.[2]

The message which Lincoln sent to Congress convinced the Jacobins that despite his coquettish glances in their direction he was still tempted by the charms of his first love, conservatism. He proposed a constitutional amendment providing for gradual, compensated emancipation in "every State wherein slavery now exists." He wanted to spin out the process of freedom over a period of thirty-seven years in order to spare "both races from the evils of sudden derangement." Such a scheme, the president claimed, was "plain, peaceful, generous, just—a way which if followed the world will forever applaud and God must forever bless."[3]

The radicals listened to the reading of the message with amazement and anger. Garfield, still trying to advance his military career in Washington anterooms, wrote: "I could hardly credit my ears when I listened to the whole message, and heard no word or sentence that indicated that the Administration intended to push the war to a triumphant conclusion. . . . The President goes into what seems to me a most weak and absurd scheme of emancipation in the year of our Lord, 1900,

[2] Julian, *Recollections*, 223; Fessenden, letter to his family, December 7, 1862, in Fessenden, *Fessenden*, 1:264; *New York Tribune*, December 11, 1862, p. 2.

[3] Richardson, *Messages of the Presidents*, 6:136–142; *Congressional Globe*, 37 Congress, 3 Session, appendix, 1–5; *New York Tribune*, December 2, 1862, p. 2.

and goes on to say that this scheme will end the rebellion sooner than it can be ended by force, and much cheaper." The nephew of old Thad Stevens assured his grim uncle that people regarded Lincoln's proposal as of "little account." The young man, striving to imitate the sarcasm of his renowned relative, estimated that at the rate the administration was proceeding, slavery would not be abolished in six hundred years. Lincoln's reversion to gradual emancipation frightened the Jacobins. They feared that he was wavering from his promise to support emancipation and that the Cabinet conservatives had smothered the September proclamation in its swaddling clothes.[4]

While the radical machine sniped at Lincoln, Burnside, convinced in his heart that he was incapable of commanding an army, was trying to figure out a plan to take Richmond. He decided to strike directly southward, throwing his troops across the Rappahannock at Fredericksburg. But when he reached the crossing he found Lee already there, strongly fortified behind stone walls—fatal walls the Union soldiers found them. Burnside resolved to attack despite the stark superiority of the Confederate position. For hours on December 13 his men flung themselves with magnificent courage against the impregnable walls and reeled back with terrific slaughter. The spectacle broke Burnside, who lost his head and wanted to lead a last forlorn charge of his old corps across the windrows of the dead. His officers restrained him and persuaded the grief-stricken general to order a retreat.

The disaster stunned the country. A great wail of despair went up as the long roll of dead and wounded swelled in sickening proportions. The war-weary people, cowed by a long succession of defeats, were ready to concede the invincibility of Lee and the hopelessness of conquering the South.[5] There was savage criticism of the administration and Republican conduct

[4] *Ibid.*, December 2, 1862, editorial and Washington correspondence; James A. Garfield to B. A. Hinsdale, December 1, 1862, in Smith, *Garfield*, 1:262–263; T. Stevens to Thaddeus Stevens, December 28 (?), 1862, in the Stevens MSS.; H. W. Cole to John Sherman, December 15, 1862, in the Sherman MSS.

[5] New York *World*, December 24, 1862; *New York Tribune*, December

of the war. There were charges that the president and Stanton had forced Burnside to fight at Fredericksburg against his will. *Harper's* ran a cartoon of an indignant Columbia asking three shrinking figures, Lincoln, Stanton, and Halleck: "Where are my 15,000 Sons—murdered at Fredericksburg?" One of Trumbull's less cultured correspondents expressed vividly the popular sentiment: "There had been no battle at Fredericksburg had the town been given just two hours in which to surrender! To save the Rebel Bitches and their snarling whelps thousands of widows have been made to weep tears of blood in the North! A nice arrangement and full of strategy aint it. But a Northern widow or orphan has ever been counted *trash* by our Government and Generals."[6]

The Jacobin bosses, superb political diagnosticians that they were, recognized in the black doldrums of the people an

26; Mrs. Lusk to Captain Lusk, in *Lusk Letters*, 252-253; William Scott to John Sherman, in the Sherman MSS.; Joseph Medill to Schuyler Colfax, in Ovando J. Hollister, *Life of Schuyler Colfax* (New York, 1886), 203; James A. Garfield to Mrs. Garfield, December 19, in Smith, *Garfield*, 1:264.

[6] *Harper's Weekly*, January 3, 1863; John Irons to Lyman Trumbull, December 20, 1862, in the Trumbull MSS.

ominous threat to the existence of the Republican Party and hence to the radical cause. They feared that the Democrats would manipulate the prevailing defeatist psychology into a peace movement that would sweep the Republicans from power and end the war upon terms dictated by the Confederacy. Ohio's worried Congressman Cutler mourned in his diary: "This is a day of darkness and peril to the country. . . . Under McClellan nothing was accomplished; now Burnside fails on the first trial. McClellan's friends chuckle and secretly rejoice over the result. The opponents of the administration are doing everything in their power to break it down. . . . [A] decisive victory by Burnside would have put them down and the administration up, but this disaster gives them courage and must weaken the administration."[7]

Alarming rumors ran through the Jacobin ranks that the Potomac army was about to revolt and proclaim its idolized "little Mac" dictator, and that the Democratic leaders were planning to call a national convention which would demand peace and recognition of the Confederacy. General Palmer warned Trumbull that the Democracy with its newly won power in Congress and the state legislatures would now try to end the war, and that the Republicans must resist the attempt by force. "Let our present army be made efficient, consolidate the radical regiments and be careful in doing so to retain only loyal incorruptible officers and let loyalty be the test in all future appointments," he wrote. "The time for balancing parties is gone by. The check of Burnside . . . will greatly promote the plans of the semi-rebels."[8]

Frightened by the swelling tide of popular dissatisfaction which threatened to engulf the administration and by their blind and helpless ignorance of what the Democrats intended to do, the radicals searched frantically for some device which

[7] Cutler diary, December 16, 1862, in J. P. Cutler, *Life of the Cutlers,* 296–297. See also A. S. Brewer to John Sherman, December 22, in the Sherman MSS.

[8] James A. Garfield to J. H. Rhodes, December 24, 1862, in Smith, *Garfield,* 1:265–266; John Palmer to Lyman Trumbull, December 19, 1862, in the Trumbull MSS.

would lift from their party the onus of Fredericksburg. As with Pope and Porter after Manassas, they determined to find a scapegoat. Immediately before and after the battle, a charge had gone the rounds that McClellan's young generals, angry with Burnside for succeeding the master, were trying to undermine him and that at Fredericksburg one of them, possibly Franklin, had deliberately kept his troops out of the fighting. The newspaper reporter Henry Villard, arriving in Washington from the battlefield, broadcast these stories right and left, and they reached the ears of radical congressmen. Here was a loophole through which the Republicans could crawl to escape the wrath of the Northern people.[9]

Obviously the Committee was the agent to do the job. On December 18 the radicals rushed through the Senate a resolution instructing the inquisitors to inquire into the late battle and "particularly as to what officer or officers are responsible for the assault which was made upon the enemy's works; and also the delay which occurred in preparing to meet the enemy." Wade, Chandler, Julian, and Covode resolved to go down to Burnside's camp at Falmouth to conduct the examination on the spot. Chandler went breathing epithets about "fool and traitor generals," and declaiming that "we mean to make thorough work of this investigation & do it at once."[10]

The radical press sent the inquisitors off with stern exhortations to run down the culprits who had betrayed the nation. "If someone has blundered," intoned Greeley, "let us see who it is, and wherever Justice dictates, let the great ax fall." The Democrats had a different explanation for the Falmouth mission. An Eastern editor reported: "One of the members of the War Committee who went down to Falmouth ostensibly to investigate the causes and responsibility of the recent disaster, stated while there that the object was to patch up the affair so

[9] Zachariah Chandler to Mrs. Chandler, December 3, 10, 1862, in the Chandler MSS.; David Dudley Field to Edwin M. Stanton, December 17, in the Stanton MSS.; James A. Garfield to J. H. Rhodes, December 24, in Smith, Garfield, 1:266; Villard, Memoirs, 2:3.

[10] C.C.W., 1863, 1:643; Chandler to Mrs. Chandler, December 18, 1862, in the Chandler MSS.

as to quiet the public mind. Our informant judged from his remarks that one purpose was to reduce the number of killed and wounded, as at first reported."[11]

The members of the Committee spent two days in camp questioning most of the generals. Significantly, they were the guests of General Sumner during their stay. It was immediately apparent that they had picked their scapegoat and that Franklin was the man. General Meade, later to feel the wrath of the Committee himself, lunched with Burnside and the Committee and reported Covode as promising that his "howl" would be raised against someone other than Burnside.[12]

In all their questions the members made it plain that they wanted to plaster an indictment on Franklin. They asked Burnside to give a reason for Franklin's failure to carry the left wing in his assault. The Commander, who was later to reverse himself, absolved his subordinate of all blame by answering, "To the great strength of the position and the accumulation of the enemy's forces there." Franklin denied sharply the implied charge that he had knifed Burnside and insisted he had attacked with all the force "that I thought it proper and prudent to put in." But they got what they wanted from "Fighting Joe" Hooker, rising rapidly in the favor of the Jacobins and pushed by Chandler as the next commander of the army. Hooker, intriguing for the Committee's support, delighted them with a blasting denunciation of Franklin's course. He declared that Franklin kept a large part of his division out of the battle and could have swept the rebels off the field, had he willed. Not forgetting to advertise the merits of Joseph Hooker, he described his own charge against the enemy as "such an attack as I believe has never before been made in this war."[13]

[11] *New York Tribune,* December 19, 1862; *Providence Post,* quoted in the *Detroit Free Press,* January 4, 1863.

[12] *New York Tribune,* December 20, 1862, army correspondence; Julian, *Recollections,* 224–225; Cochrane, *War for the Union,* 40–42; Meade to Mrs. Meade, December 20, 1862, in Meade, *Life of Meade,* 1:340.

[13] Burnside's testimony, in *C.C.W.,* 1863, 1:655; Franklin's, 661; Hooker's, 670.

When the Committee went to Falmouth, most observers expected the members to swing "the great ax" upon Burnside. Undoubtedly Wade and Chandler went with that purpose, to cut down a McClellan general who had failed dismally in his first battle. But to their amazement and enchantment they found a new Burnside, not Burnside the disciple of conservatism, but Burnside the Jacobin, breathing maledictions against slavery. He told Julian that the soldiers and the people must be taught to hate the South and its peculiar institution, and urged the congressman to head a crusade to stir up the masses. With charming naïveté, Julian later wrote that the general's "conversation disarmed all criticism." Julian told Cutler about the interview, and the latter recorded in his diary: "Julian thinks Burnside is truly convinced of the necessity of destroying slavery, and says that he has tried in vain to inspire his fellow officers with a cordial hatred of the system."[14] Burnside, on the road to Damascus, had been conveniently smitten with the radical light, and his precipitate conversion brought the Committee to his support. Wade and Chandler determined to cherish and sustain this promising recruit to radicalism.

The Committee's appearance in camp excited a tremendous furore among the common soldiers. Demoralized by the shambles of the stone walls, they had begun to question their commander's competence, and the news that a group of congressmen were investigating the causes of the defeat convinced them they had been the victims of a great blunder. In the words of General Cochrane: "Their failure before Fredericksburg had not conduced to their confidence in General Burnside, and when a committee of civilians from the Capitol, inquiringly approached his quarters . . . , with interrogatories to witnesses concerning his fitness for command, they assumed that they who had fought were certainly as competent to judge as those who had not. General Burnside's qualities as a commander thenceforth became the subject of debate at every camp fire." Henry Raymond went to Falmouth in January, and found that the soldiers had no trust in Burnside, who had "not

[14] Julian, *Recollections*, 225; William P. Cutler diary, January 20, 1863, in J. P. Cutler, *Life of the Cutlers*, 298.

only *spoken* of his incompetency but had gone before the Congressional Committee and *sworn to it.*[15]

The inquisitors returned to Washington on the night of the twentieth. To the amazement of the newspaper correspondents, they voiced no censure of Burnside. Instead they proclaimed that the army was in excellent condition and spirits, and anxious to be led against the enemy. Burnside's attack, they said, was ill-judged, but his defeat was due to the fickle fortunes of war. One member added ominously, "There are three generals who ought to be hung." For the moment Wade was content to submit to the Senate the testimony gathered at Falmouth, with no reports or comments. The Republican press, following the Committee's lead, used the material to whitewash Burnside and to revivify the shattered public morale. Let the people be calmed, advised Greeley. The disaster was not as great as at first supposed, and Burnside was a good general who would yet achieve victory.[16]

While the Committee was busy rescuing the Republican Party from the charge of inefficient conduct of the war, the radical bosses were concocting a plot to compel Lincoln to purge the Cabinet of conservative influence by throwing out Seward. They were disgusted with nearly the entire Cabinet, but above all they wanted Seward's scalp. Joseph Medill presented their case with the vivid touch of a great journalist: "Seward must be got out of the Cabinet. He is Lincoln's evil genius. He has been President *de facto,* and has kept a sponge saturated with chloroform to Uncle Abe's nose all the while. . . . Smith is a cipher on the right hand of the Seward integer— by himself, nothing but a doughface. Bates is a fossil of the Silurian era—red sandstone, at least—and should never have been quarried out of the rocks in which he was imbedded. . . . Seward, Smith, and Bates must go out."[17]

[15] Cochrane, *War for the Union,* 47–48; "Excerpts from the Journal of Henry Raymond." *Scribner's Monthly,* 19(1880):420.

[16] *New York Tribune,* December 22, 1862, Washington correspondence, December 24, 25, 27, editorials; *Leslie's Newspaper,* January 10, 1863; *Harper's Weekly,* January 10, 1863; *Senate Reports,* 37 Congress, 3 Session, vol. 1, no. 71.

[17] Joseph Medill to Schuyler Colfax, in Hollister, *Colfax,* 200.

Since autumn the hostility of the Jacobins to Seward had swelled in volume and bitterness. As long as he stood in the Cabinet at Lincoln's right hand, they despaired of ever converting the president to radicalism. More immediately, they feared that his malign sway would persuade the simple Lincoln to repudiate the emancipation proclamation. Thad Stevens frankly told Seward the radicals considered him an apostate to the antislavery cause. "I have accused the prime minister to his face for having gone back from the faith he taught us," said the old man to his Pennsylvania supporters, "and instead of arming every man, black or white, who would fight for this Union, withholding a well-meaning President from doing so." One radical journal, noted for its lavish use of epithets, sinisterly described the easygoing, tolerant Seward as "The Unseen Hand," and asked, "Is there enough left of this country to afford any further dangerous mesmerizing under the hands of Mr. Seward?" Chandler thought the secretary was the evil genius of the administration, who unless he was ousted would lead Lincoln to conclude a disgraceful peace with the Confederacy.[18]

Seward's apparent cynical indifference to moral issues, such as emancipation, infuriated the more zealous souls among the radicals. Sumner, with the contempt of a party "front" for the successful machine boss, said sanctimoniously that Seward's "contrivances and anticipations have been those merely of a politician who did not see the elemental forces engaged." A Pennsylvania radical complained, in a letter which would have delighted Seward had he seen it, that the secretary seemed to regard the rebellion and the attempt to set up an independent Southern government "as mere irregular opposition to the administration." With the fanaticism of true revolutionaries the Jacobins ascribed the repeated military disasters to the presence in the government of men like Seward, who had no faith in great guiding principles. The London *Times*, commenting on this interesting phenomenon, noted that the Amer-

[18] Stevens, quoted in the *New York Tribune*, September 11, 1862; *Wilkes' Spirit of the Times*, December 6, 1862; Zachariah Chandler to Mrs. Chandler, December 10, 1862, in the Chandler MSS.

ican Jacobins were behaving in the identical manner of their prototypes of the French Revolution: "The denunciation is precisely the same as those launched against the Girondins by the Mountain in the old French Convention. Disasters in the field have divided the Republican Party, and the zealots impute the reverses, not to the want of generals able to win victories, but to lack of faith in a principle."[19]

The Jacobins demanded that Lincoln make the Cabinet a unit, entirely radical or entirely conservative, instead of the polymorphic thing it was. "The country is in no condition to tolerate divided counsels," cried Greeley. An Ohio radical declared that the president "must be surrounded by men who are completely saturated with his views."[20] Much of the radicals' thinking on the subject of the Cabinet was dictated by their knowledge of the English system and a desire to introduce some of its features into the American scheme. One editor proposed that Cabinet members have seats in Congress: "This would bring them face to face with the people, and drag them out of those corrupt rat holes, their departments, where they can slink away, and defy public opinion for an entire four years." The Jacobins complained that Lincoln seldom troubled to consult the full Cabinet and did not consider himself bound by its collective advice. Instead he talked over important problems only with Seward. "Such a thing as a *Cabinet Council* has not been held since Mr. Lincoln became president," wrote an indignant capital corespondent. "There have been Cabinet meetings, but there have been no genuine consultations over the great questions of the day. The most important questions have been decided upon by the President in consultation only with one, or at the utmost, two of his constitutional advisers."[21]

The radicals snarled at Seward all during the autumn

[19] Charles Sumner to John Bright, October 28, 1862, in Pierce, *Sumner*, 4:106–107; A. McCoy to Joseph Holt, December 14, 1862, in the Holt MSS.; London *Times*, quoted in the *Detroit Free Press*, January 23, 1863.

[20] *New York Tribune*, November 6, 1862; New York *Independent*, December 4, 1862; R. M. Corwine to John Sherman, December 26, 1862, in the Sherman MSS.

[21] *Leslie's Newspaper*, October 31, 1863; New York *Independent*, December 25, 1862, Washington correspondence.

months, but they despaired of ever forcing Lincoln to remove him. "Seward will never yield his place willingly, and the President never will ask him to do so," Fessenden wrote gloomily. Their simmering anger boiled to the surface in December when the official correspondence of the State Department was published, disclosing Seward's instructions to American diplomats abroad to keep the slavery issue out of discussions with foreign governments, and his biting criticisms of the Jacobins and emancipation.[22] This was immediately after Fredericksburg, when the breakup of the administration seemed imminent and military disaster portended the return of the Democrats to power. Surely, thought the radicals, in this moment of discouragement Lincoln would be amenable to pressure for a reorganization of the Cabinet. They decided that the time was propitious and that it was imperative to destroy "The Unseen Hand."

Three days after the battle the Republican senators caucused in a secret meeting which lasted several hours. Trumbull, who apparently arranged the affair, told them they had been called together to determine a line of action to quiet the public mind, excited by the late disaster. Minnesota's Morton S. Wilkinson then delivered a bitter harangue against Seward, blaming all the government's failures upon the secretary, and cried that "so long as he remained in the Cabinet nothing but defeat and disaster could be expected." Grimes proposed a resolution expressing the senators' want of confidence in Seward. Wade followed with a violent speech blasting Lincoln's conduct of the war "and particularly censuring the Executive for placing our armies under the command of officers who did not believe in the policy of the government and had no sympathy with its purposes." Fessenden indorsed Grimes' resolution, and asserted that the time had come when the Senate must seize powers not given it in the Constitution and dictate to Lincoln the composition of the Cabinet, compelling him "to remove from it any one who did not coincide heartily with our views

[22] William P. Fessenden to J. M. Forbes, November 13, 1862, in Hughes, *Forbes*, 1:336–337; Thaddeus Stevens, letter of November 17, 1862, in the Stevens MSS.; Pierce, *Sumner*, 4:110–111; White, *Trumbull*, 210–212.

in relation to the war."[23] Wade demanded the appointment of a Republican general, clothed with "absolute and despotic powers,"[24] to command the entire military machine. The conservatives opposed the Grimes resolution and suggested the selection of a committee to discuss the question with Lincoln. Without coming to a decision the meeting adjourned until the next day.

At the second council John Sherman burst forth with a caustic denunciation of Lincoln, and said that nothing would be gained by changing the Cabinet. "The difficulty was with the President himself," barked Sherman. "He had neither dignity, order, nor firmness." The senators should "go directly to the President and tell him his defects. It was doubtful if even that would do any good." Finally it was determined to appoint a committee to inform Lincoln that the Senate demanded such changes in the Cabinet as would "give the administration unity and vigor." The conservative Jacob Collamer was chairman of this committee, but the other members, with the exception of Ira Harris, were radicals: Wade, Grimes, Fessenden, Trumbull, Sumner, Howard, and Pomeroy.

Collamer drew up a written statement to be read to Lincoln. This manifesto declared that the only way to save the Union was by a vigorous prosecution of the war, and that to insure success the president must be surrounded by advisers who were "cordial, resolute, unwavering supporters" of a policy which would bring victory. This condition did not exist, and changes must be made in the Cabinet which would secure "unity of purpose and action." The same principle applied to the army. It was "unwise and unsafe" to permit an officer to hold an important or separate command who did not cordially believe in the government's announced policy. Stripped of rhetorical verbiage, the document commanded the removal from the Cabinet and the army of anyone who did not believe in emancipation.

The senators met Lincoln on the evening of the eighteenth,

[23] Fessenden, *Fessenden*, 1:231–236. After the meeting Fessenden wrote a long account of the proceedings, which is reproduced in the biography.
[24] Browning, *Diary*, 1:597.

and Collamer read the indictment of the Cabinet. "Mr. Wade then rose," Fessenden's report recited, "and addressed the President, mainly on the conduct of the war, and the fact that it was left in the hands of men who had no sympathy with it or the cause, commenting at some length on the recent elections in the West, imputing the defeat of the Republicans to the fact that the President had placed the direction of our military affairs in the hands of bitter and malignant Democrats." Grimes and Howard denounced Seward for opposing emancipation. Then Fessenden demanded an end to the all-parties policy. Most of the regular army officers, he said, were "proslavery men and sympathized strongly with the Southern feeling." Yet Lincoln had lavished the important commands upon them and "disgraced" Republican generals like Frémont and Hunter. "The war should be conducted by its friends," he cried. After three hours the senators left, feeling that they had impressed Lincoln and that he would yield to their demands.[25]

Rumors swept the city that Seward had resigned, that the whole Cabinet was out, even that Lincoln had abdicated.[26] The astute president, however, had an ace up his sleeve. He asked the senatorial committee to meet him again the next evening at his office. When the solons arrived, they found to their embarrassment the entire Cabinet except Seward. Lincoln realized that he had forced them into a hole, and he immediately launched into an exposition on the unity of the Cabinet and a defense of Seward. Then he asked his advisers to corroborate his remarks. This put Chase in a horrible dilemma. Previously he had told the radical bosses that Seward's influence was responsible for the lack of Cabinet unity. Now he either had to confess before his chief that he had tattled secrets and stirred up the present crisis, or he must uphold Lincoln and repudiate what he had said to his radical allies. Obviously angered by Lincoln's clever move, he tried to wriggle out by

[25] Fessenden, *Fessenden*, 1:236–243.
[26] Henry Cooke to Jay Cooke, December 19, 1862, in Oberholtzer, *Cooke,* 1:223–224; Cutler diary, December 19, in J. P. Cutler, *Life of the Cutlers,* 297; Colonel A. Farnsworth to Captain Lusk, December 20, in *Lusk Letters,* 251–252.

saying there was "general acquiescence on public measures." The Cabinet members then left, and Lincoln informed the senators that Seward had offered his resignation but that he had not accepted it—that he feared "a general smash-up" of the administration if the New Yorker were forced out.[27]

Chase's squirmy refusal to play the rôle expected of him confused the senators, and they began to have doubts about his reliability. Fessenden called at the War Department the next morning to get some comfort from Stanton. The secretary stroked Fessenden's senatorial dignity by observing that "the interview of the evening before was the most impressive scene he had ever witnessed, and that he was particularly struck by the dignity and propriety exhibited by the senators and disgusted with the cabinet." Nevertheless the solons were right about Chase. The stagey secretary deserted them and destroyed the victory they had won by forcing Seward to resign. After much soul-searching and a talk with the persuasive Seward, Chase also sent in his resignation. Quixotically he explained to Henry Cooke that he did not want the country to think he had driven Seward from the Cabinet. The Jacobin chiefs begged him to reconsider, but he refused.[28]

Apparently Lincoln expected Chase to act foolishly. When he received the Ohioan's offer to resign, the president knew he again commanded the situation. "Now I have the biggest half of the hog," he exclaimed. He kept the Jacobins in a state of suspended confusion for a few hours, and then announced that he would not permit either secretary to leave. The radicals were checkmated. If they insisted upon Seward's ejection, Chase would go also. And bad as Chase was, they preferred his unreliability to the uncertain merits of anyone else Lincoln might appoint.[29]

[27] Fessenden, *Fessenden*, 1:243–248; Bates, *Diary*, 269–270.

[28] Fessenden, *Fessenden*, 1:248–251, from Fessenden's account of the Cabinet affair; Henry Cooke to Jay Cooke, December 20, 1862, in Oberholtzer, *Cooke*, 1:224–226.

[29] Fessenden, *Fessenden*, 1:250–251; Thaddeus Stevens, letter of December 21, 1862, in the Stevens MSS. For other accounts of the Cabinet imbroglio, see Welles, *Diary*, 1:196–203; Schuckers, *Chase*, 473–475; Welles, *Lincoln and Seward*, 81–85; Nicolay and Hay, *Lincoln*, 6:263–272; *New*

The Committee sponsored a belated and ingenious scheme to salvage some gain out of the wreckage of radical hopes. General Herman Haupt, whom Stanton had summoned from the business world to handle the transportation problems of the army, proposed to Lincoln the formation of a military council composed of the president, Stanton, McClellan, Halleck, McDowell, and two others. The president would divide with the council the responsibility for planning campaigns and determining policies. Haupt revealed to the Committee this bold plan to snatch from Lincoln his constitutional powers as commander in chief of the armed forces; immediately the members saw the advantages in the proposal, and told Haupt they would back him. Thus encouraged, the general again pressed Lincoln to agree to the council idea. "The nation has faith in you . . . but there is but little confidence in your Cabinet," he urged, "and I fear that without the most radical changes it will be impossible to increase the armies of the Union or ever to use efficiently the forces now in the field."[30] The Haupt scheme went the way of the senatorial venture. The Cabinet remained intact and conservative.

The failure of the raid on the Cabinet depressed and enraged the Jacobins. The future looked blacker than before, and their hopes that Lincoln would stand by the emancipation proclamation fell with an audible thud. Congressman Sedgwick gloomily summed up the results of the fiasco: "So the Senate is snubbed, Seward is more powerful than ever, Chase's radical friends are disgusted that he has been used to save Seward from his folly, and the great chasm into which the administration was to fall is bridged." Fessenden, in a bitter mood toward Chase, thought the affair had accomplished nothing except "to unmask some selfish cowards and perhaps frighten them into good behavior." Nevertheless, despite their blighted prospects, the radicals were still determined to force

York Tribune, December 20, 21, 22, 23, 1862; New York Evening Post, December 22; New York Times, December 20, 22, 23.

[30] Herman Haupt to Abraham Lincoln, December 22, 1862, in the Stanton MSS.; Haupt to Lincoln, December 26, ibid.

a reform of the Cabinet. The press and state bosses exhorted the congressional leaders to continue the fight.[31]

There were profound and dangerous constitutional implications in the Cabinet imbroglio. The assumption that the senators of the majority party could force the president to remove an adviser whose opinions did not square with the senators' ideas of correct party dogma was a startling innovation in the American scheme of government. Fessenden recognized that he and his colleagues were stepping outside the sphere allotted them by the Constitution. "The story of the last few days will make a new point in history," he wrote, "for it has witnessed a new proceeding—one probably unknown to the government of the country." Many observers thought the senators must have confused the American system with the British and tried to establish the doctrine of parliamentary supremacy and the responsibility of the executive to Congress. "The Constitution confers upon them no more right to demand the resignation of an obnoxious secretary than to appoint a mayor for New York city," objected *Harper's Weekly*. A conservative correspondent of John Sherman's declared that the Senate had the right to confirm men appointed to office by the president, but it possessed no power to "confirm them out again." The British press watched the affair with a keen interest and a smug conviction that the Americans were making a clumsy effort to imitate the merits of the superior English system. Pontifically the London *Times* pronounced: "The democratic government is not a tenant at will. It holds office on a lease, and within its legal term cannot be served with an ejection. The Americans are paying a heavy price for the inflexibility of their political system."[32]

[31] Charles Sedgwick to J. M. Forbes, December 22, 1862, in Hughes, *Forbes*, 1:344–346; William P. Fessenden, letter to his family, December, 1862 (no date), in Fessenden, *Fessenden*, 1:253; *New York Tribune*, December 22, 1862; Daniel Hamilton to John Sherman, December 25, and R. M. Corwine to Sherman, December 26, in the Sherman MSS.; D. L. Phillips to Lyman Trumbull, December 24, in the Trumbull MSS.

[32] Fessenden, *Fessenden*, 1:253; *Harper's Weekly*, January 3, 1863; Henry Stoddard to John Sherman, December 27, 1862, in the Sherman MSS.; London *Times*, quoted in the *Detroit Free Press*, January 23, 1863.

In reality the action of the Republican senators was a domestic political growth, nurtured by the lusty, equalitarian democratic philosophy of the period. It was an expression of the common man's belief that he or his elected representatives were smart enough to handle any problem connected with government and war. This creed manifested itself in repeated efforts by Congress, during the war and the reconstruction years, to usurp functions normally exercised by the executive branch. The constant mass criticism of military operations and the crying down of the value of military training; the House committee which investigated the number of "disloyal" persons in the employ of the government and then tried to make the department heads discharge those it labeled as Southern sympathizers; the House committee to supervise the letting of government contracts; and most important of all, the Committee on the Conduct of the War—all were facets of this democratic dogma. The move against Seward was an attempt to assert the Stevens doctrine, so essential to the success of the radical cause, that Congress was the agency which in war exercised the powers of a dictator. In trying to refashion the Cabinet by party decree the Republicans were following the drift of the times. One critic pointed out: ". . . [It] is but another step in the attempt to wrest the powers confided by the Constitution to the Executive from his hands. The formation of the Committee on the Conduct of the War . . . was the first step. This attempt to control the constitutional advisers of the President is the second, and before long, we shall see other and more important ones taken."[33]

An Illinois Republican leader, writing to commiserate Trumbull on the failure to oust "envious ambitious Seward," posed an anxious question. Would the "Unseen Hand" and his proslavery allies in the Cabinet restrain Lincoln from issuing the emancipation proclamation on the first of January? And if Lincoln held to his pledge, would not Seward and the McClellan generals stifle the enforcement of the edict? The same questions plagued other radicals. Congressman Sedgwick wrote to

[33] *Detroit Free Press*, January 14, 1863.

Forbes: "Some doubt his intention to issue the proclamation of 1st January; I do not. Many assert, more fear, that it will be essentially modified from what is promised. I do not fear this; but what I do fear is, that he will stop with the proclamation and take no active and vigorous measures to insure its efficacy." Sedgwick urged Forbes to come to Washington and use his influence with Lincoln to make the proclamation a living measure. Sumner, in an optimistic mood, assured Forbes that Lincoln would not only proclaim a strong emancipation policy, but that he had agreed to raise a Negro army of 200,000, to hold the Mississippi basin.[34] Forbes himself feared that the president would not go beyond a mere paper act of emancipation, and besought Sumner to see to it that the proclamation effected "not only emancipation but all the fruits thereof, in the perfect right to use the negro in every respect as a man, and consequently as a soldier, sailor, or laborer." The pressure of the Jacobins upon Lincoln during the last week of December was terrific. The radical machine threatened to defeat all appropriations for war supplies if the president did not publish his edict. Lincoln was quoted as saying that he would have been superseded by a dictator had he refused to proclaim emancipation.[35]

The first day of January dawned gloomy and dismal. On the night before, a smoking northeaster of driving snow and rain struck the Atlantic coast. In the morning the sun vainly tried to pierce the dark vapors, the streets were a slough of slush and mud, and a glassy blue-gray sky lowered over the Eastern seaboard.[36] The spirits of the Jacobins matched the weather as they read the emancipation proclamation.

The famous document, to be so celebrated and misunderstood by later generations, struck few chords of approval from

[31] Thomas Maple to Lyman Trumbull, December 28, 1862, in the Trumbull MSS.; Charles Sedgwick to J. M. Forbes, December 22, 1862, in Hughes, *Forbes*, 1:344–345; Charles Sumner to Forbes, December 28, 1862, *ibid.*, 352–353.

[35] Forbes to Sumner, December 27, 1862, *ibid.*, 349–350; Julian, *Recollections*, 227; *Detroit Free Press*, January 30, 1863.

[36] *New York Tribune*, January 1, 1863.

the radicals. It declared free the slaves in the rebellious states, with the exception of all of Tennessee and specified parts of Louisiana and Virginia—the only areas of the Confederacy controlled by Union forces and hence the only areas where military emancipation could be made a reality. In other words, as contemporary critics pointed out, Lincoln freed the slaves where his edict was inoperative and held them in chains where he could have set them free. Furthermore, in the whole proclamation there was no ringing declaration of antislavery sentiment nor any statement that emancipation was now one of the aims of the war. Lincoln justified his action as a measure of pure military necessity.[37]

The radical press thought the general tone of the proclamation was adequate, but Greeley and other editors blasted Lincoln savagely for excepting from its operation the areas under Union control. They called upon the president to give further proof of his devotion to the cause of freedom.[38] A conservative journal noted: "The proclamation of the President is not acceptable to the Radicals. They argue that it is not universal, and is therefore not up to the mark. They think it will not be effectual unless the President places men in the army who are in favor of it."[39] Lincoln had waited too long to espouse emancipation, said a Democratic observer, and now the radicals did not trust his sincerity: ". . . [He] has made no friends among them, for the reason that he has not done everything in their particular way, and at their designated moment."[40]

If the proclamation did not raise cries of delight from the Jacobins, it fell stillborn among the conservative Republicans. *Harper's* and the *New York Times* indorsed it, but in general it met a hostile reception in conservative circles. Lincoln's friend Browning criticized it savagely. The most dangerous

[37] Richardson, *Messages of the Presidents*, 6:157–159.

[38] *New York Tribune,* January 3, 1863; *Leslie's Newspaper,* January 17.

[39] *New York Journal of Commerce,* quoted in the *Detroit Free Press,* January 7, 1863.

[40] *Illinois State Register,* January 13, 1863, quoted in A. C. Cole, "President Lincoln and the Illinois Radical Republicans," *Mississippi Valley Historical Review,* 4(1918):427, footnote.

attack came from Thurlow Weed, Seward's manager and the boss of the silk-hat Republican machine in New York. In his newspaper organ Weed denounced the edict as turning the war into an abolition crusade, and flayed the "blind and frantic course" of the radicals, "by whom the administration is beleaguered, importuned, and persecuted."[41]

To the Democrats the proclamation was the final example of Lincoln's perfidy in soliciting Democratic support for a war to restore the Union and at the same time capitulating to the radicals on every issue. The mask was now off, they shouted, and they would have no more of Mr. Lincoln and his glib talk about an all-parties policy. Let Wade and Chandler run his war for him! An inauspicious portent for the president was the announced opposition of a powerful prelate of the Catholic church. The newspaper organ of Bishop Hughes of New York condemned the proclamation and the congressional radicals who had forced its issue.[42]

But while the radicals muttered and conservatives fell away, one strange recruit appeared in the administration ranks. In a speech at Music Hall in Boston, Wendell Phillips announced that at last he could rejoice under the banner of the United States. A disgusted editor snorted: "The proclamation may lose us Kentucky, but then it has given us Mr. Phillips. He will doubtless take the field with a formidable army of twenty thousand adjectives."[43]

Phillips, however, was willing to serve under the administration only if Lincoln delivered the conduct of the war to the radicals. "We have to proclaim that Proclamation or it will amount to nothing," he declared. "We have got just forty-five days to the fourth of March to work in. On that fourth of March Congress changes its character and becomes largely

[41] *Harper's Weekly,* January 10, 1863; *New York Times,* January 3, 1863; Browning, *Diary,* 1:578; *Albany Evening Journal,* January 13, 1863. See also *ibid.,* January 7, and *Harper's Weekly,* February 14.

[42] *Cincinnati Daily Enquirer,* January 4, 1863; New York *World,* January 3, 7; *Detroit Free Press,* January 1, 4; Hughes' organ, the *Metropolitan Record,* quoted *ibid.,* January 15, 1863.

[43] *Boston Courier,* January 7, 1863.

Democratic." He demanded of the president, "Not only a policy but civil leaders that believe in it; not only a proclamation, but a leader that the slaves know represents the Proclamation."[44]

The radical bosses did not believe that Lincoln would furnish any leadership or leaders, except of the rose-water variety. "The feeling prevails that Lincoln allows the policy of the war to be dictated by Seward, Weed, and border state men," complained Cutler. Fessenden declared of the Cabinet and the generals: "The simple truth is, there never was such a shambling, half and half set of incapables collected in one government before since the world began. I saw a letter this morning written in good English by the King of Siam to Admiral Foote, which had more good sense in it, and a better comprehensiveness of our troubles, I do verily believe, than *Abe* has had from the beginning." In order to make the faulty proclamation work, it was more imperative than ever, the radicals thought, to have in the army and the Cabinet men who believed in emancipation.[45] But they found slim proof of any intention on the part of the president to handle the patronage in correct fashion. The Missouri radicals, trying to swing the election of a Jacobin to the Senate, found the Blair faction and the federal officeholders lobbying with the legislature to pick a conservative anti-emancipationist candidate. Angrily the Missouri leaders besought Trumbull to persuade Lincoln to call off his appointees. Did the friends of freedom, they asked, have to fight Lincoln's battles and "have his governmental & Cabinet influence to fight at the same time?"[46]

The Jacobin machine still nourished the design of killing off Seward and effecting a wholesale Cabinet reorganization. "The pressure for the expulsion of Seward increases by letters

[44] *New York Tribune*, January 22, 1863.

[45] Cutler diary, January 17, 1863, in J. P. Cutler, *Life of the Cutlers*, 297–298; Fessenden, letter to his family, January 10, 1863, in Fessenden, *Fessenden*, 1:265–266; Wait Talcott to Lyman Trumbull, January 11, 1863, in the Trumbull MSS.

[46] C. H. Howland to Trumbull, January 7, 1863, and F. A. Nitchy to Trumbull, January 23, *ibid*.

and fresh arrivals," Sumner wrote hopefully. Greeley demanded a unified Cabinet which believed in emancipation, and made a trip to Washington to see about getting Seward kicked out. He left happily, assuring everyone that the evil genius would be removed in a week. Local bosses cried the Republican senators on to head a repetition of the December raid, and capital correspondents reported that such a scheme was being hatched. "There is another concerted movement on foot for a reorganization of the Cabinet, and to dictate the policy of the administration," the New York *World*'s man reported. "The program of the radicals looks to an entire recast, not only of the civil government, but of the army leaders, with a view to carrying on the war entirely in the abolition interest."[47]

On January 17 the House Republicans caucused to shape a legislative program and discuss methods of injecting some radical blood into the Cabinet. Committees were selected to report on subjects for action. Three days later another meeting was held. The members agreed not to admit to Congress men elected from any Southern state where Lincoln should attempt to reconstruct a government by military authority, on the assumption that such representatives would be upholders of slavery. The committee to draft a program to bring about a more vigorous prosecution of the war advocated that the party force Lincoln to change the Cabinet. But at still a third conference, the leaders said there was no way to move the president or secure any improvement in the situation. Lincoln wanted a divided set of advisers, so he could play off one faction against the other. Gloomily Cutler wrote in his diary: "So the upshot of the matter is that confusion is worse confounded—no one seems to have any confidence in anybody or anything. The earnest men are brought to a deadlock by the

---

[47] Charles Sumner to Francis Lieber, January 23, 1863, in Pierce, *Sumner*, 4:112, footnote; John Sherman to W. T. Sherman, January 27, in Thorndike, *Sherman Letters*, 187; *New York Tribune*, January 22, 1863; Fessenden, *Fessenden*, 1:266; Grant Goodrich to Trumbull, January 31, and J. H. Mayborn to Trumbull, February 6, in the Trumbull MSS.; New York *World*, January 20, 1863; *Detroit Free Press*, January 7, 14, Washington correspondence.

President. The President is tripped up by his generals, who for the most part seem to have no heart in their work."[48]

But if the Jacobins despaired of raising the tone of the Cabinet, they were ruthlessly determined to seize control of the military patronage. They were convinced this was their only hope of making the proclamation a drastic reality. The radical press shouted for the removal of every officer who would not pledge himself to fight for emancipation. Republican volunteer officers exhorted their senators to purge the army of Democratic generals, and hinted darkly that the McClellan clique was scheming with Northern traitors to overthrow the government.[49]

The radical bosses realized that the time had arrived when they must strike relentlessly at Democratic domination of the armies if they expected their cause to be victorious. In particular they were resolved to install a radical general in command of Louisiana and the other states of the Gulf Department. Here large areas of territory were coming under military occupation, fugitive slaves were pouring into the army camps in ever-increasing numbers, and the process of reconstruction would soon begin. Here also potent experiments with the Negroes as freemen and soldiers could be conducted. "The whole social system of the Gulf states is to be taken apart, every bit of it," exulted Wendell Phillips. If it were to be put together right, the radicals cried, uncompromising antislavery generals must do the job. Hence when it was rumored that Stanton had persuaded Lincoln to raise a large army of former slaves in Louisiana, the Jacobins demanded that Frémont be made its commander.[50]

[48] *Ibid.*, January 19, 1863, Washington correspondence; *New York Tribune*, January 19, Washington correspondence; William P. Cutler diary, January 21, 1863, in J. P. Cutler, *Life of the Cutlers*, 298–302.

[49] *New York Tribune*, January 22, 1863; *Boston Traveller*, quoted in the *Detroit Free Press*, January 31, 1863; Colonel W. F. Herrick to John Sherman, February 5, 1863, in the Sherman MSS.; J. Purdy to Sherman, January 10, *ibid.*; Colonel S. Noble to Lyman Trumbull, February 24, in the Trumbull MSS.

[50] Phillips, quoted in the *New York Tribune*, January 24, 1863; A. S. Mitchell, of the *New York Times* editorial staff, to Joseph Holt, Decem-

The president, however, had no intention of permitting the Gulf Department to become a laboratory for experiments in radicalism, and least of all a recruiting ground for a slave army. He was determined to reconstruct Louisiana by executive action and according to his own ideas. But in command at New Orleans was the raffish and radical Ben Butler, the one general with enough courage and imagination to take apart the social system of the entire area and remake it on a Jacobin pattern. Butler was a cherished favorite of the Committee and of all radicals. He had been the first general to define fugitive slaves as contraband of war and to employ them as laborers. The Jacobins applauded his ingenious and vigorous methods of squelching recalcitrant rebels, without too much regard for the niceties of the Bill of Rights or the Chesterfield code for gentlemen, and his loud advocacy of emancipation and the utilization of slaves in a military capacity. His administraton of the Gulf Department was spectacular, unbelievable, inefficient, and a constant source of delight to an astonished Northern public. He reveled in martial law and arbitrary arrests, and threw prominent residents into jail with a gusty relish. He was supposed to be gloriously guilty of bribery and corruption and to have lined his pockets with crooked money filched from contractors and the government—a reputation which he deliberately enhanced by a sardonic leering smile, a perennial crafty wink in one eye, and by his ruthless manner of disemboweling pompous stuffed shirts who pretended to be honest. He climaxed his record by getting himself accused, falsely, of stealing a set of silver spoons from one of the aristocratic families of New Orleans. He was the only Union general smart enough to handle the fiery Southern women who in New Orleans and other occupied cities insisted upon showing their contempt for the Yankee soldiery with derisive words and gestures. Other officers issued brave orders which could not be enforced against the fair tormentors, and then subsided into raving impotence. But Butler solved the problem at New

ber 24, 1862, in the Holt MSS.; Charles Sumner to J. M. Forbes, December 28, 1862, in Hughes, *Forbes*, 1:352–353.

Orleans. The North guffawed and the South frothed when he issued an order that awed the ardent ladies: "As the officers and soldiers of the United States have been subject to repeated insults from the women (calling themselves ladies) of New Orleans . . . , it is ordered that hereafter when any female shall by word, gesture or movement insult or show contempt for any officer or soldier of the United States she shall be regarded and held liable to be treated as a woman of the town plying her avocation."[51]

For obvious reasons, Lincoln did not want such a general in command of the Gulf area. In December he removed Butler and appointed in his stead Nathaniel P. Banks, whose political opinions the Jacobins suspected. At first they thought the president had recalled Butler for the purpose of investing him with a more important post. The general came to Washington for a conference at the White House, and the radicals supposed Lincoln would send him back to New Orleans to raise a slave army. One especially hopeful rumor had him becoming secretary of war. But the weeks wore on, and Butler received no assignment. Then they realized that Lincoln was hoaxing them and that their favorite was permanently out. They grasped the discouraging reality that the administration did not want a radical general in control of Louisiana or any state where reconstruction was imminent. Angrily they accused Seward and Halleck of engineering the Banks appointment in order to get rid of Butler.[52] They demanded that the president restore Butler to command. He was the only general who was right on the great issue, said Phillips. Butler hung around the city, imparting a racy tone to capital society. The Democrats in Congress attacked him for his alleged crooked financial transactions, and the radicals defended him hotly. The city was thrilled by a report that he had challenged James Brooks, the Tammany Democrat who led the assault, to a duel.[53]

[51] *New York Tribune,* September 4, 5, 1862; *O. R.,* series 1, 15:426.
[52] *New York Tribune,* January 3, 1863; *New York Times,* January 8; *Detroit Free Press,* January 14, February 22; *Harper's Weekly,* January 10.
[53] Wendell Phillips, quoted in the *New York Tribune,* January 24, February 4, 1863; *ibid.,* January 24, 25, Washington correspondence.

The removal of Butler infuriated the Committee radicals, and they determined to take up his cause. Covode sent an investigator around to the general to hear from the latter's own lips an explanation of the charges of corruption. The members talked about using their influence with Stanton to secure for Butler an independent command in the West. Early in February the general testified officially before the Committee, in a session that resembled a meeting of a mutual admiration society. He defended his administration and his financial dealings, and strongly indorsed the employment of Negro soldiers. He delighted the inquisitors with his description of how he had outsmarted the people of New Orleans on the issue of citizens of foreign countries owning slaves. He had found out that the laws of France and England did not permit subjects residing in other lands to possess slaves, so he blandly asked the residents of the city to register their citizenship, American, English, or French. Many, hoping to escape burdensome restrictions, claimed to be citizens of the last two nations. He freed the slaves of these masters, and enrolled them in a colored regiment.[54]

The Butler case only sharpened the determination of the Jacobin leaders to purge the army of Democratic influence, and supplied them with an added incentive. In January the radical machine, led by the Committee, embarked on a great drive to destroy all the conservative generals—using as weapons courts-martial, smear campaigns in the press, dismissals by the War Department, and congressional denunciation. The Democrats, at first amazed and then panic-stricken, shrieked that the Jacobins were inaugurating a "Reign of Terror."

The Committee touched off the campaign with a resounding attack in the Senate upon West Point and the traitors who had come out of it to dominate and demoralize the armies—McClellan, Buell, Porter, Stone, and Franklin. The radical senators, with Wade and Chandler directing the assault, dissected the

[54] Stephen M. Allen, the investigator, to Benjamin F. Butler, May 26, 1890, in Jessie Ames Marshall, ed., *Private and Official Correspondence of General Benjamin F. Butler during the Period of the Civil War* (privately issued, Norwood, 1917), 2:595–598; C.C.W., 1863, 3:353–364.

war records of these products of the academy and ascribed their failures to the training received at West Point, which had made them either incompetent or treasonable, and in many cases both. Wade estimated that one half of the regular officers were disloyal, aristocratic, and inept, and charged that not all the traitors had joined the Confederacy in 1861. Jim Lane of Kansas shouted that the sympathy for slavery and the South nourished by the masters of the army "has shackled this Government, shackled the President, shackled the Cabinet, and has led us to the very verge of ruin." He suggested that if defeat came, "Died of West Point pro-slaveryism" would be an appropriate epitaph for the fallen nation. The Jacobins poured vials of equalitarian wrath upon the military monopoly exercised by West Point, and decried the value of its type of military education. Wade scornfully declared that the school might produce efficient engineers and drill sergeants, but "to make a commander to take charge of your Army in the field, it has not one single qualification." Striking the same note and getting in a boost for civilian generals like Frémont, Trumbull said the West Pointers thought only in terms of fortifications and defensive war. "If this rebellion is ever to be crushed . . . you must let loose the citizen soldiery of this country upon the rebels," he cried. "The regular Army will never do it. Take off your engineering restraints; dismiss . . . every man who knows how to build a fortification, and let the men of the North, with their strong arms and indomitable spirit, move down upon the rebels, and I tell you they will grind them to powder in their power."[55]

The spectacular thrust in the Senate against the Democratic military clique was only a prelude to more practical work. In mid-January the radical ax finally came down upon Fitz John Porter. Pope's wild accusations after Manassas promoted Stanton to arrest Porter and bring him to trial before a court-martial, which got under way in November.[56] The secretary

[55] Wade's speech, in the *Congressional Globe*, 37 Congress, 3 Session, 324, 325, 326, 327; Lane's, 328–329, 330; Trumbull's, 330.
[56] The proceedings of the court-martial are in *O. R.*, series 1, vol. 12, part 2, supplement, and in *House Executive Documents*, 37 Congress, 3 Session, vol. 7, no. 71.

packed the court to make sure of a conviction. David Hunter
was president. Other members were Hitchcock, sure to vote as
Stanton dictated; Rufus King, a political general, relieved of all
responsibility after his part in first Manassas, and a hanger-on
at the War Department; B. M. Prentiss, who had been taken
prisoner at the battle of Shiloh while sitting under a tree
because he forgot to put any pickets out; James B. Ricketts, a
personal enemy of Porter's; Silas Casey, removed from command by McClellan during the Peninsula campaign; N. B.
Buford, Pope's chief of cavalry; W. W. Morris, old, respectable,
and unalert; and Garfield, convinced of Porter's guilt before
the trial started and determined to convict him as a political
duty.[57] The prosecutor was Joe Holt, judge advocate general,
who later railroaded the innocent Mrs. Surrat to death on the
charge that she had helped plan the assassination of Lincoln.

All the participants in the trial and the Republican and
Democratic press acted as if the proceedings were a political
contest between McClellan and Pope instead of a judicial
inquiry. Greeley's Washington correspondent said there was no
doubt but what Porter should be shot, and added sweepingly,
"The shooting of half a dozen imbeciles or semi-traitors,
whose shoulders glisten with silver stars, would save streams
of precious plebeian blood." The Democrats, in a frenzy of
wrath, cried that Holt and Hunter were denying Porter a
fair hearing, and that the trial was only an underhanded
scheme to attack McClellan.[58] Porter was convicted and dismissed from the service. For many weary years after the war he
tried vainly to get another and a fair trial, but Chandler, still
in the Senate, blocked his efforts. Not until the administration
of Grover Cleveland was the decision reversed and Porter's
name finally cleared. It came too late to lift the bitterness
from a disillusioned elderly man whose services in the war
had been forgotten by a later generation.

[57] For Garfield's opinion, see Smith, *Garfield*, 1:258–259.
[58] *New York Tribune*, December 11, 1862, Washington correspondence;
Harper's Weekly, January 3, 1863; New York *World*, December 30, 1862;
Chicago Times, January 24, 1863; *New York Journal of Commerce*, quoted
in the *Detroit Free Press*, January 28, 30, 1863; *New York Express*, quoted
ibid., January 28.

While Porter's trial was in its last stages, another McClellan favorite was going through the wringer. Buell, after his removal, asked Stanton for a court of inquiry to determine the truth of the charges that he had been inefficient, and the reasons for his dismissal. The radicals had a healthy fear of Buell's gifts for intrigue and his influence among the Democratic officers in the Western army. They thought he was organizing a plot to destroy Rosecrans and get himself restored to command, and that he wanted a hearing in order to place his case before the country.[59] Buell's return to power they were determined to prevent at any hazard. Stanton refused the general's request, but granted him a "military commission," which turned out to be a court-martial under another name. There were no official, only implied, charges against Buell, but there was a prosecutor, Donn Piatt, who by his questions, the witnesses he introduced, and his report, managed to smear the general's record effectively and to cast doubts upon his loyalty. The Jacobins were eminently satisfied with Piatt's work, and confident that the number-two McClellan general would never see service again.[60]

Still a third military court was at work during January, and its victim was the one-time radical favorite McDowell. The Committee precipitated the attack upon McDowell. In the previous summer reports had appeared in the press that the general, in command of the Department of the Rappahannock, had become a convert to the rose-water policy of treating civilian rebels with lavish kindness. On June 14 the *Tribune* published a letter from a private soldier, accusing McDowell of posting guards around the homes of disloyal slaveholders and providing better food and lodgings for Southern prisoners than for his own men.[61] This communication set off a tre-

[59] General J. M. Palmer to Lyman Trumbull, January 11, 1863, in the Trumbull MSS.
[60] For the proceedings of the Buell inquiry, see *O. R.*, series 1, vol. 16, part 1, especially pages 12–21, for Piatt's report. See also Donn Piatt to Joseph Holt, March 28, April 3, 1863, in the Holt MSS. For newspaper comment on the hearing, see the New York *World*, January 19, 1863; *Detroit Free Press*, January 28.
[61] *New York Tribune*, June 14, 1862, p. 1; *C.C.W.*, 1863, 3:442

mendous uproar among the Jacobins, who were astonished and
angered by such strange conduct from a general supposedly
a pillar of radicalism. Henry Wilson got a resolution through
the Senate instructing the Committee to determine the truth
of the charges. The inquisitors summoned a number of witnesses from among McDowell's subordinate officers, one of
whom was the radical General Abner Doubleday, the inventor
of baseball, who hoped to advance his career through the
Committee's aid and hence tried desperately to hang a third
strike on McDowell. Doubleday said, "The soldiers complain
that while they are doing their duty of guarding secession
houses and property the secession women insult them, drawing up their skirts as they pass them."[62]

Wade became convinced that McDowell was an apostate and
a convert to McClellanism. Using the material gathered during
the investigation, he made a bitter attack upon McDowell in
the Senate, reading one of the general's orders for a guard
around the home of a rebel, "to show the principle upon
which this accursed war is prosecuted."[63] The Committee's
inquiry and Wade's diatribe were well publicized in the press,
and McDowell's soldiers read and thought about the affair
with a growing distrust of their commander. Soon McDowell
found his position becoming unbearable. When it was rumored
that a colonel, mortally wounded in battle, wrote a note to Lincoln as he was dying, charging that he was a victim of "McDowell's treachery," the general could stand it no longer. He asked
the president for a court of inquiry.[64] He also sent a letter to
the press requesting that brother officers aid him to disprove
the Committee's accusations. One Colonel R. D. Goodwin
replied, through the press, demanding to know if McDowell
was drunk when he composed his letter: "I cannot say you were
then under the influence of liquor, as I have seen you at other

[62] *New York Tribune*, June 20, 28, 1862, Washington correspondence;
C.C.W., 1863, 3:421–449, "Protecting Rebel Property," especially pages 430–
434 for Doubleday's testimony, 442–449, for McDowell's.

[63] *Congressional Globe*, 37 Congress, 2 Session, 2930–2931.

[64] *O. R.*, series 1, vol. 12, part 2, pp. 39–40, from the proceedings of
the McDowell court of inquiry.

times, both in the field and out, but that you are one of those brazen-faced Christians who bid defiance to truth I have not the least doubt. . . . If a drunken man is incapable of holding office I am satisfied you are, for I have seen the proofs at Fairfax Court-House and in Washington." At the last the court solemnly agreed to consider the business of McDowell's drunkenness.[65]

McDowell's hearing degenerated into a trial of McClellan and a rehashing of the Peninsula campaign. McDowell was asked to explain the famous episode of the detached corps, and McClellan himself appeared as a witness. Although it had no bearing on McDowell's case, Lincoln's letter berating McClellan for leaving Washington defenseless was introduced into the record, supposedly at the insistence of the Committee. While McClellan was on the stand the inquisitors talked freely to the reporters, asserting that the general's account of the campaign was false and they would prove it in due time.[66]

Radical rejoicing over the success of the drive to purify the army knew no bounds. Porter was disgraced, Buell killed off, and McDowell disciplined. Late in January Stanton relieved Franklin of his command in the Potomac army and relegated him to an obscure post in the West. It was rumored that Stanton and the Committee were determined to drive all conservative generals from the service and that eighty officers were to be dismissed because they had condemned the removal of McClellan. The elated radicals believed that the New Jerusalem was at last in sight.[67] The Democrats were frantic with rage as they saw the military patronage slipping out of their hands. "The edict has gone forth," cried one editor. "Let every friend of McClellan prepare for the guillotine."[68]

But in the raptures of their jubilation, the radicals felt the

[65] *Ibid.*, 44–45.

[66] *Ibid.*, 91–96, 98–101, 230–231; *New York Tribune*, December 13, 1862, Washington correspondence; *Detroit Free Press*, January 20, 1863; *New York Herald*, February 25, 1863.

[67] *New York Tribune*, January 26, 27, 1863; *New York Journal of Commerce*, quoted in the *Detroit Free Press*, January 29.

[68] *Detroit Free Press*, January 24, 1863. See also *ibid.*, January 28; *New York World*, January 19; *New York Herald*, January 19.

chill of impending danger. Burnside's beaten army at Falmouth was demoralized and in a state of near mutiny, with thousands of men missing from the muster rolls. The despair of Fredericksburg still gripped the masses, and the sentiment for peace was strong. And George B. McClellan was touring the East, speaking to applauding throngs, and posing as a victim of Jacobin malice. The Democrats were booming him for the presidency. The situation called for aggressive Republican propaganda. Here too the Committee and Stanton were to do the work.

9

Propaganda:
Molding the Northern Mind and
Firing the Northern Heart

PROPAGANDA WAS one of the principal weapons employed by the Jacobin machine in its drive to impress the radical program upon the administration and the nation, and the Committee and Stanton acted as the chief agencies for its dissemination. But there were other opinion-molding groups working for the Republican cause, some of them devoted exclusively to the furtherance of radicalism and some to the general success and well-being of the Lincoln administration. No official government agency to spread propaganda existed during the war, but the job of shaping the Northern mind in a correct pattern was performed in satisfactory fashion by the many voluntary private or semiprivate organizations which sprang into being for the purpose. The Loyal League and the Loyal Publication Society, frank propaganda organs sponsored by rich, sleek Eastern business men, plastered the entire country with pamphlets. The United States Sanitary Commission enlarged its functions to produce a lurid report describing the barbarisms practiced upon Union prisoners by inhuman Confederate officials.[1]

The Jacobin leaders were sharply conscious of both the techniques and the profits of an incessant, vigorous propaganda. John M. Forbes, the New England industrialist who helped found the Loyal Publication Society, told William Cullen Bryant that the radicals could force the administration to adopt an antislavery policy only by stirring up public opin-

[1] Frank Freidel, "The Loyal Publication Society: a Pro-Union Propaganda Agency," *Mississippi Valley Historical Review*, 26(1939):359–376; Randall, *Civil War and Reconstruction*, 635–636; W. B. Hesseltine, "The Propaganda Literature of Confederate Prisons," *The Journal of Southern History*, 1(1935):62–63.

ion to support their demands upon Lincoln. "Governments are always timid about new measures without precedents," advised Forbes. "Let the press and the people speak, and government must follow." Another assiduous opinion-creator was Horace Greeley, who published in pamphlet form the speeches of the radical leaders and the Committee's reports, under the series title "The *Tribune* War Tracts." Wade became a sponsor of still a second project, formed early in the war, to supply Republican pamphlets to the voters, "The Southern Rebellion and the War for the Union."[2]

Most of the multitudinous Republican propaganda ventures were conceived in the minds of the groups or individuals who produced them, and were carried forward with no direction from a central authority and no attempt to correlate them with the efforts of other similar agencies. The one government official who tried to inspire and unify this Babel of enterprise and enthusiasm was the adept politician at the head of the War Department, himself a master of the art of manipulating public opinion. Stanton watched closely the exertions of all the voluntary propagandists, big and small, and graciously commended them for work well done. He cried on organizations like the Sanitary Commission and the Committee to investigate reports of atrocities committed by the Confederates. He wrote letters to the newspapers attacking the enemies of radicalism. An illustration of his technique is furnished in his communication to the *Tribune* in February, 1862, ostensibly to praise Grant for victories in Tennessee but actually to assail McClellan's concepts of strategy. Not only did he manage to smear McClellan with clever innuendo, but his fulsome compliments to the Lord for coming to Grant's aid evoked the applause of one of the most audible classes in the nation, the clergy. One

[2] Hughes, *Forbes*, 1:220; also 324–327; *New York Tribune*, September 1, 1861; W. C. Flagg to Lyman Trumbull, July 11, 1862, in the Trumbull MSS.; *New York Herald*, April 9, 1863. For an example of a *Tribune* Tract, see the *Report of the Congressional Committee on the Operations of the Army of the Potomac* (New York, 1863), a summary of the Committee's report on the army under McClellan. For Wade's work, see the Washington *National Intelligencer*, October 21, 1861.

gratified minister assured the secretary that the letter had awakened "a ready response from the thousands of God-fearing, patriotic clergymen in our glorious republic."[3] Stanton's frequent epistles to the newspapers, sometimes in the form of official departmental bulletins, always received front page play-up, to the fury of the Democrats, who accused him of running a propaganda machine when he should be supervising military operations.[4]

Stanton appreciated to the full the vast importance of the press as a medium for shaping mass opinion. To secure a favorable presentation of the radical program in the country's journals became his most absorbing interest and at the same time his most distressing problem. He fought under a tremendous handicap, for the Democrats controlled the Associated Press, the largest news-gathering agency in the North, which served nearly all the metropolitan newspapers. Stanton got a taste of the power of this organization soon after he took over the war office, when he made a speech before a railroad convention in Washington. He was enraged to find his remarks distorted by the Press into a eulogy of McClellan. "The fact is," he wrote to Dana, "that the agents of the associated press, and a gang around the Federal capital, appear to be organized for the purpose of magnifying their idol." The Press remained hostile to Stanton all during the war, and he abandoned any hope of being able to control it.[5] Instead he concentrated upon influencing the smaller papers, the country weeklies, and founding new organs to which he furnished financial assistance. When A. K. McClure assumed the editorship of a Pennsylvania journal the secretary agreed to supply him with "such patron-

[3] E. C. Townsend to Edwin M. Stanton, February 21, 1862, in the Stanton MSS.; *New York Tribune*, February 20, 1862; *Harper's Weekly*, March 8; Gorham, *Stanton*, 1:285–286.

[4] Hugh Campbell to Joseph Holt, May 6, 1862, in the Holt MSS.

[5] Edwin M. Stanton to Charles A. Dana, February 23, 1862, in the Dana MSS. See also Horatio Woodman to Stanton, April 27, 1865, in the Stanton MSS.; *Wilkes' Spirit of the Times*, April 9, 16, 1864. Woodman, in his letter, said the country was astonished to learn that Fitz John Porter had been found guilty by the court-martial, because during the trial the Press sent out only news favorable to his case.

age . . . as the service will admit." He threw the advertising
of the department to papers which followed the radical line.[6]
In 1864 a group of Kentucky Jacobins tried to establish a radical journal in Louisville. But the Press, supposedly at the
insistence of the Democratic politicians, refused to sell the new
sheet its services. The sponsors were ready to give up when
Stanton came to their rescue and offered, as one of the founders
wrote to Holt, to "furnish dispatches . . . that would make
ample amends for the refusal of the Associated Press." But as
always where he provided his support, the secretary insisted
upon dictating the paper's editorial policy. It must "zealously
advocate the immediate emancipation of slaves and the organization of colored troops." He fostered his Louisville enterprise
carefully, even ordering the quartermaster general in the city
to take up a financial collection for its support.[7]

Stanton employed or directed a host of agents who wrote
articles for the newspapers and wheedled editors into publishing radical propaganda. Some of these men were War
Department jobholders who added the function of propagandist to their regular duties, while others were voluntary
enthusiasts who wanted to gain the secretary's favor. One of the
latter was Horatio Woodman of Boston. During the Peninsula
campaign he wrote a series of articles for the press defending
Stanton from the charges being hurled by the Democrats that
the radicals had deliberately mutilated McClellan's army. He
informed the secretary of his service, and Stanton thanked
him effusively. The two kept up a cordial relationship for the
rest of the war, and Woodman continued to fight Stanton's
battles in the newspapers. Another henchman was John Hamilton, active in the Loyal Publication Society. Hamilton labored
to get material of the right nature inserted in the New York

[6] Edwin M. Stanton to A. K. McClure, July 22, 1863, in the Letterbooks
of Edwin M. Stanton, MS. in the Library of Congress, vol. 2; Stanton to
Benjamin F. Loan, of the Committee, February 22, 1864, in the Stanton
MSS.
[7] T. S. Bell to Joseph Holt, January 18, 1864, *ibid.*; Stanton to Joshua
Speed, February 18, 1864, in the Stanton Letterbooks, vol. 3, part 1;
General Robert Allen to Stanton, September 25, 1864, in the Stanton MSS.

papers, but he had a keen knowledge of the value of other media of dissemination as well. In the election of 1864 Joseph Holt published a report describing the activities of the secret Democratic peace societies, hinting broadly that they and McClellan were planning treason. Hamilton immediately saw the potency of the report as a campaign document, and concluded that the best way to publicize it was through the churches. "I yesterday saw the great leader of the Methodist church," he informed Holt. "At my instance he will advise an abstract of it being read throughout the churches of that sect. I propose to make an effort on the Presbyn. church, but with doubts of my success."[8] Hamilton and other operatives of Stanton demonstrated their effectiveness in 1865 when General William T. Sherman became involved in a bitter controversy with the secretary over the too lenient terms of surrender which, Stanton charged, the general had granted to a Confederate army. Stanton wanted to smear Sherman and destroy his reputation, and the success of his plot depended upon his ability to distort the general's actions and motives in the press accounts of the affair. The secretary handed out false stories to the newspapers, holding back information which would have cleared Sherman of the accusation of letting the Confederates off too easily. His agents sprang into ant-like activity, dashing off letters to the press and cajoling editors to attack Sherman. One wrote from Philadelphia that he had got an editorial from the *New York Times* inserted in the Philadelphia journals, and would have it republished "in some of our Pennsylvania interior papers." Hamilton, running the campaign in New York, suggested an ingenious scheme to win the powerful support of Bennett's *Herald*. This was judiciously to edit the correspondence between Sherman and the Confederate General Joseph E. Johnston concerning the terms of surrender. "If this be done then it seems to me it might be expedient to have the matter published in one sheet of the N. Y. Herald—with a hint or two," Hamilton told Stanton.

[8] Horatio Woodman to Stanton, June 2, 28, 1862, April 27, 1865, *ibid.;* John Hamilton to Joseph Holt, October 16, 1864, in the Holt MSS.

"This probably would secure the Herald on this subject with the Govt. J. Bennet [sic] is not accessible to money but he is to be won by the exhibition of official notice."[9]

Pamphlet writers formed an essential part of Stanton's propaganda machine. He knew the efficacy of this medium of dissemination in an America which read avidly all the political documents franked out of Washington. With great effectiveness he employed officers, as military experts, to compose pamphlets attacking McClellan. One of the most assiduous of these was General Barnard, once McClellan's chief of engineers but a bitter enemy of the Young Napoleon. Stanton used Barnard and his knowledge of the Peninsula campaign to write down McClellan in the election of 1864. Barnard prepared a report which appeared first in the press in installments and later as a pamphlet. The secretary supervised Barnard's work closely, reprimanding him frequently for failing to put McClellan in the worst light and the administration in the best. He even criticized the general's style: "Very unfortunately expressed," was his snappish verdict on one article. Another officer who placed his talents at Stanton's disposal in 1864 was the ancient General John Wool. The secretary asked Wool to write something which would establish McClellan as a gross incompetent, and the willing general replied that he was readying a document "on the subject of Major General McClellan's campaign on the Peninsula, which I think will place his generalship in its true light."[10]

Of all the Republican agencies engaged in the work of molding the Northern mind, the Committee was the most authoritative and successful. Possessed of unrivalled facilities for investigation and the immense prestige of a joint committee of Congress, it turned out the most expert propaganda productions of the war period. It also had the closest tie-up with

[9] F. E. Hayes to Stanton, April 29, 1865, in the Stanton MSS.; John Hamilton to Stanton, May 26, 1865, also May 29, *ibid.*

[10] John G. Barnard, *The Peninsula Campaign and its Antecedents* (New York, 1864); Stanton to Barnard, January 22, 1863, and Barnard to Stanton, January 22, 24, in the Stanton MSS.; John Wool to Stanton, October 29, 1864, *ibid.*

Stanton. The Committee's first adventure in propaganda occurred in the spring of 1863 when it published the reports
of its investigations in three stout volumes of vivid description
and testimony. The reports covered the entire field of the
Committee's far-flung inquiries: the Army of the Potomac,
Ball's Bluff, Frémont, and a host of minor episodes. But it was
the section dealing with McClellan's administration which
attracted the exclusive attention of the public and the press.
Indeed the members prepared the report largely for McClellan's undoing. The entire first volume was devoted to his
evil deeds, and the reports were issued for the express purpose of slaughtering his popularity with the masses and the
army and scotching the plans of the Democratic bosses to make
him president. The McClellan boom and the confident designs of the Democrats burgeoned brilliantly in the black
despair which settled upon the country after Fredericksburg.
The Committee essayed the task of changing the soil which
nourished the promising McClellan growth and applying a
killing frost to the plant itself.

Fredericksburg almost convinced the weary Northern masses
that the Confederacy could never be conquered. Burnside had
failed as McClellan and Pope and all the others had. The
long roll of dead and wounded who fell before the stone walls
brought the horrors of war home to the people with dis-
illusioning reality.[11] So staunch a Republican as Joseph
Medill was ready to concede defeat. "The feeling of utter
hopelessness is stronger than at any time since the war began,"
he confessed. "The terrible bloody defeat of our brave army
. . . leaves us almost without hope. . . . Sometimes I think
nothing is left now but 'to fight for a boundary.'" The defeatist psychology of the public portended the death of the
Republican Party. If the people repudiated the war, they
would also repudiate the party which had lost it. "Victory
alone can help us," wrote one discouraged observer. But

[11] *New York Tribune,* December 26, 1862; *Lusk Letters,* 252–253; Hughes,
Forbes, 1:342–344; James A. Garfield to Mrs. Garfield, December 19, 1862,
in Smith, *Garfield,* 1:264; William Scott to John Sherman, December 18,
in the Sherman MSS.

victory gave no sign of coming to the rescue. The weeks went by, and Burnside's cowed army continued to squat at Falmouth. In desperation the Republicans began to get up public meetings where orators tried to blow the flickering war spirit back to life.[12]

The Army of the Potomac was a seething mass of discontent and demoralization. The massacre at Fredericksburg, the culmination of a long line of failures and disasters, undermined their confidence in the generals and the government, and dulled their faith in the sanctity of the cause for which they fought. "I am sick and tired of disaster, and the fools that bring disaster upon us," a disillusioned captain wrote to his family. The correspondent of an abolitionist newspaper reported: "The men are to an alarming extent discouraged, and anxious to go home. They are stupefied by continual reverses."[13] Many asked for leave and others simply drifted away from camp without permission. Eighty thousand were missing from the muster rolls, one half of them "improperly absent."[14] One of the division officers later told the Committee: "Desertions were very numerous; the general tone of conversation in the camps was that of dissatisfaction and complaint." An agent sent down to Falmouth by the Connecticut legislature to look after the dead and wounded in the state's regiments reported in his home town newspaper: "You have no idea of the depression there is in the army at the result of the third attempt to go to Richmond."[15]

The beaten, discouraged soldiers were wildly bitter toward

[12] Joseph Medill to Schuyler Colfax, December, 1862, in Hollister, *Colfax*, 203, no date given; Richard Henry Dana to John Lothrop Motley, February 23, 1863, in Adams, *Dana*, 2:270–271; "Excerpts from the Journal of Henry J. Raymond," *Scribner's Monthly*, 19(1880):708.

[13] Captain W. T. Lusk to his family, December 22, 1862, in *Lusk Letters*, 254–257; *National Anti-Slavery Standard*, January 17, 1863, Washington correspondence.

[14] Statement of General Daniel Butterfield to the Committee, March 28, 1863, in *C.C.W.*, 1865, 1:73.

[15] *Ibid.*, 3, testimony of General Daniel Sickles; letter of L. W. Coe, December 21, 1862, in the *Waterbury American*, quoted in the *Detroit Free Press*, January 1, 1863. See also Villard, *Memoirs*, 1:375–376; *New York Tribune*, January 19, 1863, army correspondence; Thomas Worthington to John Sherman, January 19, 1863, in the Sherman MSS.

Burnside. They believed he had led them to a slaughter at Fredericksburg at the orders of the politicians, who wanted a battle fought. Ominous mutterings that they would refuse to fight another engagement under his leadership came out of the campfire discussions. The Committee's visit to Burnside's headquarters hardened the conviction of the men. Rumors scudded through the ranks that the commander had confessed to the inquisitors that he was incompetent and that Fredericksburg had been a terrible blunder. The soldiers felt only contempt for a general who swore to his own weakness. At a review soon after this, they booed Burnside.[16]

The angry growlings of the soldiers generated feelings of near-panic among administration officials and the radical chieftains. The latter feared that the army would simply disintegrate, and the war would have to end with a humiliating peace. "Our army here is almost ruined, and melting away rapidly," lamented Fessenden. Cutler doubted whether it could fight effectively "even with a good general." A stampeding terror swept the war office that the army, holding the administration responsible for Fredericksburg, was about to revolt and perhaps declare for McClellan. The *New York Times* reported that the government was considering a plan to break up the Potomac army and scatter it in widely separated units through the loyal Western armies. "The Army of the Potomac has ceased to exist," Halleck is said to have exclaimed. The *Times* correspondent, who had talked with the soldiers at Falmouth, was disposed to agree with him. "They feel that things are at loose ends—in fact they know it, for our army is one that reads and thinks," he wrote. ". . . Certainly never were a graver, gloomier, more sober, sombre, serious and unmusical body of men than the Army of the Potomac at the present time."[17]

[16] Cochrane, *War for the Union,* 44–48; John R. Adams, a chaplain with the army, to Mrs. Adams, January 1, 1863, in *Memorial and Letters of Reverend John R. Adams* (privately printed, Cambridge, 1890), 89–90; Adams to Mrs. Adams, January 31, *ibid.,* 98–99; Francis Walker, *History of the Second Army Corps* (New York, 1886), 198.

[17] Fessenden, *Fessenden,* 1:266; Charles Sumner to Francis Lieber, Janu-

Much of the fluttery uneasiness of the Republican leaders arose from their knowledge that the sullen resentment of the soldiers might force Lincoln to restore McClellan to command. Immediately after Fredericksburg the Democratic press had started to yell for the return of the great organizer who could rejuvenate the demoralized army. Soon a flood of letters began to appear in the Democratic newspapers, supposedly written by soldiers and officers in the Potomac army to their home town editors. They called for the restoration of "little Mac," blamed the administration for Burnside's defeat, and expressed opposition to the emancipation proclamation. The Republicans accused Democratic journalists of concocting these productions in an attempt to scare the country into thinking the army would not fight unless McClellan were its leader. Greeley quoted a letter alleged to have come from a New York chaplain, charging the Republican politicians with having sabotaged McClellan in the Peninsula and slaughtered the army at Fredericksburg. Indignantly Greeley exclaimed: "All this is well known here to be false—wickedly, atrociously false. Yet the journals which originated and reiterated it do not retract it. They send it flying through the camps of the Grand Army on the heels of a sad repulse, and it is still at work there . . . , causing all manner of discouragement, demoralization, and disaffection."[18]

It is quite probable that some of the letters were ghostwritten in Democratic editorial rooms. But it seems certain that the great majority were genuine articles. The American soldier of the Civil War retained the sturdy critical faculties of a voter even after he got his uniform on, and writing a letter to the "Public Pulse" of his local paper to lambaste his commander was as natural to him as writing one in peacetime to accuse the county clerk of being a crook.[19] Whoever the

---

ary 17, 1863, in Pierce, *Sumner*, 4:114; Cutler diary, January 26, 1863, in J. P. Cutler, *Life of the Cutlers*, 300; entry of January 22 in Welles, *Diary*, 1:226; *New York Times*, January 16, 1863.

[18] *New York Herald*, January 10, 1863; *Washington Republican*, quoted in the *Detroit Free Press*, January 15; *New York Tribune*, January 8, 1863.

[19] Evidence that the soldiers really wanted McClellan is furnished in

authors, the tone and plentitude of the letters frightened the Jacobins. A New York officer declared: "A large number of the rank and file, I think it would almost be safe to say a majority, express their belief in our inability to conquer the South from the cross purposes of our different military and political leaders and their failure to act in concert."[20] From a Rhode Island private came the statement, "The whole army is sick of this miserably managed war." He added that the soldiers would follow no one but McClellan, but they knew "somebody at Washington wanted to crush him." Another Rhode Islander revealed the appearance of a dangerous cynicism among the soldiers about the justice of the Union cause and the glories of dying for it. Fredericksburg, he said, had caused the soldiers to "lose much of that patriotic ardor which led us to sacrifice our home comforts for the sake of our 'poor, bleeding country.' "[21]

Many of the letters were from officers who claimed to have been Republicans but who were now bolting the party because they could not stomach the emancipation proclamation and the mismanagement of the war. Among the private soldiers the new emancipation policy excited disgust and opposition.[22] Henry Raymond picked up a story that the New Jersey regiments in Burnside's army had declared that they would not fight in an antislavery war because their state had just elected a Peace Democrat to the Senate, thereby demonstrating its opposition to the administration program. Hooker later furnished the Committee with an accurate picture of the army's dangerous state of mind: "At that time perhaps a majority of the officers, especially those high in rank, were hostile to the policy of the government in the conduct of the war. The emancipation proclamation had been published a

a letter of John R. Adams to Mrs. Adams, January 1, 1863, in *J. R. Adams Letters*, 89.

[20] Buffalo *Courier*, quoted in the *Detroit Free Press*, January 16, 1863.

[21] Letters from the *Providence Post*, quoted *ibid.*, January 22, 1863.

[22] Letters from the *Concord Patriot* and the *Hartford Times*, quoted *ibid.*, January 29, 1863; *Indianapolis Journal*, quoted *ibid.*, January 31, 1863.

short time before, and a large element of the army had taken
sides antagonistic to it, declaring that they would never have
embarked in the war had they anticipated this action of the
government."[23]

The Jacobins realized that the pulsing restlessness of the
army might burst at any moment into a storm that would
shatter the administration. They knew that demoralization
stalked the campfires, but they believed the Democratic press
was inspiring and magnifying the angry mutterings and the
threats to fight for no general but McClellan. They also knew
the cause of the genuine dissatisfaction that existed—the army
was reading the wrong propaganda in the form of Democratic
newspapers and hence thinking the wrong politics. Republican officers complained that their men saw only the organ of
the Peace Democracy, filled with virulent attacks upon the
administration and sly talk about the hopelessness of winning
the war. A warning about the effects of the Democratic propaganda came to John Sherman from a correspondent who had
a son in the army: "There are some things that must be done
at the north. The class of papers to which the Cin[cinnati]. Enquirer, and Chicago Times, belong must be suppressed, or, at
least, not allowed to come and circulate within army lines.
They have exercised, and are exercising, a very depressing influence upon our men—causing many desertions; and much
discontent. . . . Another evil growing out of this matter is—
writing to the men advising them that they should not support
the Proclamation; and enclosing printed extracts from all the
treasonable newspapers at the north bearing upon this
point."[24]

[23] "Excerpts from the Journal of Henry Raymond," *Scribner's Monthly*,
19(1880):421; *C.C.W.*, 1865, 1:112.

[24] *New York Tribune*, January 23, 1863, army correspondence; "Excerpts
from the Journal of Henry Raymond," *Scribner's Monthly*, 19(1880):420,
quoting General Wadsworth; Lucius Fairchild to Mrs. Fairchild, January
30, 1863, in the Lucius Fairchild MSS. in the Library of the State Historical
Society of Wisconsin; Colonel Hans C. Heg to Mrs. Heg, February 16, 1863,
in Theodore C. Blegen, ed., *The Civil War Letters of Colonel Hans Christian Heg* (Northfield, 1936), 189–190; J. L. Miner to John Sherman, February 7, 1863, in the Sherman MSS.

The caucus of House Republicans which met on January 20 to discuss ways of getting the Cabinet reformed also considered the alarming condition of the army and the influence of Democratic propaganda upon it. "It was asserted that the Army of the Potomac had been drilled into an anti-Republican engine . . . ; that large numbers of the Herald and the World were circulated gratuitously among the soldiers, while other papers were practically excluded," wrote Cutler in his diary. A committee was appointed to report a plan for barring the Democratic journals from the army. Later the committee proposed that Congress adopt articles of war empowering the government to suppress the circulation of papers that created disaffection in the armed forces, to punish the proprietors and sell their presses.[25] The administration, without waiting for congressional authorization, acted on the problem early in February. It announced that henceforth newspapers with objectionable editorial policies could not be sent to the army. The New York *World,* which had as much to do with causing the new policy as anyone, cried indignantly, "The administration hopes by this means to prevent a knowledge of the growing discontent from reaching the soldiers, for fear it would affect their morale."[26]

The growing discontent which the *World* exulted over was born of the defeatist psychology and the war-weariness that seemed to dominate the masses. The demand for peace swelled mightily in the months of inactivity after Fredericksburg. "The people are bewildered and in a fog," Cutler observed gloomily. The clever reporter "The Lounger," who wrote a gossip column for *Harper's,* declared: "The purpose of the nation is relaxed. It is no longer resolved, as it was eighteen months ago, to subdue the rebellion at all costs." He added an ominous note: "There is a large party at the North which hates another Northern party more than it does the rebels."[27] This

[25] Diary of W. P. Cutler, entry of January 21, 1863, in J. P. Cutler, *Life of the Cutlers,* 298; *ibid,* 301, 303.

[26] New York *World,* February 16, 1863; *Detroit Free Press,* February 16.

[27] Cutler's diary, February 2, 1863, in *Life of the Cutlers,* 302. See also the entries on pages 297, 300; *Harper's Weekly,* January 31, 1863, "The Lounger."

was the Peace Democracy, the "Copperheads," that wing of the party which had refused to enter Lincoln's coalition and whose leaders believed the Union should be restored by negotiation and on Southern terms. In the popular despondency after Fredericksburg their cause was sprouting vigorously. Democratic peace clubs mushroomed all over the North. Governor Morton of Indiana informed Stanton that these societies were scheming to take the Northwest out of the Union if the war continued; they had obtained a strong foothold in the military camps at Indianapolis. In Illinois the lower house of the legislature, under Democratic control, passed a resolution demanding a cessation of hostilities and an armistice. Everywhere the peace sentiment, organized by the Democrats, was welling up to the surface. The Republicans were dismayed. "The leaders of the Democratic Party are fast swinging that powerful organization into an attitude of serious hostility to the war and the Government," Medill cried. "The public discontent waxes greater daily." Lincoln, always an unerring judge of shifts in public opinion, told Sumner his greatest fear was not of military failure, but of "the fire in the rear."[28]

While the Republicans shivered before the rising blast of popular disapproval of the war, the Democratic bosses started to boom McClellan for the presidency in 1864. In January the general embarked on what was supposed to be a pleasure tour of the New England states. His procession through the Eastern cities, however, suspiciously resembled a political expedition by a receptive candidate, and he showed more interest in making stump speeches than in viewing the beauties of the countryside. The Democratic press painted his journey as a series of triumphal conquests and wildly enthusiastic receptions. Everywhere the tone of his remarks was definitely conservative and partisan. At Boston he was entertained at the

[28] Oliver P. Morton to Edwin M. Stanton, January 2, 1863, in Rhodes, *History of the United States*, 4:223, footnote; *New York Tribune*, January 10; A. S. Brewer to John Sherman, December 22, 1862, in the Sherman MSS.; *Chicago Tribune*, January 14, 1863; Joseph Medill to Schuyler Colfax, in Hollister, *Colfax*, 203; Charles Sumner to Francis Lieber, January 17, 1863, in Pierce, *Sumner*, 4:114.

home of Edward Everett, and Andrew and the other state officials were pointedly ignored in the ceremonies of welcome. Portland wanted the general as its guest. He declined graciously, and spoke of the growing conservatism in New England as a hopeful sign for the future. The Democratic majority in the New York legislature invited him to visit Albany, and passed resolutions commending his record as commander of the Army of the Potomac. The city corporation of Albany joined its voice to the legislature's request. The gleeful Democrats asserted that he would carry every Eastern state in 1864.[29] Angered and frightened by these surprising manifestations of McClellan's popularity, the radicals retaliated by howling that the general was an embittered man who had permitted himself to be made the tool of Democratic politicians.[30]

Fear and dismay clutched at the Jacobins in that tense month of January when the army seethed with talk of mutiny, the peace sentiment swelled daily in volume, and McClellan made his bid for the presidency. They knew that only a vigorous counteroffensive could save the Republican cause. Their weapon must be propaganda, powerful, vivid propaganda that would restore the army's morale, inspire the masses, and demolish McClellan. Obviously the agency with the prestige and material to deliver this thrust was the Committee. The problem of destroying the Young Napoleon was peculiarly of a military nature. His political appeal rested upon the claim that he was a high-minded officer and a military genius who had been prevented by partisan machinations from winning the war. If the radicals could show him up as an incompetent and a sham, they would remove his chief talking point, and at the same time prove that he was unfit to hold the office of president. But such a judgment must come from a body whose opinions on military matters the country respected. Who so completely met this criterion as the great Committee which Congress in its wisdom had set up to aid the president

[29] New York Herald, January 27, February 12, 1863; New York World, January 29; Boston Post, January 31, February 3; Detroit Free Press, February 4, 7; New York Express, February 20; Pierce, Sumner, 4:113–114.
[30] St. Louis Missouri Democrat, February 6, 1863.

in the conduct of the war? The radical bosses told the inquisitors to go to work.

The Committee, which had dropped the investigation of the Army of the Potomac in the previous July, suddenly resumed its inquiry in late January. Chandler boasted that they were preparing a report which would kill McClellan as dead as a herring.[31] Wade summoned Hitchcock, Heintzelman, Sumner, and Barnard to appear as witnesses. Together the inquisitors and these ancient enemies of McClellan raked up the failures of the Peninsula campaign. They rehashed the defects of McClellan's plan to attack Richmond from the east; his refusal to obey Lincoln's orders to leave Washington properly defended; the slow march up the Peninsula and the strangely neglected opportunities to seize the rebel capital; the escape of Lee after Antietam. McClellan himself testified on February 28, and underwent a thorough grilling.[32] Describing his reception to his wife, the harassed general wrote: "I went before the Committee today. They were very polite, and gave me something to do which will occupy me for a couple of days at least. . . . I have many—very many—bitter enemies here—they are making their last grand attack—I *must* and *will* defeat them. . . . I am in a battle and must fight it out."[33] The members were just starting to work on McClellan. They called him again on March 2 and subjected him to a rough and searching cross-examination. Gooch badgered him with tricky questions which were really accusations: "Immediately after the battle of Fair Oaks, could you not have advanced on Richmond?" The squirming general asked permission to read a prepared statement, but Wade said with sardonic relish that the Committee desired specific answers to specific questions.[34]

[31] Zachariah Chandler to Mrs. Chandler, January 22, 1863, in the Chandler MSS.

[32] *C.C.W.*, 1863, 1:302–305, Hitchcock's testimony; 346–359, Heintzelman's; 363–369, Sumner's; 389–393, Barnard's; 419–431, McClellan's.

[33] George B. McClellan to Mrs. McClellan, February 26, 1863, in William Starr Myers, *A Study in Personality: George Brinton McClellan* (New York, 1934), 407.

[34] *C.C.W.*, 1863, 1:431–441.

Wade ran the investigation through into March. The parade of witnesses hostile to McClellan continued—Casey, Halleck, Governor Sprague, Hooker, and Keyes. Only a handful appeared to speak for McClellan, and of these Franklin alone possessed any prominence.[35] Hooker, who had but recently succeeded to the command of the Army of the Potomac with radical backing, gave the members exactly what they wanted. Asked to ascribe a reason for the collapse of the Peninsula campaign, he replied flatly, "I do not hesitate to say that it is to be attributed to the want of generalship on the part of our commander." With that profound self-admiration which colored all his pronouncements, Hooker assailed McClellan for besieging Yorktown and observed grandly, "I would have marched right through the redoubts" and into Richmond in two days. He neglected to explain how he would have marched fifty miles in forty-eight hours against Lee's army.[36]

As the Committee drilled its witnesses week after week, titillating rumors of what was going on in the secret hearings seeped out to the press. It was announced late in February that the Committee would issue a report in a few days, and that the revelations in the document would electrify the country and blast not a few reputations. "In reporting it to the Senate, Mr. Wade will call attention to some of the most important points," said one correspondent. "The campaigns before Washington, on the Peninsula and in Maryland, are ventilated fully. It will make the most important record of the war, and it is said that attempts are already making to suppress its publication."[37]

These tantalizing hints redoubled in number in March, crowding other news out of the columns of the capital correspondents. The *Tribune* exultantly claimed that the forthcoming report would demolish McClellan completely, and destroy the plans of the Democrats to get him restored to the

---

[35] See *ibid.*, 441–447, for Casey's testimony; 452–454, for Halleck's; 565–569, for Sprague's; 575–589, for Hooker's; 602–614, for Keyes'; 621–628, for Franklin's.

[36] *Ibid.*, 575–578.

[37] *Philadelphia Inquirer,* February 20, 1863; *New York Times,* February 18; *Detroit Free Press,* February 26.

command of the Eastern army. Another intriguing item whispered that the report "will contain evidence of a nature calculated to lead at least one Major General to call for a court of inquiry."[38] It was stated that someone, possibly Lincoln himself or Seward, was making frantic efforts to get portions of the document suppressed. The Copperhead press charged angrily that Wade was handing out these stories to the Associated Press every few days in order to whet public interest and to prejudice the case against McClellan before the evidence was released.[39] If this was what Wade was doing, his advertising was a complete success. The country stirred with excitement as the first week in April approached, when rumor said the report would be published. Like a crowd at a Roman game, the people were waiting to see the radical lion charge upon the gladiator McClellan. Apprehensively one of the general's journalistic supporters cried that the report "will convict McClellan of incompetency or treason. . . . The Committee will perform their dirty work faithfully and round off the injury they have already done to the country by a copious libel upon its greatest general."[40]

In the committee rooms the inquisitors worked with frenzied haste to ready the portion of the report which dealt with McClellan. They wanted to get in in the hands of the Associated Press by the first day in April. Chandler wrote to his wife that they had been going until midnight for days. Governor Johnson of Tennessee, in town on official business, was helping his old colleagues. Chandler was buoyantly confident of what the report would accomplish. It "kills Copperheads dead," he boasted, it would kill McClellan "deader than the prophets," and it would make the administration "squirm." He said they were going to show the report to Mrs. Lincoln. "She is down upon Seward, McClelland [sic] & the whole crew & wants to see & talk with us."[41]

[38] *New York Tribune*, March 3, 1863, Washington correspondence; *Detroit Free Press*, March 25, 31, 1863.
[39] *Ibid.*, April 2, 1863; Rochester *Union*, quoted *ibid.*, March 27, 1863.
[40] *Detroit Free Press*, April 3, 1863.
[41] Julian, *Recollections*, 230; Zachariah Chandler to Mrs. Chandler, March 31, 1863, in the Chandler MSS.

With a consummate knowledge of the techniques of securing a good press, Wade sent copies of the completed report to the metropolitan newspapers and the Associated Press on Saturday, April 4, for simultaneous publication on Monday. It was rumored that the entire force in the government printing office was working on the document. The Washington correspondents knew on Saturday, without having seen the report, the nature of its attack upon McClellan. Summaries appeared in the New York papers on Monday. The principal reason back of the extreme haste with which the report was whipped together and issued became immediately apparent. It was printed in three solid pages by the *Washington Chronicle*, and rushed in bales to Burnside's army at Falmouth. Not until April 9 did Wade give out the less important sections dealing with Frémont, Stone, and first Manassas.[42]

The report on the Army of the Potomac was a sixty-six page affair covering the period from the time McClellan assumed command in 1861 to Antietam. A minor section cleared Burnside of any censure for the disaster at Fredericksburg and threw the blame upon Franklin. Proudly the Committee stated that it had taken the testimony of nearly two hundred witnesses, almost all of whom were military men, and one hundred of whom were generals.

The report started off with a thrust at Lincoln, insinuating in unmistakable terms that his vacillation was responsible for the failure to crush the rebellion. Certainly Congress had done its part in voting men and supplies, the authors cried, and could not be blamed for the incubus of "delay and inaction" which had lain like a dead weight upon the armies since the day the war began. To determine the causes of the perpetual procrastination which characterized the direction of military operations had been the primary objective of the Committee's investigations, and because the war in the East was a splendid epitome of the inefficiency that prevailed everywhere, the members had turned their attention particularly to the Army of the Potomac:

[42] *Detroit Free Press*, April 6, 10, 17, 1863, Washington correspondence; *New York Tribune*, April 5.

In the history of that army is to be found all that is necessary to enable your committee to report upon "the conduct of the war." Had that army fulfilled all that a generous and confiding people were justified in expecting from it, this rebellion had long since been crushed, and the blessings of peace restored to this nation. The failure of that army to fulfill those expectations has prolonged this contest to the present time, with all its expenditure of life and treasure, for it has to a great extent neutralized, if not entirely destroyed, the legitimate fruits which would otherwise have been reaped from our glorious victories in the west.[43]

After this conciliatory beginning the document settled down to a detailed and jaundiced account of McClellan's misadministration of the army. It described his inexplicable refusal to advance in the fall of 1861 when the weather was good, his pigheaded opposition to the corps organization, the mystery in which he surrounded his plans, his insane scheme to attack Richmond by the Peninsula route, his inadequate provisions for the defense of Washington, the bungled Peninsula campaign, the knifing of Pope, and the suspicious failure to bag Lee after Antietam. Dancing between the lines of the whole narrative was the implication that disloyalty explained every one of McClellan's actions.

Bitterly the report condemned the West Point theory of winning the war with strategy, and pointed to McClellan's campaign as a horrible example to be avoided by future commanders: "More than any other wars, rebellion demands rapid measures. . . . Though delay might mature more comprehensive plans, and promise greater results, it is not the first case in which it has been shown that successful war involves something more than abstract military principles."[44]

Feeling that it had disposed of McClellan, the Committee turned to the task of rejuvenating the popular morale. Victory, it promised, was just around the corner. The Union armies had failed only because they were commanded by generals who believed in the policy of delay. With the adminis-

[43] *C.C.W.*, 1863, 1:3–4.
[44] *Ibid.*, 28–29.

tration at last showing a willingness to entrust the war to generals like Hooker who believed in fighting, things would be different. The Committee expected the campaign of 1863 to be a brilliant triumph. With these bright auguries the people were exhorted to sustain the struggle to the bitter end.[45]

The Committee's broadside threw the Democrats into angry confusion. It was an expert piece of propaganda, and McClellan's supporters immediately realized the damaging effects it would have on his political fortunes. They howled that it was a Republican campaign document for 1864, issued under the respectable imprimatur of Congress. Bennett charged that "so one-sided a document never before emanated from a Congressional committee." The *World* called the report "a sustained, minute, and malignant assault," occupied "with the conduct, not of the war, but of General McClellan."[46] Weeks later, when the Committee released its mass of testimony and the Democrats got a chance to study it, they were able to point out glaring inconsistencies and errors in the report. Thus the Committee claimed that Hooker would have smashed the enemy at Williamsburg had not muddy roads prevented needed ammunition from reaching him, then it condemned McClellan for not advancing after the battle, sneering at his excuse that the roads were muddy. Again the report said McClellan could have captured Richmond after Malvern Hill, but on the next page declared that the army was so decimated by sickness that it had to be withdrawn from the unhealthful Peninsula, where it never should have been sent in the first place, because Richmond could not be captured from that direction.[47] Indignantly the *World*, whose own scientific objectivity might have been questioned, shouted, "The volumes

---

[45] *Ibid.*, 60–66.

[46] *Detroit Free Press*, April 8, 9, 1863; *New York Herald*, April 10, 1863; also April 6; New York *World*, April 6, 1863.

[47] *C.C.W.*, 1863, 1:20, 26–27. For examples of Democratic analysis of the report, see the *Detroit Free Press*, April 9, 1863; Hurlbert, *McClellan*, 218–219; G. S. Hilliard, *Life and Campaigns of George B. McClellan* (Philadelphia, 1865), 231–232; Hiram Ketchum, *General McClellan's Peninsula Campaign* (New York, 1864), 16–19, 28, 37–38.

of the Committee contain no approach to a complete history. They publish garbled, selected, and distorted evidence, and cut or suppress altogether the most important documents."[48]

Upon the Republicans the report produced an effect like that of a pardon on a man about to be executed. They saw in this powerful propaganda document the weapon with which they could strike down the menace in the form of McClellan that threatened their political existence. The Republican press spread the report over the front page and backed it up with enthusiastic editorial commendation. Greeley called it "a clear and impartial history of the great army which the nation raised with unexampled liberality and rapidity and with unexampled generosity intrusted it to an untried commander." The *Times* praised it as "an able, interesting, and important document," and said the strictures on McClellan were not harsh enough. Constantly and effectively, the Republican editors hammered on the theme of McClellan's incompetence and possible treason, as demonstrated by the report, and asked scornfully, Is this the man the Democrats want the country to take as its president?[49]

Almost immediately observers noticed that the report was nearly as rabid in its attacks upon Lincoln and the administration as against McClellan and the Democrats. By broad implication the president was censured for appointing and sustaining in power such a stumbling incompetent as the Committee pictured McClellan to be, and for filling the important commands with generals who did not want to win victories. The Committee intimated that Lincoln had interfered with Burnside's plans after Fredericksburg at the request of McClellan's pets, and was in no small degree to blame for the demoralization in the army. In administration circles the report was recognized as a hostile piece of Jacobin propaganda. Welles wrote in his diary: "Little good can be expected of these partisan supervisors of the Government at any

[48] New York *World*, April 27, 1863.
[49] *New York Tribune*, April 6, 1863; *New York Times*, April 6, 7, 1863; New York *Independent*, April 9, 1863; *Detroit Advertiser and Tribune*, April 8; *Cincinnati Gazette*, April 9.

time. They are partisan and made up of persons not very competent to form correct and intelligent opinions of Army or Navy operations, or administrative purposes."[50]

Using the Committee's material as ammunition, the radicals, to the delight of the Democrats, began to fire shots at Lincoln as well as McClellan. One of John Sherman's supporters wrote to the senator: "I have just been reading the report of the War Committee & I am astonished that the President confided in McClellan as long as he did. McClellan and Buel [sic] has cost the country millions." Greeley said the report was a "fearful exposé" of Lincoln's mismanagement of the war. The New York *Independent*, accusing the president of condoning the alleged plot of the McClellan officers to overthrow Burnside, sneered at "the weak and inexcusable forbearance of Mr. Lincoln to punish the very highest misdemeanors known to military law, even when necessary to sustain the very power of his chief commander."[51] A shrewd Democratic observer offered the suggestion, with a great deal of truth behind it, that one of the Committee's objectives was to destroy Lincoln's chances of securing the Republican nomination in 1864.[52]

In fact the Democrats themselves began to use the Committee's material to prove that such an incompetent administration must be voted out and their party voted in. Bennett declared the report was "a satire on the President." A Western Copperhead organ exclaimed: "It shows such a want of administrative ability in the President, such a constant intermeddling in questions beyond his knowledge, that it must inevitably lower not only the President but the government in the estimation of the world." To have the Democrats exploit the Committee's labors for an attack upon the administration was an embarrassing development which the radicals had not foreseen. "The report of Wade and Chandler's War

[50] Welles, *Diary*, 1:262.

[51] William Patterson to John Sherman, April 12, 1863, in the Sherman MSS.; Horace Greeley in the New York *Independent*, April 9, 1863; editorial in the New York *Independent*, April 9, 1863.

[52] *Detroit Free Press*, April 12, 1863.

Committee is a tartar the Republicans have caught," chortled a Democratic editor. "They were so anxious to prejudice the public mind against McClellan that they commended the whole report in extravagant terms, and are circulating it to the extent of their powers, without detecting the deep censure it casts upon the President by accusing him . . . of being incompetent to the discharge of his duties."[53]

Not until the last week in April did the Committee release the testimony upon which the reports were based. The Democrats charged that this procedure was a trick to prejudice the minds of readers, whose opinions would be fixed by the report before they examined the evidence. The real reason for the delay, however, was the slowness of the government printing office. The inquisitors knew the value of circulating the report in book form as a campaign document, and during April the entire printing force worked feverishly to ready the testimony for publication. The material was set up in stereotype so that additional copies could be run off at any time.[54]

When completed, the reports and testimony made three large volumes. They formed the chief arsenal of Republican orators and editors in the elections of 1863 and the presidential contest of the following year, when McClellan was the Democratic standard-bearer. Republican workers deluged congressmen with requests for copies.[55] Greeley published summaries of the material in pamphlet form. To the report on the Army of the Potomac he accorded the distinction of "*Tribune* War Tract, number one," and beneath its official title danced the in-

[53] *New York Herald*, April 10, also 28, 1863; *Detroit Free Press*, April 8, also 18, 1863; *Buffalo Commercial*, quoted *ibid.*, April 18, 1863.

[54] New York *World*, April 29, 1863; *Detroit Free Press*, April 6, 7, 1863; F. M. Rees, chief of the government printing office, to John Sherman, April 21, 1863, in the Sherman MSS.

[55] Letters to John Sherman in the Sherman MSS. from A. P. Russell, April 27, 1863; A. E. Buss, May 1; A. Denny, June 1; J. G. Sharp, of the Sandusky *Commercial Register*, August 7; F. March, August 1, September 28; D. E. Pinkerton, November 2. See also E. C. Bittinger to Joseph Holt, December, 1863, in the Holt MSS.; Simon Stevens to Thaddeus Stevens, November 28, 1863, in the Stevens MSS.; C. H. Allen to Lyman Trumbull, January 26, 1864, in the Trumbull MSS.

triguing subheads: "Cause of its inaction and ill success. Its
several campaigns. Why McClellan was removed."[56]
The enormous effectiveness of the Committee's adventure
in propaganda was demonstrated by the host of Democratic
writers who rushed into print to refute the charges against
McClellan in the reports. In the campaign of 1864, the Democrats were continually on the defensive, vainly trying to vindi-
cate their candidate's military record and to erase impressions which the Committee had fixed in the popular mind in
1863.[57]

☆

Peoples and nations seemingly cannot fight wars without
hating savagely the enemy whom they fight. Their loathing is
an inclusive thing which blankets the enemy's culture and
institutions and concentrates on the parts of his social system
which differ from their own. If this hatred does not exist
when the war begins—as it almost always does, because it is
an important contributing cause of war—the government or
some agency acting with the government's consent must call
it into being with the abracadabra of propaganda, and sustain
it with constant doses of the same stimulant until the struggle
is victoriously ended. In the Civil War the mission of arousing
and maintaining a mass hatred of the enemy, of firing the
Northern heart, was performed by the same voluntary private
or semiprivate organizations that labored to mold the Northern
mind. Here too the Committee was active, and its prestige and
facilities for investigation made it the leader of all the other
propaganda agencies.

Northern propagandists found their task immeasurably fa-
cilitated by the existence of a convenient stereotype—the cruel

[56] *Report of the Congressional Committee on the Operations of the
Army of the Potomac* (New York, 1863). See also the *Tribune* War Tract,
number three, *How Bull Run Battle Was Lost. The Ball's Bluff Massacre.
Department of the West—Fremont* (New York, 1863). Democratic opinion
of these pamphlets is given in the *New York Herald*, April 9, 1863;
Ketchum, *McClellan*, 3, 16.

[57] Ketchum, *McClellan*; Hilliard, *McClellan*; Hurlbert, *McClellan*; Ken
dall, *Letters Exposing Abraham Lincoln*.

slaveholder epitomized by Simon Legree. Thirty years of abolitionist preachings had instilled in the popular mind definite thought patterns and reactions regarding the Southern people and their social system. It was widely believed that slavery had brutalized the Southern character, that the owner of human chattels was a dour, repulsive fiend, animated by feelings of savage hatred toward Negroes and Northern whites. "A foaming fountain of insecurity and alarm, of violence and crime and blood, the institution of slavery is," cried the Reverend William H. Furness to his Philadelphia flock at the outbreak of war. Other men of the cloth warned their congregations that the North was facing a foe whose lower civilization rested upon "anarchy, fraud, and treason," and whose government was an "unrelenting, bloody tyranny."[58] Horace Greeley predicted that the Confederacy would wage a war of barbarity, consonant with the character of "a people to whose natural ugliness of disposition is added the ferocity of exasperated wild beasts." Exhausting his arsenal of adjectives, an editorial writer for the *New York Times* informed his readers: "The Southern character is infinitely boastful, vainglorious, full of dash, without endurance, treacherous, cunning, timid, and revengeful."[59] Such intense emotional fixations needed only the impetus of a flood of atrocity stories to unleash a venomous hatred of the South that carried through the war and persisted long after the conflict itself had ended.

Early in its career the Committee discovered pressing and imperative reasons for preaching a crusade of hate. Probing the causes of the Union defeats at Manassas and Ball's Bluff, the members learned from McDowell and Meigs that the superior dash and courage of the Confederates had given them the victory. This desirable military quality, the officers asserted, was the result of a hatred for the North that dominated the

[58] William H. Furness, *A Discourse Delivered on the Occasion of the National Fast* (Philadelphia, 1862), 12; *New York Tribune*, September 30, 1861, quotations from the sermons of fifteen New York and Boston ministers.

[59] *Ibid.*, December 14, 1861; *New York Times*, May 4, 1861. See also Grant Goodrich to Lyman Trumbull, July 29, 1861, in the Trumbull MSS.

Southern soldiery. The interested questions which Wade shot at the generals signified that he grasped the necessity of inculcating similar sentiments into the Northern masses, from which came the volunteer armies. The opinion expressed by McDowell and Meigs was widely supported in the North. One of Greeley's army correspondents described for his readers a group of Southern prisoners whom he inspected at close range. They were "gaunt, sunburnt, stolid, and savage," he wrote, fierce fighting men, "educated to that fanatic hatred of the Yankees which supplied the fuel to the devastating fire of rebellion. . . . I thought what would Kidd, Blackbeard, Morgan, have given for such fellows as these." Julian awoke to the importance of creating a war psychosis when he talked to Burnside at Falmouth, and the general told him the Union reverses were due to a lack of fighting spirit among the soldiers, who did not "adequately hate" their enemy. "This spirit was a military necessity," Julian concluded.[60]

If these motives for propaganda were purely military, the Committee knew others wholly political. From the first days of the war the radical press had shrewdly emphasized reports of the inhuman treatment which the rebels meted out to Southern Unionists. Would the government refuse to confiscate the property of such barbarians? cried the editors indignantly.[61] The Committee bosses recognized the political value of this potent appeal. They also realized that the officers and soldiers must be taught to hate slavery if the radical war policies, confiscation and military emancipation, were to be administered effectively.

Equipped with an adequate appreciation of the political and military advantages to be gained by the dissemination of atrocity propaganda, the Committee soon found an opportunity to display its talents. In the summer of 1861, immediately after the battle of Manassas, the press published lurid stories of the Confederates mutilating the bodies of the Union

[60] *C.C.W.*, 1863, 1:139, 155; *New York Tribune*, May 14, 1862, p. 1; Julian, *Select Speeches*, 33.
[61] *Leslie's Newspaper*, August 24, 1861; *New York Tribune*, September 16, 1861; *ibid.*, May 30, 1862, p. 1, army correspondence.

dead on the field and inflicting barbarous cruelties upon Northern prisoners. "We are told," shrieked the *New York Times*, "of their slashing the throats of some from ear to ear; of their cutting off the heads of others and kicking them about as footballs; and of their setting up the wounded against trees and firing at them as targets or torturing them with plunges of bayonets into their bodies."[62] Although eleven paroled surgeons captured at Manassas asserted upon their return to Washington that the newspaper accounts were without foundation, this note of reason went unheeded in the hymn of malice that the Republican press was chanting with increased vigor. An apprehensive conservative journal ventured the hope that the war spirit of the nation would not degenerate into emotions of "savage ferocity."[63] It gave every indication of doing so as the newspapers whooped up their campaign. Soon indignant citizens were reading of insidious attempts to poison Union soldiers, the wrecking of passenger trains in the Border States, the unspeakable outrages committed upon Southern Unionists, and the inhuman treatment meted out in Richmond prisons.[64] In September the press added a new and startling charge to this impressive list of Southern barbarities. It was announced that the Confederate government had enrolled large bodies of the Southwestern Indians in its army and was prepared to unleash the horrors of savage warfare in the Border States. Thirteen hundred bloodthirsty warriors, armed with butcher knives, tomahawks, and rifles, had joined Ben McCulloch's army in Missouri, claimed a thrilling rumor. Quotations from Southern newspapers increased the turmoil produced by this fresh discovery

[62] *New York Times*, July 25, 1861; *Harper's Weekly*, August 17, contains a highly imaginative sketch of the scenes that supposedly ensued after the battle.

[63] Washington *National Intelligencer*, August 14, 1861, interview with the surgeons, August 16, editorial.

[64] *Lexington Observer and Reporter*, quoted in the *New York Tribune*, September 1, 1861; *New York Tribune*, September 2, 6, 7, October 31, editorials; *ibid.*, September 2, letter of a soldier; *Leslie's Newspaper*, August 24, September 14. For accounts of prison conditions, see the *New York Times*, August 18, September 30; *Harper's Weekly*, November 2; *New York Tribune*, December 14.

of rebel depravity. "It will be a grand sight," exulted the *Memphis Avalanche*, "to see a cavalry brigade of those wild and fierce horsemen of the desert, subject to the discipline of civilized warfare, fighting the battles of the South. Our Indian army will strike terror into the craven hearts of our mercenary invaders."[65] The knowledge that Jefferson Davis had enlisted "the tomahawk and scalping knife" in his desperate cause did not surprise a North rapidly becoming hardened to Southern savagery. "War, in its mildest form, is full of horrors; but the South seems inspired with a devilish ingenuity in enhancing its enormities," one editor declared. The Indian auxiliaries of the Confederacy caused real terror in the Border States. A Louisville journal exhorted every Kentuckian to meet the invading redskins and "drive them back ere the tread of hostile shoes and moccasins shall be on our streets, on our threshold, and in our parlors, or perish in the firm and fierce endeavor. . . . Rise as your fathers rose; strike as your father struck."[66]

The persistence of these charges and rumors prompted Charles Sumner to present a resolution in the Senate on April 1, 1862, instructing the Committee to collect evidence regarding "the barbarous treatment by the rebels, at Manassas, of the remains of officers and soldiers of the United States," and the employment of "Indian savages" by the Confederacy and the behavior of "said savages" in battle. Sumner declared that the people of the North were in a conflict with a people lower in the scale of civilization than themselves, and he wanted a record of Southern barbarism for the use of future historians.[67]

As early as February the inquisitors had asked witnesses appearing on other business about the Manassas cruelties, and on the day following the passage of Sumner's resolution they went to work with a vengeance. Two surgeons captured at Manassas, people who had visited the field after the battle to

[65] Washington *National Intelligencer*, August 28, 1861; *Memphis Avalanche*, quoted *ibid.*, September 2, 1861; *New York Tribune*, September 6, 19.
[66] *Leslie's Newspaper*, September 14, 1861; *Louisville Journal*, October 31, 1861, quoted in the Washington *National Intelligencer*, November 5.
[67] *C.C.IV.*, 1863, 3:449; *Harper's Weekly*, April 19, 1862.

claim the bodies of relatives or friends, and returned prisoners from Richmond thronged the committee rooms. The surgeons testified that the Confederate authorities had inflicted needless brutalities upon the Union wounded, refusing them food, water, shelter, and proper medical attention. Only young and inexperienced doctors were permitted to operate on the Union soldiers, and these surgeons, the Committee's report

Atrocity Propaganda in Harper's Weekly, *June 7, 1862*

charged, "seemed to delight in hacking and butchering" their helpless patients. The returned prisoners described for the Committee the wretched conditions in Richmond prisons, accusing the Confederate officials of consciously following a policy of brutality by depriving the inmates of proper food and shelter and permitting the guards to torture them.[68]

These disclosures of Southern barbarity were eminently satisfactory to the propaganda-conscious inquisitors, but they found even more telling indictments of the Confederate government in the testimony relating to the desecration of the

[68] *C.C.IV.,* 1863, 3:449–452, 461–465, 468–474, 485–487, 487–490. Some of this evidence was hearsay, and most of it reflected more upon the poor administration of the Southern prisons than upon the character of the officials.

Union dead. Witnesses who had gone over the field several weeks after the battle and talked to Negroes and whites in the neighborhood furnished sensational if hearsay and unreliable evidence on this point. The Committee learned that for two weeks after the engagement the bodies of Northern soldiers lay naked and unburied upon the ground, while rebel women walked over the field, "gloating over the horrid sight." Several witnesses stated they had found bodies with the head or other portions chopped off. Others had heard that the Confederates boiled the dead bodies to obtain the bones as relics, that they pried shinbones out and used them as drumsticks, and that they carved rings and ornaments from the thighbones. One Confederate was alleged to have cut off the head of a dead Union officer, remarking as he did so that he intended to preserve the skull to drink a brandy punch out of at his wedding.[69] The star witness on the mutilation count was Governor Sprague of Rhode Island, who had visited Manassas weeks after the battle. Sprague was blatantly dogmatic about the motives of the Confederates. Asked whether the Confederates had intentionally buried Union soldiers face downward as a mark of indignity, he barked, "Undoubtedly; beyond all controversy." Why had the rebels mutilated the bodies? "Sheer brutality; nothing else."[70]

Wade wrote a report of the Manassas inquiry in the latter part of April and released it to the press immediately—the only publication which the Committee issued before the appearance of its complete reports in 1863. "Rebel Barbarities—Manassas" was a powerful, vivid, moving document, studded with lurid quotations from the testimony and vigorous commentaries by Wade. The most eloquent paragraphs were those detailing "the treatment of our heroic dead," where "the fiendish spirit of the rebel leaders was most prominently exhibited," and where Wade's best descriptive phrases were displayed. He ap-

[69] *Ibid.*, 451, 453–454, 458–461, 473–477. It is apparent that most of these stories were told to the witnesses by Negroes and that the Negroes got them from the Confederate soldiers, who were amusing themselves by spinning tall tales for the superstitious slaves.
[70] *Ibid.*, 474–476.

pealed to the people of the North to fight until the end
against the barbaric authors of these outrages:

They have now crowned the rebellion by the perpetration of
deeds scarcely known even to savage warfare. . . . Our fellow
countrymen, heretofore sufficiently impressed by the generosity
and forbearance of the government of the United States, and
by the barbarous character of the crusade against it, will be
shocked by the statements of these unimpeached and unim-
peachable witnesses; and foreign nations must, with one accord,
consign to lasting odium the authors of crimes which, in all
their details, exceed the worst excesses of the Sepoys of India.
. . . It was reserved for your committee to disclose as a concerted system their insults to the wounded, and their mutilation and desecration of the gallant dead.[71]

The Committee did not submit a report on the employment
of Indians by the Confederacy. Wade stated that time had
not permitted the members to conduct a proper investigation
of the subject, which would have necessitated a trip to the
West. However a number of documents transmitted by Western
officers were included in the testimony. These charged that
Indians fought with the Confederates in the battle of Pea
Ridge, and that dead Union soldiers were found scalped
and mutilated after the engagement.[72]

The Committee's story of the atrocities at Manassas horrified
the North. An editorial writer in *Harper's Weekly* called the
report "one of the most melancholy documents in history. It
is not surprising, however, for no one who has thoughtfully
read the many records of the aspects and characteristics of a
society based upon slavery was unconscious of its essential
and necessary barbarism." After pondering the Southern system a little more, the editor added thoughtfully: "Their civilization is a mermaid—lovely and languid above, but ending in
bestial deformity." The report immediately became the theme
of Northern propagandists. The popular illustrated weeklies
published sketches based upon its vivid paragraphs, depicting

[71] *New York Tribune*, May 1, 1862, p. 3; *C.C.W.*, 1863, 3:453, 455–457.
[72] *Ibid.*, 490–491.

villainous Southerners decapitating dead Union soldiers and Indians tomahawking a bloody path into Northern homes. Pamphleteers composed sensational summaries, and excerpts from the testimony formed the basis for some purple passages in one work of fiction. Julian reviewed the investigation and the evidence in a speech before the House in May, which demonstrated how the Jacobins intended to wrest political profits from the creation of a hatred psychosis. The people of the North, cried Julian, were locked in a struggle for existence with a relentless adversary who would not abide by the rules of warfare set up by civilized nations, an adversary who "gives arsenic to our soldiers, mocks at the agonies of wounded enemies, fires on defenceless women and children, plants torpedoes and infernal machines in its path, boils the dead bodies of our soldiers in cauldrons, so that it may make drinking cups of their skulls, spurs of their jawbones and finger joints, as holiday presents for the 'first families of Virginia,' and the 'descendants of the daughters of Pocahontas.' " Could anyone believe that the rose-water policy would conquer such a foe as this?[73]

[73] *Harper's Weekly*, May 17, 1862; *ibid.*, June 17, October 25, 1862, February 7, 1863; *Leslie's Newspaper*, April 4, 1863; John Russell Bartlett, *The Barbarities of the Rebels* (Providence, 1863); anonymous, *The Rebel Pirate's Fatal Prize* (Philadelphia, 1862), 40–43; Julian, *Select Speeches*, 7.

10

Fighting Joe Hooker
and the Finest Army on the Planet

ALTHOUGH BURNSIDE transformed himself into a Jacobin before
the approving inquisitors of the Committee at Falmouth, his
abrupt conversion did not save either his soul or his command.
The Committee went back to Washington resolved to cherish
and uphold this welcome recruit to the cause. The testimony
which Wade submitted to the Senate cleared Burnside of the
onus of Fredericksburg and dumped the blame upon Franklin.
The members let it be known that they would fight any attempt to remove Burnside. But politics, even as practiced by
Wade and Chandler, could not save Burnside. The Committee
could not change his pathetic conviction that he was incapable of handling an army or rescue him from the results
of his repetitious incompetence and indecision. The Committee
could not still the din of the campfire debates at Falmouth,
where the demoralized soldiers vented their opinion that the
commander was a blunderer. It could not stop the flood of indignant soldier letters in the newspapers. Least of all could
Wade and Chandler protect their inept protégé from the
aspiring intrigues of his subordinate generals to oust him
from the command. The camp at Falmouth became a hive of
deceit and conspiracy and gossip. Loyalty to Burnside did not
exist among the officers in either the McClellan or the Republican faction. The leading schemers were the radical
Hooker, who wanted Burnside's job, and the conservative
Franklin, who was probably working for the restoration of
McClellan.

After Fredericksburg, Burnside fluttered between a desire
to get rid of a responsibility he had never wanted by resigning
his command and an ambition to recoup his reputation by a

vigorous smash against the enemy. He worked out a new plan of operation which called for another crossing of the river and another assault upon Lee. This sounded suspiciously like Fredericksburg over again, and his generals, including Hooker, Franklin, and Sumner, the commanders of the three "Grand Divisions," raised objections when Burnside laid his proposal before a council. Burnside, however, went ahead with his preparations for the attack. There followed one of the strangest episodes of the war. Military usage recognized the right of subordinates to criticize the plans of their superior in the secrecy of army councils, but stipulated that the criticism must not go outside of those bounds. The Civil War threw this rule in the garbage pail. Officers did a lot of loose talking to newspaper reporters, other officers, and even to privates, about the faults of their commanders. Sometimes, as in the case of Buell, the result was a complete breakdown of discipline, and the commanding general lost his job. The primary reason back of this wholesale disregard for the niceties of the military code was the gigantic influence which politics played in the hiring and firing of generals. Disgruntled subordinates were always careful to make their denunciations loud enough to carry to the sensitive ears of the politicians in Washington, who were always ready to listen to such complaints and to intrude their influence in the game of army politics. The best listener and meddler was the Committee, which from the beginning had encouraged officers to speak out against their superiors. Now it secured superb if somewhat embarrassing cooperation from Burnside's generals.

A few days after Burnside had announced his plan, Franklin and his crony W. F. Smith decided to take their protests over the commander's head to Lincoln. They dispatched a letter to the president condemning Burnside's proposed operations and suggesting a counterplan of their own. This was a serious breach of military etiquette, but it was only the prelude to more startling developments. On December 30 Generals John Cochrane and John Newton, officers in Franklin's division, came up to Washington from Falmouth to peddle criticisms of Burnside. Cochrane, who conceived the trip, was a political general, a Democrat before the war began and a radical and emancipationist immediately afterward. Significantly the two looked first for the Committee, to tell the inquisitors that Burnside had lost the confidence of the army and should be removed—that his project to attack Lee would result in another ghastly failure. Finding no one at the committee rooms, they decided that Lincoln was the next best, and took their story to him. They so alarmed the president that he telegraphed Burnside not to start a forward movement without official permission.[1]

Cochrane's and Newton's tattling was the finish for Burnside. Characteristically he thought that their opinion of him was probably correct. He offered his resignation to the government, telling Lincoln that Stanton and Halleck should go out with him in order to restore confidence to the people.[2] The president calmed the general and told him to hang on. But Burnside's position rapidly became unbearable. The story of Cochrane's and Newton's errand leaked out to the newspapers, and a shocked public learned that Burnside's officers distrusted his competency. Soon the press began to publish accounts of what the subordinates thought about the commander. Hooker talked blatantly to the reporters about the new regime that would prevail if Joe Hooker were in command.[3] Maddened by Hooker's jibes and the almost open insubordination of his generals, Burnside took a foolish and fatal step. He prepared an order dismissing from the service Hooker, W. T. H. Brooks, Newton, and Cochrane, and relieving from duty Franklin, Smith, and three other officers. The or-

[1] William B. Franklin and W. F. Smith to Abraham Lincoln, December 20, 1862, in the Stanton MSS.; *O. R.*, series 1, vol. 21, 868–870; *C.C.W.*, 1863, 1:730–740, Newton's testimony; *ibid.*, 740–746, Cochrane's testimony; Cochrane, *War for the Union*, 47–52; O. R., series 1, 1:900.

[2] Ambrose E. Burnside to Lincoln, January 1, *ibid.*, 941–942; "Excerpts from the Journal of Henry Raymond," *Scribner's Monthly*, 19(1880):422.

[3] *New York Times*, January 16, 25, 1863; *New York Herald*, January 10; *Detroit Free Press*, January 23, February 1, Washington correspondence; *Cincinnati Commercial*, quoted *ibid.*, February 1; Villard, *Memoirs*, 1:348; "Raymond's Journal," *Scribner's Monthly*, 19(1880):422.

der accused Hooker of "unjust and unnecessary criticisms of the actions of his superior officers," and of being "unfit to hold an important commission during a crisis like the present." Burnside read the order to Henry Raymond of the *New York Times,* who was visiting at Falmouth. The astonished journalist remarked that Hooker might resist the execution of the decree. Burnside's reply, as Raymond recorded it in his diary, was that he "would *swing him* before sundown, if he attempted such a thing." Raymond took it upon himself to rush back to Washington to warn Lincoln about the crisis in the army. He found the president at a levee and drew him into a corner to relate his story. Lincoln was already worried about the pulsing intrigues going on at Falmouth, and Raymond's information increased his anxiety. He told the editor he would stop Burnside from issuing the order but he feared he would have to appoint Hooker to the command of the Potomac army. Hooker was "stronger with the country to-day than any other man," said the president sadly.[4]

Forbidden by the president to dismiss his throat-cutting subordinates, Burnside came to Washington and insisted that his resignation be accepted. He spent the entire morning of the twenty-fourth of January conferring with Lincoln, Stanton, and Halleck. On the next day it was announced that Burnside, at his own request, had been relieved of the command of the Army of the Potomac, and that Hooker had been assigned to the place. The same order relieved Franklin of duty.[5]

The bosses of the Jacobin machine were delighted with the appointment of Hooker. He had won the favor of the Committee by his advocacy of emancipation and his violent denunciations of the McClellan clique. After Fredericksburg the inquisitors had hoped to boost him into the command. Then Burnside's switch to radicalism at Falmouth made a change seem unnecessary. But when it became evident in the latter

---

[4] *O. R.*, series 1, 21:998–999; "Raymond's Journal," *Scribner's Monthly,* 19(1880):703–706.

[5] *O. R.*, series 1, 21:1004–1005; Washington *National Intelligencer,* January 26, 1863; *Detroit Free Press,* January 31, 1863, Washington correspondence.

part of January that Burnside would have to go, the Jacobins demanded Hooker for the command. Nevertheless, despite their pleasure at the accession of "Fighting Joe," they regretted the passing of Burnside, and determined to send him off with a clean record as far as Fredericksburg was concerned. It was decided to have the Committee resume its investigation of the causes of the disaster and in addition to probe the charges that certain subordinates, not Hooker, had interfered with Burnside's plans. Here the radicals saw an opportunity to smear Franklin, and through Franklin, McClellan. They saw too a chance to attack Lincoln for listening to the talebearing of Cochrane and Newton. Greeley's correspondent announced that the Committee intended to dig into the knifing of Burnside, and that Franklin and several other officers would get courts-martial as a result.[6]

On January 26 the Senate passed a resolution, offered by Wilson, instructing the Committee to determine what plans Burnside had made for an advance after Fredericksburg and "whether any subordinate generals . . . have written to or visited Washington to oppose or interfere with the execution of such movements."[7] Burnside appeared as the first witness. This time he reversed his earlier statement to the Committee that Franklin had not carried the left wing during the battle because of the great strength of the enemy's position. Now he charged his subordinate with delaying the attack in disobedience of orders until the chance of victory had disappeared. There were no "willful acts of bad faith" on Franklin's part, Burnside said, but he had shown "a lack of alacrity." The Committee was enthusiastic about Burnside's testimony and his willingness to bedaub Franklin with the blame for Fredericksburg.[8] After the session ended the members conducted

[6] Zachariah Chandler to Mrs. Chandler, January 22, 1863, in the Chandler MSS.; *New York Tribune*, January 24, 1863, Washington correspondence; *Detroit Free Press*, January 31, Washington correspondence.

[7] *C.C.W.*, 1863, 1:57.

[8] *Ibid.*, 716–723; Zachariah Chandler to Mrs. Chandler, February 7, 1863, in the Chandler MSS.; New York *Independent*, February 12, Washington correspondence.

the general over to Congress for a reception. A correspondent who saw the way the wind was blowing described the scene: "Major-General Burnside was today examined by the Committee on the Conduct of the War and was afterwards accompanied by them to each house of Congress, where he was warmly welcomed privately by members."[9] Shrewd capital reporters concluded after this episode that the Committee was out for the sole purpose of getting Franklin. General Meade, who came to Washington in March to testify, had the same opinion. "My conversations with Burnside and Wade satisfied me that Franklin was to be made responsible for the failure at Fredericksburg," Meade wrote, "and the committee is seeking all the testimony they can procure to substantiate this theory of theirs."[10] Franklin himself met the inquisitors late in March, and they made him run a gauntlet of hostile and searching questions. Describing the ordeal to McClellan, Franklin wrote that he had been "drawn through the War Committee. . . . They went over everything very unfairly. Their evident intention was to get up something that would ruin, 1st you, and 2nd me—that is so far as my evidence is concerned."[11]

The Committee published its findings on the Burnside case as a part of the larger report on the Army of the Potomac which was released in April. The inquisitors exonerated Burnside completely of the blame for Fredericksburg and claimed that the battle had been lost by Franklin's refusal to attack with his full force. The Republican press seized on this section of the report to praise Burnside and attack the administration. Burnside, cried the *Tribune,* was "a brave, earnest, devotedly loyal soldier," who had been sabotaged by the McClellan gang while Lincoln looked on with tacit approval. The attack upon Franklin in "Ben Wade's party pamphlet," as the *World*

[9] *Detroit Free Press,* February 9, 1863, Washington correspondence; *New York Tribune,* February 10, Associated Press item.

[10] *Detroit Free Press,* February 12, 1863, Washington correspondence; *Cincinnati Gazette,* quoted *ibid.,* February 12; George G. Meade to Mrs. Meade, March 17, 1863, in Meade, *Life of Meade,* 1:358–360. For Meade's testimony, see *C.C.W.,* 1863, 1:690–692.

[11] William B. Franklin to George B. McClellan, April 6, 1863, in Myers, *McClellan,* 408. For Franklin's testimony see *C.C.W.,* 1863, 1:707–712.

labeled the report, stirred the Democrats to fiery expressions of wrath. They accused the Committee of painting Burnside's blunders with a "palliating pencil" and blackening Franklin's honor with broad strokes of false evidence. A Western Copperhead organ charged that the Committee was systematically trying to destroy all the conservative generals: "Their office has been to kill off all military reputations which might hereafter aspire to high positions." Franklin, in temporary retirement at York, Pennsylvania, contributed to the polemical flood a bitter and effective pamphlet, *A Reply . . . to the Committee*, which the Democrats circulated enthusiastically.[12]

One section of the Committee's report described the visit of Cochrane and Newton to Washington and their interview with Lincoln. With broad inferences the Committee censured the president for listening to the tattling officers. Solemnly and with magnificent aplomb, the Committee asserted that such civilian interference with military affairs was destructive of discipline and should be avoided. This portion of the document touched off a lively controversy which had its comical and embarrassing moments. Cochrane, who was supposed to be a radical, rushed to Franklin's defense and assailed the Committee in letters written in the blowsy literary style of which he was a master. The Republican press denounced the president for receiving the two generals and interfering with Burnside's plans.[13] To the anger of the Republicans, the Democrats joined the din, shouting that an administration which fostered intrigues in the army should be thrown out.[14] Sometimes the Committee's sword cut both ways.

☆

[12] *Ibid.*, 52–57; *New York Tribune*, April 6, 1863; New York *Independent*, April 9, 1863; New York *World*, April 10, May 2, 1863; *Detroit Free Press*, May 7, 1863; William B. Franklin, *A Reply of Major General William B. Franklin to the Report of the Joint Committee of Congress on the Conduct of the War* (New York, 1863), especially pages 5, 10, 18–20, 23–24.

[13] *C.C.W.*, 1863, 1:57–60; Cochrane, *War for the Union*, 43, 52–53; *Leslie's Newspaper*, April 25, 1863; *New York Tribune*, April 6, 9, 1863; New York *Independent*, April 9.

[14] New York *World*, April 25, 1863; *Detroit Free Press*, April 12; Rochester *Union*, quoted *ibid.*, April 15.

On January 26, 1863, Count Gurowski admitted a note of optimism to the pages of his dismal diary. Hooker had become the commander of the Army of the Potomac, Gurowski wrote, "and patriotic hearts thrill with joy." "Fighting Joe" was a thrilling figure. Handsome, cleanshaven, with thick curling hair and bright, confident eyes, he looked and talked like a son of Mars. Only a weak chin marred his imposing exterior. He was an excellent corps commander, and brave to the point of recklessness, often leading his men in the charge across a fire-filled field. Pope recalled him at second Manassas, riding a white horse at the head of his regiment, "a very handsome young man, with florid complexion and fair hair, and with a figure agile and graceful."[15] Hooker's character was that of a spoiled small boy. He was vain and self-centered, selfish and artful, and at times extremely likeable.

Hooker intrigued long and earnestly to secure the Potomac command. In the early days of the war he was known as a conservative, and he aroused the anger of the Committee by opening his camp to searchers for fugitive slaves.[16] But he was too sharp not to see that the political future lay with the radicals. He wore his principles loosely, and soon he was snuggling up to the Jacobin bosses. In the middle of the Peninsula campaign he tried to get an interview with Stanton to reveal McClellan's mismanagement of affairs.[17] He told the Washington reporters that Lincoln had waited too long to issue an emancipation proclamation and that the government would not be able to win the war unless it destroyed slavery. Loudly and on every occasion he denounced McClellan and his satellites.[18] The Jacobins began to think that "Fighting Joe" might

[15] Adam Gurowski, *Diary, November, 1862 – October, 1863* (New York, 1864), 109–110; John Pope, "The Second Battle of Bull Run," in *Battles and Leaders of the Civil War*, 2:465.
[16] *C.C.W.*, 1863, 3:634–641, testimony of General Sickles, April 10, 1862.
[17] W. W. Tilghman to Edwin M. Stanton, May 22, 1862, in the Stanton MSS.
[18] *New York Tribune*, September 4, 1862, Washington correspondence; James A. Garfield to Mrs. Garfield, October 12, 1862, in Smith, *Garfield*, 1:251; Joseph Hooker to Edwin M. Stanton, November 9, 1862, in the Stanton MSS.

be the general they had been seeking. John Pope advised Halleck to throw out McClellan as commander of the Eastern army and appoint Hooker to the post: "You will find him a true man and one of incalculable use to you with that army." One of Stanton's intimates, Mark Skinner, asked anxiously whether the secretary had determined how Hooker stood on the great question: "I ventured to ask you the last time I had the pleasure of seeing you what Hooker's notions on the subject of retaining or abolishing slavery are. You said that you would ascertain." Skinner thought that Hooker should make a flat-footed declaration of support for the radical war policies, and the Jacobin machine could then work for his elevation to McClellan's place. Hooker evidently gave the desired assurances, for soon the radical press began to boom him for the command of the Eastern army. When Lincoln removed McClellan after Antietam, the Jacobins urged that the appointment should go to Hooker, but Halleck's opposition was supposed to have killed off his chances.[19] Undaunted by failure, "Fighting Joe" continued to scheme and talk. He criticized Burnside bitterly, in letters to Stanton and in conversations with reporters. His journalistic supporters continued to advertise his merits. After Fredericksburg Hooker saw the command within his grasp. At Falmouth he played the tune the Committee wanted with his denunciation of Franklin's course in the battle, and at the same time he pushed his own cause. Gurowski thought the Committee's testimony showed that of all the generals in Burnside's army, Hooker alone possessed "the capacities and resources of a captain."[20] Hooker must have been surprised and grievously disappointed when the Committee decided to support Burnside. But he did not cease his burrowing intrigues to undermine the commander,

[19] John Pope to Henry W. Halleck, September 30, 1862, in *O. R.*, series 1, vol. 12, part 3, p. 818; Mark Skinner to Edwin M. Stanton, October 20, 1862, in the Stanton MSS.; *Wilkes' Spirit of the Times*, October 11, 1862; *New York Tribune*, October 28, Washington correspondence, November 14, editorial; *C.C.W.*, 1865, 1:112, 175, Hooker's testimony.

[20] Joseph Hooker to Edwin M. Stanton, December 4, 1862, in the Stanton MSS.; Villard, *Memoirs*, 1:348; *Wilkes' Spirit of the Times*, December 6, 1862; Gurowski, *Diary, 1862–1863*, pp. 54–55.

and it was he, more than Franklin, Cochrane, or Newton, who finally drove the harassed Burnside to resign.

Lincoln assigned "Fighting Joe" to the command with extreme reluctance and only because he thought it wise at the moment to placate the Jacobins. He regarded Hooker as a slippery schemer who was not to be trusted. The president had formed this opinion when he learned that Hooker had talked loudly, at Falmouth and Washington, about the necessity of placing a dictator at the head of the government. In the nadir of Union hopes following Fredericksburg, many people began to fear and say that the democratic system was incapable of prosecuting a successful war. Sinister rumors floating around Washington whispered that an attempt would be made to depose Lincoln and set up a temporary military dictatorship, with some general, possibly Ben Butler, playing the rôle of strong man. Hooker acted as though he would welcome the part. One of the *Times* reporters told Raymond the general had declared openly that he was for ousting the president: "Nothing would go right, he said, until we had a dictator, and the sooner the better." Lincoln was more irritated than alarmed by Hooker's mouthings. Correctly he judged that the general's bark was greater than his courage, and he gently informed Hooker that it took more than blatant threats to overthrow a government. On the day after he appointed Hooker to the command, Lincoln wrote him a fatherly letter: "I have heard, in such a way as to believe it, of your recently saying that both the army and the government needed a dictator. Of course it was not for this, but in spite of it, that I have given you the command. Only those generals who gain successes can set up dictators. What I now ask of you is military success, and I will risk the dictatorship."[21]

The Jacobins hailed the appointment of Hooker as an augury that Lincoln meant to entrust the direction of the war to Republicans. Greeley's Washington correspondent crowed

[21] Doster, *Lincoln,* 13; Ward Lamon, *Recollections of Abraham Lincoln* (Washington, 1911), 193–194; "Raymond's Journal," *Scribner's Monthly,* 19 (1880):422; Lincoln to Hooker, January 26, 1863, in Lincoln, *Works,* 8:206.

that it portended the forced departure from the armies of the "half-loyal, half-hearted, heavy and slow generals." Greeley himself predicted that Hooker would uproot from among the generals the "pro-slavery subservience to West Point traditions, of indifference to the cause of the Republic" which had paralyzed the Union's military efforts. Wendell Phillips bestowed his blessing upon the new commander as the hope of radicalism.[22] The Democratic press frothed with denunciations of Hooker the intriguer and the fawner at the footstool of power. Sarcastically the Democrats pointed out that with a radical general in command the Republican newspapers did not set up their usual clamor for an "On to Richmond" movement, which had sabotaged the plans of generals like McClellan.[23]

The Jacobins were reported to have convinced Lincoln that the war must be won in the next few months or the struggle abandoned, with some foreign nation mediating a peace agreement. If victory did not come, the people would vote the Republican Party out of existence at the spring and fall elections. Therefore the administration had decided to back Hooker to the limit, in a desperate now-or-never effort. Other rumors swirling out of Washington claimed that Lincoln would oust Hooker, Stanton, and Halleck as soon as Congress adjourned and restore McClellan to command and appoint two conservatives to the Cabinet.[24] It was whispered that the Jacobin machine had served Lincoln with an ultimatum—he must get rid of Seward and the conservatives in the Cabinet and the army or the radicals would push through Congress a vote of want of confidence in the administration. An apprehensive Democratic editor claimed "that Wade and Chandler and that set are determined, if they can, to reinaugurate the reign of terror,

[22] *New York Tribune*, February 3, 1863, Washington correspondence; *ibid.*, February 27, 1863, editorial; Phillips, quoted *ibid.*, February 4, 1863. See also the *Chicago Tribune*, January 27.

[23] *Detroit Free Press*, January 28, 29, February 6, 17, May 5, 1863; Rochester *Union*, quoted *ibid.*, January 30, February 20.

[24] Rochester *Union*, quoted *ibid.*, January 30, 1863; *New York Herald*, January 27, February 19, 1863, Washington correspondence; *Detroit Free Press*, March 3.

to fill the land with nigger soldiers, and under the protection of their bayonets" carry out the radical program.[25]

Most of these stories originated in the fevered imaginations of the Democrats, but some of them had a basis of fact. Although Hooker and Rosecrans dominated the military scene and no Democratic general held an important independent command, the radicals resented the preponderance of Democratic or conservative officers in the subordinate positions. They feared Seward's influence in the Cabinet and they wanted Halleck removed. They demanded appointments for Butler and Frémont. Chandler declared that Seward was an out-and-out traitor who must be destroyed before the cause could triumph. Julian delivered a strange, complaining speech in the House denouncing the administration for letting Democrats run the war: "Democratic policy holds in its hands all the great machinery of this war, and directs it according to its own will."[26]

The news from the Gulf Department stirred the smouldering resentment of the radicals to flaring anger and hardened their determination to purge the army of conservative generals. Here General Banks had assumed command after Lincoln removed Ben Butler. Banks was a Massachusetts politician before the war, a Democrat who broke with his party on the slavery issue and joined the Republicans. Ordinarily the Jacobins would have applauded the selection of Banks for the important Gulf post; but they preferred Butler to Banks or any other general for the job of reconstructing Louisiana according to radical ideas. They knew that the president had plans of his own for Louisiana and that he was determined to prevent the state from becoming a laboratory for radical experiments. They could not down their suspicions that Banks was going to New Orleans as Lincoln's agent, to set up and administer a conservative reconstruction program.

With the Jacobins eyeing him threateningly, Banks took up

[25] *Ibid.*, January 28, 1863.
[26] Zachariah Chandler to Mrs. Chandler, February 7, 1863, in the Chandler MSS.; William P. Fessenden, letter to his family, February 21, in Fessenden, *Fessenden*, 1:266; Julian, *Speeches on Political Questions*, 203–207.

his duties. He found his most immediate problem to be of a social rather than a military nature. The slaves, lured by the promise of a new life, were leaving the plantations in alarming numbers and congregating around the army camps. Having no means of supporting themselves, they looked to the military authorities for food and clothing. Not only were they a burdensome drain upon the resources of the army, but their absence from home menaced the state with an economic crisis. If the laboring class remained in supported idleness, no crops would be planted or harvested, and the agricultural system would break down completely. The situation was critical, and Banks acted promptly. On January 29 he issued an order establishing by military fiat a new labor system for Louisiana. It was one of the most comprehensive attempts made during the war to solve the problems created by the sudden destruction of slavery.

The order directed that all persons without visible means of support must "maintain themselves by labor. Negroes are not exempt from this law. Those who leave their employers will be compelled to support themselves and families by labor upon the public works. Under no circumstances whatever can they be maintained in idleness, or allowed to wander . . . without employment." A commission was set up to confer with "planters and other parties, to propose and establish a yearly system of Negro labor, which shall provide for the food, clothing, proper treatment, and just compensation for the Negroes." The compensation was not to be "exorbitant or onerous" upon employers; when a planter accepted such a labor contract, "all the conditions of continuous and faithful service, respectful deportment, correct discipline, and perfect subordination shall be enforced on the part of the Negroes by the officers of the Government." Another section instructed the quartermaster's department to put unemployed colored people to work on abandoned farms, "under the control of suitable agents or planters," and under regulations that would "tend to keep families together, to impart self-supporting habits to the negroes." Banks issued another order on February 18 which forbade recruiting officers to take Negroes off plantations and enroll them in the army.[27]

Banks' measures stirred the Jacobins to fierce protest. Their worst fears were realized: Banks was a conservative and at Lincoln's command was about to wreck the radical plans for the reconstruction of Louisiana and the Gulf area. They denounced him wildly. Phillips called him a "faltering, stupid general," who was toadying to the slaveholders and trying to force the Negroes back into servitude. The Boston *Commonwealth,* supposedly the newspaper voice of Charles Sumner, declared that Banks was a "Turveydrop," and added bitterly: "Better a thousand times that New Orleans should be today in the hands of an open rebel than of this man, who makes our war a crime and shame before the world."[28] The Democratic press, probably to the general's embarrassment, rushed to his defense. The leading Copperhead journal of the nation suggested that he would make an admirable secretary of war, and other Democratic papers claimed he was a follower of McClellan.[29]

The angry radicals now began to watch Banks' every move, and they found increasing fuel for their wrath. They charged that he was blocking the enlistment of Negro soldiers, and that his course stamped him as a new but notorious member of the proslavery clique. The Reverend Henry Ward Beecher's politico-religious weekly accused him of permitting the civil officers in Louisiana, elected after the state seceded, to resume their functions. "Movements are made toward reconstruction without destroying slavery in Louisiana," complained this source of criticism. The same journal claimed that Banks was using soldiers to return fugitive slaves, protecting the property of rebels, and allowing the whites to torture Negroes.[30]

[27] *O. R.,* series 1, 15:666–667, 678.

[28] Wendell Phillips, quoted in the *New York Tribune,* February 3, 1863; *ibid.,* February 4, 10, March 4, editorials; *Harper's Weekly,* February 21; Boston *Commonwealth,* quoted in the *Detroit Free Press,* March 7, 1863.

[29] New York *World,* February 17, 1863; *Detroit Free Press,* February 6, 12.

[30] Boston *Commonwealth,* quoted *ibid.,* April 23, 1863; *Detroit Adver-*

The Banks administration determined the Jacobins to strike for absolute control of the military patronage, especially in areas like Louisiana where the policies of reconstruction would be worked out and put into effect. Here the Jacobins were resolved to have uncompromising radical generals in command. They wanted men of the kind recommended to the Committee by General Silas Casey, whom McClellan had relieved of duty during the Peninsula campaign because of incompetence. Casey told the approving inquisitors that the time had come when the war must be managed exclusively by officers "whose hearts are in the matter. A man with half the ability, if his heart is in the matter, is better than a man with double the ability if his heart is not in it."[31] The radical bosses were certain about the hearts, if not the abilities, of Butler and Frémont. They demanded that these two generals be assigned to important commands in the South.

They wanted Butler restored to New Orleans. The rakish general was still in Washington in February, fraternizing with the radical politicos and pulling strings to get an appointment. He testified before the Committee and delighted the members with his vigorous indorsement of the employment of Negro soldiers and his description of the ease with which a slave army could be recruited in Louisiana—if a general with the right heart were in command. He treated his admiring audience to a lecture on the entire theater of the war and the correct conduct of military operations. A waggish reporter wrote to his paper: "General Butler has been before the Committee on the Conduct of the War. His testimony exhibited a knowledge of military details in every department in the country, as well as the condition of Southern harbors, rivers, and bays, and the condition of the rebels for defence."[32]

The Committee radicals were ready to throw in all their chips for Butler. Wade and Chandler were anxious to get

tiser and Tribune, April 24; New York Independent, May 28, June 11, 1863.

[31] C.C.W., 1863, 1:447.

[32] Ibid., 3:353–364; Detroit Free Press, February 4, 1863, Washington correspondence.

Butler a command in the West, to build up Western support for the general as "the coming man" in politics after the war had ended.[33] At intervals during January and February, reports thrilled the radicals that the Committee had persuaded Lincoln to send Butler back to New Orleans. In Senate speeches Chandler and Wilson defended the general hotly against Democratic charges that his administration in Louisiana had been marked by wholesale corruption. But despite the best efforts of the Jacobins, Butler did not get an assignment. It was rumored that Seward had thrown his full influence against Butler's restoration to command.[34]

The Jacobins fared no better with their plans for Frémont. They demanded that the administration send him to North Carolina to recruit a huge Negro army which he would then lead in a march of conquest through the lower South. Rumors came out of Washington that the Committee was successfully pressing Lincoln to appoint the general to this command. In the House Julian lauded Frémont's record extravagantly, and threatened the administration with dire punishment if it refused to give him an appointment: "I believe no commander in the public service has thus far shown more military genius, or been more successful, considering the circumstances of his command. . . . I can never think of the woes and sorrows with which this war has deluged our country within the past twelve months, without deploring the malign influences which led the administration to strike down a Republican major-general in the midst of a glorious career, and in defiance of the sentiments of the people, while Democratic generals who were lauded by every rebel sympathizer throughout the country . . . have been persistently kept at the head of our great military departments."[35]

[33] J. M. Shaffer to Benjamin F. Butler, May 28, 1863, in *Butler Correspondence*, 3:77–79.

[34] *New York Tribune*, January 24, 1863; *Detroit Free Press*, February 26, 27, 1863; *Congressional Globe*, 37 Congress, 3 Session, 1334, 1337; New York *Independent*, May 21, 1863; Rochester *Union*, quoted in the *Detroit Free Press*, February 22, 1863.

[35] St. Louis *Missouri Democrat*, February 6, 1863; *New York Tribune*, February 12; Rochester *Union*, quoted in the *Detroit Free Press*, February 22; Julian, *Speeches on Political Questions*, 207–209.

Frémont's future looked bright, especially when Stanton promised to work for his advancement. The Pathfinder himself came to Washington early in March to confer secretly with his allies of the Committee about the nature of his appointment. Lincoln, however, had not the slightest intention of giving Frémont an assignment, although he skillfully fended off the Jacobins with vague promises when they praised the general's merits. By mid-March they saw through the president's excuses and delays and realized that he would do nothing for their favorite. In an angry mood, Julian went to the White House to make a personal appeal and returned rebuffed and angrier.[36]

The Committee's report on the Western Department, released with its other publication in April, stirred anew the hopes of Frémont's partisans. The inquisitors applied liberal daubs of whitewash to the episodes in his career which shrieked of inefficiency, and commended lavishly his administration at St. Louis and his foresightedness in grasping the need for an emancipation proclamation before the president did. The report spurred the Jacobins to renew their clamor for an appointment for Frémont. Again optimistic rumors swept through the radical ranks that he would be assigned to the command of a great army of freed slaves. Thad Stevens, who should have known better, believed these stories. "I learned from the President . . . that he was about to offer to the General the command of the Negro army, which he hoped would soon be 100,000 strong," he wrote. "I hope Frémont may accept it, and beat all the white troops in action, and thereby acquire glory."[37] Again Lincoln was playing with the Jacobins; Frémont continued to languish without employment.

[36] Robert Bonner, editor of the *New York Ledger*, to Edwin M. Stanton, March 2, 1863, in the Stanton MSS.; Stanton to John C. Frémont, March 21, in the Stanton MS. Letterbooks, vol. 1. *Detroit Free Press*, March 10, 1863, Washington correspondence; *New York Tribune*, March 10, 1863, Washington correspondence, March 24, editorial; Julian, *Recollections*, 229–230.

[37] *C.C.W.*, 1863, 3:5–6; *New York Tribune*, April 10, 1863; Bartlett, *Frémont*, 82; Brotherhead, *Fremont*, 5; Charles A. Dana, *Recollections of the Civil War* (New York, 1898), 5; Thaddeus Stevens, letter of June 9, 1863, in the Stevens MSS.; *New York Independent*, May 7.

The president's refusal to award commands to Butler and Frémont infuriated the Jacobins. They cried warningly that the emancipation proclamation, unless enforced by its friends, would be only a barren husk. The radical press charged that Seward and Halleck were deliberately blocking the appointments of antislavery generals in order to prevent the enlistment of Negro soldiers. Scornfully the Boston *Commonwealth* declared: "This talk about our having an emancipation policy is idiotic. We have never had such a policy, nor anything like it."[38]

While the Jacobins were mixing unsuccessfully in army politics the spring elections loomed at hand. Again the administration and the Republican Party would have to submit their policies to the voters for approval. The Jacobins remembered the smashing Democratic victories of the previous autumn's contests, when the Republicans went into the campaign disunited. Still shaken by that debacle, the bosses determined to preserve a semblance of party harmony until the elections were over. Temporarily they were willing to sing low in their criticisms of Lincoln. The administration was bad enough, but another Copperhead triumph would be disastrous. Joseph Medill counselled: "Our view is, that we ought to do all we can to strengthen the hands of the administration until the crisis is past. . . . An awful responsibility rests upon our party. If it carries the war to a successful close, the people will continue it in power. If it fails, all is lost, Union, party, cause, freedom, and abolition of slavery."[39]

The unity of the Republicans was entirely on the surface. Beneath the calm exterior presented to the public the two factions were still at each other's throats. Both expressed scornful contempt for Lincoln. Young Richard Henry Dana, visiting Washington in February and March, was appalled by the stream of abuse which the politicians directed at the man in the White House. "As to the politics of Washington," he

[38] *Detroit Advertiser and Tribune*, April 24, 1863; New York *Independent*, May 21; *Boston Commonwealth*, quoted in the *Detroit Free Press*, April 23, 1863.

[39] Joseph Medill to A. S. Hill, March 20, 1863, in Rhodes, *History of the United States*, 4:241, footnote.

wrote, "the most striking thing is the absence of personal loyalty to the President. It does not exist. . . . If a Republican convention were to be held tomorrow, he would not get the vote of a State." Murat Halstead, the brilliant editor of the conservative *Cincinnati Gazette,* warned John Sherman that the moderates were disgusted with Lincoln's weak-kneed pandering to the radicals: "There is a change in the current of public sentiment out West—a reaction against the Butlerites. If Lincoln was not a damn fool, we could get along yet. He is an awful, woeful ass, and therefore all the enemies of the government look to him to give them all the capital that is necessary as a political instrument to give them power. But what we want is not any more nigger—not any if you please."[40]

These subterranean rumblings did not find their way out of cloakroom caucuses and capital barrooms. Grimly the Republicans closed their ranks to smash down the Democrats in the elections. The national committee sent over forty speakers, including a battery of generals, into Connecticut to stump every corner of the state. Stanton told the Republican governor, up for re-election, that the War Department stood ready to furlough home to vote as many Republican soldiers as could safely be spared from the army. It was reported that a huge slush fund was available to swing the New England states, that the manufacturers of that section, who "are declaring dividends of one hundred and one hundred and fifty per cent have contributed liberally toward the electioneering fund."[41] Factory employers threatened to discharge their workers if they did not vote Republican and to close their plants in the dire event of a Democratic victory. To the joy of the radicals, Lincoln for the first time hurled the influence of the federal officeholders in the contested states into the struggle.[42]

[40] Richard Henry Dana to Charles Francis Adams, March 9, 1863, in Adams, *Dana,* 2:264; Murat Halstead to John Sherman, February 8, 1863, in the Sherman MSS.

[41] *New York Express,* April 1, 1863; Edwin M. Stanton to William A. Buckingham, March 21, 1863, in the Stanton MS. Letterbooks, vol. 1; Rochester *Union,* quoted in the *Detroit Free Press,* March 10, 1863.

[42] *Boston Courier,* April 6, 1863; New York *Independent,* May 7, 1863, Washington correspondence.

Despite these prodigious efforts the Republicans barely scraped through in New England. Their gubernatorial candidates won by majorities that were uncomfortably narrow, and in some cases the victories were the result of a split between the War and Peace Democrats. The Democracy carried the Chicago mayoralty election.[43] Certainly the voters had not returned a clear-cut declaration of approval of Republican prosecution of the war.

Temporarily the disappointing outcome of the elections sobered the radicals and tended to keep them in line behind Lincoln. They were afraid to precipitate open strife in the party when the administration was in evident danger of repudiation by the people. Then too they were cheered at reports that the president was moving steadily in the direction of radicalism. Beecher's organ said that the administration was at last preparing the machinery to enlist Negro soldiers and that military emancipation would be pushed to the limit. Seward's influence in the Cabinet had declined, with the result that the president's advisers now constituted a unit. Stanton had declared that he intended to sweep the armies clean of Democratic generals.[44]

More encouraging to the Jacobins than Lincoln's apparent conversion to radicalism was the news coming out of Falmouth. There Hooker was whipping the demoralized army he had inherited into magnificent condition. The depleted muster rolls again were filled, and the soldiers were ready to follow their dashing commander unquestioningly. It was an army, boasted Stanton to Sumner, which "ought to be able to go on its belly to Richmond." Hooker announced that he intended to move against Lee as soon as good weather set in, and at intervals he came up to Washington to discuss his plans with Lincoln, Stanton, and the Committee.[45] The general's conversation swaggered with threats of what he would do to Lee and Jackson

[43] New York *World*, April 7, 1863; *Detroit Free Press*, March 14, April 7; *Chicago Times*, April 23.

[44] New York *Independent*, April 16, 30, May 7, June 4, 1863.

[45] Pierce, *Sumner*, 4:114; *New York Herald*, March 12, 1863, Washington correspondence.

once he caught up with them. He had "the finest army on this planet," he declared proudly. He added a remark which arose later to plague him: "My plans are perfect. . . . May God have mercy on General Lee, for I will have none." His confidence was infectious. The country expected him to smash the Confederacy with one great victory, to tumble "the whole card-castle of slavery," as Charles Sumner ecstatically predicted.[46] Democratic critics pointed out that "Fighting Joe" had placed himself in a perilous position. He had denounced as incompetents all the generals who were his rivals, he had promised victory, he had raised high the hopes of the people. If he failed, his own words would rise up to damn him.[47] Such admonitions went unheeded by the joyously expectant radicals. Sumner quoted Hooker as saying he "did not mean to drive the enemy, but to bag him." "It is thought he is now doing it," Sumner wrote happily on the very day when Lee was crushing the finest army on the planet at Chancellorsville.[48]

Hooker worked out a brilliant plan of operations. He would throw his army across the Rappahannock above Fredericksburg and advance to attack Lee in the dreary stretch of country to the south known as "the Wilderness." He made the crossing without loss, and his magnificent army of 130,000 menaced Lee's 60,000. Then suddenly "Fighting Joe" lost his daring. He drew back to a defensive position near Chancellorsville and waited for the Confederates to attack. Lee, playing a dangerous game, split his small force and sent Jackson to fall on the Union flank. Hooker could have crushed Lee while Jackson was on the march, but he was palsied with indecision. Jackson struck and crumpled a surprised Union division, and at the same time Lee surged in along Hooker's front. There followed the strange spectacle of an army driving before it an enemy twice its size. When the Confederate assault opened, Hooker was standing on the porch of a house directing the battle. A

[46] Pierce, *Sumner*, 4:133–134; *Harper's Weekly*, April 4, 1863; George Smith to George W. Julian, May 2, in the Giddings-Julian MSS.
[47] *New York Herald*, April 30, 1863.
[48] Charles Sumner to Francis Lieber, May 3, 1863, in Pierce, *Sumner*, 4:138–139.

shot from a Confederate battery struck the building, and a falling pillar crashed upon him. Before he lost consciousness he ordered a retreat. Once more a defeated Union army forded the Rappahannock and stumbled back into Falmouth.

The first reports from Chancellorsville had heralded a Union victory. But in a few days the country knew that the Army of the Potomac had suffered another great disaster. The popular depression was the greater because Hooker had raised hopes high with his glowing talk of certain victory.[49] Lincoln and Halleck went down to Falmouth to confer with Hooker. An alert reporter, watching Lincoln emerge from the commander's quarters, wrote sympathetically, "The President's countenance seemed to bear traces of sore disappointment."[50]

Immediately the Democrats raised a roaring clamor for Hooker's removal and the restoration of McClellan. They howled that the army was demoralized and would not follow Hooker. They scouted the story of the porch pillar falling on the commander, and charged he had been sodden drunk during the battle.[51] Valiantly the radicals rallied to Hooker's defense. He was the idol of his soldiers, one editor declared, and would yet lead the nation to victory. Wendell Phillips announced that Hooker must be sustained because he was a fighting general and an emancipationist. "Let me make the generals, and I don't care who makes the proclamations," Phillips added. Medill, in the *Chicago Tribune,* insisted that fickle fortune had swung the victory to Lee at Chancellorsville, and accused the McClellan gang of trying to exploit the situation to get rid of Hooker. The Washington correspondent of Beecher's journal assured his readers that no one in the government wanted to oust Hooker, but that there were encouraging signs that Halleck was facing dismissal. Thaddeus Stevens conducted

[49] *New York Tribune,* May 8, 1863; *New York Times,* May 9; *Chicago Tribune,* May 8; *Harper's Weekly,* May 16.
[50] *New York Herald,* May 9, army correspondence. See also New York *Independent,* May 14, Washington correspondence.
[51] New York *World,* May 8, 1863; Washington *National Intelligencer,* May 8, June 18; *Detroit Free Press,* May 9.

an investigation of the stories that Hooker had been drunk during the fighting, and stamped them as atrociously false.[52] Stevens was a practising expert on the influence of liquor, and his opinion should have stilled all whispers.

The behavior of the Jacobins differed strangely from their conduct when a Democratic commander suffered a disaster. Now there was no savage criticism of the administration, no press campaign for an army purge; the Committee raised no hue and cry against the commanding general or his subordinate. So eager were the radicals to save Hooker that they publicly disavowed any purpose of making political capital out of the popular dissatisfaction by moving for a reform of the Cabinet. It must have startled contemporaries to hear Horace Greeley, the proprietor of the "On to Richmond" cry, counsel his readers to be patient and to refrain from censoring the government: "We must all exercise patience. We strongly hope to have the pleasure of diffusing joyful intelligence before the end of the week, but shall endeavor to bear reverses with equanimity if we must."[53]

The most sensational departure from the usual radical program was the refusal of the Committee to take any action; apparently the inquisitors were afraid of what they might turn up if they ventured a formal investigation. Wade and Chandler, accompanied by Wilson, journeyed to Falmouth to talk with Hooker and the corps commanders. The conservative generals, hoping to displace Hooker, had set on foot an intrigue to get the command for Meade, but Wade and Chandler sensed their design and pointedly ignored Meade and his supporters during the interviews. The Committee was determined to uphold "Fighting Joe." Seward was engineering a conspiracy to remove Hooker, Chandler said, but the Committee would block his efforts. On their return to Washington the senators loudly

[52] Philadelphia *Press*, May 11, 1863; Wendell Phillips, quoted in the *New York Tribune*, May 12, 1863; *Chicago Tribune*, May 15, 18, 1863; New York *Independent*, May 14, Washington correspondence; Thaddeus Stevens, letter of May 18, 1863, in the Stevens MSS.
[53] New York *Independent*, May 14, 1863, Washington correspondence; *New York Tribune*, May 10, 1863.

informed everyone that the army was in splendid fighting condition and champing to be led to victory by Hooker.[54]

But not all the efforts of the Committee and the Jacobin machine could protect Hooker from the weapon of army intrigue—the weapon which he himself had forged to destroy Burnside and which now with poetic justice recoiled fatally upon him. Hooker later told the Committee that Halleck and the McClellan clique had schemed to bring about his downfall before Chancellorsville, and that they brought their plot into the open after the battle. If "Old Brains" had been acting "in the rebel interest," Hooker charged, he could not have done more to damage the army's morale and its confidence in the commander.[55] Republican subordinate officers corroborated Hooker's testimony. Daniel Butterfield thought there was "a conspiracy against him among the corps commanders." Sickles declared that "the partisans of General McClellan, then in high command, were hostile to General Hooker."[56] Lincoln heard about the plans being hatched at Falmouth from Governor Andrew Curtin of Pennsylvania, who was pushing Meade to succeed Hooker. Disturbed by Curtin's news, the president wrote Hooker a warning letter: "I must tell you that some of your corps and division commanders are not giving you their entire confidence. This would be ruinous if true." Lincoln interviewed most of the corps generals about the condition of the army, but he never revealed to Hooker what they told him.[57]

The whole situation was a distressing replica of the days after Fredericksburg when Hooker instigated and led an intrigue to unseat Burnside. The result was the same—the army and the country lost faith in the commanding general. It became only a question of time until Hooker, finding his posi-

---

[54] George G. Meade to Mrs. Meade, May 20, 1863, in Meade, *Life of Meade*, 1:379; Zachariah Chandler to Mrs. Chandler, May 29, 1863, in the Chandler MSS.; New York *Independent*, May 28, 1863, Washington correspondence.

[55] *C.C.W.*, 1865, 1:111–112, 142, 175–176.

[56] *Ibid.*, 83, Butterfield's testimony; 14–15, Sickles'.

[57] Meade, *Meade*, 1:379; *C.C.W.*, 1865, 1:150–151.

tion unbearable, would resign. He soon found a pretext. Lee, after Chancellorsville, decided upon another invasion of the North and struck toward the Pennsylvania border. Hooker followed in a parallel line, ready to offer battle. Wishing to augment his force with every available man, he asked Halleck for the garrison at Harper's Ferry. Halleck refused to let him have it. Then Hooker went to Washington and handed Lincoln his resignation, claiming that Halleck was trying to sabotage his plans. Stanton and Chase begged him to remain, but he had had enough.[58] Lincoln appointed Meade to the command.

Strangely, the radical press did not regret Hooker's passing. Both the *Tribune* and the *Independent* admitted that he had been a failure, and both questioned the sincerity of his devotion to the antislavery cause.[59] But the radicals of the Committee were enraged at Halleck. In the following year, when the inquisitors were trying to get Hooker restored to the Potomac command, they conducted an investigation of the Chancellorsville campaign and the events which followed, and presented a report charging that the conservative generals had not sustained Hooker properly during the battle. They accused Halleck and the McClellan clique of entering into a conspiracy to destroy Hooker. If Hooker had enjoyed the cooperation of Halleck as Meade did, the Committee declared, he would have smashed Lee's invasion.[60] Wade termed the change in commanders on the eve of a crucial battle "a rash and unwise act," indulged in by Halleck because he was willing "to jeopard the army to personal considerations."[61]

[58] *Ibid.*, 176–178; Pierce, *Sumner*, 4:142.
[59] *New York Tribune*, June 29, July 1, 1863; New York *Independent*, July 2.
[60] *C.C.W.*, 1865, 1:xlviii, liii–liv.
[61] *Ibid.*, 82, 303.

11

Meade and the Issue of Reconstruction

THE COUNTRY knew little about George Gordon Meade when he assumed command of the Army of the Potomac in those melancholy days of late June as Lee drove northward into Pennsylvania. One editor thought his appointment must have been an "official accident."[1] The austere, reticent Meade did not know the art of self-advertising as practised by some of his more ambitious colleagues. A stern honesty ruled all his actions, and his strict code hindered his advancement in a time when other military men did not hold these qualities in such high regard. He had a thin, scholarly face framed in a luxuriant beard and sparse hair. His body was tight and nervous, his disposition high-strung and irritable. He had a bad habit of flaring out in fits of scolding anger, and he needlessly aroused the enmity of many people. His soldiers, who respected but did not love him, called him "the old snapping turtle." As a commanding general, Meade was exceedingly competent, but he lacked the boldness and imagination which make genius. He was a good defensive fighter. When offensive movements were called for, he had a little too much of McClellan's caution.

The Jacobin bosses resented the selection of Meade. They knew him as a member of the Democratic clique and a friend of McClellan, and suspected that he was under the dominance of Halleck. In their suspicion-charged minds they accused him of disloyalty, because he and Henry A. Wise, the Virginia secessionist leader, had married sisters.[2]

Meade grasped the military reins at a moment when the North was shaking with fright. Lee's host was rolling into Pennsylvania and the radical press was screaming that the

---

[1] New York *Independent,* July 9, 1863.
[2] *C.C.W.,* 1865, 1:303, 327; R. A. Maxwell to William P. Fessenden, September 20, 1864, in the Fessenden MSS.

rebels could dare an invasion because their government, unlike the Lincoln administration, was animated by a great single purpose of victory.[3] At Gettysburg Meade and his army, who had barely got acquainted with each other, met the redoubtable and seemingly invincible Lee. Here in the first hot days of July occurred the tremendous battle sometimes called the high-water mark of the Confederacy. Lee hurled his legions, headed by Longstreet and Pickett, against Meade's strong defensive positions. The Confederate attack could not budge Meade, and finally Lee, his army shaken and weakened, had to retreat. As the gray-clad soldiers pointed southward, the North rang with relief and joy. Meade was hailed as a savior, even by the radicals. Greeley predicted that the commander would hunt down and disperse Lee's beaten band, and the war would be over.[4]

But Meade made no move to pursue Lee. The Confederates slipped over the Potomac in safety, while the Union army snailed after them at a circumspect distance. Then the Jacobins began to snipe at Meade and wrench at the laurels they had helped to place on his brow. Stanton declared in disgust that "since the world began, no man ever missed so great an opportunity of serving his country as was lost by his neglecting to strike his adversary at Williamsport." Charles A. Dana, who had decided to back Grant as the coming man, informed the latter's friends that Meade's failure to bag Lee had aroused bitter criticism but that there was no talk yet of removing him. Pious old Eleutheros Cooke, of the great banking family, thought Meade had committed blasphemy in not catching the rebels. "Providence had done His part in swelling the Potomac" to prevent Lee's passage, Eleutheros said, but the Union commander had refused to cooperate with the Deity. Meade's prestige as the victor of Gettysburg temporarily preserved him from an open radical attack, especially by the Committee, but the Jacobins started a persistent whispering campaign to steal

[3] New York *Independent*, July 2, 1863.

[4] Horace Greeley, article *ibid.*, July 9. See also the editorial in the same issue; *New York Tribune*, July 7; *Harper's Weekly*, July 18; Henry D. Cooke to John Sherman, July 9, 1863, in the Sherman MSS.

his glory. They claimed that he did not deserve the credit for Gettysburg—that the Republican corps commanders had planned and won the battle. They pointed to his continued inactivity during the summer as proof of his incompetence.[5]

Gettysburg was not the only victory which thrilled the country in July. On the glorious Fourth when Lee began his retreat, Vicksburg, the great Confederate stronghold on the Mississippi, surrendered to Grant. Extravagant predictions that the South would be crushed in a few months resounded on all sides. The Jacobins were not elated at these auguries of triumph. The immediate destruction of the Confederacy and the end of the war was exactly what they did not want. If peace came now it would, they feared, be a peace of compromise and appeasement. Seward and Montgomery Blair would persuade Lincoln to negotiate a settlement on the basis of the *status quo,* perhaps with slavery left intact, and certainly without striking down the political and economic power of the Democratic slavocracy. The prospect frightened Charles Sumner. Victories, he cried, were more dangerous to the radical cause than defeats. He wanted "more delay and more suffering" before there was any talk of peace. "Before this comes," he wrote, "I wish two hundred thousand negroes with muskets in their hands, and then I shall not fear compromise."[6]

Senator Trumbull, at home in Illinois after the adjournment of Congress, puzzled over the possible effects of impending victory and peace upon the radical policies. He asked Chandler for counsel. Would Meade and Grant smash the rebellion within the next hundred days? Would Lincoln back down on the emancipation proclamation? Would the administration

[5] Edwin M. Stanton to A. K. McClure, July 22, 1863, in the Stanton MS. Letterbooks, vol. 2; Charles A. Dana to General James H. Wilson, July 21, 1863, in James H. Wilson, *Life of Charles A. Dana* (New York, 1907), 249–250; Eleutheros Cooke to Jay Cooke, July, 1863, in Oberholtzer, *Cooke,* 1:265–266, footnote; New York *Independent,* July 30, 1863, Washington correspondence; *Wilkes' Spirit of the Times,* August 29.

[6] Horace Greeley to J. H. Stevens, August 16, 1863, in the Greeley MSS.; New York *Independent,* July 23, Washington correspondence and editorial, July 30, editorial; Charles Sumner to E. L. Pierce, July 29, 1863, in Pierce, *Sumner,* 4:142; Sumner to John Bright, July 21, *ibid.,* 142–143.

"patch up a compromise with traitors"? Chandler replied in a letter that breathed optimism. He looked for the speedy collapse of the Confederacy. "We have, in my judgment, reached the critical point of the war. . . . Now we must fight one more tremendous battle and if we are successful the bubble will burst. Are we quite ready?" Chandler said yes. He had no fear that slavery would ever rise alive from the ashes of the war. "The slavery question is settling itself with great rapidity. Every Negro regiment of a thousand men presents just one thousand unanswerable arguments against the revocation of the Presidents proclamation." Chandler scoffed at the notion that Lincoln would withdraw the proclamation. "I have little fear that the President will recede. He is as stubborn as a mule when he gets his back up and it is up now on the Proclamation. Seward and Weed are snaky, but this peculiar trait of stubborness (which annoyed us so much 18 months ago) is now our salvation."[7]

Other radicals re-echoed Chandler's faith that emancipation would and must endure. The New York *Independent,* which from the first had feared that Lincoln might waver, threateningly warned him to stand firm. Victory was now within reach, its editor informed him, only because the administration had adopted, almost too late, the radical war program. Let Lincoln adhere to the policy which had generated the recent military triumphs: "Having of late won battles by the mailed hand, let him not now be beguiled by the friends of the enemy into striking a soft blow with a silken glove."[8]

Lincoln soon found an opportunity to soothe the apprehensions of the worried Jacobins. In late August he was invited to address a Union meeting in his home town, Springfield, sponsored by men who objected to making emancipation one of the aims of the war. He declined in an open letter, published in the newspapers, to the chairman of the local committee. The letter was a public declaration that he would sustain the

[7] Lyman Trumbull to Zachariah Chandler, August 4, 1863, in the Chandler MSS.; Zachariah Chandler to Lyman Trumbull, August 6, 1863, in the Trumbull MSS.
[8] New York *Independent,* August 6, 1863.

emancipation edict to the end. Chiding those who still opposed freedom for the slaves, he asserted that every man who professed support for the Union cause must also support the proclamation, because emancipation was the surest way to crush the rebellion. He promised that he would never revoke any part of the proclamation. The radicals were delighted. Slow but sure Abraham was on the right track and meant to stay there. They applauded his pledge of devotion to radicalism as a token of better things to come. *Harper's* "Lounger," watching the Washington scene, concluded that Lincoln knew how to play the political game: "The conservative Republicans think him too much in the hands of the radicals; while the radical Republicans think him too slow, yielding, and half-hearted." But both factions had to accept his leadership—for the moment.[9] The Jacobins again shouted his praise in September, when it was announced that the administration was about to suspend the *habeas corpus* in certain Northern states. They took this to mean that the government meant to deal sternly with Copperheads in the approaching fall elections. Beecher's *Independent* hailed the president's too-long-delayed resolve to squelch traitors, and at the same time pointedly informed him that the radicals would oppose his nomination for a second term: "Rising to the dignity of the time, the President during his third year has shown a comprehensive policy and a wisdom in its execution which promise to broaden his sun at its setting." A contributor to the *Independent* declared enthusiastically that the radicals now ruled the administration; the great triumvirate of Stanton, Chase, and Holt was supreme.[10]

The Jacobins faced the fall elections with swaggering confidence and a determination to wipe out the losses of the

[9] Letter to James C. Conkling, August 26, 1863, in Lincoln, *Works*, 9: 95–102; New York *Independent*, September 10, 1863, p. 2; *ibid.*, September 10; *New York Tribune*, September 3; J. M. Forbes to Charles Sumner, September 8, in Hughes, *Forbes*, 2:58–59; Mary Lewis to George W. Julian, September 4, in the Giddings-Julian MSS.; *Harper's Weekly*, August 29, 1863, "The Lounger."

[10] New York *Independent*, September 17, 1863; *ibid.*, October 15, letter of "A Massachusetts Man," p. 1.

previous year when the Democrats had come perilously close to gaining control of Congress. The Republican national committee threw batteries of speakers into every state. Wade, Chandler, and Julian stumped the Northwest, proclaiming the insidious effects of Democratic influence upon the conduct of the war. But the most potent force working for Republican victory was Stanton. He dashed off letters to Fessenden, Hannibal Hamlin, and other party leaders, offering to furlough home enough soldiers to swing the elections. "I will thank you to inform me of anything that can be done by this Department towards achieving a patriotic success in New York this fall and it shall surely be done to the extent of my power," he wrote to O. B. Matteson.[11] The soldier votes which Stanton poured into the ballot boxes carried the day in several states, notably Pennsylvania, where Curtin held on to the governorship by a narrow margin. "This state has really been carried by *fraud*," one Republican admitted to Sherman, "but we have control of the State which is very important." Another said Curtin would have been defeated "if it had not been for the soldiers etc we got at the last."[12]

The Republicans swept every Northern state except New Jersey, "which does not count," *Harper's* explained exultantly. The conservatives interpreted the results as a popular ratification of the administration's policies, now "fairly and squarely endorsed by the people," proclaimed *Harper's*. Greeley, strangely friendly to Lincoln since July, advanced the same opinion. He urged the party to forget its factional differences and follow the president's leadership unitedly.[13] But the Jacobins viewed the astonishing Republican successes in an entirely different light. The people had placed a permanent seal of approval upon the radical war program, and emancipa-

[11] Edwin M. Stanton to O. B. Matteson, October 16, 1863, in the Stanton MS. Letterbooks, vol. 3, part 1; Stanton to R. P. Spaulding, Cleveland, September 10, *ibid.*; Stanton to William P. Fessenden, August 3, and to Hannibal Hamlin, August 20, *ibid.*, vol. 2.

[12] Alfred Denny to John Sherman, October 15, 1863, in the Sherman MSS.; V. H. Painter to Sherman, October 24, *ibid.*

[13] *Harper's Weekly*, October 31, November 14, 1863; *New York Tribune*, October 22, 23, 1863.

tion was at last safe from any attack, whether it came from Democrats or from the appeasing Seward. The elegant and literary John Lothrop Motley crowed: "The elections I consider of far more consequence than the battles, or rather the success of the antislavery party and its steadily increasing strength make it a mathematical certainty that, however the tide of battle may ebb and flow with varying results, the progress of the war is steadily in one direction." The Jacobin press cried that the returns were a mandate to the administration from the North to advance further and faster in the direction of radicalism and the New Jerusalem. "Do these elections indorse the policy of the government?" asked one editor. "They do more. Approving what the government has done, they say— this is too little, do more. . . . The elections were an indorsement of the government's forward, not backward measures, of its aggressive, not its conservative, zeal, and of its iron hand, not of its silk glove method with the rebellion."[14]

Immediately after the election victories, the old strife between the radicals and the conservatives blazed up with fiercer vigor. No longer did the Jacobins have to repress their hostility to the administration out of a rankling fear that the party's standing with the voters was uncertain and precarious. Radical propaganda had educated the masses to accept emancipation and Negro soldiers. Flushed with triumph the bosses now determined to mold public opinion to support new radical issues. With the end of the war apparently close at hand, the Jacobins faced the problem of the reconstruction of the South and the terms upon which the seceded states would be permitted to come back to the Union. The radicals had a design for the New South already worked out. Some of the details were lacking, but the main outline was starkly clear. They demanded conditions for readmission which would insure Republican domination of the Southern political system and give the deathblow to the power of the slaveholding aristocracy.

[14] George W. Curtis, ed., *Correspondence of John Lothrop Motley* (New York, 1889), 2:143; New York *Independent*, October 15, 1863; *ibid.*, November 5.

They were too smart, in 1863 when the people had barely begun to consider the subject of reconstruction, to talk about their purpose of forcing Negro suffrage upon the South. This was the surest way of establishing Republican control in Dixie, but they realized that large doses of propaganda would have to be administered before they could educate the public to support this position. Fervently the Jacobins believed that Lincoln was not the man to handle the process of reconstruction. They feared that his kindly nature and conservative temperament would lead him to contrive a policy which would bring back the seceded states with the slavocracy unscathed and unpunished and the former slaves still mere hewers of wood for the ruling class. Because they distrusted the president, the radicals insisted that Congress was the proper constitutional authority to frame a program of reconstruction. But Lincoln acted as if it was the business of the executive and a legitimate exercise of his war powers. In August he asked his henchman the detested Banks to set up a civil government in Louisiana, backed by the bayonets of the army. The general was zealous to carry out Lincoln's wishes but wanted full authority. Lincoln told him he was "master of all," and urged a free state reorganization of Louisiana in the shortest possible time. Banks then proposed an ingenious scheme. He would issue an order calling an election to choose a governor and other state officials, but the order would declare slavery inoperative and void. His purpose was to spare the people the distasteful task of condemning slavery themselves, and thus to attract more voters. He promised, if Lincoln agreed to this plan, to establish a government whenever the president wished.[15] A friend of Julian's, indignantly reading the press accounts of Banks' work, asked harshly, "Is this the justice to be meted out to traitors?"[16]

The Jacobins began in midsummer to ponder the problem of

[15] Abraham Lincoln to Nathaniel P. Banks, August 5 and November 5, 1863, Banks to Lincoln, December 6, 16, in Nicolay and Hay, *Lincoln*, 8: 421–422, 423–424, 427; Lincoln to Banks, December 24, *ibid.*, 427–428; Banks to Lincoln, December 30, *ibid.*, 428–430.

[16] Mary Lewis to George W. Julian, September 16, 1863, in the Giddings-Julian MSS.

reconstruction. Sumner hoped one of the Gulf states, possibly Florida, could be inducted into the Union under congressional supervision, with a new constitution abolishing slavery. This would be a controlling precedent for the admission of other states. Sumner declared that there "can be no talk of admission into the Union except on the basis of the actual condition at the moment, with slavery abolished by the Proclamation. We fear the Secretary of State may intrigue the other way." The radical press sent up trial balloons in every direction to test public sentiment. Who should direct the process of readmission, Congress or the president? What conditions should be imposed upon the conquered states? Emphatically the editors declared that only loyal men should be permitted to participate in the restored Southern governments and that Congress had the right to decide if representatives and senators elected from those states were entitled to their seats. The Jacobins missed the powerful voice of the *Tribune* in the press campaign to drum up support for their plans. Greeley was still honeymooning with the administration. He announced that he favored a speedy re-establishment of the Union and no harsh measures of punishment for the defeated Southern people. To the disgust of the radicals he wanted to entrust the job to Lincoln.[17]

The Jacobin bosses judged that the best way to control the process and machinery of reconstruction was to force the party to ditch Lincoln as its standard-bearer for 1864 and secure the nomination of an inexorable radical. Already a candidate who fitted their pattern was in the lists—Salmon P. Chase. A boom for the pompous secretary had got under way in August, and the radicals watched it hopefully. Beecher's organ pushed his cause openly. The paper's capital correspondent asserted that of all the leaders in the party, Chase was incomparably "the greatest, the strongest, the boldest." Chase made an open bid for radical support when he went into Maryland in the fall election to campaign for the emancipation

[17] Charles Sumner to John Bright, August 4, 1863, in Pierce, *Sumner*, 4:143; *Leslie's Newspaper*, September 26, 1863; New York *Independent*, August 20, 27, September 10, editorials; *ibid.*, August 27, letter of the Reverend S. H. Tyng; *New York Tribune*, November 23, 1863.

faction in the Republican Party, which was fighting to wrest control from the Blair clan and the federal officeholders. By autumn the secretary's candidacy had taken on threatening proportions. Trumbull's informants reported that Chase might go to the convention with all the Northwest in his bag of delegates. In Washington the secretary observed the swelling sentiment in his favor with smug gratification. Coyly receptive and ponderously obvious, he announced that he stood ready to serve his country in any capacity. He considered Mr. Lincoln to be an extremely well-meaning, goodhearted person. But the nation wanted courage and firmness in the leader it would choose to guide it through the years of reconstruction. Chase feared Lincoln did not possess these qualities.[18]

The president watched the growing Chase boom with anxiety but he made no open move to puncture it. Neither would he declare what his reconstruction policy was, nor assail the program the radicals were advancing. But if Lincoln cannily preferred to remain silent, thus protecting himself from attack until public opinion developed on the issue, the Blair brothers, who often acted as his hatchet men, were itching to hack down Chase's presidential ambitions. Fanatically loyal to Lincoln, they hated the bombastic secretary and the radicalism for which he stood. Frank, who had got himself elected to the House from the St. Louis district, was fighting a desperate battle in Missouri to prevent the radicals from getting control of the party. Nevertheless he decided to come to Lincoln's aid. He wrote a public letter to the president, denouncing Chase for permitting his treasury agents to engage in questionable financial deals. Then in a savage speech he flayed the secretary as a political Judas, sitting in the Cabinet, posing as a loyal supporter of the administration, and all the time driving the stiletto into his chief. Bitingly Blair condemned the Jacobins

[18] New York *Independent*, October 15, November 5, 1863, Washington correspondence; W. Barber to Lyman Trumbull, October 30, 1863, and G. T. Brown to Trumbull, November 12, in the Trumbull MSS.; Horace White to William P. Fessenden, November 2, 1863, in the Fessenden MSS.; Salmon P. Chase to William Sprague, November 26, 1863, in Schuckers, *Chase*, 494–495.

and their plans to impose harsh penalties upon the defeated South. Reconstruction, he cried, should be left to the president.[19]

Blair's vitriolic attack upon their champion threw the Jacobins into wild fits of rage. The Missouri organ of the radicals charged that Frank was doing Lincoln's dirty work and that the administration machine was out to prevent Chase's nomination. In Washington the radical politicos buzzed with wrath as they read the speech. They could not believe, wrote Beecher's correspondent in describing their feelings toward Blair, "that men capable of such brutalities of speech will have much influence with the President in the settlement of the Missouri troubles."[20]

But apparently such men had. In early October the other half of the Blair combination, Montgomery, spoke at Rockville, Maryland. He lashed the Jacobins for presuming to say that Congress should direct the machinery of reconstruction. He advocated mild terms for the South and an early restoration of the rebellious states. Although cautious conservatives declared that the postmaster general voiced only his private sentiments, it was generally assumed that he had presented the administration's program and that Lincoln would defy the Jacobin machine on the reconstruction issue. Immediately the angry radicals demanded that the president eject Blair from the Cabinet. Thad Stevens exclaimed that if Montgomery were retained it was time to look for a successor to Lincoln.[21]

The Jacobin anger flared higher when the radical faction in Missouri made a determined attempt to destroy the Blair machine and Lincoln supported the Blairs. The Blair group controlled the state government, and through the governor the state militia. Its program was conservative, even proslavery, the radicals charged. They claimed that Frank used

[19] Smith, *Blair Family*, 2:165–167.

[20] St. Louis *Missouri Democrat*, September 23, 1863, quoted *ibid.*, 166; New York *Independent*, October 8, 1863, Washington correspondence.

[21] Smith, *Blair Family*, 2:237–245; *Harper's Weekly*, October 24, 1863, "The Lounger"; Thaddeus Stevens to Salmon P. Chase, October 8, 1863, in the Stevens MSS.

the militia to terrorize opponents of his regime. The loyal antislavery people of the state were helpless before his legalized banditti, the radical leaders shouted, because General John M. Schofield who commanded the Missouri area took his orders from the Blairs and refused to furnish military protection to their enemies. Since the first year of the war the radicals had labored mightily to overthrow the Blair influence, but their best efforts failed. Lincoln allowed Frank to dispense the federal patronage in Missouri, and the phalanx of job-holders had carried every contest for the conservatives. "The National officeholders," complained an irritated radical, "by the liberal use of their money have exerted a very pernitious [sic] influence in damaging the Radical cause." To the Jacobin bosses Lincoln's Missouri policy seemed like an ominous reversion to the old detested all-parties nation. The *Independent's* Washington correspondent reported that Lincoln's advisers had no conception of the importance of building up Republican machines in the states. They acted as if it were "a matter of no particular moment" whether "in a state the patronage of the administration is given to Republicans or their traitorous opponents."[22]

In late September a determined delegation of seventy Missouri radicals arrived in Washington to see Lincoln. Their purpose was to strike at the root of Blair power by forcing a change in the patronage policy. They demanded an end to the "intolerable pro-slavery oppression" of the Blair machine. They asked the president to remove Schofield and give them Ben Butler. They wanted the government to disband the terrible state militia. Immediately the Jacobin leaders, sensing an opportunity to strike at the Blair influence in the administration, rushed to the support of the petitioners.[23]

The Missouri question was a mass of thorns tossed into Lincoln's lap, and he handled it gingerly. A grapevine rumor asserted that he would try to please both factions by keeping

[22] J. B. Clark to Thaddeus Stevens, November 7, 1863, in the Stevens MSS.; New York *Independent*, October 15, 1863, Washington correspondence.

[23] *Ibid.*, October 1, Washington correspondence, October 8, editorial.

Schofield and curtailing the powers of the state government. But at the last he decided to stay with the Blairs. One observer thought Lincoln suspected that the visit of the Missourians was a radical scheme to damage his chances of renomination: "The President has got his head full of the ideas that the recent 'Missouri delegation' was a corrupt caucus to make Gen Butler the next President—a point on which he is very sensitive."[24] Lincoln informed the protestants in writing that he could not accede to their demands. He refused to dismiss Schofield or interefere with the state government.

His reply goaded the Jacobins to scornful wrath and strengthened their opinion that he was unfit to reconstruct rebels. Even conservative *Harper's* grieved that he had ranged himself "upon the side agreeable to the rebels." The *Independent* exploded with rage. "The letter to the Missouri delegation is a scrawny fruit from the stalk that yielded the golden apple to the Illinois convention," said the editor, recalling Lincoln's ringing defense of emancipation in August. "The President has turned his face to smile coy smiles upon its enemies. . . . He has not committed a graver fault since the day he quenched Fremont's proclamation." Heatedly the editorial accused Lincoln of backsliding from the faith and trying at the last moment to suffocate the great radical reforms. "But now that we are drawing nigh to the Promised Land, are we to be led back to the flesh pots of Egypt? Are we to return once more to the early trifling with the rebellion? Did the President strike slavery so hard on the first of January that he now seeks to parry the blow?"[25]

While the clamor over the Missouri fight still filled the air, Seward handed the Jacobins another jolt. In a speech at his home town of Auburn he discussed the approaching problem of reconstruction. The urbane secretary announced his support of emancipation as one of the aims of the war. "The insurrec-

[24] *Ibid.*, October 8, Washington correspondence; Horace White to William P. Fessenden, November 7, 1863, in the Fessenden MSS.

[25] *Wilkes' Spirit of the Times*, October 10, 1863; J. B. Clark to Thaddeus Stevens, November 7, in the Stevens MSS.; *Harper's Weekly*, November 28, 1863, "The Lounger"; New York *Independent*, October 29, 1863.

tion will perish under military power, necessarily and therefore lawfully exercised," he proclaimed, "and slavery will perish with it." Then he outlined a plan for bringing the South back into the Union at the earliest moment. Despite all the sins of the rebels he would welcome them lovingly: "Nevertheless I am willing that the prodigal son shall return. The doors, as far as I am concerned, shall always be open to him." These rose-water sentiments, supposedly spoken with the administration's approval, disgusted the Jacobins. Seward was starting Lincoln's campaign for renomination, they sneered; he wanted to have old Abe under his thumb for four years more.[26] A little later Seward repeated his proposals at Gettysburg, referring to the Southern people as "our misguided brethren." This was too much for *Harper's* "Lounger," who thought that for the good of the party a halt must be called to the secretary's saccharine mouthings. "Now fine words butter no parsnips," he exclaimed. "Open enemies must not be treated as friends in disguise. They are not to be cozened, they are to be conquered."[27]

With relief and hope the Jacobins turned from the fumblings of Lincoln and his Sewards and Blairs to the opening of Congress in December. They relied upon the presence of the party leaders in Washington to force the president back to the faith. Nine tenths of the Republican members were radicals, boasted Beecher's journal, and the radicals would dominate Congress and determine the nature of all important war legislation. As the Jacobin chieftains grimly took their seats, the capital correspondents looked eagerly for the stalwart figure of Wade. "A sight of him is an excellent medicine for a weak spine—among the politicians," wrote the *Independent*'s realistic commentator.[28]

Lincoln's message to Congress pleased and puzzled the radicals. He repeated his unswerving devotion to emancipation.

[26] *Ibid.*, November 12; *Wilkes' Spirit of the Times*, November 21, 1863.
[27] *Harper's Weekly*, December 19, 1863.
[28] New York *Independent*, November 26, 1863, editorial, December 3, 10, Washington correspondence.

"I shall not attempt to retract or modify the emancipation proclamation, nor shall I return to slavery any person who is free by the terms of that proclamation or by any of the acts of Congress." The radicals applauded this declaration of fidelity, although in the light of recent events they were inclined to distrust the president's sincerity.[29] But bundled up with the message was a "Proclamation of Amnesty and Reconstruction." It was Lincoln's plan for reconstructing the South, announced at last and somewhat disguised as an exercise of his pardoning powers. With certain limited exceptions, such as high Confederate officials, he offered a pardon to all persons in the insurrectionary states who would take an oath to support the Constitution and the acts of Congress and his own proclamations concerning slavery. When in any state ten per cent of the number of voters in 1860 had sworn this oath, they could set up a state government, republican in form, and he would extend to it executive recognition. If the new government wished to adopt some provision which would recognize and declare the permanent freedom of the former slaves, the national government would not object.[30]

The Jacobins could not stomach this mild and tender proposal which threatened to lose them all the gains of the war. The president wanted to bring unrepentant traitors back to power, they cried indignantly. What would become of the freed slaves if the masters still held the reins of government? They would still be chattels. Lincoln's terms were too lenient and generous, and his one tenth idea was preposterous. The disgusted Fessenden thought that "Abraham's proclamation, take it altogether, was a silly performance. . . . Think of telling the rebels they may fight as long as they can, and take a pardon when they have had enough of it." Acute observers

[29] Richardson, *Messages of the Presidents*, 6:190. For the complete message, see *ibid.*, 179–191; *Congressional Globe*, 38 Congress, 1 Session, appendix, 1–4; *New York Tribune*, December 10, 1863, Washington correspondence and editorial; *Harper's Weekly*, December 26; New York *Independent*, December 17, Washington correspondence and editorial.

[30] Lincoln, *Works*, 9:218–223; Richardson, *Messages of the Presidents*, 6:213–215.

predicted that the reconstruction issue would split the party in a new fight.[31]

All during December the political front rumbled with threats of trouble to come. Again the Jacobins were talking about a Cabinet housecleaning, and demanding the resignations of Blair and Bates. It was rumored that fifty members of Congress had signed a petition to the president asking for the dismissal of the postmaster general. The Chase boom continued to gather strength, to the secret anxiety of administration leaders.[32] On the day after Lincoln announced his reconstruction policy, Chase's supporters in Washington held a meeting to discuss ways of pushing their candidate's cause. Horace Greeley acted as if he were about to bolt into the Chase camp.[33] Wendell Phillips proclaimed that the abolitionists would not accept Lincoln as the nominee for 1864, but would gladly take Butler or Frémont.[34]

Nor was all quiet on the Potomac, where bombshells hurled from the radical camp burst dangerously around General Meade. After Gettysburg, Meade placed his army before Washington, but he did not venture a forward movement. All through the dog days he lay idle, while the radicals whispered the story that the corps commanders had really won the great battle in Pennsylvania and would have smashed Lee with a vigorous pursuit but for the commander's criminal vacillation.[35] At the approach of fall Meade crossed the Potomac and engaged the Confederates. But his efforts were halting, and he always drew back at the slightest sign of danger.

[31] New York *Evening Post*, December 10, 1863; New York *Independent*, December 17; Fessenden to his family, December 19, 1863, in Fessenden, *Fessenden*, 1:266–267; *Harper's Weekly*, December 19, 1863.

[32] New York *Independent*, December 17, 1863, Washington correspondence; Smith, *Blair Family*, 2:248; Henry Raymond to Schuyler Colfax, December 5, 1863, in Hollister, *Colfax*, 217–218.

[33] Charles R. Wilson, "The Original Chase Organization Meeting and *The Next Presidential Election*," *Mississippi Valley Historical Review*, 23(1936):62; Randall, *Civil War and Reconstruction*, 609, footnote; *New York Tribune*, December 24, 1863, account of a speech by Greeley.

[34] Bartlett, *Frémont*, 100.

[35] *Wilkes' Spirit of the Times*, August 29, 1863; Welles, *Diary*, 1:472–473.

His apparent exaggerated caution was the result of his attempt to follow Lincoln's instructions to keep the army always between the enemy and the capital. But the radicals screamed taunts at Meade's inaction and delays. He was wasting the ideal autumn weather, they cried, when he should be on the road to Richmond. He was tied up with the McClellan gang, and counseled only with the treacherous Democratic generals who had stabbed Pope and Burnside. He did not believe in fighting. Let the administration recall Joe Hooker to the command! Beecher's correspondent, repeating the opinions of the Jacobin bosses, declared that Meade was cautious to a fault and skilled only in retreat.[36] The general himself expected that the clamor of the radicals would force his removal. General M. R. Patrick later told the Committee of Meade's gloomy resignation following the unsuccessful battle of Mine Run in November: "After our return he came to my tent very much depressed, and said that he was conscious that his head was off."[37]

In December the radical outcry against Meade arose in a new crescendo. Demands for his removal thickened the Washington air. The radical press abounded in sneers at his failures and ultimatums for the return of "Fighting Joe."[38] One editor spoke of the soldiers on the Potomac as "The Doomed Army," doomed by West Point, proslavery incompetence and treason. He wanted all the West Pointers banished to some isolated spot until the war was safely ended.[39] Meade tried to answer his savage critics in a letter which was published in the Demo-

[36] *Leslie's Newspaper*, October 10, 1863; *Wilkes' Spirit of the Times*, October 3, 24, 31; *Harper's Weekly*, November 7; New York *Independent*, October 22, 1863, Washington correspondence, also October 29, November 5.

[37] *C.C.W.*, 1865, 1:474.

[38] *Wilkes' Spirit of the Times*, December 5, 19, 26, 1863; New York *Independent*, December 10, Washington correspondence; *New York Tribune*, December 2, Washington correspondence. See also Murat Halstead to John Sherman, December 14, in the Sherman MSS.; Captain N. Ellmaker to Thaddeus Stevens, December 5, in the Stevens MSS.; Agassiz, *Meade's Headquarters*, 59–60.

[39] *Wilkes' Spirit of the Times*, December 12, 1863.

cratic newspapers. He excused his cautious movements by declaring that he was opposed to sacrificing his soldiers' lives needlessly.[40] To the Jacobins this was disgusting West Point traditionalism. One congressman reportedly exclaimed that "it would be better to strew the road to Richmond with the dead bodies of our soldiers rather than that there should be nothing done!"[41]

A bit of doggerel verse, anonymously authored, went the rounds in Washington, repeated with special delight by the radicals. It recalled the famous message which the French king, Francis I, sent to his wife when he was captured at the battle of Pavia in the sixteenth century, "All is lost, save honor."

> *The night of Pavia's bloody day,*
> *The words that Francis wrote to her*
> *Whose brave heart watched him far away—*
> *Were, 'Tout est perdu sauf l'honneur.'*
>
> *This evening General Meade may say*
> *Amid the camp fires' light and stir,*
> *Thanking his stars he got away—*
> *'Rien n'est perdu sauf l'honneur.'*[42]

[40] New York *World,* December 15, 1863; *New York Tribune,* December 16.

[41] Agassiz, *Meade's Headquarters,* 61.

[42] New York *Independent,* December 10, 1863, Washington correspondence.

12

The Election of 1864

THE BURNING RESENTMENT of the Jacobin bosses at Lincoln's determination to reconstruct the South by executive action and his refusal to oust the conservatives from the army and the Cabinet flared into open rebellion in 1864. Led by Wade and Chandler, the radical machine made a spectacular attempt to prevent Lincoln's nomination, and later, after the failure of their plot, to force him to withdraw as the Republican candidate. Seldom in American political history have the party leaders dared to dump overboard their incumbent chief after four years of office. Such a step saddles a party with the handicap of repudiating its program and advertising the blunders of its stewardship. The organization goes into the campaign with a depressing defeatist psychology, and victory for the opposition is almost certain. But in 1864 the radicals, in their panting eagerness to control the reconstruction process, chanced this danger. They plunged the Republicans into such savage internecine strife that only the triumphs of Sherman saved the party from disaster in November.

Long before the end of Lincoln's first term the Jacobins began to cast about for a likely candidate with whom to displace him in 1864. In the spring of 1863 Horace Greeley decided that General Rosecrans, who enjoyed a brilliant military reputation he was soon to lose, might be the man. Greeley sent an agent West to plumb the general's political opinions, and received a satisfactory report. But Rosecrans proved to be the wrong horse. After the failure of his Tennessee campaign he was removed, and Greeley abandoned him.[1]

---

[1] James R. Gilmore, *Personal Recollections of Abraham Lincoln and the Civil War* (Boston, 1899), 86–101, 146; Albert G. Riddle, *Life, Character, and Public Services of James A. Garfield* (Cleveland, 1880), 69; Garfield to Salmon P. Chase, in Smith, *Garfield*, 1:276.

No prodding was necessary to kindle the ambitions of Salmon P. Chase to take Lincoln's place in the White House. The strutting master of the Treasury Department was a quadrennial candidate for the presidency before and after 1864. Convinced that he was of larger political stature than the Illinois lawyer who had sneaked the nomination from him in 1860, Chase entered the Cabinet blissfully confident that the voters would yet recognize his transcendent abilities and call him to the office he was born to fill. As early as 1862 he began to make plans to take over Lincoln's work, and his friends started to construct an organization. He courted the favor of Greeley, and used the great propaganda machine built up by his ally, Jay Cooke, to sell the national bonds to advertise his merits. In the spring of the next year he let it be known that he was in a receptive mood, and his supporters openly suggested him as a successor to Lincoln. Soon the elements of dissatisfaction within the party clustered around his candidacy. A few editors and many pint-sized bosses gave him their public indorsement. Privately leaders like Grimes, Morton, Wadsworth, and Greeley assured him that he was their first choice.[2] Elated by these favorable reactions, Chase took to the stump in the fall elections in order to let the people get a good look at him. In reality the evidences of Chase strength were highly illusory. He did not have the open support of a single powerful party chieftain. The radical directory in Washington preferred him to Lincoln, but they were smart enough to keep silent until they could be certain of the popular reaction to his boom. They had their ears to the ground, but they were not sure what it was saying.

As the movement for Chase gathered momentum, another candidate stepped forward to angle for radical support. This was the troubled soldier Frémont. Since his failure to secure a command in 1863 he had sulked in New York, coddling his

[2] Albert B. Hart, *Salmon P. Chase* (*American Statesmen Series,* Boston, 1899), 309; Bartlett, *Frémont,* 87–88; *ibid.,* 88–89, Chase to Greeley, May 21, 1862, Greeley to Chase, September 29, 1863; Oberholtzer, *Cooke,* 1:360–361; Donnal V. Smith, *Chase and Civil War Politics* (Columbus, 1931), 85–88.

wounded vanity and nursing a conviction that he was the victim of a West Point plot. Characteristically he decided to seek vindication in the political arena. Urged on by his wife and friends, he announced in the spring that he would accept the nomination. The Chase managers encouraged his boom, believing that eventually it must collapse and they would garner his supporters. Immediately the Frémont movement attracted to its standard the antislavery Germans of the West and the New England abolitionists. Phillips denounced both Chase and Lincoln, and advised his followers to vote for the Pathfinder, the first general who was right on the great issue.[3] The presence of two radical candidates posed a difficult problem for the Jacobin bosses. They would gladly have taken either before Lincoln, but they doubted whether the secretary or the general had any real popular support. Therefore they remained publicly aloof from the campaigns of both. If they struck Lincoln, they knew they must have public opinion behind them to succeed, and at the moment Father Abraham seemed the idol of the masses.

Of the president's hold upon the people's affections, the Jacobins had abundant and discouraging proof. General Palmer reported to Trumbull that the Western army was almost solid for his re-election. Other correspondents told the senator of Lincoln's mounting strength in the Northwest. In January and February the state machines scrambled to climb on the rolling Lincoln bandwagon. The Republican organizations in ten states went on record in favor of his nomination. When the powerful string of Republican newspapers published by John W. Forney came out for old Abe, even Chase and the Cookes wanted to give up the fight. Norman B. Judd, the ambassador to Berlin, counseled the Jacobins to have patience. To Trumbull he wrote: "When I last saw you—your conviction was that L. would be reelected. I tell you combinations can't prevent it—Events possibly may. But until some event occurs is it wise or prudent to give an impression of hostility for no earthly good."[4]

---

[3] Bartlett, *Frémont*, 89–91.
[4] John M. Palmer to Lyman Trumbull, December 18, 1863, January 24.

The radicals could do nothing but follow Judd's sage advice, and Count Gurowski recorded in his diary their feelings of angry impotence. The great majority of the Republican members of Congress were opposed to Lincoln's nomination, he wrote, but the people would force them to accept him. Gurowski thought the Jacobin leaders should speak out against Lincoln and organize opinion for some other candidate, preferably Ben Butler. But Lincoln had lulled them with promises of Cabinet reform: "I may be mistaken, but the honest, patriotic radicals will be caught. They believe that if reelected, Lincoln will change his Cabinet." The Washington scene seethed with Jacobin rage, the more savage because it was helpless. Those expressions of personal disrespect for Lincoln, which so shocked young Richard Henry Dana and other wartime visitors to the capital, crackled fiercely wherever the politicians gathered. Congressman Riddle heard Henry Wilson denounce Lincoln in the very waiting room of the White House itself. Garfield, now a member of the House, observed wearily: "I hope we may not be compelled to push him four years more."[5] An abolitionist editor conceded that Lincoln was the best storyteller in the country, but declared that he possessed not one qualification to solve the problems of reconstruction: "He is hardly the man to handle this country, while its heart is over-generous with reconstituted peace, so that due guarantees may be exacted from its enemies." Greeley, his brief love affair with the administration ended, was breathing affection for Chase and Frémont in his columns. He recommended that the Republican convention, scheduled for early June, be postponed until late summer. By that time, he hoped, the enthusiasm for Lincoln would have cooled, and the radicals could name the nominee. Only Trumbull sounded a note of optimism. He wrote to an Illinois friend:

1864, in the Trumbull MSS.; H. G. Pike to Trumbull, February 1, 1864, W. H. Hanna to Trumbull, February 5, *ibid.;* Barlett, *Frémont,* 105–107; Henry Cooke to Jay Cooke, January 14, 1864, in Oberholtzer, *Cooke,* 1: 361–362; Norman B. Judd to Lyman Trumbull, January 2, 1864, in the Trumbull MSS.

[5] Gurowski, *Diary, 1863–1865,* pp. 60, 67, 69, 86; Riddle, *Recollections,* 267; Smith, *Garfield,* 1:375.

The feeling for Mr. Lincoln's reelection *seems* to be general, but much of it I discover is only on the surface. You would be surprised in talking with public men we meet here, to find how few when you come to get at their real sentiments are for Mr. Lincoln's reelection. There is a distrust & fear that he is too undecided & inefficient ever to put down the rebellion. You need not be surprised if a reaction sets in before the nomination in favor of some man supposed to possess more energy & less inclination to trust our brave boys in the hands, & under the leadership of Generals who have no heart in the war.[6]

The master politician in the White House gauged accurately the angry mutterings of the Jacobins. "He is fully apprehensive of the schemes of the Radical leaders," wrote Bates in his diary. ". . . He is also fully aware that they would strike him at once, if they durst; but they fear that the blow would be ineffectual, and so, they would fall under his power, as *beaten enemies.*"[7]

Lincoln's star continued to rise in February. The abolitionist press raged openly against him, but the radical journals remained discreetly silent or chirped weakly about postponing the convention.[8] The Chase movement was bogged down in its own insignificance. The powerful bosses would not touch it. Julian, offered a place on the secretary's central committee, refused scornfully with some biting remarks about Chase's "overweening ambition." Chase's end was near; the dying days of the month saw his boom collapse suddenly and with an utter lack of dignity. His Washington brain-trusters, with almost unbelievable stupidity, did not realize the strength of the popular swing to Lincoln. They dared to fight him openly. They got an anonymous political writer to prepare a pamphlet entitled *The Next Presidential Election,* a savagely malignant

[6] *Wilkes' Spirit of the Times,* January 30, 1864; *New York Tribune,* January 14, 1864; Lyman Trumbull to H. G. Pike, February 6, 1864, in the Trumbull MSS.

[7] Entry of February 13, 1864, in Bates, *Diary,* 333; *ibid.,* 334; Welles, *Diary,* 1:525.

[8] *Wilkes' Spirit of the Times,* February 6, 13, 1864; New York *Independent,* February 18; New York *Evening Post,* February 23, 1864.

attack upon Lincoln, which they circulated in bales, particularly in Ohio. It boomeranged right back. Indignant Buckeye Republicans asked John Sherman why he had permitted his name to be connected with such a scurrilous libel upon the president.[9] The intensely hostile reception of the pamphlet should have warned the Chase managers to go slow, but unheedingly they took another and fatal step. On February 20 Senator Pomeroy, who was running the Chase campaign, issued a manifesto for Chase. The "Pomeroy Circular" declared that with Lincoln as the candidate the party was certain to be defeated in November, demanded a more vigorous prosecution of the war, and asserted that Salmon P. Chase possessed in a high degree the talents necessary to crush the rebellion and reconstruct the South. The protest fell stillborn. Greeley praised it cautiously,[10] but it aroused angry condemnation, and damaged Chase more than Lincoln. Confused and humiliated, the secretary offered to resign. Lincoln told him to stay, probably feeling that Chase was less dangerous in the Cabinet than out. Two days after the Pomeroy document appeared, the Republican National Committee indorsed Lincoln for renomination by a majority of four to one. At the same time the Republican members of the Ohio and Indiana legislatures voted approval of old Abe.[11]

The Pomeroy fiasco did not surprise the Jacobin bosses. So great was Lincoln's popular support, said Garfield, that any movement to displace him "will not only be a failure but will tend to disturb and embarrass the unity of the friends of the Union." Garfield advised the radicals not to alienate Lincoln or he would fall back into the hands of the conservatives. Greeley, still hopeful, wrote that Lincoln was "not out of the woods. I shall keep up a quiet but steady opposition and, if

[9] Clarke, *Julian*, 250–251; Charles R. Wilson, "The Original Chase Organization Meeting and *The Next Presidential Election*," *Mississippi Valley Historical Review*, 23(1936):64–65. See *ibid.*, 71–76, where the pamphlet is reproduced. It came into Ohio under Sherman's frank.

[10] *New York Tribune*, February 24, 25, 1864; *New York Times*, February 23; Pierce, *Sumner*, 4:196; Hart, *Chase*, 312.

[11] Entry of February 22 in Welles, *Diary*, 1:529–530; Bartlett, *Frémont*, 91.

we should meantime have bad luck in war, I guess we shall back them out."[12]

Chase's candidacy now wobbled badly, and the Lincoln manager decided to try for a knockout blow. On February 27 Frank Blair arose in the House to deliver a virulent attack upon the Treasury Department's trade regulations for occupied areas in the South, charging corruption and asking for a congressional inquiry. The Jacobin leaders, unenthusiastic though they might be about Chase as a presidential contender, still were of no mind to see him smeared by a Blair. Led by Stevens they rushed to the defense. The wily Thad suggested that the War Committee was the proper agency to make such an investigation, and a resolution by Garfield instructed the inquisitors to look into the matter. Blair knew he was beaten. Later the Committee decided the investigation was impractical.[13]

Chase himself had concluded that his cause was hopeless. He asked Greeley and Garfield if he should withdraw from the race, and they advised him to do so. Garfield told him to get out of a contest where "he had no hope of success and could only distract the party." On March 5 the secretary announced that he was no longer a candidate. His act of self-obliteration did not fool Lincoln's friends into thinking that radical opposition to the president's nomination had ceased. "It proves only that the *present* prospects of Mr. Lincoln are too good to be openly resisted, at least, by men within the party," Bates observed.[14] Joshua Giddings counseled Julian not to mourn over Lincoln's apparent ascendancy, but to sustain the administration and work for a reform of the Cabinet. Greeley too resigned himself to four more years of Lincoln. "I am not at all confident of making any change; but I do believe I shall make things better by trying," he confided to a friend. "There

---

[12] Smith, *Garfield*, 1:375–376; Horace Greeley to Beman Brockway, February 28, 1864, in the Greeley MSS.

[13] *Congressional Globe*, 38 Congress, 1 Session, Appendix, 46–51; Smith, *Blair Family*, 1:256–260; C.C.W., 1865, 1:xviii.

[14] Horace Greeley to Salmon P. Chase, March 2, 1864, in Bartlett, *Frémont*, 92; Henry Cooke to Jay Cooke, March 1, 4, in Oberholtzer, *Cooke*, 1:362; Smith, *Garfield*, 1:376; entry of March 13, 1864, in Bates, *Diary*, 345.

are those who go as far as they are pushed, and Mr. Lincoln is one of these. He will be a better President . . . for the opposition he is now encountering."[15]

There were still elements in the party which would not concede the nomination to Lincoln. The out-and-out radical newspapers pronounced him too "seasoned with conservatism," and sneered that his widely advertised popular support consisted of federal jobholders. As Chase faded from the scene, the forces backing Ben Butler began to push their man to the front. Bates heard disturbing rumors that the Missouri radicals were lining up for Frémont.[16] Bryant and Greeley were shouting in the press for the postponement of the convention from June to September, and Henry Raymond angrily charged this was a radical trick to defeat Lincoln. Gurowski noted in his diary that "the best men" among the congressional radicals were "sullen and taciturn on Lincoln's reelection."[17]

During April the Jacobins kept their ears pressed to the ground, hoping to catch an upsurge of dissatisfaction with Lincoln. The ground, however, was sending up confusing tidings. The straining politicians at Washington heard continued reports of Lincoln's great personal popularity.[18] They heard also disturbing news of the people's weariness with the prolongation of the war and of the growing strength of the Democrats. An Illinois radical warned Trumbull: "If the Democrats nominate McClellan and we nominate Mr. Lincoln and some of the dissatisfied should start out on Butler or Fremont, we should be whipped. Some will now only vote for Fremont, others only for

[15] Joshua R. Giddings to Mrs. George W. Julian, March 7, 1864, in the Giddings-Julian MSS.; Horace Greeley to Mrs. R. M. Whipple, March 8, 1864, in the Greeley MSS.
[16] *Wilkes' Spirit of the Times*, March 5, 12, 19, 1864; New York *Evening Post*, March 8; Gurowski, *Diary, 1863–1865*, p. 154; letters to Butler from T. W. Wentworth, E. Locke, R. M. McMurdy, in *Butler Correspondence*, 3:513–515, 553–554; 4:136–137; entry of March 19, 1864, in Bates, *Diary*, 349.
[17] New York *Evening Post*, March 21, 1864; *New York Tribune*, April 1; *New York Times*, April 8; entry of March 22, 1864, in Gurowski, *Diary, 1863–1865*, pp. 146–147.
[18] A. Hamilton to Schuyler Colfax, April 10, 1864, in the Colfax MSS.; F. R. Payne to Lyman Trumbull, May 1, in the Trumbull MSS.

Butler, almost all would like a change, but they have no one to change for." Forbes, willing to support Lincoln because he was "a pilot who takes his orders from the crew," feared that unless the rebellion was crushed by September the Democrats would take the election. So also thought Garfield, who wrote apprehensively: "We are on the brink of the most fearful precipice. . . . The President is bound hand and foot by the Blairs and they are dragging him and the country down the chasm."[19]

While the leaders of the Jacobin machine fumed and fretted and could not make up their minds, the conglomeration of radical Germans from St. Louis and abolitionists from New England who were directing Frémont's campaign decided upon direct action. Realizing that Lincoln was certain of the Republican nomination, they determined to present the Pathfinder as the candidate of a third party. Early in May they sent out a call for a convention to meet in Cleveland. The important party bosses stood coldly aloof from the movement, although some of them, such as Greeley and Andrew, secretly urged the Frémont men on. It was a motley crowd of delegates that assembled in Cleveland on the thirty-first to shout Frémont's praises and name him as their standard-bearer. Every shade of opposition to the administration was there, from militant abolitionists to disgruntled Democrats. Cheered by an eloquent letter from Wendell Phillips promising his support for Frémont, the delegates adopted an uncompromising radical platform. It called for a constitutional amendment abolishing slavery in all the states, loyal or rebellious; a reconstruction policy, to be formulated by Congress, which would protect the rights of freedmen; a single term for the presidency; and the confiscation of the lands of rebels and their distribution among soldiers and settlers.[20] General Cochrane, he who had once carried tales to Lincoln, was nominated for vice-president.

Outside of the convention hall the Cleveland nominations

[19] W. A. Baldwin to Trumbull, April 4, *ibid.;* John M. Forbes to George W. Curtis, April 28, 1864, in Hughes, *Forbes,* 2:89–90; James A. Garfield to J. H. Rhodes, April 28, 1864, in Smith, *Garfield,* 1:376–377. See also Horace Greeley to Beman Brockway, April 9, in the Greeley MSS.

[20] Nevins, *Frémont,* 2:658–659; Bartlett, *Frémont,* 100–103.

aroused little enthusiasm. The strong men of the party gave no word of approval. Julian thought the whole affair was a sad mistake, and Chandler thought it would prove useful only as a rallying point should popular dissatisfaction with Lincoln develop in the future. General Palmer told Trumbull that the Frémont ticket had no support in the Western army. Even the abolitionist press was strangely cool.[21] Frémont himself, in his letter of acceptance, talked as though he were only a stalking-horse candidate. Should the Republican convention, he wrote, select "any man whose past life justifies a well-grounded confidence in his fidelity to our cardinal principles, there is no reason why there should be any division among the really patriotic men of the country. To any such I shall be most happy to give a cordial and active support."[22]

In the first week of June, the Republicans—who still called themselves the Union party—held their convention in Baltimore, after the Jacobins had made a last gallant and unsuccessful effort to postpone the date. The radical chieftains went to Baltimore sullen and indifferent, resigned to accepting a nomination they could not prevent.[23] Smoothly the Lincoln managers put through the selection of the president. The radicals did not dare a peep of opposition, but they had the satisfaction of taking a fling at the Cabinet in the platform, which as a declaration of party principles bore a distinctly radical tinge. It resoundingly indorsed emancipation and the employment of Negro soldiers, and called for a continued vigorous, unrelenting prosecution of the war. The sixth resolution, adopted at the demands of the Jacobins, read: "That we deem it essential to the general welfare that harmony should prevail in our national councils, and we regard as worthy of public confidence

[21] Clarke, *Julian*, 251; *Life of Chandler*, 266; John M. Palmer to Lyman Trumbull, June 8, 1864, in the Trumbull MSS.; *Wilkes' Spirit of the Times*, June 11, July 30, 1864.

[22] Nicolay and Hay, *Lincoln*, 9:42.

[23] *Ibid.*, 57–58; New York *Independent*, June 2, 1864; entry of June 5, 1864, in Gurowski, *Diary, 1863–1865*, pp. 246–247; Julian, *Recollections*, 243; Horace Greeley, *The American Conflict* (Chicago, 1864–1866), 2:655; Henry Wilson, *History of the Rise and Fall of the Slave Power in America* (Boston, 1872–1877), 3:545.

and official trust those only who cordially indorse the principles proclaimed in these resolutions and which should characterize the administration of the government." This was delightedly interpreted by the radical press as an ultimatum for the removal of Blair and Seward.[24] It was rumored that Lincoln had made a deal with the Jacobins to oust Blair in return for their support. The report had some basis of fact. The postmaster general, always ready to sacrifice himself for Lincoln, gave him an undated letter of resignation immediately after the convention. Lincoln was to fill in the date whenever he decided that the retention of Montgomery was damaging his chances of re-election.[25]

The pulsing undertone of hostility to the president at the Baltimore convention did not escape the administration leaders. "It did indeed nominate Mr. Lincoln," wrote the indignant Bates, "but in a manner and with attendant circumstances as if the object was to defeat their own nomination." Unmistakably evident to all observers was the fact that the Jacobin bosses had not yet accepted Lincoln, even though the party in formal convention had chosen him as its candidate. Greeley observed curtly that old Abe was not the best man the Republicans could have put up, and then lapsed into a chilly silence. Grimes, Andrew, Trumbull, Wilson, and other leaders still hoped that events would conspire to force Lincoln's withdrawal.[26] Old Gurowski, recording what he heard the congressional radicals say, wrote, "Many, many have not yet made up their minds to go for him, and what is still worse, to go for his Sewards and Blairs. . . . It is . . . probable that a new Republican convention may be called, and a new nomination made. This, how-

[24] Horace Greeley, *Proceedings of the First Three Republican National Conventions of 1856, 1860, and 1864* . . . (Minneapolis, 1893), 226; Nicolay and Hay, *Lincoln*, 9:69; New York *Independent*, June 20, 1864.

[25] Smith, *Blair Family*, 2:266; letter of Montgomery Blair in the New York *World*, March 14, 1868.

[26] Entry of June 10, 1864, in Bates, *Diary*, 374–375; *New York Tribune*, June 9, 1864; Gurowski, *Diary, 1863–1865*, pp. 69, 91, 258; Salter, *Grimes*, 279; Peleg W. Chandler, *Memoirs of Governor Andrew* (Boston, 1880), 111–114.

ever, depends upon the events of the war."[27] A little later the Count added a note of mysterious optimism: "Events may bring forth strange complications. . . . The tomorrow may play Lincoln a trick. Patience!"[28] The attitude of the last-ditch radicals was expressed by *Wilkes' Spirit of the Times* which, in a lather of rage and epithets, denounced "this albino administration, and its diluted spawn of pink eyed patriots—this limp result of the feeble embraces of half-furnished conservatives and limited emancipators."[29]

Toward the end of the month something happened which drove deeper the wedge between Lincoln and the radicals. Chase got mixed up in a patronage fight with one of the New York senators, and Seward sided with the latter. Professing to believe that Lincoln through Seward was interfering with his right to appoint his own agents, Chase offered his resignation. He had done this many times before, but the president had always refused to let him go. Undoubtedly the secretary expected the same procedure to be repeated. But to his and everyone else's vast surprise, Lincoln accepted the resignation. His friends claimed that Chase wanted to get out because of the galling attacks of the Blair faction and "the insult with which the President followed them up." An indignant radical editor said that the best man in the Cabinet had been driven from it by the schemings of Seward and Thurlow Weed, "that raven of the lobby." In administration circles it was feared that Chase was leaving to reorganize his presidential campaign, and that he would try to take over the Frémont movement.[30] The radicals viewed the affair as simply another deplorable example of Lincoln's willingness to yield to Seward.

But the Jacobins had more important things to worry about

[27] Entry of June 9, 1864, in Gurowski, *Diary, 1863–1865*, pp. 251–252.
[28] Entry of June 29, *ibid.*, 267.
[29] *Wilkes' Spirit of the Times*, June 18, 1864.
[30] Warden, *Chase*, 617; Schuckers, *Chase*, 484–487; Doster, *Lincoln*, 236; Lincoln, *Works*, 10:140–141; H. C. Fahnestock to Jay Cooke, June 30, 1864, in Oberholtzer, *Cooke*, 1:420–421; *New York Herald*, June 30; *Wilkes' Spirit of the Times*, July 9, 1864; entry of June 30, 1864, in Bates, *Diary*, 381.

in July than the wounded feelings of Chase; for in that month they openly challenged Lincoln to battle on the issue of reconstruction. After his proclamation in December the president had gone ahead with his plans. Under his supervision Banks had set up a new state government in Louisiana. Then a loyal government was established in occupied Arkansas under the protection of the army, and representatives from this state appeared in Washington to claim their seats in Congress. The radicals viewed the president's handiwork with alarm and mounting anger. Phillips warned Julian that Lincoln would carry the votes of these military creations in his pocket and that he would weld them into a political alliance with the conservatives which would control the government and smash the radical revolution and all its hopes: "But let such a majority as I have described once get its hand on the helm and the Revolution may easily be checked with aid of the Administration, which is willing the negro should be free but seeks nothing more for him."[31]

Trumbull and some of the other leaders were determined to deny admission to the Arkansas representatives, thus placing the stamp of congressional disapproval upon Lincoln's governments and his entire reconstruction policy. But Wade proposed a better scheme to wreck the president's program. In February the brilliant, fiery young Maryland radical, Henry Winter Davis, had piloted through the House a bill which embodied the Jacobins' ideas of reconstruction. When the bill came over to the Senate, Wade took charge of it. He made repeated attempts to get it before the Senate, pleading that the Arkansas question was ancillary to the Davis measure, which laid down rules for readmission of all the disloyal states.[32] Ultimately, on July 1, he secured consideration of the bill.

The Wade-Davis bill differed drastically from Lincoln's plan. It required a majority of the white voters in a state, instead of ten per cent, to take an oath of allegiance before a new govern-

---

[31] Wendell Phillips to George W. Julian, March 27, 1864, in the Giddings-Julian MSS.; *Detroit Advertiser and Tribune*, June 14.

[32] *Congressional Globe*, 38 Congress, 1 Session, 2906, 3362, 3363–3365.

ment could be established. It excluded a larger number of people from the right to vote or hold office, on the grounds that treason must be punished. It required each state seeking admission to insert in its constitution a clause abolishing slavery. It declared emancipation by congressional enactment. One section proclaimed that "all persons held to involuntary servitude or labor in the States referred to are emancipated and discharged therefrom, and they and their posterity are declared to be forever free."[33]

And yet the Wade-Davis measure did not represent the real policy of reconstruction which the radicals planned to fasten upon the subjugated South. It restricted the suffrage to whites, and they wanted to extend it to the Negroes in order to insure the growth and dominance of a native Republican party. It admitted that the seceded states still retained some rights under the Constitution, and the Jacobins believed in the "conquered provinces" theory later expounded by Stevens. It did not provide for the confiscation of rebel property, and they were determined upon drastic seizure of plantations for distribution among the former slaves. The purpose of its backers was to get the best kind of bill possible at the moment, and thus to forestall Lincoln in his attempt to bring back the rebellious states unpunished and unrepentant. They trusted that events and the effect of their propaganda upon the people would enable them to secure the passage of a "thorough" reconstruction measure later. Congressman James G. Blaine said of the Wade-Davis proposal: "It was commonly regarded as a rebuke to the course of the President in proceeding with the grave and momentous task of reconstruction without waiting the action or invoking the council of Congress." Julian admitted that this "somewhat incongruous bill," if it had passed, would have proved "a stumbling-block in the way of the more radical measures which afterwards prevailed."[34]

[33] *Ibid.*, 3448–3449.
[34] See James A. Woodburn, *Life of Thaddeus Stevens* (Indianapolis, 1913), 316–317, for Stevens' objections to the bill; Blaine, *Twenty Years of Congress,* 2:42; Julian, *Recollections,* 247–248.

Wade spoke vigorously for his bill. He contended that the time had come when Congress must announce with unmistakable clarity upon what terms it would permit the Southern states to come back into the Union, because Lincoln, actuated by a lust for power, was usurping the power to direct the process of reconstruction.

The Executive ought not to be permitted to handle this great question to his own liking. It does not belong, under the Constitution, to the President to prescribe the rule. It belongs to us. The President undertook to fix a rule upon which he would admit these States back into the Union. It was not upon any principle of republicanism, because he prescribed the rule to be that when one tenth of the population would take a certain oath, they might come in as States. When we consider that in the light of American principle, to say the least of it it was absurd. . . . Until majorities can be found loyal and trustworthy for State government, they must be governed by a stronger hand.

Thus Wade squarely challenged Lincoln to declare who was to control reconstruction, Congress or the president. The bill was agreed to by both Houses on July 2, one hour before the final adjournment of Congress for the session.[35]

Lincoln had come to the president's room at the Capitol to sign bills passed in the last-minute rush. When the Wade-Davis measure was put before him, he laid it aside and went on with other work. Several Jacobin senators, including Chandler and Sumner, stood around, in an evident agony of excitement about the fate of the reconstruction bill. Finally Chandler in bold tones asked the president whether he meant to approve it. Lincoln replied that he could not, that he had had no opportunity to study the bill, and it was too important "to be swallowed in that way." Angered, Chandler cried, "If it is vetoed, it will damage us fearfully in the Northwest. The important point is that one prohibiting slavery in the reconstructed States." Calmly accepting battle with the Jacobins, Lincoln answered, "That is the point on which I doubt the author-

---

[35] *Congressional Globe*, 38 Congress, 1 Session, 3450, 3491, 3518.

ity of Congress to act."[36] Chandler left the room in a rage to spread the news that Lincoln had killed the bill with a pocket veto. The information reached the House as the members were rushing out after the adjournment. Henry Winter Davis, overcome by a paroxysm of fury, stood by his desk waving his arms wildly, denouncing the president in a speech to an empty hall.[37]

Savagely the leaders of the Jacobin cabal condemned Lincoln for daring to veto the bill. "Wait, wait, Mr. Lincoln!" cried Gurowski ominously. "You have not yet heard the last on account of this escamotage."[38] Their anger flared higher when on July 8 Lincoln issued a proclamation explaining why he had not approved the measure. Rather patronizingly he said that the Wade-Davis bill contained some good ideas and that he might even follow a few of its suggestions. But he was opposed to committing the government to any one inflexible plan of reconstruction. "What an infamous proclamation!" exploded Thad Stevens. "The President is determined to have the electoral votes of the seceded states. . . . The idea of pocketing a bill & then issuing a proclamation as to how far he will conform to it."[39] In their rage the Jacobins forgot that they had defeated congressional recognition of Lincoln's governments in Arkansas and Louisiana.

Opinion among the Republican masses in the country seemed to indorse Lincoln's disposal of the bill and his proclamation. A substantial portion of the party press applauded what it termed his policy of "masterly inactivity." Few were the journals like the *Cincinnati Gazette* which dared to denounce the president openly as a power-hungry dictator overriding the rights of Congress. This paper's Washington correspondent had reported with elation the passage of the Wade-Davis measure:

[36] Nicolay and Hay, *Lincoln*, 9:120–121.

[37] Noah Brooks, *Washington in Lincoln's Time* (New York, 1895), 168.

[38] Blaine, *Twenty Years of Congress*, 2:43–44; Wilson, *Rise and Fall of the Slave Power*, 3:525–528; Warden, *Chase*, 625; Nicolay and Hay, *Lincoln*, 9:124; entry of July 6, 1864, in Gurowski, *Diary, 1863–1865*, p. 274.

[39] Richardson, *Messages of the Presidents*, 6:222–223; Eben G. Scott, *Reconstruction during the Civil War* (Boston, 1895), 411–412; Thaddeus Stevens to Edward McPherson, July 10, 1864, in the Stevens MSS.

"The most signal triumph of radical principles this session, the country owes to Ben Wade for forcing through the Senate Winter Davis' great reconstruction bill." In its editorial columns the paper lashed the president's argument against an inflexible plan, sneering at his state governments, "kept alive by military nursing": "They need a government of inflexible law."[40] The Democrats, always gleeful at the prospect of a cat and dog fight within the Republican ranks, flayed Lincoln and the radicals impartially.[41]

The Jacobin bosses mistakenly thought they had found an issue upon which to oppose Lincoln. The gloomy outlook of the military situation in July further encouraged them to think the moment had arrived when they could strike him successfully. Grant had come East to take command of the entire military machine and to direct the operations of the Potomac army. He had tried to go to Richmond by the Wilderness route and had got nowhere with terrific slaughter. Another Union general, the country wailed, had been added to the endless roster of Lee's victims, and again the dangerous cry for peace was heard.[42] It found an ardent representative in the eccentric Greeley. He badgered Lincoln into making contact with some Confederate agents who had arrived in Canada, presumably to conclude a peace settlement. The sceptical president dispatched Greeley to Niagara to conduct the negotiations. The editor did not want the honor, and went with extreme reluctance. Characteristically he bungled the whole affair, not even mentioning to the Southerners that Lincoln's prime condition for peace was Confederate acceptance of the destruction of

[40] Boston Daily Advertiser, July 9, 1864; Milwaukee Sentinel, July 11; Springfield Weekly Republican, July 16, 23; Cincinnati Daily Gazette, July 4, 1864, Washington correspondence, July 7, 12, editorials.

[41] New York Herald, July 6, 10, 1864; Columbus Ohio Statesman, July 11; Philadelphia Age, July 12.

[42] H. C. Fahnestock to Jay Cooke, July 4, 26, 1864, in Oberholtzer, Cooke, 1:412, 414; Jay Cooke to Henry Cooke, August 2, ibid., 415–416; Charles A. Dana to James H. Wilson, July 2, August 2, in Wilson, Dana, 334, 341–342; excerpts from Doster's diary during July, in Doster, Lincoln, 247–251; T. H. Hicks to William P. Fessenden, July 11, in the Fessenden MSS.

slavery. John Hay had to make a hurried trip to Niagara, bearing the president's real terms. The agents had no authority to conclude an agreement, and the proceedings finally fizzled out ingloriously.[43]

At the same time Lincoln authorized another unofficial peace move. He permitted two enthusiastic visionaries, J. R. Gilmore, Greeley's friend, and Colonel Jaquess, a former Methodist college president, to go to Richmond to contact the Davis government. They claimed they had information indicating that the Confederacy desired to end the war. Again Lincoln, sceptical, insisted that any settlement must be based upon the abolition of slavery. The president's peace feelers aroused the suspicions of the Jacobins. They felt that he should have consulted the party leaders in Congress before taking action, and they feared he would grant the South too lenient terms.[44]

As military failures and war-weariness conspired to lower Lincoln's stock, the Jacobins took hope. Perhaps there was yet time to force him to withdraw and to substitute a radical candidate as the party's standard-bearer. John Sherman thought this was imperative. He declared that Lincoln lacked the "energy, dignity of character to either conduct the war or to make peace."[45] The expectations of Butler's supporters rocketed as Lincoln seemed to slip in popular favor. One of them who was in Washington hobnobbing with the radical bosses reported to the general that Wade had said "he believed you would be triumphantly elected Pres. if you were nominated—and thinks there would be scarcely any trouble with that." An ardent young Butlerite proposed the perfect presidential ticket, Benjamin F. Butler and Benjamin F. Wade: "Two earnest men for country, humanity, God's truth,

[43] Edward C. Kirkland, The Peacemakers of 1864 (New York, 1927), 68, 73, 76, 96; Greeley, American Conflict, 2:664–666; Nicolay and Hay, Lincoln, 9:186–192. See O. R., series 3, 4:503–504, for Lincoln's public announcement of his peace terms.

[44] Gilmore, Recollections, 240–244; Life of Chandler, 269; Bates, Diary, 388–389.

[45] Gurowski, Diary 1863–1865, pp. 272, 304–305, 309; John Sherman to William T. Sherman, July 24, 1864, quoted in Bartlett, Frémont, 118–119.

and Eternal Justice."[46] The Butler managers optimistically hoped that Frémont would leave the race and throw his support to their man. There was talk of persuading both Lincoln and the Pathfinder to withdraw, and of a new convention that would nominate a candidate capable of leading the party to victory. The president, when he heard of this scheme, announced that he was in the contest to stay.[47]

But Wade and Chandler were ready at last to force Lincoln from his position at the head of the ticket, whether he would or no. Their plan was to organize a bolt of the party by the Jacobins, to detach most of Lincoln's support, and then to place another candidate in the field. The time was ripe to strike the president. It was just after Greeley's peace fiasco, which left with the Republicans the impression that Lincoln had been willing to negotiate a too-generous peace with the rebels. Grant had still to achieve an important success and his sickening losses in the Wilderness had stunned the public. The country growled its dissatisfaction with the conduct of the war.

The blow fell with lightning swiftness. On August 5 there appeared in the *Tribune* a communication signed by Wade and Davis—the famous "Wade-Davis Manifesto." It was a detailed, withering, and malignant denunciation of Lincoln's reconstruction policy and his veto of the bill passed in July. The authors said their protest was called forth by the president's unconstitutional encroachments upon the authority of Congress, as evidenced by his proclamation of July 8 and by his determination to reconstruct the South by executive power and with no regard for the wishes of Congress. They condemned his governments in Louisiana and Arkansas as "mere creatures of his will . . . mere oligarchies, imposed on the people by military orders under the form of election." They accused Lincoln of setting up these governments for the sole purpose of capturing their electoral votes. Of his proclamation they said, "A more studied outrage on the legislative authority

[46] J. K. Herbert to Benjamin F. Butler, July 4, 1864, in *Butler Correspondence*, 4:464; Mason C. Weld to Butler, July 26, *ibid.*, 546–547.

[47] Edgar Conkling to Butler, July 18, *ibid.*, 512; Carl Schurz, *Reminiscences* (New York, 1907–1908), 3:102–104.

of the people has never been perpetrated." Lincoln had presumed too much on the patience of the radicals. "But he must understand that our support is of a cause, and not of a man." Finally the authors asked the Republicans to repudiate Lincoln. "Let them consider the remedy of these usurpations, and, having found it, fearlessly execute it."[48]

The manifesto exploded in Washington with sudden violence, throwing "politicians of every stamp into the wildest confusion," as one reporter wrote. Old Gurowski chortled with elation: "Better late than never. Two *men* call the people and Mr. Lincoln to their respective senses." The Butler forces exulted at the evident terror which the document created in the administration camp. Montgomery Blair was reported to have cried bitterly, "We have Lee & his —— on one side, and Henry Winter Davis & Ben Wade and all such hell cats on the other." The manifesto excited the Jacobins to new hope; they felt confident now of destroying Lincoln.[49] Correspondingly it took the heart out of the conservatives. Welles could think of no better retort than to charge that Wade had been bitten by the presidential bug. Blair feared that Lincoln could not overcome the force of the attack unless "we meet with reasonable success in arms." The alarm of the administration supporters jumped higher at a rumor that Wade and Davis would follow up their protest with a demand in Congress for the impeachment of the president. The president's leading newspaper champion, Raymond's *Times*, betrayed its fright in an angry editorial which screamed that Wade and Davis were dangerous revolutionary radicals: "They have sustained the war, not as a means of restoring the Union, but to free the slaves, seize the lands, crush the spirit, destroy the rights and blot out forever the political freedom of the people inhabiting the Southern States."[50]

[48] *New York Tribune,* August 5, 1864; Scott, *Reconstruction during the Civil War,* 412–425.

[49] Brooks, *Washington in Lincoln's Time,* 170; Gurowski, *Diary, 1863–1865,* pp. 309–310; J. K. Herbert to Benjamin F. Butler, August 6, 1864, in *Butler Correspondence,* 5:8–9; *Life of Chandler,* 272.

[50] Entry of August 6, 1864, in Welles, *Diary,* 2:95–96; Montgomery Blair

The radicals were jubilantly confident that the manifesto had set in motion a tremendous popular revulsion against Lincoln. They felt certain they could get him out of the race, either by appealing to him to withdraw for the good of the party, or by nominating another candidate.[51] On August 14, Greeley, Davis, and over twenty other party leaders met secretly at the home of David Dudley Field in New York. They decided to circulate privately a call for a convention to meet in late September "to consider the state of the nation and to concentrate the union strength on some one candidate who commands the confidence of the country, even by a new nomination if necessary."[52]

The elation of the Jacobins was unfounded, as they might have realized if they had studied the press reactions to the manifesto more carefully. Greeley cautiously pronounced it "a very able and caustic protest," but he went no farther and added that he did not regret the veto of the Wade-Davis bill. Even Bryant ventured only a guarded approval. An overwhelming majority of the Republican newspapers denounced the authors as wreckers of party unity, and repudiated the sentiments in the manifesto. The great organ of radicalism in the West, the *Chicago Tribune,* condemned them bitterly. So did the Detroit journal which had been Chandler's staunchest supporter in Michigan politics. Led by the Forney papers, the conservative Eastern press rallied to the president.[53] The most

to D. H. McPhail, August 12, 1864, in Smith, *Blair Family,* 2:278; New York *World,* August 12, 1864, Washington correspondence; *New York Times,* August 9, 1864.

[51] Entry of August 11 in Gurowski, *Diary, 1863–1865;* J. K. Herbert to Benjamin F. Butler, August 11, in *Butler Correspondence,* 5:35–37; Mrs. Butler to Butler, August 13, *ibid.,* 47–48; J. W. Shaffer to Butler, August 17, *ibid.,* 67–69; Horace Greeley to George Opdyke, August 18, in the New York *Sun,* June 30, 1889, p. 3.

[52] The issue of the New York *Sun* for June 30, 1889, page 3, contains documents and letters of the Republicans active in the move to displace Lincoln. See also Pierce, *Sumner,* 4:196–197; Pearson, *Andrew,* 2:159–160.

[53] *New York Tribune,* August 5, 1864; New York *Evening Post,* August 8, 1864; *Chicago Tribune,* August 11; *Detroit Advertiser and Tribune,* August 23, 30. See also the Milwaukee *Sentinel,* August 6, 11; *Cleveland Herald,* quoted *ibid.,* August 11; *Wisconsin State Journal* (Madison),

enthusiastic commendation for the document came from the Democrats, who used its arguments as ammunition to assail Lincoln and the Republican Party.[54]

The refusal of the abolitionists and those elements in the party who stood closest to them to indorse the manifesto should have warned the leaders of the bolt that their cause was hopeless. If the most radical groups would not oppose Lincoln, there was small hope that any others would. And such respectable figures among the abolitionists as Gerrit Smith, the veteran crusader against slavery, and the editors of the *Anti-Slavery Standard* censured Wade and Davis. In a public letter, Smith reproached the authors of the protest for periling a Republican victory and urged united support for Lincoln.[55] Republican conventions in Ohio's Western Reserve, Wade's own stamping ground and the strongest antislavery section in the nation, adopted resolutions condemning him for splitting the party at a critical hour. Garfield, whose district lay here, was suspected of having helped prepare the manifesto, and his indignant constituents threatened not to renominate him. Frightened, he went before the convention and denounced the protest.[56] The last-ditch Missouri radicals, to the surprised delight of Bates, announced that they were for Lincoln and no one else. Watching the strange antics of the Republicans with an air of cynical amusement was Bennett of the *Herald*. He predicted that all the bolters would be back in Lincoln's camp as soon as they forced him to concede their terms:

Whatever they say now, we venture to predict that Wade and his tail; and Bryant and his tail; and Wendell Phillips and his tail; and Weed, Barney, Chase and their tails; and Winter

---

August 11; Harrisburg *Daily Telegraph*, August 17, 1864; *Boston Daily Advertiser*, August 9; *Harper's Weekly*, August 20; *Springfield Weekly Republican*, August 13; *Albany Evening Journal*, quoted in the *Wisconsin State Journal*, August 11.

[54] *New York Herald*, August 6; New York *World*, August 6, 12; Columbus *Crisis*, August 17; Philadelphia *Age*, August 6.

[55] *Detroit Advertiser and Tribune*, August 23, 1864.

[56] *Ibid.*, August 30; *New York Times*, August 26; entry of August 26 in Welles, *Diary*, 2:121–122; Smith, *Garfield*, 1:378–379.

Davis, Raymond, Opdyke and Forney who have no tails; will all make tracks for Old Abe's plantation, and will soon be found crowing and blowing, and vowing and writhing, and swearing and stumping . . . , declaring that he and he alone, is the hope of the nation, the bugaboo of Jeff Davis, the first of Conservatives, the best of Abolitionists, the purest of patriots, the most gullible of mankind, the easiest President to manage, and the person especially predestined and fore-ordained by Providence to carry on the war, free the niggers, and give all the faithful a fair share of the spoils.[57]

But the Jacobin bosses, strangely blind to the signs of the times, blithely continued their plans to nominate a radical candidate. The responses to the call for a convention inspired optimism. Davis, John Jay, Butler, Greeley, Chase, Richard Smith of the *Cincinnati Gazette,* and Sedgwick were among those who promised support. Davis wrote that Wade was sanguine, but advised against an open break until after the Democratic convention. Somewhat ambiguously, Frémont pledged his cooperation. But the conspirators could not draw Sumner into their circle. He was for persuading Lincoln to withdraw voluntarily. If this could not be accomplished, then the radicals would have to support him to prevent a Democratic victory.[58]

At this moment the Democrats came to Lincoln's aid. They held their convention in Chicago in the last days of August; they nominated McClellan, and adopted a peace platform written by the boss Copperhead, Clement L. Vallandigham. The prospect of the archfoe of the Committee in the White House, advised by the archadvocate of peace with the Confederacy, was calculated to sober even the bitterest radicals and make them think of repairing the party ranks. McClellan and Vallandigham were infinitely worse than Lincoln and Seward. The leaders organizing the bolt knew this, and they knew also

[57] Entry of August 14, 1864, in Bates, *Diary,* 398; *New York Herald,* August 24, 1864.

[58] New York *Sun,* June 30, 1889, p. 3; Kirkland, *Peacemakers of 1864,* p. 193, footnote; Sumner to Francis Lieber, September 3, 1864, in Pierce, *Sumner,* 4:198.

that if they went ahead with their plans they would insure Democratic victory.[59] Out in Detroit Zachariah Chandler knew it, and he shivered at the possibility. He decided that the breach in the party must be closed at all costs. Hurriedly he packed his grip and headed for Washington, stopping off en route to see Wade. His plan for restoring harmony was to yank Frémont out of the race and persuade Lincoln to remove Blair from the Cabinet, since this concession would make it easier for the radicals to come to the president's support. By the twenty-sixth of August he was in the capital contacting the administration leaders, convinced that Lincoln's election hung upon the success of his mission. On September 3 he laid his project before Lincoln.[60]

But the little knot of conspirators in New York still thought they would defeat Lincoln with their convention. Greeley, Bryant, Theodore Tilton of the *Independent,* the political theorist Francis Lieber, and others busied themselves with plans. Hopes ran high. On August 30 another meeting convened at Field's house. A committee was appointed to sound out the Republican governors. But at this second conference the schemers received a stunning blow: Andrew and his New England machine refused to come in. The doughty governor had seen Lincoln's published account of the Gilmore-Jaquess peace mission, and Lincoln's insistence upon Southern acceptance of emancipation as a condition of peace satisfied him. He announced that he would support the president.[61]

The conspiracy was tottering, and General William Tecum-

[59] For radical reaction to the Chicago convention, see the *New York Tribune,* September 3, 1864; *Wilkes' Spirit of the Times,* September 10; Gurowski, *Diary, 1863–1865,* p. 329; Zachariah Chandler to Mrs. Chandler, September 8, in the Chandler MSS.; W. M. Dunn to Joseph Holt, September 3, in the Holt MSS.

[60] Chandler to Mrs. Chandler, August 27, 28, September 2, 1864, in the Chandler MSS.; *Life of Chandler,* 273–274; J. K. Herbert to Benjamin F. Butler, September 3, in *Butler Correspondence,* 5:120–121.

[61] Pearson, *Andrew,* 2:161–162; Hughes, *Forbes,* 2:101; *Wilkes' Spirit of the Times,* September 3, 1864; Whitelaw Reid to D. D. Field, September 2, in the New York *Sun,* June 30, 1889; Thomas S. Perry, ed., *Life and Letters of Francis Lieber* (Boston, 1882), 350–351.

seh Sherman now dealt it the final blow. Sherman and his army had gone unnoticed by the public during the summer, when Grant was struggling before Richmond; they had disappeared into the depths of the lower South on their way to Georgia. Then on September 2 the news flashed over the North that Sherman had captured Atlanta, splitting the Confederacy in two and rendering victory almost certain. The country went mad with joy. In the ringing exultation the Republican leaders plainly saw re-election for Lincoln and defeat for the Democrats. And as Sherman's troopers swept down Peachtree street, the plotters who had gathered at Field's saw the handwriting on the wall. Sullenly they dropped their plans for a convention and prepared to scurry back into the party fold. One by one they ranged themselves on the side of the administration. On September 6 Horace Greeley announced that he was supporting the one true Union candidate, Abraham Lincoln.[62]

In the meantime Zack Chandler was busy in Washington on his project to patch up the rents in the party. He easily got a promise from Lincoln to remove Montgomery Blair from the Cabinet in return for his own pledge to persuade Frémont to withdraw. Lincoln felt no compunctions about sacrificing the willing Blair if by so doing he could ease the way for the radicals to support the administration. He told several other leaders, as well as Chandler, that he intended to get rid of the postmaster general.[63] Chandler then went to New York to work on Frémont. From his headquarters at the Astor House he conferred daily with the general and his advisers. He found Frémont in a surly mood but anxious to get out of a hopeless contest and tempted by the chance to strike down one of the

[62] Zachariah Chandler to Mrs. Chandler, September 6, 1864, in the Chandler MSS.; Merriam, Bowles, 1:413; Letters in the New York Sun, June 30, 1889, from Charles B. Sedgwick, Whitelaw Reid, Chase, and others; Sedgwick to J. M. Forbes, September 5, 1864, in Hughes, Forbes, 2:101; Ida Tarbell, Life of Abraham Lincoln (New York, 1907), 2:202; New York Tribune, September 6; Gurowski, Diary, 1863–1865, p. 344.

[63] Life of Chandler, 274–276; Nevins, Frémont, 2:664; Smith, Blair Family, 2:227; Isaac N. Arnold, History of Abraham Lincoln and the Overthrow of Slavery (Chicago, 1866), 390–391; S. G. Laughlin, Missouri Politics during the Civil War (Iowa City, 1921), 147.

hated Blairs. Finally Frémont agreed to withdraw. On September 22 he announced his decision and grudgingly asked his friends to vote for Lincoln.[64]

The next day, coming out of a Cabinet meeting, Blair surprised Bates by saying that the president had asked him to resign as a move to appease the Jacobins. The distressed Bates wrote in his diary: "The result will, probably, be to ensure Mr. L's election . . . and the Radicals, no doubt, hope that they will constitute the controlling element in the new party thus formed, and as such will continue to govern the nation." Blair was willing to immolate himself and resigned immediately.[65]

Blair's downfall stirred the Jacobins to wild expressions of jubilation. Chandler, back in Washington, received profuse congratulations from his admiring colleagues. He himself was elated beyond measure. To Wade he wrote: "I have been running a nightly express between here & New York the past week but have now closed that business. H. Winter Davis has just left my room. He is delighted with my success & cant see how it was done. . . . I can assure you that I am receiving a perfect ovation for what I have done."[66] Chandler promptly got drunk to celebrate the great victory, and boasted in his cups that he would have Welles' scalp on his belt before the election.[67]

Midway in the negotiations between Chandler and Frémont and Lincoln, a rumor went out of Washington that the chairman of the War Committee, one of the authors of the famous manifesto, was about to take the stump for Lincoln. He entered the campaign on the seventeenth at Meadville, Pennsylvania,

[64] Zachariah Chandler to Mrs. Chandler, September 6, 8, 18, 1864, in the Chandler MSS.; Nevins, *Frémont*, 2:665.

[65] Entry of September 23, 1864, in Bates, *Diary*, 412–413; Montgomery Blair to Mrs. Blair, September 23, in Smith, *Blair Family*, 2:288.

[66] Entry of September 24 in Gurowski, *Diary, 1863–1865*, p. 359; Julian, *Recollections*, 248; Benjamin F. Wade to Zachariah Chandler, October 2, in the Chandler MSS.; Chandler to Wade, September 24, *ibid.* Most of the letters of Chandler and Wade here quoted appear in W. A. Harbison, "Zachariah Chandler's Part in the Re-election of Abraham Lincoln," *Mississippi Valley Historical Review*, 22(1935):267–276.

[67] J. K. Herbert to Benjamin F. Butler, September 26, 1864, in *Butler Correspondence*, 5:167–168.

in a thundering speech that was described in the press as "a terrific assault upon the Copperhead policy."[68] It was remarked that in this and in his later speeches he spoke against the Democrats rather than for the administration, and that he seemed to avoid mention of the president's name.[69] In his heart Wade still detested Lincoln. He spoke bitterly to intimates about the "flunkies" in the party who had deserted him and Davis. He confided to Chandler that only party loyalty prompted him to support Lincoln: "But to save the nation I am doing all for *him* that I possibly could do for a better man."[70]

Most Jacobins shared Wade's feelings of sullen resentment as they settled down to the job of beating McClellan. One congressman said the Republicans had to defeat "a creature who owes all his strength—as does the rebellion itself—to the fact that he was so long tolerated—along with the Border State counsellors—by the President himself." An Illinois leader declared that Lincoln was unfit in almost every respect to head the nation, but that the party would have to swallow him as the alternative to a more bitter Democratic pill. It "could not risk a change—a change of Presidents might be a change of everything—Generals, Cabinet, etc."[71]

There was no change. The people returned Lincoln to the White House, and kept the Republican Party in control of the government. Beecher's *Independent* said the election was a popular mandate for the radical policies, and the president would recognize it as such. The Jacobins would have no further trouble with him: "The President of the fourth of March, 1865, is not the man who came into power in 1861.

[68] *New York Tribune,* September 12, 22, 1864; Kirkland, *Peacemakers of 1864,* pp. 193–194, footnote.

[69] See his speech at Cincinnati, published in the *Cincinnati Gazette,* October 24, 1864, and reproduced as a pamphlet, *Facts for the People.*

[70] J. K. Herbert to Benjamin F. Butler, September 26, in *Butler Correspondence,* 5:167–168; Benjamin F. Wade to Zachariah Chandler, October 23, 1864, in the Chandler MSS.

[71] Congressman Thomas Williams to Edwin M. Stanton, October 13, 1864, in the Stanton MSS.; G. T. Allen to Lyman Trumbull, October 4, in the Trumbull MSS.

The Abraham Lincoln of today is an abolitionist, an emancipator, and is ready to take still bolder strides toward radicalism, if it be necessary to save the country."[72] Other Jacobins doubted the reality of Lincoln's conversion, but they comforted themselves with the knowledge that they could always, with much labor, push him up to the radical mark. "Abraham has the heart of the people," wrote one radical grimly, "but he must not treat treason hereafter so tenderly. He must encourage the growth of Hemp."[73]

[72] New York *Independent,* November 17, 1864, Washington correspondence.

[73] *Wilkes' Spirit of the Times,* November 26, 1864; Thomas Shankland to Joseph Holt, November 8, in the Holt MSS.

43

Grant and the Final Victory over Lincoln

IN THE EARLY SPRING of 1864, when Lincoln was riding high in the affections of the masses and the Jacobin politicos masked their bitter hostility behind the smile of party regularity, Ulysses S. Grant came to Washington to assume supreme command of all the Union armies, with the new rank of lieutenant general, specially created for him by act of Congress. He came out of the West, the hero of Vicksburg and Chattanooga, welcomed by the president and applauded by the radicals, who claimed him as their own military discovery.

There had been a time when they had not thought so highly of the stumpy, bearded, taciturn, cigar-chewing, sloppily dressed general. In 1862, after the terrible battle of Shiloh, where the Confederates caught Grant by surprise and almost smashed his army, the Jacobins had tried to pillory him. They accused him of gross negligence and of being drunk during the fight. There was talk of an investigation by the Committee, but the inquisitors could not make the long trip to the West. However they asked General Lew Wallace, appearing as a witness on other business, to give them an account of Shiloh. Wallace had been present at the engagement, arriving well after it started because he got lost on the way to the field. He replied that Grant had bungled things completely and was undeniably incompetent. This seemed to convince Wade, for the Committee became sharply hostile to Grant. His closest friend, General Sherman, described Grant in the summer of 1862, sitting in his tent "almost weeping at the accumulated charges against him by such villains as Stanton of Ohio, Wade and others. He had made up his mind to leave for good. I begged him, and he yielded."[1]

[1] *New York Tribune*, May 5, 1862; *Chicago Tribune*, May 24; Gustave

The Jacobins assailed Grant so savagely because he was known as a Democrat. Officers in his army reported that he was completely under the dominance of General John A. Logan, the Democratic boss of southern Illinois, who had joined his staff. "There is not among all his generals that I know of, one single leading Republican," a colonel wrote. And later, when Grant issued an order permitting the Copperhead *Chicago Times* to circulate in the army, the same officer said of him: "Visions of the next Presidency are undoubtedly flitting through his dull brain."[2] A prominent leader of the Illinois Republicans gave his opinion that Grant was a typical, disloyal product of "that abominable and aristocratic hole West Point," and an abolitionist paper lumped him with the treasonable McClellan gang, opposed to emancipation and the use of Negro soldiers.[3] In 1863, when Grant began to loom as the most successful general of the war, the Republicans feared that the Democrats would make him their candidate in 1864.[4]

Realizing that Grant was the coming man and that they could not break him, the Jacobins resolved to annex him. In March of 1863 Stanton sent General Lorenzo Thomas out to the West to arrange for the enlistment of Negro soldiers, with special instructions to impress upon Grant the importance of employing former slaves in the army: Thomas was to make Grant understand that no officer was "regarded as in the discharge of his duties" who threw any obstacles in the way of the government's policy of "using every man to bring the war to an end." At the same time Stanton sent Charles A. Dana of the *Tribune* to travel with Grant's army as an observer for the War Department. In reality Dana was to report whether

Koerner to Lyman Trumbull, April 14, in the Trumbull MSS.; General John M. Palmer to Trumbull, April 24, 1862, *ibid.; C.C.W.*, 1863, 3:337–343; William T. Sherman to Mrs. Sherman, in M. A. De Wolfe Howe, ed., *Home Letters of General Sherman* (New York, 1909), 278.

[2] Colonel S. Noble to Lyman Trumbull, January 6 and February 24, 1863, in the Trumbull MSS. See also G. T. Allen to Trumbull, January 26, 1863, *ibid.*

[3] J. K. Dubois to Trumbull, May 7, 1862, *ibid.;* Boston *Commonwealth,* quoted in the *Detroit Free Press,* April 23, 1863.

[4] J. Tell to Trumbull, August 11, 1863, in the Trumbull MSS.

Grant was qualified to handle a larger job. He was also to find out if the general was a chronic drunkard, as rumor asserted.[5]

Grant, who was much more of a politician than most people imagined, correctly gauged the direction of the political winds and their relation to military promotions. He decided to become a radical. Soon he was advocating the employment of Negro soldiers. Greeley's Washington correspondent reported with elation in the fall of 1863 that among the generals there was no more ardent advocate of emancipation and colored soldiers.[6] In this dazzlingly successful general, who had turned out to be a radical, the Jacobin bosses saw an opportunity to grasp control of the military patronage and to smash the Meade influence in the Potomac army. They began to talk about calling him East to take over the command of all military operations. Stanton, still not sure of his man, sent General Hunter to study the rising luminary and make a recommendation. Hunter submitted a completely laudatory report. By December it was assumed in political circles that Grant would shortly become the dictator of the armies. The Jacobins were jubilant. Sumner viewed him as a genius, and Motley said he was the man for whom the nation had been waiting. General Palmer told Trumbull to have no worries about the orthodoxy of Grant's political opinions. They were eminently sound: "He is a soldier and of course regards Negroes at their value as military material." Palmer added shrewdly that the radicals must make Grant one of them. As the great hero of the war, he was almost certain to be the next president.[7]

Immediately after Congress convened in December, Trum-

[5] Edwin M. Stanton to Lorenzo Thomas, March 25, 1863, in the Stanton MS. Letterbooks, vol. 1; Dana, *Recollections*, 21; Wilson, *Dana*, 200–201. Dana's dispatches to Stanton are in two boxes of MSS. in the Library of Congress.

[6] *O. R.*, series 1, vol. 24, part 1, p. 31; *ibid.*, part 3, p. 547; *New York Tribune*, September 2, 1863, Washington correspondence.

[7] David Hunter to Edwin M. Stanton, December 15, 1863, in the Stanton MSS. Hunter spent three weeks with Grant. Pierce, *Sumner*, 4:172; Curtis, *Motley Correspondence*, 2:146; *New York Tribune*, December 14, 1864, Washington correspondence; John M. Palmer to Lyman Trumbull, January 24, 1864, in the Trumbull MSS.

bull presented a bill to give Grant the new rank of lieutenant general, the highest title in the military hierarchy and one held by no other man since George Washington. Trumbull and the other Jacobin leaders who supported the measure praised Grant lavishly, and ostentatiously claimed him as radical property. The bill passed in February, and Grant came to Washington the following month to assume supreme command. The delighted radicals hailed his coming. He would purge the armies of conservative generals, they thought. Halleck and Meade were through. L. Maria Child, the stern feminine radical, wrote to Julian: "I take courage from the fact that Gen. Grant is at last at the head of military affairs. I have long wished to see him there."[8]

In the meantime the Committee, Congress having granted it a new lease of life and enlarged powers, was planning its activities for the coming year. The members held a conference with Stanton, and "agreed upon certain principles" to govern them in their investigations. The radical press cried the inquisitors on to bring out the truth about the crucifixion of Hooker and to expose Meade's fraudulent claims that he was responsible for Gettysburg. A vigorous campaign was under way in the newspapers to force the ouster of Meade and to get "Fighting Joe" restored to the command. Wade and Chandler needed no urging to move against Meade. They were determined to destroy him. In mid-February they went to Lincoln and demanded that he remove Meade and all his conservative subordinates. Lincoln refused.[9]

But the inquisitors were confident. They had rosy visions of working with the radical Grant to clean out the ratholes in the Potomac army. Chandler sent the new commander a list

[8] *Congressional Globe*, 38 Congress, 1 Session, 586–594; White, *Trumbull*, 225-226; entry of March 12, 1864, in Gurowski, *Diary, 1863–1865*, p. 136; *New York Tribune*, March 9; *Chicago Tribune*, March 15; L. Maria Child to George W. Julian, March 27, in the Giddings-Julian MSS.

[9] *C.C.W.*, 1865, 1:ix, from the Committee's journal for January 27, 1864; Edwin M. Stanton to Benjamin F. Wade, January 27, in the Stanton MS. Letterbooks, vol. 3, part 2; *Wilkes' Spirit of the Times*, January 23, 1864; *Detroit Advertiser and Tribune*, quoted *ibid.*, February 27; entry of February 20 in Gurowski, *Diary, 1863–1865*, p. 113.

of the officers infected with "McClellanism," with a recommendation for their removal.[10] Grant shattered their hopes immediately. After he arrived in Washington and took over the direction of affairs, he made no changes in the personnel of Meade's officers. He treated Meade with marked friendliness. He would have nothing to do with the Committee's war against "the old snapping turtle." The Jacobins began to have doubts about Grant. One editor pointed out that most of his officers in the West had been Democrats, and that his closest friend, Sherman, who had succeeded him in the Western command, was an outspoken opponent of emancipation. And most sinister of all, Hooker had not received an independent command. Grant was mixing the same old "West Point brew": "It was misfortune enough that men who do not represent the ardor or resolution of the People should be at the helm of the civil Government; but it is deplorable, indeed, nay utterly alarming, that the great issues of the impending struggle should be confined to generals of feeble natures and inferior ability, not one of whom represents that popular sentiment which is the *avant-courier* of Destiny and which is pressing on this war." Hooker himself, serving in the West, told Chandler that Grant hated him and that the latter's friends were trying to engineer him out of the army.[11]

In late February the Committee, without waiting for Grant, had started a campaign to destroy Meade. Wade continued it, even when the commander refused to become a part of the plot. The inquisitors summoned officers from Meade's army to appear before them to relate the history of Gettysburg. The first witnesses were generals from the Republican faction, known enemies of Meade. From the questions put to them, they could easily guess what kind of story the Committee wanted—official substantiation of the whispered rumors that the corps commanders had forced Meade to fight at Gettysburg and deserved the credit for the victory, and that Meade had

[10] *Life of Chandler,* 240.
[11] *Wilkes' Spirit of the Times,* March 26, 1864; Joseph Hooker to Zachariah Chandler, May 3, 1864, in the Chandler MSS.

been guilty of criminal negligence in not pursuing Lee after the battle. Sickles, Doubleday, and A. P. Howe responded in the proper fashion, with scathing criticisms of the commander.[12] They also declared that Meade and his closest advisers were disloyal to the government and opposed to fighting a war which had emancipation as one of its aims. Doubleday charged: "There has always been a great deal of favoritism in the Army of the Potomac. No man who is an anti-slavery man or an anti-McClellan man can expect decent treatment in that army as at present constituted. . . . I think there have been pro-slavery cliques controlling that army, composed of men who would not have been willing to make a compromise in favor of slavery, and who desired to have nobody put in authority except those who agreed with them on that subject. . . . I cannot but think that there has been an indifference to say the least . . . to the success of our army." Howe said there was "too much Copperheadism" among the generals; they "do not like the way the negro question is handled, and . . . there are some who have no faith in this war, who have no heart in it." Of Meade, he observed, "My impression is that there is a want of heart, of earnestness of purpose in the man who is in command."[13]

As the Committee's investigation got under way, the Jacobin machine unleashed a savage attack upon Meade. Wilkinson, speaking in the Senate, demanded his removal. There was a great hue and cry in the press. Greeley's capital correspondent reported that the inquisitors, after gathering enough material to convict Meade, would force the president to remove him.[14] Official Washington tingled with anticipation.

Meade arrived in the capital on the fourth of March, in answer to a summons from the Committee. He was stunned, as he wrote to his wife, "to find the whole town talking of certain grave charges of Generals Sickles and Doubleday that

[12] *C.C.W.*, 1865, 1:295–304, Sickles' testimony; 305–312, Doubleday's; 312–329, Howe's.

[13] *Ibid.*, 1:311, Doubleday's testimony; 325–328, Howe's.

[14] *Congressional Globe*, 38 Congress, 1 Session, 897–898; *New York Tribune*, March 4, 7, 8, Washington correspondence.

had been made against me in their testimony before the Committee on the Conduct of the War." Meade went to the committee rooms the next day and found only Wade there. "He was very civil," Meade wrote in describing the scene for his wife, "denied there were any charges against me, but said the Committee was making up a sort of history of the war and was now taking evidence to enable it to give an account of the battle of Gettysburg and my administration since commanding the army." This smooth piece of double-dealing did not fool Meade. After he finished testifying, he saw Stanton. The secretary, still chronically unable to follow a straight course, confided that the Committee was plotting to get Hooker restored to the command.[15] Meade heard a rumor that Wade and Chandler had already gone to Lincoln with a demand for his removal. On the twelfth the general again saw Wade. The chairman still tried to blandish Meade with fair words. "He took great pains to endeavor to convince me that the Committee was not responsible for the newspaper attacks on me, and I might rest assured there was no disposition on their part to do me injustice."[16]

These were Judas words. Wade and Chandler were holding back only until they could collect all the damning evidence they wanted. In late March they decided to strike. They called on Lincoln on the twenty-third. The account of the interview which Wade had entered on the Committee's journal stated that they demanded of Lincoln "the removal of General Meade and the appointment of someone more competent to command." The president asked them what general they would recommend, and they replied that Hooker was their first choice. They threatened to attack the administration in Congress unless Lincoln made a change: "They stated that Congress had appointed the Committee to watch the conduct of the war, and unless this state of things should be soon changed it would

[15] George G. Meade to Mrs. Meade, March 6, 1864, in Meade, *Meade,* 2:169. For Meade's testimony, see *C.C.W.,* 1865, 1:329–351.

[16] Meade, *Meade,* 1:172–173; Meade to Mrs. Meade, March 14, *ibid.,* 2:177–178; *Life of Chandler,* 245; Colonel Theodore Lyman to Mrs. Lyman, March 5, 1864, in Agassiz, *Meade's Headquarters,* 78–79.

become their duty to make the testimony public which they had taken with such comments as the circumstances of the case seemed to require." Lincoln said nothing and he did not remove Meade. The Committee members fumed with wrath. Their rage was the greater because Grant had not come to their aid.[17]

The president's support of Meade and Grant's apparent backsliding from the faith destroyed the Jacobins' roseate visions of controlling the military patronage. Conservative domination of the armies seemed as strong as ever. In Louisiana the hated Banks, having completed his job of setting up a state government for Lincoln, embarked on an expedition up the Red River. The genesis of this movement was the desire of the State Department to effect an occupation of Texas for the purpose of impressing the French government, which had seized the opportunity presented by American civil strife to establish a puppet emperor in Mexico in defiance of the Monroe Doctrine. Banks had previously tried to occupy Texas by going up the coast, but he found the difficulties insuperable. Then Halleck advised him to take his army up the Red River and down into northern Texas. Lincoln indorsed the scheme because it would bring more of reconstructed Louisiana under Union control. The government also hoped the expedition would secure possession of large supplies of cotton, at that time desperately needed for Northern mills and for export to England. Against his judgment, Banks undertook the campaign. The expedition was poorly organized, partly because of the commander's preoccupation with civil affairs; some of his troops were lent by other generals and recalled after he started his march. In the circumstances the failure of the project was not surprising. Defeated at Sabine Crossroads in April, Banks retreated to New Orleans.

Immediately the radical hue and cry burst forth. The Jacobins charged that Banks, while on the expedition, had engaged in corrupt speculation in cotton and reaped huge profits. A man who had accompanied the army wrote, in a

[17] *C.C.W.*, 1865, 1:xix; Gurowski, *Diary, 1863–1865*, p. 183.

letter that was turned over to Stanton by its recipient, that
Banks was too mild in his treatment of rebels, refused to confiscate property, had failed to "make the people realize there
is a war in the land." The *Independent* demanded that Congress investigate the blundering regime of the perpetrator of
"The Serf System in Louisiana." Grimes accurately described
the feelings of the congressional radicals when he said, "Everybody curses Banks loud and deep." Sumner thought "that
Banks' military character has suffered very much, hardly more
than he has suffered as a statesman by his proceedings for reconstruction."[18]

While the Jacobins screamed epithets at Banks, the Committee was busily engaged in another project to fire the
Northern heart. Its second adventure in the production of
atrocity propaganda was a double-edged attempt to sustain a
war psychosis and to smear Lincoln for his refusal to order
measures of retaliation inflicted upon Confederate prisoners in
return for alleged inhuman treatment of Union soldiers in
Southern prisons. In lurid accounts of conditions in the Confederacy's prisons, the Northern press accused the Davis government of deliberately following a policy designed to destroy
the inmates. There were loud demands that the North retali-
ate, eye for eye and tooth for tooth. Wade and Chandler urged
the president to make a declaration that he would resort to
reprisals if the Confederacy did not abandon its savage program. To their disgust, Lincoln took no action. He further
angered the radical leaders by refusing to answer the threat
of the Confederate authorities that since they did not consider
Negro soldiers as equals they would not accord them the protection of the laws of war. This pronouncement, with its probable effect of discouraging the enlistment of colored men in the
army, alarmed the Jacobins. Vainly they pressed Lincoln to
promise drastic measures of retaliation upon Confederate pris-

[18] Russell Hinckley to Lyman Trumbull, April 28, 1864, in the Trum-
bull MSS.; S. A. Ballou, letter of April 25, in the Stanton MSS.; New
York *Independent*, April 28, May 5, 1864; James W. Grimes to Mrs.
Grimes, April 24, in Salter, *Grimes*, 260–261; Charles Sumner to Francis
Lieber, in Pierce, *Sumner*, 4:193.

oners if "the Southern barbarians" carried out their "hideous threats."[19]

Wade and Chandler soon found an opportunity to force Lincoln's hand when, in April, a wave of hysteria gripped the North at the reported massacre of a Negro garrison and its white officers at Fort Pillow, Tennessee. The alleged assassins were General Nathan Bedford Forrest, whose simple recipe for victory was "to get there the fustest with the mostest men," and his famous, hard-riding "Critter Company." The profane, illiterate Forrest and his band of native Tennesseans had fixed ideas about the Negro's proper station in society. They thought of him as a little above the animals. Consequently they had been inflamed to savage rage when the Union employed Negro soldiers, and they vented their wrath at Pillow. The fort fell easily. As Forrest's grim troopers swarmed over the parapets, the frightened colored soldiers scurried for cover like rabbits. The attackers hunted them down, and a scene of bloody carnage ensued. There was no organized massacre, but a great deal of needless slaughtering took place. After the battle, Forrest could boast that the river in front of the fort was dyed with blood for two hundred yards.[20]

The reports of Forrest's gory work horrified the North. The newspapers supplied the public with sensational and, in some respects, exaggerated accounts. The great illustrated weeklies dramatized the scenes at Pillow with vivid sketches. Immediately the Jacobins set up a clamor for measures of retaliation upon Confederate prisoners. They charged that Abraham Lincoln was the real murderer of the Negro garrison. If he had threatened reprisals when the Confederacy first announced that it would not grant colored soldiers the protection of the laws of war, the Fort Pillow tragedy would never have occurred. Bending before the storm the president promised in a speech

[19] *New York Times*, December 5, 1863, March 5, 12, 31, 1864; *Harper's Weekly*, December 5, 1863; *New York Tribune*, March 5, 1864; Gurowski, *Diary, 1863–1865*, p. 191; New York *Independent*, June 4, 1863.

[20] The battle occurred on April 12. For descriptions see Eric Sheppard, *Bedford Forrest* (London, 1930), 168–172; John A. Wyeth, *General Nathan Bedford Forrest* (New York, 1899), 344–362.

at Baltimore that if the Fort Pillow rumors were substantiated by some official body, he would inaugurate a system of retaliation. One radical editor commented ominously: "The President, who overlooked previous massacres, has publicly declared that when official accounts of the affair arrive there shall be retaliation. We trust this shall be so; otherwise, the troops, mocked by a Government that uses them and then allows them to be slaughtered, will rush on the places where the rebel prisoners are confined, and wipe out in indiscriminate slaughter the account of Ft. Pillow."[21]

Assurance of action from Lincoln was all the Jacobin bosses wanted. They sped through both houses of Congress a joint resolution directing the Committee to investigate the facts of the affair at Pillow.[22] The Committee eagerly accepted the assignment and designated Wade and Gooch to proceed to the West and collect evidence on the spot. The two inquisitors set out on their mission armed with orders from Stanton instructing the military authorities to furnish them full cooperation. At Cairo, Mound City, Fort Pillow, Memphis, and elsewhere, they took evidence from seventy-eight witnesses, eighteen of whom had not been present at the Pillow massacre. This list included hospital surgeons who had cared for the wounded survivors, soldiers of the garrison who had escaped unharmed, and people who had visited the fort after the battle.

Their evidence collected, Wade and Gooch returned to Washington and submitted their information to the full Committee. On May 4, while the members were discussing the report Wade had written, the chairman showed them a letter he had just received from Stanton. The wily secretary, ever alert to what was good propaganda, suggested that the inquisitors go to Annapolis and examine a group of Union sol-

<hr />

[21] *Harper's Weekly*, April 30, 1864, editorial and sketch; New York *Independent*, April 21, 28, May 5; *Leslie's Newspaper*, May 7, editorial and sketch; I. J. Sharpless to Joseph Holt, April 24, in the Holt MSS.; S. A. Ballou, letter of April 25, in the Stanton MSS.; S. H. Morse to George W. Julian, no date, in the Giddings-Julian MSS.; Lincoln, *Works*, 10:49; *Leslie's Newspaper*, May 7, 1864.

[22] *Senate Reports*, 38 Congress, 1 Session, no. 63, p. 1, "Ft. Pillow Report," hereafter cited as "Ft. Pillow Report." The resolution was passed on April 16.

diers just returned from Southern prisons. "The enormity of the crime committed by the rebels towards our prisoners for the last several months is not known or realized by our own people, and cannot but fill with horror the civilized world when the facts are revealed," he wrote. "There appears to have been a deliberate system of savage and barbarous treatment and starvation."[23] Hurriedly the Committee approved Wade's report on Fort Pillow, and two days later they proceeded to Annapolis to revel in more examples of Southern barbarity. A report of the evidence taken from the prisoners was whipped into shape immediately, and on May 9 Wade released the two reports to the press as one document.

These reports were the most expert atrocity-propaganda productions of the war period. The Fort Pillow narrative was a vivid description of the scenes which took place after Forrest's vengeful troopers stormed the fort and scattered the frightened garrison. The excesses committed, declared the report, were not the results of momentary passions but of a deliberate policy to discourage the use of Negro soldiers:

The rebels commenced an indiscriminate slaughter, sparing neither age nor sex, white or black, soldier or civilian. The officers and men seemed to vie with each other in the devilish work; men, women, and even children were deliberately shot down, beaten, and hacked with sabres; some of the children not more than ten years old were forced to stand up and face their murderers while being shot; the sick and wounded were butchered without mercy, the rebels even entering the hospital and dragging them out to be shot, or killing them as they lay there unable to offer the least resistance.[24]

The testimony hardly justified this sweeping indictment. A great deal of needless killing of the garrison undoubtedly occurred,[25] but the captain of a Union gunboat in the river near the fort testified that before the battle he had removed all the

---

[23] Edwin M. Stanton to Benjamin F. Wade, May 4, 1864, in *C.C.W.*, 1865, 1:xxv; *House Reports*, 38 Congress, 1 Session, no. 63, p. 1, "Returned Prisoners," hereafter cited as "Returned Prisoners Report."

[24] "Ft. Pillow Report," 4.

[25] *Ibid.*, 13–14, 44, 51, 94. One survivor said that the Confederate officers made an attempt to restrain their men. *Ibid.*, 40.

women, children, and sick Negroes to the safety of a nearby island.[26]

Not content with butchering the garrison, the report continued, Forrest's men indulged their savage hatred for Negroes and Northerners by torturing the wounded and the prisoners. The attackers had fired the huts and tents in which the wounded lay, and the helpless inmates had died horribly. The rebels had nailed prisoners by their clothes to walls or floors and then set the dwellings ablaze.[27] Again the Committee was making a charge which the evidence did not entirely sustain. The witnesses who described the burnt bodies were people who had visited the fort after the battle, and most of them did not examine the remains closely enough to know accurately that Forrest's troops had nailed men to walls.[28] Only one witness offered reliable testimony on this point; he had found, on the day after the engagement, the body of a Negro nailed to a tent floor.[29] On the other hand, a soldier present during the fighting said the Confederate officers tried to remove the wounded from the burning tents.[30] The report hurled a final accusation that the fiendish rebels had not given the Union dead a decent burial, but had thrown the bodies into a shallow trench and left portions of heads and limbs "protruding through the earth in every direction. The testimony also established the fact that the rebels buried some of the living with the dead, a few of whom succeeded in digging themselves out, or were dug out by others, one of whom your committee found in Mound City hospital and there examined."[31] This statement was a flagrant misrepresentation of the evidence. The witness referred to, a colored private, testified that he had feigned death during the fighting in order to escape attack. His act was good enough to fool the Confederates, who started to bury him with the dead. Then an officer noticed that the man was alive, and had him removed and given care.[32]

[26] *Ibid.*, 86.   [27] *Ibid.*, 5.
[28] *Ibid.*, 27, 30, 31, 94, 107–108.
[29] *Ibid.*, 91–92, testimony of Eli Bangs.
[30] *Ibid.*, 82–83.   [31] *Ibid.*, 5.
[32] *Ibid.*, 18–19, testimony of Daniel Taylor.

Accompanying the Fort Pillow account was the shorter but equally vivid report on the Annapolis prisoners. Embellished with pictures of eight wasted victims of the Richmond prisons, this narrative detailed the sufferings, privations, and tortures endured by Union soldiers who fell into Confederate hands. Although the evidence gathered at Annapolis contradicted itself violently and much of it came from surgeons rather than from the prisoners themselves, the Committee did not hesitate to conclude that the "inhuman practices" of the Confederate authorities were the result of a determination "to reduce our soldiers in their power, by privation of food and clothing, and by exposure, to such a condition that those who may survive shall never recover so as to be able to render any effective service in the field."[33]

The techniques of the conscious propaganda appeared on every page of the two reports. The many sweeping accusations which did not square with the evidence showed a deliberate purpose to twist and distort the facts in order to implant the desired opinions in the mass mind. Using the excuse of grammatical necessity, the Committee "dressed up" the testimony of the illiterate Negroes in the Fort Pillow inquiry, and got results of unusual eloquence. More important was the employment of pictures in the Annapolis document. "We found," said Chandler, "that language failed to convey to the mind a correct idea of the condition of these men, and we were compelled, in order to give an approximate idea of the treatment our prisoners had received, to have photographs of those skeletons before the people of the United States, that they might realize the barbarities that had been perpetrated upon them." Julian spoke complacently of the two reports as "a special installment of our proceedings, for popular use."[34]

The reports produced a tremendous public sensation. Backed

[33] "Returned Prisoners Report," 3. The testimony revealed more of the inefficient organization of the Confederate prison system and the general scarcity of supplies in the South than it did of any concerted, deliberate system of cruelty toward the prisoners.

[34] *Congressional Globe,* 38 Congress, 2 Session, 496; Julian, *Recollections,* 238–239.

by the great prestige of the Committee, they attained a wide circulation and a large audience. Twenty thousand extra copies were printed for the Senate and franked out over the country. Pamphlet versions told the lurid story in briefer form. *Harper's Weekly* embellished the printed account with a full-page picture of the Fort Pillow massacre in which villainous and depraved-looking rebels, with round shoulders and hollow chests, were shown murdering and hacking large, handsome, but curiously helpless, Negro soldiers. The dailies splashed the story over the front pages, beneath screaming headlines that summarized the most extreme accusations in the report. One indignant citizen, after having read the documents, recorded in his diary: "It is horrible, atrocious. History records no instances of such deliberate ferocity. . . . Let Lincoln send a copy of this book to every home. It is better than the draft, or his greenbacks."[35]

The popular reaction to the reports gratified the Committee. But the documents failed to achieve the end for which they had been prepared—to induce Lincoln to adopt the system of retaliation which he had promised at Baltimore. Stanton worked out a six-point program, and the Committee pressed its merits. But the president refused to come to a decision. The inquisitors, in profound disgust, temporarily abandoned the fight.[36]

In May the taciturn Grant started his campaign, throwing the Union armies into action on a wide front. Sherman's host in the West plunged into the lower South, striking toward Georgia. The Army of the Potomac moved against Richmond, with Grant directing its operations. Technically Meade was

[35] *Congressional Globe*, 38 Congress, 1 Session, 2171; *Rebel Barbarities, Official Accounts of the cruelties inflicted upon Union Prisoners and Refugees at Ft. Pillow, Libby Prison, etc.* (New York, 1864); Frank Moore, ed., *The Rebellion Record* (New York, 1864–1868), 7:80–98; *Harper's Weekly*, May 21, 1864; *New York Tribune*, May 6, 10, 1864; *New York Herald*, May 6; entry of July 4, 1864, in General William E. Doster's diary, quoted in Doster, *Lincoln*, 243. See also the minutes of the Congregational Association of Michigan in *The Congregational Churches of Michigan*, 1870.

[36] Edwin M. Stanton to Abraham Lincoln, May 5, 1864, in the Stanton MS. Letterbooks, vol. 3, part 2; Flower, *Stanton*, 235–236.

still commander, but Grant accompanied the army and gave the orders. The Jacobin bosses watched Grant with a critical eye, ready to attack him if the moment seemed propitious. Grant elected to move southward against the Confederate capital through the tangled, wooded, gloomy region known as the Wilderness. Here the defending army of Lee had every advantage. In the dense, dark underbrush the two armies fought furiously. Stubbornly Grant hurled his troops against the strong Confederate positions and saw them fall back, shattered and shaken. After weeks of bloody battering, Grant was no farther than when he started. The country cried out in horror at his roll of dead and wounded, and the radicals proclaimed him a failure. Then Grant abruptly switched plans. He took his army over the James and prepared to attack Richmond from the east. This was the scheme which McClellan had advocated back in the Peninsula days. Then the Jacobins had sneered that such a plan was unworkable and doomed to fail, but now they asked pointedly why the stupid Grant had not adopted this obviously sound and only practical way to take Richmond before?[37] Bursting with rage, Ben Wade stumped down to the White House to berate Lincoln and demand the removal of Grant. "You are the father of every military blunder that has been made during this war," he cried at the president. "This government is on the road to hell, sir, by reason of your obstinacy, and you are not a mile from there this minute." Quietly Lincoln observed that a mile was about the distance to the Capitol, where Congress met. Wade glared, seized his hat and cane, and left.[38] At Meade's headquarters the staff officers uneasily discussed rumors that Grant was about to get the guillotine.[39]

[37] James W. Grimes to Mrs. Grimes, May 10, 18, 1864, in Salter, *Grimes,* 261–262; diary of Salmon P. Chase, May 23, in Warden, *Chase,* 594; *Chicago Tribune,* May 12; New York *Independent,* May 12; Grimes to Mrs. Grimes, June 19, 1864, in Salter, *Grimes,* 263.

[38] Nathaniel Wright Stephenson, ed., *An Autobiography of Abraham Lincoln* (New York, 1926), 416–417.

[39] Colonel Theodore Lyman to Mrs. Lyman, August 1, 1864, in Agassiz, *Meade's Headquarters,* 203–204.

As the bloody summer of 1864 ended, the Jacobins were snarling viciously at the Grant clique and the administration. "Fighting Joe" Hooker had just asked to be relieved of duty in the West because he had been placed under the command of a junior officer. The radicals cried that the Grant gang had driven him out of the army and that Halleck had engineered a conspiracy to destroy their favorite. Of Halleck's part in Hooker's downfall, a radical editor declared: "The malice of that cold, calculating owl, who broods in the shadows of the War Department, distilling evil upon every noble character which rubs his envy, has again triumphed over General Hooker." And at the same time, continued the indignant journalist, the administration sustained in power such a notorious incompetent as "Nothing Positive" Banks.[40] This was at the same moment when the Jacobins were confidently perfecting their plans to call a convention to place a new presidential candidate in the field and to force Lincoln out of the race. Sherman's capture of Atlanta abruptly exploded their plot and saved Lincoln. It also saved Grant from a Jacobin attack. Military victory promised triumph in November, and the radical bosses closed the breach in the party. They wanted harmony—until the election was safely over. They also temporarily dropped their hostility to Grant and his friends. Sherman, after his victory in Georgia, swung eastward in his triumphal march to the sea. The stubborn Grant was edging steadily toward Richmond. The Jacobins were too shrewd to assail successful generals.

When Congress met in December the atmosphere in the Republican camp was that of a marriage feast. Lovingly and with a proprietary manner the Jacobins caressed that best of radicals, Abraham Lincoln, who had just emerged victorious from a savage struggle with the Copperheads because of Jacobin aid. Loudly and with an undertone of warning menace meant for White House ears they proclaimed that the new Lincoln would carry forward to victorious conclusion the principles of radicalism. Lincoln's message to Congress seemed to

[40] *Wilkes' Spirit of the Times,* August 20, 1864.

corroborate their boasts. He called for a vigorous prosecution of the war and pledged that he would oppose any peace terms which did not include the destruction of slavery. He advocated the passage of a constitutional amendment abolishing the hated institution, and repeated his unwavering support of the Emancipation Proclamation. Beecher's *Independent* voiced the opinion of the delighted radicals when it exclaimed, "God bless Abraham Lincoln." Greeley declared that the warfare between radicals and conservatives had ended forever; the party was now a united phalanx. Sumner had discussed with Lincoln "the duty of harmony between Congress and the Executive," and the optimistic senator believed that Lincoln would let Congress write a reconstruction bill which would enforce Negro suffrage upon the South. The powerful Union League clubs started a movement to get more radicals into the Cabinet, blissfully confident that Lincoln would fall in with their scheme.[41]

In the Senate Wade exultantly voiced his conviction that the final triumph of the Jacobin revolution was at hand. No longer was the war being prosecuted for the vain and empty purpose of restoring the Union with slavery intact, he boasted. It had become a crusade to destroy slavery, and the struggle would not end until "the monster" breathed his last. The Republican Party, he cried, would force the Southern states to purge themselves of all the inequities of their social system before it permitted them to come back into the Union: "We will govern them until they do right. . . . Let this war go on long enough to compel these men when they ask for justice at our hands to do justice by their own people." Threateningly Wade warned Lincoln not to impede the radical program. The Republican platform of 1864 had obligated the president to destroy slavery. "That is the platform upon which we put him, and he said that he assented to it. If he backed out of it, he would be the most

[41] Richardson, *Messages of the Presidents*, 6:252, 254–255; New York *Independent*, December 8, 1864; *Wilkes' Spirit of the Times*, December 17; *New York Tribune*, December 9, 1864; Charles Sumner to Francis Lieber, December 27, 1864, in Pierce, *Sumner*, 4:204–205; A. Chester to Lyman Trumbull, January 18, February 17, 1864, in the Trumbull MSS.

infamous man that ever obtained the confidence and votes of the people by false pretences." The Jacobins were leading a great popular revolution, Wade continued, and no man could halt it. "The sternness of their principle has revolutionized this whole continent. . . . In the hour of victory, when we have the solution of the great question which we have so long contended for within our reach, do you suppose we are now to back down and permit you to make a dishonorable pro-slavery peace after all this bloodshed and all this sacrifice of life and property?" he asked the conservatives. "It cannot be. Such revolutions never go backward."[42]

Lincoln's actions in January justified Wade's arrogant confidence: the president seemed eager to speed the course of the revolution. In the previous year the Senate had adopted an amendment to the Constitution abolishing slavery, but the measure had failed of passage in the House. Now the administration suddenly threw all its influence behind the amendment. It rode to easy victory in the House, and was sent to the states for ratification.[43]

Jacobinism was rolling at flood tide, and its lashing power seemed about to engulf the last few conservative bulwarks. Wade and Chandler seized the opportunity of the moment to move again for a system of retaliation upon Confederate prisoners, for the professed purpose of forcing the Southern government to cease its barbarous treatment of Union inmates of its prisons. Equipped with information concerning Southern prison conditions gathered from General Butler and other witnesses, Wade offered a resolution authorizing the president to invoke reprisals. His measure would have exacted an eye for an eye and a tooth for a tooth, with the reprisals being carried out under the direction of men who had suffered in Confederate prisons.[44] In flaming words he accused the Confederacy of inaugurating a policy compounded of "brutality, inhumanity, exposure, and starvation," for the "base and ac-

[42] *Congressional Globe*, 38 Congress, 2 Session, 162, 164, 165.
[43] *Ibid.*, 531.
[44] *C.C.W.*, 1865, 2:49; *ibid.*, vol. 3, "Treatment of Prisoners" report; *Congressional Globe*, 38 Congress, 2 Session, 267, 363–364.

cursed purpose" of destroying the manhood of Union prisoners and thus rendering them unfit for military service after they were exchanged. He avowed himself willing to accept any measures of retaliation: "I will make the South a desolation, and every traitor shall lose his life, unless they treat our men with humanity. . . . I will go to an extreme in that direction." The Jacobin supporters of the resolution could not resist hurling a few gibes at Lincoln for his stubborn refusal to inaugurate retaliation. "The President," Wade cried, "has not nerve enough to come up to the mark, and say, 'The soldiers whom I have called into the field shall be treated like men and prisoners of war when they are captives.' I wish to God he had more courage; but I must confess that he has been been perfectly reckless of his duty for a long time."[45] Chandler said that the Committee had labored to persuade Lincoln to adopt measures of reprisal ever since the time when it had investigated the condition of the returned prisoners at Annapolis: "We then hoped and believed that the administration would adopt, and adopt immediately, a system of retaliation that would prove efficacious. In that hope we were disappointed."[46]

The conservative Republicans could not stomach Wade's drastic proposal. Much less could they stand the overbearing arrogance which he exhibited during the debates and the savage sentiments which he voiced. Even radicals like Sumner and Wilson were repelled, and opposed the measure. Wilson feelingly declared that as he listened to Wade and Chandler he "thought that the old slave-masters had come back again. I thought that I witnessed all their insolence, and something more than their coarseness." The brilliant McDougall bitingly compared Wade to Marat, the terrible figure who came out of the cellars of Paris during the French Revolution to drench France in the blood of the Reign of Terror.[47] Because of conservative opposition, the resolution failed. Its opponents so emasculated it with amendments that Wade in disgust

[45] *Ibid.*, 268–269, 434, 495.
[46] *Ibid.*, 496.
[47] *Ibid.*, 499, Wilson's speech; 497, McDougall's. See also Pierce, *Sumner,* 4:211.

abandoned the fight. Sullenly he and Chandler noted that the administration had given them no aid in their battle.[48]

The fate of the retaliation bill heralded an approaching break in the honeymoon that had existed since the election between the Jacobins and Lincoln and the conservatives. The radicals could not rid themselves of the suspicion that Lincoln would prove an unfaithful mate and would try to resume amorous relations with his former loves, the Democrats and the conservatives. Nor could they resist taunting him, as Wade and Chandler had done in the debates on retaliation, because his past associations had been of a shady and disreputable character. They watched him like hawks for any indication that he was straying from the path of fidelity. In late January they learned that he had permitted old Frank Blair to go to Richmond to open informal peace negotiations with the Confederate authorities. The president had no faith that Blair could accomplish anything, but he judged that no harm could come of letting him try. The Jacobins buzzed with wrath when they heard of Blair's mission. Immediately they leaped to the conclusion that Lincoln was thinking of making a rose-water peace.[49] As a result of Blair's work the Confederate government dispatched envoys to confer with Lincoln and Seward. They met the president and the secretary on a transport vessel in Hampton Roads, and Lincoln presented his terms: an immediate end of the war, reunion, and Southern acceptance of emancipation. This was more than the Confederacy was willing to concede, and the conference adjourned without coming to any agreement.

In Washington the radicals seethed with anger and suspicion while Lincoln and his evil genius talked with the rebel envoys. Wild rumors scudded through the city to alarm the radicals: Lincoln had offered to abandon emancipation, confiscation, and the amendment abolishing slavery if the South

[48] Zachariah Chandler to Mrs. Chandler, January 16, 27, 1865, in the Chandler MSS.

[49] Chandler to Mrs. Chandler, January 25, *ibid.;* New York *Independent,* January 26, February 2, Washington correspondence; James L. Bates to Edwin M. Stanton, January 23, in the Stanton MSS.

would lay down its arms. Bitterly the radicals denounced the president for lowering the dignity of his office by treating with the emissaries of treason. Zack Chandler said that Lincoln had taken a long trip for nothing and had come back with a flea in his ear. "Fools meet & separate," was the old senator's scornful verdict on the meeting.[50]

So excited were the Jacobins that Sumner introduced a resolution in the Senate calling upon Lincoln to furnish information about what had taken place at Hampton Roads. This touched off a snarling debate in which the hitherto-banked fires of factional controversy flared up in open warfare. The attenuated bonds holding radicals and conservatives together were revealed, as frayed tempers long held in leash snapped completely. Administration senators, led by Doolittle, rushed forward to contend that the resolution was an attack upon the president. Doolittle singled out Wade as the leader of a Jacobin plot to sabotage the administration's program for peace and reconstruction. In a savage reply, Wade flayed both Lincoln and Doolittle in intemperate language. He was not afraid to attack the president, he proclaimed. Sneeringly he observed that it was not honorable for senators to be Lincoln's "mere servants, obeying everything that we may ascertain to be his wish and will, because he is not always wiser than the whole of us or a majority of us." Wade denounced Lincoln for meeting the Confederate commissioners. He would continue to denounce the president whenever the occasion demanded, he stated, even though the miserable Doolittle like a Cerberus "stood in the way barking."[51] Lincoln transmitted the desired information, and the Jacobins quieted down when they saw his terms. But the episode had revealed the radicals' deep distrust of Lincoln and their abiding conviction that he could not be trusted to handle the problems of peace and reconstruction. Gideon

[50] Brooks, *Washington in Lincoln's Time,* 224; New York *Independent,* February 9, 1865, Washington correspondence; James A. Garfield to Hinsdale, February 5, 1865, in Smith, *Garfield,* 1:381; J. D. Cox, *Reminiscences,* 2:397–398; Zachariah Chandler to Mrs. Chandler, February 6 and February 10, 1865, in the Chandler MSS.

[51] *Congressional Globe,* 38 Congress, 2 Session, 657, 659–660.

Welles predicted apprehensively in his diary that the Jacobin cabal would attempt to impose upon the conquered states conditions that went far beyond Lincoln's terms of Southern acceptance of emancipation. The old secretary saw looming ahead a bitter struggle over the issue of reconstruction.[52]

His analysis was correct. The problem of reconstruction and who should control its process, Congress or the president, had lain dormant since before the election. Now in the early months of 1865 it was clear to all observers that the Confederacy would soon collapse. With the approach of victory and peace, reconstruction became a dominant issue to the exclusion of all other questions. Upon what terms were the Southern states to be received back into the Union? Who would determine the conditions of readmission—Wade and Chandler or Lincoln? The president stood where he had stood in the previous summer. He would welcome home any seceded state which ceased resistance to the government and recognized the fact of emancipation. He would have no harsh punishment of a defeated people. He still held to his promise that whenever ten per cent of the voters in any state took an oath of allegiance and set up a loyal state government, he would give that government executive recognition. Under his plan, so fiercely reviled by Wade and Davis in their manifesto, new governments had been established in Louisiana, Arkansas, Tennessee, and Virginia. The Jacobins had moved far beyond their position as announced in the Wade-Davis bill. No longer were they content to accept emancipation as the great result of the war. Now they demanded as the price of readmission a program which would insure Republican political control of the South. They had no mind to see unrepentant Southern Democrats returning to Congress and in alliance with their Northern fellows destroying the economic measures passed by the Republicans during the war: the protective tariff, the national banking system, and the homestead bill. They demanded the suffrage for the freed slaves and the disfranchise-

[52] New York *Independent*, February 16, 1865, Washington correspondence; entry of February 10, 1865, in Welles, *Diary*, 2:238–239.

ment of a substantial portion of the Southern white population. Some of them, like Stevens, advocated the distribution of confiscated rebel property among former slaves. They demanded that until their policies became a reality the seceded states be governed by the military as "conquered provinces." Over the issue of reconstruction Lincoln and the Jacobins fought their last titanic battle. Again the Jacobins were to defeat their great antagonist.

The Jacobin bosses were grimly confident that they could whip Lincoln on the reconstruction issue. They believed that public opinion had moved up to their position and that the people would support a program which included the suffrage for the Southern Negroes as one of its cardinal principles. They chose to precipitate the inevitable struggle with the president; their object was to defeat congressional recognition of Lincoln's ten per cent governments. Early in February the radicals prepared to jam through Congress a resolution declaring that the eleven seceded states were not entitled to representation in the electoral college. This struck directly at Lincoln's four reconstructed states. Wade, who led the debate for the Jacobins, bitterly denounced Lincoln's reconstruction plan as "the most absurd and impracticable that ever haunted the imagination of a statesman." The proclamation which Lincoln had issued when he pocketed the Wade-Davis bill was, cried Wade, "the most contentious, the most anarchical, the most dangerous proposition that was ever put forth for the government of a free people."[53] The resolution passed both houses, and Lincoln signed it under protest. He may have hoped to conciliate the Jacobins by yielding. It was a useless concession. The radicals had the bit in their teeth and they were running hard.

Late in February the senators and representatives elected by reconstructed Louisiana knocked at the doors of Congress asking for recognition and admission. This the Jacobin chieftains were determined to prevent. Wade, Chandler, and Sumner led the fight to deny seats to the petitioners. Fearful that

[53] *Congressional Globe,* 38 Congress, 2 Session, 559–560.

they could not command a majority to defeat the resolution recognizing the Louisiana government, the three resorted to obstruction and delay. They spoke interminably, they demanded the yeas and nays on every question. And finally they triumphed. The Senate, its patience worn thin, "dispensed" with the resolution. In the heated debates on the measure, Wade accused Lincoln of seeking to set up state governments in the South by military force and in violation of the Constitution: "If the President of the United States operating through his major generals can initiate a State government, and can bring it here and force us, compel us, to receive on this floor these mere mockeries, these men of straw, who represent nobody, your Republic is at an end."[54]

While the Jacobin machine in Congress was fighting and defeating Lincoln on the reconstruction issue, the Committee was busily at work behind the scenes. Immediately after Congress gathered in December the inquisitors met to plan their activities for the session, and they turned their first attention to General Banks. That officer, with no pressing military duties to perform, had come to Washington in the autumn to lobby for congressional recognition of the government he had sired in Louisiana. Rumor whispered that he would receive a Cabinet appointment, and Mrs. Lincoln, who disliked him heartily, besought Sumner to use his influence to prevent such a calamity.[55] The radical leaders were determined to crush any attempt to give official sanction to the Louisiana government. They decided to strike a blow at it by smearing the record of its founder, the hated Banks. The general received a summons to appear before the Committee to answer questions about his Red River campaign. He testified on December 14 and again on January 13, in an atmosphere that crackled with hostility. The Committee grilled him thoroughly, with searching questions which dealt not only with Red River but also with his work in reconstructing Louisiana and his alleged speculations in cotton.[56] For the moment the Committee did

[54] See *ibid.*, 1101–1111, 1126–1129, for the debates.
[55] Pierce, *Sumner*, 4:221.
[56] *C.C.IV.*, 1865, vol. 2, "Red River," 3–28, 84.

not publicly attack Banks, but Wade held the information drawn out of him and other witnesses ready for instant use. He employed some of its effectively in the debates when the Jacobins defeated the administration's attempt to secure congressional recognition for Louisiana.

At the same time the Committee started an investigation aimed at Gideon Welles, the secretary of the navy. The acid old man was almost fanatically devoted to Lincoln and he detested the radicals. In particular he made no secret of his contempt for the inquisitors, whom he labeled as "mischievous busybodies, and a discredit to Congress." The radicals and the Committee reciprocated his feelings with interest. They took pot shots at his administration of the naval department whenever the opportunity offered. In the summer of 1864 there was widespread newspaper criticism of the small monitors being constructed by the navy. These vessels, critics asserted, were unseaworthy and should never have been built. Sensing a chance to attack Welles, the Jacobins secured the adoption of a Senate resolution instructing the Committee to investigate the matter.[57] For some undisclosed reason the members took no action at the time. But in December, when the strength of radicalism seemed to be sweeping all before it and the radical forces entertained hopes of reforming the Cabinet, the Committee suddenly undertook an inquiry into the subject of the monitors. Some of the members traveled to the Boston and New York naval yards to collect testimony. Naval officers and experts were summoned to appear in Washington for questioning. Months later the Committee was to present a report bitterly condemning Welles for permitting the construction of twenty worthless ships and accusing the department of making gross errors in drawing up the plans for the monitors.[58]

On February 16, with the inquiry virtually completed but with the testimony still in the form of shorthand notes, Wade

[57] Welles, *Diary*, 1:226; *New York Tribune*, July 28, 1864; *C.C.W.*, 1865, 1:xxvi.

[58] *Ibid.*, xxvii, xxix; *ibid.*, vol. 3, report on the "Light-Draught Monitors."

arose in the Senate to deliver a stinging attack upon Welles and to accuse the secretary of inefficiency in the administration of his department. Speaking for the Committee, Wade proposed a fundamental and far-reaching change in the organization of the naval department. He introduced a measure to establish a board of admiralty, to be composed of six men appointed by the president. This board was to advise the secretary, who must get its opinion before any vessels could be built or altered or any new type of guns constructed. All bids were to be opened in its presence. The Committee's investigation of the monitors made it clear, he declared, "that there should be somebody responsible for the manner in which your appropriations are expended." He demanded that the members of the proposed board be carefully selected. He wanted no armchair experts: "I want the board to be men who will have to navigate the vessels, high officers, who will have to stake their lives finally upon the success of the ships they order to be built; captains, commodores, admirals, practical men, who know all about that which they are doing, and who have really got to test the experiments they make, and test it, too, at the hazard of their lives."[59]

Wade's proposal did not have the ghost of a chance. Other senators asked sarcastically why the War Committee was sponsoring legislation dealing with the navy. Even Wade's radical associates thought the spectacle somewhat strange. Grimes, a staunch Jacobin and chairman of the Senate committee on naval affairs, tore Wade's evidence to shreds. He accused the Committee of conducting an unfair examination and advised it to stick to its trade. With crushing force the Senate voted down the measure. Welles rejoiced to his diary that this "deliberate and mendacious assault" upon his department had failed.[60]

No sooner had the Committee organized for action in December than it determined to try another lunge at its old enemy Meade. The weapon which Wade meant to use against

---

[59] *Congressional Globe*, 38 Congress, 2 Session, 823–825.
[60] *Ibid.*, 864–865; Salter, *Grimes*, 268–270; Welles, *Diary*, 2:240.

the general was the bloody tragedy of the Petersburg mine crater, which had shocked the nation in the previous summer. At Petersburg, the gateway to Richmond, the Army of the Potomac faced Lee's dwindling but still formidable army, waiting behind its earthworks and redans for Grant to attack. This the taciturn commander would not risk. The horrors of the Wilderness were still too fresh in his mind. He settled down to a siege, and his men began to dig their way toward Petersburg, burrowing slowly forward beneath a circling line of trenches. A Pennsylvania colonel in Burnside's corps worked out a project to run a mine under the Confederate position, and Burnside indorsed the scheme enthusiastically. Meade, however, was sceptical; but he gave Burnside permission to go ahead. For a month the colonel's regiment labored at their mine, and on July 30 they exploded it, blowing a huge crater in the Confederate lines. The Union troops charged forward and piled into the crater, only to find to their horror that, because of their own numbers and the steepness of the sides, they could not get out. The Confederates stood on the edge and shot down the helpless, milling men. The tremendous slaughter horrified the North, and rumor asserted that Meade would be removed. Burnside charged that Meade had wanted the plan to fail and had done everything he could to make it fail. Burnside claimed that he had intended to use a body of colored troops for the charge into the crater, men who had been drilled especially for the job, but that Meade had forbidden this because of a prejudice against Negro soldiers. Angrily Meade replied that the mine scheme was fantastic and that Burnside should have known better than to try it. A military court of inquiry investigated the controversy and cleared both officers of any blame. But the Jacobins sniffed another opportunity to attack Meade, and they did not let the matter drop. As soon as Congress met, they put through the Senate a resolution directing the Committee to probe the facts of the butchery at the crater.[61]

The Committee accepted the assignment with relish. Four

[61] C.C.W., 1865, vol. 1, "Battle of Petersburg."

of the members, headed by Chandler, went down to the camp of the army near Petersburg to interview the leading actors in the crater tragedy. Julian later said that they talked to Grant at dinner and that the commander disgusted them by getting drunk before the meal was over.[62] The inquisitors first examined their favorite, Burnside. He repeated his accusation that Meade had wanted the mine project to fail and had forbidden the employment of the colored soldiers because of prejudice. Then the apprehensive Meade appeared. He explained his objections to the mine, but asserted that he had thrown no obstacle in Burnside's way. His reason for not permitting the Negroes to head the charge, he said, was a desire to protect the army from the criticism that it was forcing the colored soldiers to take the post of greatest danger.[63] Meade came away bitterly convinced that the Committee was out to get evidence which would indict him and uphold Burnside. He asked the Committee to examine several of his staff officers, and Chandler consented. These witnesses, Meade reported indignantly, "came out laughing, and said as soon as they began to say anything unfavorable to Burnside, they stopped them and said that was enough, clearly showing they only wanted to hear evidence of one kind." When Grant testified, he angered the inquisitors by indorsing Meade's opposition to the mine scheme and censuring Burnside. He declared that Meade was right about the Negro troops, although he conceded that these men would have performed more efficiently than the white soldiers.[64]

Early in February the Committee presented a report on the affair of the crater. The document showered praise upon Burnside for devising and executing the project of the mine. The plan would have succeeded and Petersburg would have fallen, declared the Committee, had it not been for the stubborn, envious opposition of Meade. By omitting part of Grant's

[62] *Ibid.*, 1:xxviii; Julian, *Recollections*, 249.
[63] *C.C.W.*, 1865, 1:13–30, "Battle of Petersburg," Burnside's testimony; 30–41, Meade's.
[64] George G. Meade to Mrs. Meade, December 20, 1864, in Meade, *Meade*, 2:253–254; *C.C.W.*, 1865, 1:109–112.

testimony the report made it appear that the commander had condemned Meade for refusing to employ the colored soldiers.[65]

The Committee's blast frightened Meade. He feared that Grant's seeming censure would stir up public opinion against him and enable the Committee to force his removal. But Grant, indignant at the manner in which the Committee had distorted his testimony about the Negro troops, came generously to Meade's support. To the harassed and apprehensive Meade, Grant wrote consoling words, and in his quiet way castigated the inquisitors: "Their opinions are not sustained by knowledge of the facts nor by my evidence nor yours either do I suppose. General Burnside's evidence apparently has been their guide and to draw it mildly he has forgotten some of the facts."[66] Grant's prompt defense of Meade saved the latter from an attack by the Committee. But the commander's action and his earlier testimony in favor of Meade had aroused the fury of the committee radicals. Their rage leaped to a savage pitch when Grant at the same time boldly challenged them by removing their cherished favorite, Ben Butler, from command.

Grant swung the ax on Butler because the breezy political general had shouldered his way into the command of an expedition against Fort Fisher in North Carolina, then had so bungled matters that the project had resulted in a humiliating failure. This fort on the Cape Fear river guarded the only remaining important Southern port to which Confederate blockade runners could bring their precious cargoes. For a long time Welles and his advisers had been considering plans to stop up this leak in the tight Northern blockade. They believed the fort was so strong that nothing short of a combined land and sea assault could reduce it. Therefore they requested the help of the army. Grant, drawing his circle of death always closer around the Confederacy, saw the wisdom of destroying

[65] *Ibid.*, 1–12.
[66] Meade to Mrs. Meade, February 9, 1865, in Meade, *Meade*, 2:261–262; Grant to Meade, February 9, *ibid.*, 344.

the last point of entry through which supplies from Europe could reach the beleaguered South. He agreed to furnish Welles with 6,500 men from the army in front of Richmond, and sent General Godfrey Weitzel to lead them. At Hampton Roads the navy began to assemble a huge armada of warships and transports under the command of the salty old sea dog Admiral David D. Porter. Glowing enthusiasm marked the first preparations, but the work soon bogged down as official jealousy between the army and the navy sprang up to prevent any effective cooperation. Delay followed delay while generals and admirals bickered. To add to the general irritation, the irrepressible Northern press insisted upon advertising the expedition to the enemy, with detailed accounts of the number and equipment of the vessels in the Roads and with accurate speculations as to their destination. The sponsors of the expedition were on the point of abandoning it in disgust, when Butler obtruded himself onto the scene. His ingenious mind had devised a scheme to reduce the fort with little risk to the attacking forces. This was simply to drift a boat loaded with powder under the walls and have it exploded. The resulting concussion, claimed Butler, would knock down the walls and the soldiers could rush in and take possession. Butler's burbling optimism reinvigorated the flagging ardor of the naval officials, and they plunged anew into the work of preparation. Finally in December the fleet was ready to move. To Grant's resentful surprise Butler announced that he was going to accompany the expedition, the scene of operations being in his department and the powder boat his own conception. Grant, well aware of Butler's incompetence as an officer, was disturbed at the prospect, but mistakenly he made no opposition. He handed his written orders to Weitzel over to Butler for transmission to Weitzel. The orders were for the army to land after the naval bombardment and attack the fort. If they could not capture it, they were to entrench and await further orders. Butler never showed the instructions to Weitzel. With a marked atmosphere of strain prevailing among the commanding officers, the expedition got under way. There was bad blood between Porter and Butler, and Weitzel did not know what his status was.

The armada arrived before Fort Fisher. Blithely Butler directed the explosion of the powder boat, while the other ships hurriedly retreated seaward to escape the terrific concussion which was to demolish the ramparts. The powder boat burst with a roar, and when the smoke had cleared away the walls of the fort stood as strong as they had been before, utterly untouched by the explosion. The garrison thought a boiler had burst in one of the besieging ships. Porter, undoubtedly pleased that Butler's scheme had fizzled, then took his vessels in to bombard the fort. The fire from the defending guns gradually dwindled, and the navy started to land the soldiers, preparatory to an assault upon the works. When a third of the men had reached the shore, Butler suddenly announced that he would not permit any more to be landed and that those who were before the fort must be returned to the ships. Bad weather was in the offing, he declared, and a choppy sea would make it impossible to land the entire force; besides he believed the fort was too strong to be captured. Porter ranted in profane anger but he could not move Butler. Without the cooperation of the army, any attack was hopeless. Sullenly the admiral yielded, and the expedition steamed back to Fort Monroe.[67]

The failure of the attack aroused intense excitement in the North. The Jacobin press, fearful that Lincoln might exploit the situation to remove Butler, jumped eagerly to the general's defense, with angry accusations that Porter and the navy were to blame for the collapse of the expedition.[68] But editorials could not save Butler. On January 10 the blow fell. Grant ordered that the Massachusetts politician be relieved from

[67] Nicolay and Hay, *Lincoln*, 9:54–63; Admiral David D. Porter, *Incidents and Anecdotes of the Civil War* (New York, 1886), 262; James R. Soley, *Admiral Porter (Great Commander Series*, New York, 1903), 414–423; Butler, *Butler's Book*, 774–824.

[68] New York *Independent*, January 5, 12, 1865; *Wilkes' Spirit of the Times*, January 7; *New York Tribune*, January 2, Washington correspondence, January 9, Fort Monroe correspondence.

duty, and the Jacobins bellowed with anguished wrath. Greeley's Washington correspondent, always close to the radical
leaders, reported that Grant and the West Point gang had conspired to strike down Butler. Grant had engineered "a scheme
to get a troublesomely earnest Radical out of the way, and to
dispose of a dreaded politician. The Copperheads of Washington and Georgetown are jubilant tonight over his removal."[69]
In Congress the Jacobin bosses moved quickly and characteristically. Henry Wilson presented a resolution directing the
Committee to investigate the real facts behind the failure of
the attack on Fisher. The Committee, also moving quickly and
characteristically, invited Butler to appear for questioning.
There were confident assertions in radical circles that the inquisitors would speedily renovate his reputation and get him
restored to command.[70]

The ebullient general bustled into town on January 16. As
he entered Willard's Hotel an admiring throng in the lobby
gave him an ovation, and soon the Jacobin politicos were
crowding his rooms to tender their support. The conservatives watched the spectacle with apprehension. Meade gloomily predicted: "This is the beginning of a war on Grant."
Gideon Welles wrote in his diary that the Committee had
summoned Butler to Washington to "help the mischief-makers
make trouble and stimulate intrigue and faction. Allied with
Wade and Chandler and H. Winter Davis, he will not only aid
but breed mischief. This is intended."[71]

Butler met the Committee on the seventeenth. The inquisitors had already prejudged the case, and their only purpose
was to assemble evidence which would help the general.
Chandler told his wife that the West Pointers were out to
destroy Butler and that the Committee meant to save him.
The session lasted for four hours. The questions which Wade

[69] *Ibid.*, January 12, Washington correspondence; *Wilkes' Spirit of the
Times,* January 21; New York *Independent,* February 2.

[70] *C.C.W.,* 1865, 2:i; *New York Tribune,* January 14, Washington correspondence, January 17, editorial.

[71] *Ibid.*, January 17, Washington correspondence; George G. Meade to
Mrs. Meade, January 14, 1865, in Meade, *Meade,* 2:256; entry of January
14, 1865, in Welles, *Diary,* 1:224.

and other members asked and Butler's responses had clearly been prepared and discussed beforehand by all the principals. Butler was given the widest latitude in his answers, and his testimony consisted of a series of long prepared statements. There was no cross-examination. The general declared that Grant had asked him to assume command of the expedition because Weitzel and Porter were enemies and because Weitzel was a young, inexperienced officer. After the bombardment of the fort, Butler said, he had started to land the troops. Then the sea became so rough that he had had to stop and bring back the men already transported ashore. There had been no violation of Grant's orders to land and to entrench if the fort could not be taken, because in reality a landing had not been effected. Furthermore all the available information indicated that the fort was undamaged and too strong to be assaulted. Butler had talked to a captured Confederate officer, who "seemed to be a very communicative gentleman, willing to tell us all that he could," and this man had assured him that an attack was hopeless. Butler heaped the blame for the defeat of the expedition upon Porter. The admiral, he charged, had failed to do his part—to batter down the walls of the fort. Hence the army could never have carried the works. Asked to state the cause of his removal, Butler declared that the West Point caste wanted to hound him into disgrace because he was the last civilian general who had an important command. With a sneer at Grant's large losses in the Wilderness, Butler accused the commander of being "as unjust as he is reckless of other men's lives and reputations."[72]

At this point, the subject of Fort Fisher having been exhausted, it might have been expected that the Committee would excuse Butler. But Wade asked the general if he wished to comment upon any other of his acts that had been criticized. Butler did. To a chorus of approving expressions from the Committee, he described and defended his arbitrary arrests, his military record, his appointments, and his financial deals. His last statement, in response to a leading question by

[72] Zachariah Chandler to Mrs. Chandler, January 16, 1865, in the Chandler MSS.; C.C.W., 1865, 2:1–35.

Wade, was a volley at Grant for refusing to exchange prisoners with the Confederacy. Grant's policy was designed to prevent any augmentation of the waning rebel armies, but to the Northern public his position seemed inhuman and cold-blooded. The press was crying for exchange and the liberation of Union boys from the hellhole prisons of the South. Butler condemned Grant and advocated exchange. He also criticized the administration for not adopting a system of retaliation.[73]

Butler's defense delighted the Jacobins. Jubilantly Greeley's correspondent wrote that the general's testimony had been sensational. It had lifted the veil which "has so closely covered many of the disasters and blunders that have cost the country such treasures of blood and money in front of Petersburg."[74]

After his appearance before the Committee, Butler retired to his home at Lowell. From here he bombarded Wade with documents impeaching Porter and with names of suggested witnesses who would testify that he had acted wisely in not attacking at Fisher. He entered into a correspondence with Weitzel, in which he flattered the young officer's vanity and promised to bring influence to bear to get him an advanced commission. Then he coached Weitzel on the proper kind of evidence to give the Committee. In a snarling speech toward the end of January Butler flayed Grant for refusing to ex-change prisoners, and the Jacobin press applauded.[75]

Early in February Wade summoned Grant to appear in Washington for questioning. Reluctantly the commander left his duties in front of Richmond to face the inquisitors, whose implacable hostility he now realized. The Committee sub-jected Grant to a thorough grilling, but the stubborn general held his own. He asserted flatly that he had not wanted Butler to accompany the expedition, that the powder boat scheme

[73] *Ibid.*, 45–49.

[74] *New York Tribune*, January 18, 1865, Washington correspondence.

[75] Benjamin F. Butler to Benjamin F. Wade, February 1, 1865, enclos-ing a letter from W. H. Merriam, in *Butler Corerspondence*, 5:530–531; Butler to Wade, February 7, enclosing a letter from R. S. McHay, *ibid.*, 540–542; Butler to Weitzel, January 23, 1865, Weitzel to Butler, January 25, Butler to Weitzel, January 30, *ibid.*, 512–515; *New York Tribune*, Janu-ary 30, 1865; New York *Independent*, February 2.

was fantastic, and that Butler had violated orders in not landing and entrenching. The best efforts of the clever lawyers of the Committee could not shake his testimony. When Wade tried to make him admit that the coast was too dangerous to effect a landing, Grant drily pointed out that a second expedition had just accomplished the feat and occupied Fort Fisher. Nor did Wade get anywhere with an effort to trip Grant on his policy regarding the exchange of prisoners. The general walked out of the room with the dialectical honors. Wade secured more satisfactory results with Weitzel. That officer remembered his instructions from Butler and in the main presented testimony favorable to the Massachusetts politico. After the meeting Weitzel dispatched a note to Butler, calling attention to the fact that he had followed orders. Confidently he assured Butler that the inquisitors had a true picture of events at Fort Fisher: "I found the entire committee strongly in your favor. . . . That committee will bring you out all right."[76]

The controversy between Butler and his allies of the Committee and Grant raged on for months. Wade continued the investigation, haling Porter and other witnesses to Washington. The radical press cried for Butler's restoration to command. Finally late in March the Committee resolved to go to Fort Fisher to take evidence on the spot. Rumors of this decision inspired the Jacobins to gloating expressions of victory over Grant. Wendell Phillips exhorted Julian to dig up the truth and come back with evidence which would "protect Butler's fame."[77]

The inquisitors did not leave Washington until the tenth of April. The days before their departure had witnessed fast-moving and tremendous events. Lee's weary little army abandoned its lines before Richmond and crawled away to the

[76] *C.C.W.*, 1865, 2:51–56; *ibid.*, 3:76–77, Grant's testimony; *ibid.*, 2:73–81, Weitzel's; Godfrey Weitzel to Benjamin F. Butler, February 12, 1865, in *Butler Correspondence*, 5:548–549.

[77] Philadelphia *Press* and *Pittsburgh Commercial*, quoted in the New York *Independent*, March 23, 1865; Wendell Phillips to George W. Julian, March 27, 1865, in the Giddings-Julian MSS.; *C.C.W.*, 1865, 1:xxxiv; Zachariah Chandler to Mrs. Chandler, April 6, in the Chandler MSS.

South. Blue soldiers marched into the rebel capital as roaring exultation swept the North. Lee hoped to join his forces with the army of Joseph E. Johnston, facing Sherman in North Carolina, but Grant barred the way at every attempt. Lee realized the game was up. He resolved to ask for terms, and entered into a correspondence with Grant. On April 9 the great Confederate captain came into the Union headquarters at Appomattox and surrendered the Army of Northern Virginia. The drama of the Confederacy was approaching its end.

Lincoln journeyed to captured Richmond soon after Union forces occupied the city, and talked to a self-appointed spokesman of the Virginia state government about reconstruction. The president pledged that if the Virginia legislature would come together and vote to restore the state to the Union and to withdraw its troops from the war, he would extend executive recognition to the legislature as the *de facto* government of Virginia. He gave Weitzel, the commander in Richmond, an order to permit the legislature to assemble.[78] Reconstruction, immediate and magnanimous, was the dominating thought in Lincoln's mind as victory and peace dawned brighter and nearer. On his return to Washington he laid his policy before the people, in the last speech of his life. A rejoicing crowd gathered on the lawn of the White House on the evening of April 11 to serenade the president. He spoke to them of his hopes and plans for the years ahead. He pleaded for the acceptance of the seceded states back into the Union. He would have no hangings, no bloody revenge. He would make it easy for the South to return. He would not insist that the Southern states give the suffrage to the Negroes as a condition of readmission. He hoped that the South would grant the vote to the more intelligent Negroes and to those who had been soldiers, but there must be no compulsion from the national government. The speech was Lincoln's challenge to the Jacobins. If they wanted war on the issue of reconstruction, he would fight them.[79]

[78] *O. R.*, series 1, vol. 46, part 3, p. 612.
[79] Lincoln, *Works*, 11:84–91.

The Jacobins welcomed war. Even before Lincoln flung down the gauntlet, they had launched their preparations. The radical press dragged out the Committee's atrocity reports and reminded Northern readers of the horrors of the Confederate prison-pens and of the massacre at Pillow. The perpetrators of these outrages must be punished, shrilled the editors. Lee and Davis and other prominent Confederates, the real authors of Southern barbarities, should be hanged to the highest gallows. The seceded states, which had chosen these devils as rulers, must be denied readmission to the Union. Were bloody and unrepentant traitors to return to political power?[80] Grant's lenient terms to Lee enraged the Jacobins. The Union commander had placed the principal officers of the Army of Northern Virginia on military parole, thus protecting them temporarily from the vengeance which the radicals demanded. It was whispered that this was Lincoln's work. On the day before Lincoln spoke to the crowd at the White House, the Jacobins held their own meeting on the steps of Willard's Hotel to denounce the president's "bribe of unconditional forgiveness," as Greeley's correspondent labeled Grant's terms. Ben Butler headed the cast of speakers, and the theme was harsh and retributive justice for the South and execution for its high military and civil leaders.[81]

The savage hostility of the radicals did not dismay Lincoln, who had expected opposition, but it made him cautious. He knew that he was entering a struggle to the death with cunning and implacable foes, and that he could not afford to give them the slightest advantage. In this mood he decided that his order giving the Virginia legislature permission to assemble had been imprudent, because it presented the Jacobins with the opportunity to accuse him of extending recognition to a rebel organization. Acting upon the advice of the Cabinet, he revoked the order. But he was too late. The newspapers, unaware of his reversal, published on the twelfth Weitzel's call to the legislators.

[80] New York *Independent*, April 13, 1865; *Leslie's Newspaper*, April 15.
[81] *New York Tribune*, April 11, 1865.

The inquisitors left Washington before the storm of controversy broke. They proceeded on their way, with happy expectations of stopping off for a few gloating days in fallen Richmond and Charleston. On the twelfth they reached Richmond, and here to their enraged surprise they first heard of Lincoln's order for the meeting of the Virginia legislature. They were disgusted by the president's "display of misguided magnanimity." Julian wrote: "We were all thunderstruck, and fully sympathized with the hot indignation and wrathful words of the chairman of our committee."[82] Immediately the members changed their plans. They knew that they must return to Washington. Butler was forgotten. The last great battle with Lincoln had started, and they were miles away. Back they rushed to place themselves at the head of the Jacobin attack. They arrived on the fourteenth. They found the radicals buzzing with fury over Lincoln's speech of three days before and the call to the Virginia legislators. The Jacobin machine was marshalling its forces for open war upon the president.

That night Lincoln attended Ford's Theatre, and the crazed actor John Wilkes Booth performed the last tragedy of the Civil War with an assassin's bullet. In the grey hours of the dawn of the next day, Lincoln died, and Stanton took over the control of the government. Hysteria and rage engulfed the country. Men assumed that the Confederate government had plotted the murder, and Stanton, supplying the newspapers with reports, fanned this opinion into unreasoning belief. "The commencement, the progress, and the close of the rebellion—treason, wanton barbarity, assassination," screamed a Jacobin editor.[83] As the fury of the people blazed higher, the Jacobin leaders again raised their cry for vengeance upon the South. Now there were none to oppose them. Ironically Lincoln's death had killed also his policy of mercy. The vindictive spirit of the Jacobins became the faith of the nation.

[82] Julian, *Recollections*, 251–254; *C.C.W.*, 1865, 1:xxxvi.
[83] *Leslie's Newspaper*, April 29, May 6, 13, 20, 1865; New York *Independent*, April 27.

14

Epilogue

ON THE FIFTEENTH of April, while a drizzling rain fell upon the horrified capital, Andrew Johnson took the oath of office as president of the United States. The rugged, homespun Tennessean who now stepped forward from the obscurity of the vice-presidency to head the nation was a War Democrat. He had been placed on the ticket with Lincoln in 1864 to give color to the claims of the Republicans that they were a Union party. Johnson was from East Tennessee, that mountain region which possessed a social structure utterly unlike that of the rest of the state. It was a land of small farmers, intensely democratic, and Johnson was their spokesman. He hated the planter aristocrats. From the beginning he had opposed secession. In the tense days when the lower South was leaving the Union, he had stood in the Senate, a courageous figure from a slave state, to denounce the slavocracy as the manipulators of a great conspiracy to wreck the American democratic system. After the outbreak of war he supported every measure of the administration to crush the Confederacy. He announced that during the nation's crisis he would forget party ties. His speeches excited the admiration of the Republicans, and the radical bosses, looking for a safe Democratic senator to place upon the Committee when it was created, selected Johnson. Here he worked hand in glove with Wade and Chandler, following their lead in all the Committee's varied activities. His cooperation was so complete that he even indorsed Wade for re-election to the Senate in 1862. Ardently he joined the Jacobin members in their war against McClellan. Johnson believed the Young Napoleon was under the thumb of the Peace Democrats, the Copperheads, whom Johnson considered to be little better than traitors. He feared that these men would use McClellan's military prestige to seize control of the party and make the politically ambitious general president after the war was over. As one of the most prominent Democrats in the country and a possible candidate for the White House himself, Johnson did not intend that this should happen. Hence he aided the efforts of the inquisitors to pull McClellan down. He was not with them when they succeeded. In March of 1862 he resigned to become military governor of Tennessee, and he rejoiced from afar at the Committee's final victory over Mc-Clellan. Johnson always maintained a deep interest in the Committee's activities, especially when they were directed at McClellan. The Tennessean was in Washington on official business in 1863 at the time his former colleagues were preparing their report on McClellan's stewardship of the Army of the Potomac, designed to blast his presidential availability. Johnson came to the committee rooms and helped to write this Republican campaign document. Greater love than this no War Democrat could have.[1]

Brutally honest to the last, the Jacobins rejoiced at Lincoln's death. They knew Johnson favorably through his work on the Committee. They had applauded him when in April he went to Lincoln with demands that the Confederate leaders be executed. Johnson's vindictiveness was a reflection of his hatred for the slaveholding aristocracy, but the radicals thought it meant that he was one with them on their program of vengeance and Negro suffrage for the South. They viewed his accession to the presidency as "a godsend to the country." Zack Chandler intoned that God had kept Lincoln in office as long as he was useful and then had placed another and a better man in his place.[2]

On the day Johnson took office, the radicals caucused to discuss the rosy future suddenly opened before them by divine intervention. They decided to instruct Johnson to reform the Cabinet and to inaugurate the radical reconstruction program.

[1] Harry Williams, "Andrew Johnson as a Member of the Committee on the Conduct of the War," *The East Tennessee Historical Society's Publication* (1940), No. 12, pp. 70–80.

[2] Julian, *Recollections*, 255; Zachariah Chandler to Mrs. Chandler, April 22, 1865, in the Chandler MSS.

At the same time the inquisitors, delighted that their staunch comrade of former days was at the head of the government, were exploring ways and means of making themselves his unofficial advisers. They were certain that Johnson would follow their guidance upon the reconstruction issue, that "the presence and influence of the Committee, of which Johnson had been a member, would aid the administration in getting on the right track."[3] But they feared that the conservatives, especially the busy Blairs, might get to the president first. To prevent this, Wade addressed a letter to Johnson asking for an interview: "I have been instructed by the Committee on the Conduct of the War to inform you that your old associates upon that committee would be pleased to wait upon you at such time as may suit your convenience. They have just returned from the city of Richmond, where they saw and heard many things which they deem it would be well to make known to you at the present time."[4]

Intrigued by this tantalizing hint and eager for the counsel of men he knew well, Johnson readily agreed to meet the inquisitors the next day at his temporary headquarters in the Treasury Building. Wade, unable to contain his exultation, cried, "Johnson, we have faith in you. By the gods, there will be no trouble now in running the government." Johnson's reply was eminently satisfactory. He said that treason, like rape, must be punished, and that the leaders of treason must suffer. Wade approvingly advised him to hang a baker's dozen of the principal rebels. Rejoiced beyond measure, the members left to record in their journal that the conference had been "exceedingly satisfactory."[5]

They spread their jubilation around Washington. Wade continued to see the president, and a few days later he reported with elation that Johnson had condemned Lincoln's reconstructed government in Louisiana. "Bluff Ben" was fairly sure he had convinced Johnson that any reconstruction meas-

[3] Julian, *Recollections*, 255, 257.

[4] *C.C.W.*, 1865, 1:xxxvi.

[5] Julian, *Recollections*, 257; *Life of Chandler*, 280–282; Riddle, *Wade*, 268; *C.C.W.*, 1865, 1:xxxvi.

ures should be delayed until Congress met, but he was slightly disturbed because the president could not be persuaded to expel the conservatives in the Cabinet. The Committee stuck to Johnson like a plaster all during April, and Chandler optimistically predicted that its influence upon the administration would be permanent.[6] Capital rumor whispered that Johnson wanted to dismiss Stanton, but that the Committee had ordered him to retain the war secretary.[7] Johnson still talked the language of radicalism. Punishment for the leaders of the South dominated his thoughts, and in speeches to visiting state delegations he talked of nothing but hangings and revenge. The radical press chorused approval. All was serene in the Jacobin sky.[8]

Then like a bolt out of the blue came terrifying news from Sherman in North Carolina. The outspoken, spare, red-haired Sherman stood high on the Jacobins' list of generals who could not be trusted. He was opposed to the employment of Negro soldiers and he was a known supporter of Lincoln's reconstruction policy. The Jacobins had never dared to attack him openly, because he was too successful. But they watched him with hostile eyes as he swung across the lower South in his triumphal march to the sea. They circulated stories that he detested Negroes and that he refused to let fugitive slaves come into his lines. Halleck, alarmed by the threatening gestures of the radicals, warned Sherman to be on guard. "Whilst almost everyone is praising your great march through Georgia and the capture of Savannah," he wrote, "there is a certain class, having now great influence with the President and very probably anticipating still more on a change of Cabinet, who are decidedly disposed to make a point against you—I mean in regard to 'Inevitable Sambo.' They say that you have mani-

<hr>

[6] Charles Sumner to F. W. Bird, April 21, 1865, in Pierce, *Sumner*, 4:241; Benjamin F. Wade to Benjamin F. Butler, in *Butler Correspondence*, 5:617–618; Zachariah Chandler to Mrs. Chandler, April 23, 25, 1865, in the Chandler MSS.

[7] John H. Clifford to Edwin M. Stanton, April 25, 1865, in the Stanton MSS.

[8] New York *Independent*, April 27, 1865; *Leslie's Newspaper*, April 29, May 6.

fested an almost *criminal* dislike to the negro, and that you are not willing to carry out the wishes of the government in regard to him, but repulse him with contempt."[9]

After capturing Savannah, Sherman had slashed into the Carolinas, driving Joe Johnston's dwindling army before him. Johnston hoped to join his forces with Lee, and to make a last desperate stand before the gates of Richmond. His plan crashed sickeningly when he learned that Lee had surrendered on April 9. Johnston realized that this was the end of the Confederacy. He decided to treat with Sherman, despite the fretful opposition of Jefferson Davis, who fatuously wanted to continue the war. Johnston asked Sherman for a meeting, and the two generals discussed terms in a little farmhouse near Durham. Here on the eighteenth they concluded the remarkable agreement which the Jacobins were to label derisively the Sherman-Johnston Treaty. Johnston fired Sherman's vivid imagination by offering to surrender all the Confederate armies between the Potomac and the Rio Grande. Sherman saw himself in the great rôle of the victorious military chief who after crushing the enemy brought a just and lasting peace to the nation. In March he had talked to Lincoln at Grant's headquarters near Richmond, and the president had told him to conclude agreements with Southern civil authorities and to promise executive recognition to state governments, if by so doing he could hasten the coming of peace. Lincoln spoke at length about his hopes for an immediate restoration of the Union and his opposition to a program of revenge. His policy coincided with Sherman's own generous sentiments, and the general returned to the field determined to carry out Lincoln's wishes. The president's death intensified Sherman's purpose. He would make a peace which would honor Lincoln's memory. He saw his chance when Johnston promised to deliver up all the remaining Confederate armies. Sherman pledged that if this were done the executive would recognize the existing state governments, guarantee the political rights of the people, and

[9] *New York Tribune*, January 23, 1865, Washington correspondence; Henry W. Halleck to William T. Sherman, December 30, 1864, in *O. R.*, series 1, 44:836.

grant a general amnesty. He dispatched the agreement to Washington by courier for Johnson's signature, serenely confident that he had acted as Lincoln would have and that a grateful government would approve.[10]

Sherman was unaware of the rapid changes which had taken place on the political front after he talked to Lincoln in March. He had no knowledge of the savage struggle between Lincoln and the Jacobins which had blazed up when the president came back from captured Richmond and pleaded for mercy for the South. He could not know how the murder of Lincoln had aroused the North to angry hysteria and a roaring demand for revenge. He did not know of Johnson's alliance with the radicals. If he had known, he would have realized that Lincoln's policy was dead and that the agreement with Johnston would be killed as soon as it reached Washington.

Sherman's courier arrived at the capital on the twenty-first and delivered the treaty. That night the Cabinet met with Johnson and Grant to discuss its terms. Stanton dominated the proceedings. Wild with excitement, he denounced Sherman for negotiating with rebels. He pointed out that Lincoln had instructed Grant on March 3 not to discuss political questions in any conferences with Lee which might take place over the surrender of the latter's army; the president reserved the determination of such questions to himself and would not permit generals to handle them. Sherman had disobeyed Lincoln's order, cried Stanton. He did not say that the war office had never transmitted Lincoln's instructions to Sherman. Stanton's fierce denunciations swept Johnson and the Cabinet members off their feet. Quickly it was decided that the president could not approve the agreement. Grant was directed to inform Sherman to resume hostilities or to conclude a purely military arrangement for the submission of Johnston's army. Grant left for Raleigh that night to bear the disheartening news to Sherman in person.[11]

[10] *Memoirs of General William T. Sherman By Himself* (New York, 1875), 2:356–357.
[11] Welles, *Diary,* 2:294–295.

Stanton and the Jacobins thought they could now destroy Sherman, and the secretary started the campaign with a smear attack upon him in the press. On April 22 he handed out a public statement which was a tissue of falsehoods. He accused Sherman of maliciously disobeying Lincoln's order of March 3. He charged that the general had let Jefferson Davis escape with millions of dollars in gold, and hinted that Sherman was to get a share of the boodle. He declared that Sherman had recognized treason and rebellion by treating with Johnston.[12]

The Jacobin editors caught the cue. Forney telegraphed to Stanton that he was launching an immediate attack upon Sherman. From the whole radical press there arose a scream of condemnation. Sherman was a traitor. He wanted to be elected president with Southern votes. He was about to march his army on Washington and overthrow the government and re-establish slavery.[13] "Alas, Sherman," mourned one journalist who charged, "General Sherman would have ignored the whole scope, purport, object, and value of this war, by condoning treason."[14] In bitter words George Wilkes declared that the Sherman treaty was only another example of West Point treason, the sequel to Grant's permission for Lee's soldiers to retain their arms: "These West Point gentlemen seem to be outbidding each other for favor with their recreant southern schoolmates; and the late performances remind us of the remark we made in these columns as early as 1862, to the effect that the aspiring graduates of that academy seemed either to regard the war as a big joke, or simply a piece of business provided for their benefit, and by means of which they might ultimately divide the country among themselves."[15]

The storm of denunciation mounted higher with the passage of every hour. The public, moved to morbid expressions of grief by the passage of Lincoln's funeral cortège

[12] *New York Tribune,* April 24, 1865; *New York Times,* April 24; J. D. Cox, *Reminiscences,* 2:499-505.

[13] John B. Forney to Edwin M. Stanton, April 24, 1865, in *O. R.,* series 1, vol. 47, part 3, p. 292; New York *Independent,* May 4, 11, 1865; Boston *Transcript,* quoted in *Leslie's Newspaper,* May 13; *New York Tribune,* April 24; *Chicago Tribune,* April 24.

[14] *Leslie's Newspaper,* May 6.   [15] *Wilkes' Spirit of the Times,* April 29.

through the country and convinced beyond reason that the martyred president had been the victim of a rebel plot, was ready to swallow any fantastic tale. It was easy for the Jacobins to paint Sherman as a would-be dictator. Chase, now chief justice of the Supreme Court, and George Bancroft, the prolific historian of the American Revolution, delivered funeral eulogies of the dead Lincoln in which they exploited the solemn situation to attack Sherman for usurping power and consorting with traitors. Demands for the removal of the general thickened the air. Mingled with the shrilling chorus of condemnation was a note of fear—fear of what the impetuous Sherman might do. Observers warned Stanton that the Northern conservatives were flocking to the general's support and that the opposition to the radical reconstruction program would center around him. But outweighing these political considerations was the hair-raising possibility that Sherman would hurl his wild Westerners against Washington in open revolt. "Pay off Sherman's army as soon as possible, and let everybody know that Mr. Stanton is Secretary of War," Fessenden begged of Stanton.[16]

The Jacobin bosses decided to call in the Committee to finish off Sherman. His treaty had enraged the inquisitors. To them it seemed "a wanton betrayal of the country to its enemies," and they were convinced that Sherman had acted deliberately and with Lincoln's authority. Early in May they asked Stanton to order Sherman and Grant to appear in Washington for questioning. The generals attempted to dodge the interview with the excuse that their military duties would not permit them to leave the field. But the Committee was not to be denied. Wade told Stanton to issue "peremptory orders" for them to come.[17] They came reluctantly, as men who knew they must face an ordeal.

[16] Chase and Bancroft, quoted in *Leslie's Newspaper*, May 27; Senator William Sprague to Edwin M. Stanton, April 24, in *O. R.*, series 1, vol. 47, part 3, p. 272; *Wilkes' Spirit of the Times*, May 6, p. 20; Horatio Woodman to Stanton, April 27, Edwards Pierrespont to Stanton, May 14, William P. Fessenden to Stanton, May 23, in the Stanton MSS.

[17] Julian, *Recollections*, 258; Zachariah Chandler to Mrs. Chandler, April 25, 1865, in the Chandler MSS; *C.C.W.*, 1865, 1:xxxviii.

Sherman met the Committee on the twenty-second. Ben Wade conducted the inquiry. He wanted to know why Sherman had made a political agreement with Johnston and if Lincoln had been behind the negotiations. In a defiant mood, the general replied that his treaty followed Lincoln's often-expressed wishes for a quick and humane peace. Lincoln had authorized him in "general terms" to deal with "civil authorities, governors, and legislatures, even as far back as 1863," he revealed. Bitterly he exclaimed, "Had President Lincoln lived, I know he would have sustained me." The outspoken general boldly informed Stanton's secret allies that the secretary was a two-faced scoundrel.[18]

The Committee's handling of Sherman delighted the Jacobins. Senator Howard, after reading the printed account of the testimony, was certain that the Committee had killed Sherman with the people. "No person can now doubt that at least *one* leading motive for his 'treaty' with Johnston was the hope of reaching the presidency," Howard wrote to Stanton. "His whole treaty & report shows a foregone determination to recognize the rebel state governments & to make himself . . . the *'savior of the South'* & the restorer of *peace*. This would insure him their *votes*." Immediately the radical press seized upon the testimony to hurl more abuse at Sherman.[19]

The Jacobin bosses feared that Sherman's criticisms might have damaged Stanton with the public. Stanton was a valuable property: they expected to run him for the presidency in 1868, hence they could not afford to have any blots upon his record. They decided to have the Committee put Meade and Grant on the stand and ask them to state in what manner Stanton had conducted the affairs of his department. Stanton himself asked Wade to summon the two generals.[20]

Ready to play its part, the Committee called first Meade and then Grant. To both Wade addressed almost identical

[18] *Ibid.*, 3:4–14.
[19] Jacob M. Howard to Edwin M. Stanton, June 1, 1865, in the Stanton MSS.; *Wilkes' Spirit of the Times*, June 3, 10, 1865.
[20] Flower, *Stanton*, 387–388.

questions: in what manner had Mr. Stanton performed his duties in regard to the supply of the armies and the support of the military operations under your charge? Meade replied that he had no complaint. Not satisfied with this pale approval, Wade snapped, "What do you say of the talent and ability with which Mr. Stanton had conducted his department?" Meade said Stanton had shown "great ability." Grant was much more cooperative. He assured the inquisitors that Stanton's work had been admirable. Wade inquired if there had ever been "any misunderstanding with regard to the conduct of the war, in any particular, between you and the secretary of war since you have been in command?" Grant said there had been none.[21]

Stanton's friends hailed the testimony as establishing his political future. "Since Grant and Meade put their opinions upon record touching your administration you need have no solicitude about your fame," wrote an admirer to the secretary.[22]

From March to May the Committee held few formal meetings. The inquisitors were working feverishly preparing their final reports for publication. Zack Chandler proudly informed his wife that the reports would make history. He and Wade knew exactly the kind of history they wanted to give the voters—history that would persuade people of the rightness of the radical cause during the war and of the justice of the radical program for the South now that the war had ended.[23]

In May the reports appeared, three bulging volumes of documented radical propaganda. They were something to gladden the heart of the most exacting Jacobin. One section was devoted to a eulogy of Joe Hooker's command of the Army of the Potomac. Another consigned Meade to the limbo of incompetent generals for his actions at Gettysburg and

---

[21] C.C.W., 1865, 1:523-524.
[22] D. C. Chipman to Edwin M. Stanton, May 30, 1865, in the Stanton MSS.
[23] Zachariah Chandler to Mrs. Chandler, March 6, 11, and April 27, 1865, in the Chandler MSS.; New York Tribune, March 11, Washington correspondence.

Petersburg. The fame and future of Ben Butler were amply provided for with a glowing tribute to his bravery at Fort Fisher. A report on the Red River expedition disposed of "Nothing Positive" Banks and scathingly condemned the reconstruction policy of the dead Lincoln.[24]

The Committee appealed fervently to the people not to forget the atrocities of the Southern prison-pens at Andersonville and Libby, the carnage at Fort Pillow, and the countless other barbarities committed by a South which now sought restoration to the Union. Feelingly Wade described the return of the soldiers and sailors to "the ways of peace and the pursuits of civil life, from which they have been called for a time by the danger which threatened their country." Then he exhorted:

Yet while we welcome those brave veterans on their return from fields made historical by their gallant achievements, our joy is saddened as we view their thinned ranks and reflect that tens of thousands, as brave as they, have fallen victims to that savage and infernal spirit which actuated those who spared not the prisoners at their mercy, who sought by midnight arson to destroy hundreds of defenceless women and children, and who hesitated not to resort to means and to commit acts so horrible that the nations of the earth stand aghast as they are told what has been done.[25]

The Jacobins had need to wave "the bloody shirt," for they had lost Andrew Johnson. The president slipped away from them as suddenly as he had joined them. Early in May they began to suspect that he was backsliding to his former Democratic faith. Despite the urgings of Wade, Johnson would not come out for Negro suffrage forced upon the South by the national government.[26] There could be no real and lasting alliance between Johnson and the Jacobins. Although he might

[24] *C.C.W.*, 1865, vol. 1, "Army of the Potomac–Hooker," "Army of the Potomac–Meade," "Battle of Petersburg"; *ibid.*, vol. 2, "Ft. Fisher," "Red River Expedition."

[25] *Ibid.*, 1:iii–iv.

[26] Julian, *Recollections*, 263; J. W. Shaffer to Benjamin F. Butler, May 14, 1865, quoting Wade, in *Butler Correspondence*, 5:619.

talk vindictively of punishing the Bourbon aristocrats, he felt only an intense revulsion for the heart of the radical program—suffrage for the Southern Negro and special privileges for Northern industrialists. Fundamentally he was a representative of the white small-farmer class and an old-fashioned advocate of the Jeffersonian doctrine of states' rights. The break came on May 29. He issued a proclamation of general amnesty and a proclamation setting up a civil government in North Carolina.[27] He followed this with similar documents for the remaining unreconstructed states. His conditions for the readmission of a state differed from Lincoln's in that he required a loyal majority of voters instead of ten per cent. But in every other respect they were identical. He made no mention of the vote for the former slaves, and he assumed that reconstruction was the business of the president rather than of Congress.

Once again the Jacobins faced a hostile president. Once again they knew they must fight the battle of reconstruction. But they felt no misgivings, only a fierce joy. They had conquered Lincoln, they would conquer Johnson. With a grim confidence, they entered the savage years of the tragic era.

[27] Richardson, *Messages of the Presidents*, 6:310–314.

BIBLIOGRAPHY AND INDEX

BIBLIOGRAPHY

MANUSCRIPTS

LIBRARY OF CONGRESS

BUTLER, BENJAMIN F. Butler Papers.
CHANDLER, ZACHARIAH. Chandler Papers.
COLFAX, SCHUYLER. Colfax Papers.
DANA, CHARLES A. Dana Papers.
DOOLITTLE, JAMES R. Doolittle Papers.
FESSENDEN, WILLIAM PITT. Fessenden Correspondence.
GIDDINGS, JOSHUA, and JULIAN, GEORGE W. Giddings-Julian Correspondence.
GREELEY, HORACE. Greeley Papers.
HEINTZELMAN, SAMUEL P. Journal.
HOLT, JOSEPH. Holt Papers.
JOHNSON, ANDREW. Johnson Papers.
SHERMAN, JOHN. Sherman Papers.
STANTON, EDWIN M. Stanton Papers.
STEVENS, THADDEUS. Stevens Papers.
TRUMBULL, LYMAN. Trumbull Papers.

STATE HISTORICAL SOCIETY
OF WISCONSIN

DOOLITTLE, JAMES R. Doolittle Manuscripts.

GOVERNMENT DOCUMENTS

COMMITTEE ON THE CONDUCT OF THE WAR. *Reports.* 8 vols. Washington, 1863–1866.
HOUSE OF REPRESENTATIVES OF THE UNITED STATES. *Reports of Committees,* First Session, Thirty-Eighth Congress, vol. 1, no. 67, *Report on Returned Prisoners.*
SENATE OF THE UNITED STATES. *Reports of Committees,* First Session, Thirty-Eighth Congress, no. 63, *Ft. Pillow.*
War of the Rebellion: A Compilation of the Official Records of the Union and Confederate Armies. 128 vols. Washington, 1880–1901.

NEWSPAPERS

Albany Evening Journal, 1863.
Boston Courier, 1863.
Boston Daily Advertiser, 1863–1864.
Chicago Times, 1862–1863.
Chicago Tribune, 1861–1865.
Cincinnati Gazette, 1862–1865.
Columbus *Crisis,* 1864.
Detroit Advertiser and Tribune, 1861–1865.

Detroit Free Press, 1861–1865.
Frank Leslie's Illustrated Newspaper (New York), 1861–1865.
Harper's Weekly (New York), 1861–1865.
Harrisburg *Daily Telegraph,* 1864.
Milwaukee *Sentinel,* 1864.
Missouri Democrat (St. Louis), 1861–1863.

387

National Anti-Slavery Standard (New York), 1861–1865.

National Intelligencer (Washington), 1861–1863.

New York *Commercial Advertiser*, 1861–1862.

New York *Evening Post*, 1861–1865.

New York Express, 1862.

New York Herald, 1861–1865.

New York *Independent*, 1861–1865.

New York *Sun*, 1861.

New York Times, 1861–1865.

New York Tribune, 1861–1865.

New York *World*, 1861–1865.

Ohio Statesman (Columbus), 1864.

Philadelphia *Age*, 1864.

Philadelphia Inquirer, 1862.

Springfield Republican, 1864.

Wilkes' Spirit of the Times (New York), 1861–1865.

Wisconsin State Journal (Madison), 1864.

BOOKS, PAMPHLETS, AND ARTICLES

ADAMS, CHARLES FRANCIS. *Richard Henry Dana: A Biography*. 2 vols. Boston, 1890.

ADAMS FAMILY. *A Cycle of Adams Letters*, edited by Worthington C. Ford. 2 vols. Boston, 1920.

ADAMS, JOHN R. *Memorial and Letters of Reverend John R. Adams*. Cambridge, 1890.

AMBLER, CHARLES H. *Francis H. Pierpont*. Chapel Hill, 1937.

ARNOLD, ISAAC N. *History of Abraham Lincoln and the Overthrow of Slavery*. Chicago, 1866.

ASHLEY, JAMES. "Abraham Lincoln." *Magazine of Western History*, 14:23–35 (May, 1891).

BALTZ, JOHN D. *Honorable Edward D. Baker*. Lancaster, Pennsylvania, 1888.

BARNARD, JOHN G. *The Peninsular Campaign and Antecedents*. New York, 1864.

BARNES, THURLOW WEED. *Memoir of Thurlow Weed*. Boston, 1884.

BARTLETT, JOHN R. *The Barbarities of the Rebels*. Providence, 1863.

BARTLETT, RUHL J. *John C. Frémont and the Republican Party (Ohio State University Studies: Contributions in History and Political Science, no. 13)*. Columbus, 1930.

BATES, EDWARD. *Diary of Edward Bates, 1859–1866*, edited by Howard Beale (*Annual Report of the American Historical Association, 1930*, vol. 4). Washington, 1933.

BIGELOW, JOHN. *Retrospections of an Active Life*. 5 vols. New York, 1909.

BLAINE, JAMES G. *Twenty Years of Congress: From Lincoln to Garfield*. 2 vols. Norwich, 1884–1886.

BOUTWELL, GEORGE S. *Speeches and Papers Relating to the Rebellion and the Overthrow of Slavery*. Boston, 1867.

BROCKETT, LINUS P. *Men of Our Day*. Philadelphia, 1868.

BROOKS, NOAH. *Washington in Lincoln's Time*. New York, 1895.

BROTHERHEAD, WILLIAM. *General Fremont*. Philadelphia, 1862.

BROWNING, ORVILLE HICKMAN. *Diary of Orville Hickman Browning*, edited by Theodore C. Pease and James G. Randall (*Collections of the Illinois Historical Library*, vol. 20; *Lincoln Series*, vol. 2). Springfield, 1927.

BUEL, CLARENCE C., and JOHNSON, ROBERT U., eds. *Battles and Leaders of the Civil War.* 4 vols. New York, 1887.

BUTLER, BENJAMIN F. *Butler's Book.* Boston, 1892.

———— *Private and Official Correspondence of General Benjamin F. Butler during the Period of the Civil War,* edited by Jessie A. Marshall. 5 vols. Norwood, 1917.

CHANDLER, PELEG W. *Memoir of Governor Andrew.* Boston, 1880.

CHANDLER, ZACHARIAH. *Conduct of the War.* Washington, 1862.

CHASE, SALMON P. *Diary and Correspondence of Salmon P. Chase (Annual Report of the American Historical Association,* 1902, vol. 2). Washington, 1903.

CHITTENDEN, LUCIUS E. *Recollections of President Lincoln and His Administration.* New York, 1904.

CLARKE, GRACE JULIAN. *George W. Julian (Indiana Historical Collections,* vol. 11). Indianapolis, 1923.

COCHRANE, JOHN. *The American Civil War.* New York, 1861.

———— *The War for the Union.* New York, 1875.

COLE, ARTHUR C. "President Lincoln and the Illinois Radical Republicans." *Mississippi Valley Historical Review,* 4:417–436 (March, 1918).

COLFAX, SCHUYLER, and STEVENS, THADDEUS. *Speeches of Messrs. Colfax of Indiana and Thaddeus Stevens of Pennsylvania, in Reply to Messrs. Diven and Blair's Attacks on General Frémont.* Washington, 1862.

COMMITTEE ON THE CONDUCT OF THE WAR. *How Bull Run Battle Was Lost. The Ball's Bluff Massacre. Department of the West—Fremont (Tribune Association War Tracts,* no. 3). New York, 1863.

———— *Report of the Congressional Committee on the Operations of the Army of the Potomac (Tribune Association War Tracts,* no. 1). New York, 1863.

Congregational Churches of Michigan for the First Fifty Years. Printed by order of the Association of Congregational Churches of Michigan. n. p., 1892.

CONKLING, ALFRED R. *Life and Letters of Roscoe Conkling.* New York, 1889.

COX, JACOB D. *Military Reminiscences.* 2 vols. New York, 1900.

CUTLER, JULIA P. *Life and Times of Ephraim Cutler, with Biographical Sketches of Jervis Cutler and William Parker Cutler.* Cincinnati, 1890.

DANA, CHARLES A. *Recollections of the Civil War.* New York, 1898.

DOSTER, WILLIAM E. *Lincoln and Episodes of the Civil War.* New York, 1915.

EDMUNDS, JAMES M. "Zachariah Chandler." *Republic,* 4:193–208 (April, 1875).

ELLET, CHARLES. *Army of the Potomac.* New York, 1862.

FAHRNEY, RALPH R. *Horace Greeley and the Tribune in the Civil War.* Cedar Rapids, Iowa, 1936.

"Federal Generals and a Good Press," selections from the James Gordon Bennett Papers. *American Historical Review,* 39:284–297 (January, 1934).

FESSENDEN, FRANCIS. *Life and Public Services of William Pitt Fessenden.* 2 vols. Boston, 1907.

FIELD, HENRY M. *Life of David Dudley Field.* New York, 1898.

FLOWER, FRANK A. *Edwin McMasters Stanton.* Akron, 1905.

FORBES, JOHN MURRAY. *Letters and Recollections of John Murray Forbes,* edited by Sarah F. Hughes. 2 vols. Boston, 1899.

FRANKLIN, WILLIAM B. *A Reply of Major-General William B. Franklin to the Report of the Joint Committee of Congress on the Conduct of the War.* New York, 1863.

FREIDEL, FRANK. "The Loyal Publication Society, a Pro-Union Propaganda Agency." *Mississippi Valley Historical Review,* 26:359–376 (December, 1939).

FRY, JAMES B. *Operations of the Army under Buell.* New York, 1884.

FURNESS, WILLIAM H. *A Discourse Delivered on the Occasion of the National Fast.* Philadelphia, 1861.

GILMORE, JAMES R. *Personal Recollections of Abraham Lincoln and the Civil War.* Boston, 1899.

GODWIN, PARKE. *A Biography of William Cullen Bryant.* 2 vols. New York, 1883.

GOOCH, DANIEL W. *Any Compromise a Surrender.* Washington, 1861.

———— *Secession and Reconstruction.* Washington, 1864.

GORHAM, GEORGE C. *Life and Public Services of Edwin M. Stanton.* 2 vols. Boston, 1899.

GRANT, ULYSSES S. *Personal Memoirs of Ulysses S. Grant.* 2 vols. New York, 1885–1886.

GREELEY, HORACE. *The American Conflict.* 2 vols. Chicago, 1864–1866.

———— *Proceedings of the First Three Republican National Conventions of 1856, 1860, and 1864.* Minneapolis, 1893.

GUROWSKI, ADAM. *Diary, March 4, 1861–November 2, 1862.* Boston, 1862.

———— *Diary, November, 1862–October, 1863.* New York, 1864.

———— *Diary, 1863–1864–1865.* Washington, 1866.

HALLOCK, WILLIAM H. *Life of Gerard Hallock.* New York, 1869.

HARBISON, WINFRED A. "Zachariah Chandler's Part in the Re-election of Abraham Lincoln." *Mississippi Valley Historical Review,* 22:267–276 (September, 1935).

HARRIS, WILMER C. *Public Life of Zachariah Chandler.* Lansing, 1917.

HART, ALBERT B. *Salmon P. Chase (American Statesmen Series).* Boston, 1899.

HAY, JOHN. *Letters of John Hay and Extracts from his Diary.* 3 vols. Washington, 1908.

HEG, HANS CHRISTIAN. *The Civil War Letters of Colonel Hans Christian Heg,* edited by Theodore C. Blegen. Northfield, Minnesota, 1936.

HESSELTINE, WILLIAM B. "The Propaganda Literature of Confederate Prisons." *Journal of Southern History,* 1:56–66 (February, 1935).

HILLIARD, GEORGE S. *Life and Campaigns of George B. McClellan.* Philadelphia, 1865.

HITCHCOCK, ETHAN ALLEN. *Fifty Years in Camp and Field: the Diary of Major-General Ethan Allen Hitchcock, U.S.A.,* edited by W. A. Croffut. New York, 1909.

HOLLISTER, OVANDO J. *Life of Schuyler Colfax.* New York, 1886.

HOWARD, JOHN R. *Remembrance of Things Past.* New York, 1925.

HURLBERT, WILLIAM H. *General McClellan and the Conduct of the War.* New York, 1864.

JOY, JAMES F. "The Committee on the Conduct of the War." *Detroit Free Press,* January 10, 1863.

JULIAN, GEORGE W. *Political Recollections, 1840–1872.* Chicago, 1884.

——— *Select Speeches of George W. Julian.* Cincinnati, 1867.

——— *Speeches on Political Questions, 1850–1868.* New York, 1872.

KELLEY, WILLIAM D. *Lincoln and Stanton.* New York, 1885.

KENDALL, AMOS. *Letters Exposing the Mismanagement of Public Affairs by Abraham Lincoln.* Washington, 1864.

KETCHUM, HIRAM. *General McClellan's Peninsula Campaign.* New York, 1864.

KIRKLAND, EDWARD C. *The Peacemakers of 1864.* New York, 1927.

KOERNER, GUSTAVE. *Memoirs of Gustave Koerner,* edited by Thomas J. McCormack. 2 vols. Cedar Rapids, Iowa, 1909.

LAMON, WARD. *Recollections of Abraham Lincoln, 1847–1865.* Washington, 1911.

LAUGHLIN, SCEVA B. *Missouri Politics during the Civil War.* Iowa City, 1921.

Life of Zachariah Chandler, by the Detroit Post and Tribune. Detroit, 1880.

LINCOLN, ABRAHAM. *An Autobiography of Abraham Lincoln,* edited by Nathaniel W. Stephenson. New York, 1926.

——— *Complete Works of Abraham Lincoln,* edited by John G. Nicolay and John Hay. Colter edition. 2 vols. New York, 1905.

LUSK, WILLIAM T. *War Letters of William Thompson Lusk.* New York, 1911.

LYMAN, THEODORE. *Meade's Headquarters, 1863–65: The Letters of Theodore Lyman,* edited by George R. Agassiz. Boston, 1932.

MACARTNEY, CHARLES E. *Lincoln and His Cabinet.* New York, 1931.

McCLELLAN, GEORGE B. *McClellan's Own Story.* New York, 1887.

MAURICE, SIR FREDERICK. *Statesmen and Soldiers of the Civil War.* Boston, 1926.

MEADE, GEORGE. *Life and Letters of George Gordon Meade.* 2 vols. New York, 1913.

MEIGS, MONTGOMERY C. "General M. C. Meigs on the Conduct of the Civil War." *American Historical Review,* 26:285–303 (January, 1921).

MENEELY, ALEXANDER HOWARD. *The War Department, 1861 (Columbia University Studies in History, Economics, and Public Law,* no. 300). New York, 1928.

MERRIAM, GEORGE S. *Life and Times of Samuel Bowles.* New York, 1885.

MICHIE, PETER S. *General McClellan (Great Commander Series).* New York, 1901.

MOORE, CHARLES. "Sullivan M. Cutcheon." *Michigan Pioneer and Historical Collections,* 30:96–109. Lansing, 1905.

MOTLEY, JOHN LOTHROP. *Correspondence of John Lothrop Motley,* edited by George W. Curtis. 2 vols. New York, 1889.

MYERS, WILLIAM S. *A Study in Personality: General George Brinton McClellan.* New York, 1934.

NEVINS, ALLAN. *Frémont, the West's Greatest Adventurer.* 2 vols. New York, 1928.

NICOLAY, JOHN G., and HAY, JOHN. *Abraham Lincoln: A History.* 10 vols. New York, 1890.

OBERHOLTZER, ELLIS P. *Jay Cooke.* 2 vols. Philadelphia, 1907.

PEARSON, HENRY G. *James S. Wadsworth of Geneseo.* New York, 1913

———— *Life of John A. Andrew.* 2 vols. Boston, 1904.

PERRY, THOMAS S. *Life and Letters of Francis Lieber.* Boston, 1882.

PHILLIPS, WENDELL. *Speeches, Lectures, and Letters.* Boston, 1881.

PIERCE, EDWARD L. *Memoir and Letters of Charles Sumner.* 4 vols. Boston, 1887–1893.

PIERSON, WILLIAM W. "The Committee on the Conduct of the War." *American Historical Review,* 23:550–576 (April, 1918).

PORTER, DAVID D. *Incidents and Anecdotes of the Civil War.* New York, 1886.

RANDALL, JAMES G. *The Civil War and Reconstruction.* Boston, 1937.

RAYMOND, HENRY J. "Excerpts from the Journal of Henry J. Raymond," edited by Henry W. Raymond. *Scribner's Monthly,* 19:57–61, 419–424, 703–710 (November, 1879; January, 1880; March, 1880).

———— *Life and Public Services of Abraham Lincoln.* New York, 1865.

Rebel Barbarities: Ft. Pillow, Libby Prison. New York, 1864.

Rebel Pirate's Fatal Prize. Philadelphia, 1862.

RICHARDSON, JAMES D., ed. *A Compilation of the Messages and Papers of the Presidents, 1789–1897.* 10 vols. Washington, 1896–1899.

RIDDLE, ALBERT G. *Life of Benjamin F. Wade.* Cleveland, 1886.

———— *Life, Character, and Public Services of James A. Garfield.* Cleveland, 1880.

———— *Recollections of War Times.* New York, 1895.

RUSSELL, WILLIAM H. *My Diary, North and South.* Boston, 1863.

SALTER, WILLIAM. *Life of James W. Grimes.* New York, 1876.

SCHOFIELD, JOHN M. *Forty-Six Years in the Army.* New York, 1897.

SCHOULER, WILLIAM. *History of Massachusetts in the Civil War.* 2 vols. Boston, 1868–1871.

SCHUCKERS, JACOB W. *Life and Public Services of Salmon Portland Chase.* New York, 1874.

SCHURZ, CARL. *Speeches, Correspondence, and Political Papers of Carl Schurz,* edited by Frederic Bancroft. 3 vols. New York, 1907–1908.

SCOTT, EBEN G. *Reconstruction during the Civil War.* Boston, 1895.

SHANKS, JOHN P. C. *Vindication of Major-General J. C. Fremont.* Washington, 1862.

SHEPPARD, ERIC W. *Bedford Forrest, the Confederacy's Greatest Cavalryman.* London, 1930.

SHERMAN, WILLIAM T. *Home Letters of General Sherman,* edited by M. A. De Wolfe Howe. New York, 1909.

SHERMAN, WILLIAM T., and SHERMAN, JOHN. *The Sherman Letters,* edited by Rachel S. Thorndike. New York, 1894.

SMITH, DONNAL V. *Chase and Civil War Politics (Ohio Historical Collections,* vol. 2). Columbus, 1931.

SMITH, THEODORE C. *Life and Letters of James A. Garfield.* 2 vols. New Haven, 1925.

SMITH, WILLIAM E. *The Francis Preston Blair Family in Politics.* 2 vols. New York, 1933.

SMITH, W. G. *Life and Letters of Thomas Kilby Smith.* New York, 1898.

SOLEY, JAMES R. *Admiral Porter (Great Commander Series).* New York, 1903.

STANTON, HENRY B. *Random Recollections.* Johnstown, New York, 1885.

STEPHENSON, NATHANIEL W. *Lincoln: An Account of His Personal Life.* Indianapolis, 1924.

STEVENS, HAZARD. *Life of General Isaac Ingalls Stevens.* 2 vols. Boston, 1900.

STEVENS, THADDEUS. *Speech on Bill to Raise Additional Soldiers, February 2, 1863.* Washington, 1863.

SUMNER, CHARLES. *The Works of Charles Sumner.* 15 vols. Boston, 1874–1883.

SWINTON, WILLIAM. *Campaigns of the Army of the Potomac.* New York, 1882.

TARBELL, IDA. *Life of Abraham Lincoln.* 2 vols. New York, 1907.

TAYLOR, EMERSON G. *Gouverneur Kemble Warren.* Boston, 1932.

THAYER, WILLIAM R. *Life and Letters of John Hay.* 2 vols. Boston, 1915.

TRUMBULL, LYMAN. "Trumbull Correspondence." *Mississippi Valley Historical Review,* 1:101–108 (June, 1914).

VILLARD, HENRY. *Memoirs of Henry Villard.* 2 vols. Boston, 1904.

WADE, BENJAMIN F. *Facts for the People.* Cincinnati, 1864.

———— *Traitors and Their Sympathizers.* Washington, 1862.

WALKER, FRANCIS. *History of the Second Army Corps.* New York, 1886.

WARDEN, ROBERT B. *Account of the Private Life and Public Services of Salmon Portland Chase.* Cincinnati, 1874.

WELLES, GIDEON. *Diary of Gideon Welles,* edited by John T. Morse. 3 vols. Boston, 1911.

———— *Lincoln and Seward.* New York, 1874.

———— "Three Manuscripts of Gideon Welles," edited by Alexander Howard Meneely. *American Historical Review,* 31:484–494 (April, 1926).

WHITE, HORACE. *Life of Lyman Trumbull.* Boston, 1913.

WILLIAMS, GENERAL THOMAS. "Letters of General Thomas Williams, 1862," edited by G. Mott Williams. *American Historical Review,* 14:304–328 (January, 1909).

WILSON, CHARLES R. "The Original Chase Organization Meeting and *The Next Presidential Election.*" *Mississippi Valley Historical Review,* 23:61–79 (June, 1936).

WILSON, HENRY. *History of the Rise and Fall of the Slave Power in America.* 3 vols. Boston, 1872–1877.

———— "Jeremiah S. Black and Edwin M. Stanton." *Atlantic Monthly,* 26:463–475 (October, 1870).

WILSON, JAMES H. *Life of Charles A. Dana.* New York, 1907.

WINSTON, ROBERT W. *Andrew Johnson, Plebeian and Patriot.* New York, 1928.

WOODBURN, JAMES A. "Attitude of Thaddeus Stevens toward the Conduct of the Civil War." *American Historical Review,* 12:567–583 (April, 1907).

———— *Life of Thaddeus Stevens.* Indianapolis, 1913.

WYETH, JOHN A. *General Nathan Bedford Forrest.* New York, 1899.

INDEX

Abolitionists, connection with radicals, 6; and atrocity propaganda, 255; back Frémont for president, 308, 314, 315; attack Lincoln, 310; condemn Wade-Davis manifesto, 327; on Grant, 335

Adams, Charles Francis, Sr., on emancipation, 10

Adams, Charles Francis, Jr., on effect of Manassas, 33

Allen, G. T., on Democratic generals, 195

Altoona conference, 185–186

Andrew, John A., protests return of runaway slaves, 95; supports Hunter's emancipation proclamation, 137; and Altoona conference, 185; backs Frémont candidacy, 314; and election of *1864*, 316, 329

Anti-Slavery Standard, on Wade-Davis manifesto, 327

Arkansas, reconstruction in, 318, 321, 324

Army, politics in, 118–119, 120–122, 135–136, 193–194, 204–205, 214, 223–224, 237–241, 242, 248, 256, 263, 264, 285–287, 293, 304–305, 308, 335–336, 338, 368, 376–379

Army Board, 125, 128. *See also* Ethan Allen Hitchcock

Associated Press, 232–233

Atrocity stories, 254–262, 342–348, 371, 383

Baker, Edward, demands war of conquest, 11; death, 46–47, 94

Baldwin, W. A., on Democratic strength, 313–314

Ball's Bluff, battle of, 46, 94

Bancroft, George, condemns Sherman, 380

Banks, Nathaniel P., Republican general, 121, 274; in command of Gulf Department, 222, 274–276; attacked by radicals, 274, 341–342; orders on Negroes, 275–276; plan for reconstruction, 295, 318; and Red River campaign, 341; testifies before Committee on the Conduct of the War, 358; Committee's report on, 383

Barlow, Samuel, 78

Barnard, John G., Republican general, 118; writes propaganda pamphlets, 235; testifies against McClellan, 245

Bates, Edward, advises Lincoln to command army, 84; on Stone case and McClellan, 101–102; fears effect of radical attacks, 113; quoted on radicals and McClellan, 134–135; and Cabinet intrigue against McClellan, 178; Medill's opinion of, 205; on election of *1864*, 310, 312, 313, 316, 327; on Blair's resignation, 331

Beecher, Henry Ward, *see* New York *Independent*

Bennett, James Gordon, indorses Stanton, 91; on Committee on the Conduct of the War's report on McClellan, 250, 252; on radical attempt to bolt the party, 327–328. See also *New York Herald*

Blaine, James G., on Wade-Davis bill, 319

Blair, Frank, Sr., pleads McClellan's cause, 190; attacks Chase, 312. *See also* Blair family

Blair, Frank, Jr., and Missouri, 39; attacks Frémont, 48–49, 109; defends Halleck, 60; in Frémont investigation, 108; attacks Chase, 297–298. *See also* Blair family

Blair, Montgomery, Cabinet mem-

Harris, Ira, demands Cabinet changes, 209

Haupt, Herman, on McDowell's attack on Richmond, 132–133; proposes military council, 212

Hay, John, characterizes radicals, 5; on attempt of radicals to force army advance, 45; quoted on Lincoln and McClellan, 111–112; on McClellan's occupation of Manassas, 123; on radical intrigues against McClellan, 126; on Halleck, 150; and Greeley's peace mission, 323

Heintzelman, Samuel P., and Committee on the Conduct of the War, 80; and organization of army into corps, 121; on McClellan and army politics, 131, 135, 155–156; testifies against McClellan, 245

Hickman, John, threatens destruction of South, 11; denounces Lincoln's plan for compensated emancipation, 158

Hill, Adams S., on Lincoln's conservatism, 163

Hitchcock, Ethan Allen, summoned to Washington, 125; approves McClellan's plans for defense of Washington, 127; serves on Porter's court-martial, 225; testifies against McClellan, 245

Holt, Joseph, prosecutor in Porter court-martial, 225; and Mrs. Surrat, 225; and report on Democratic peace societies, 234

Hooker, Joseph, backed by radicals for command, 203, 271, 304, 337, 338; denounces Franklin, 203, 271; on army after Fredericksburg, 240–241; testifies against McClellan, 246; intrigues against Burnside, 263–264, 265, 271–272; Burnside orders dismissal of, 265–266; Lincoln on, 266; commander of Army of the Potomac, 266, 270–273, 282–284, 285–287; characterized, 270; intrigues against Mc-

Clellan, 270; adopts radical views, 270, 272; chided by Lincoln, 272; and battle of Chancellorsville, 283–284; officers intrigue against, 285–287; resigns command, 287; accuses Grant of enmity, 338; leaves army, 350; Committee on the Conduct of the War's report on, 382

Howard, Jacob, on second confiscation bill, 164; denounces Seward, 210; condemns Sherman, 381

Howe, A. P., condemns Meade, 339

Hunter, David, suceeds Frémont in Western Department, 49; indorses emancipation, 55; in Frémont investigation, 108; issues emancipation proclamation, 136–138; at Porter's court-martial, 225; sent to investigate Grant, 336

Illinois State Register, on emancipation proclamation, 216

Indians, rumored serving in Southern armies, 257–258, 261

Ives, Malcolm, correspondent of *New York Herald*, 87

Jackson, T. J. ("Stonewall"), in second battle of Manassas, 174; in battle of Chancellorsville, 283

Jacobins, *see* Radical Republicans

Jaquess, Colonel, and peace mission, 323, 329

Jay, John, favors party bolt, 328

Johnson, Andrew, member of Committee on the Conduct of the War, 65, 373; characterized, 68–69, 373; opposes McClellan, 69, 373–374; on McClellan and Potomac blockade, 116–117; asks removal of Buell, 193; aids investigation of McClellan, 247, 374; becomes president, 373; military governor of Tennessee, 374; interview with Committee on the Conduct of the War, 375; and reconstruction, 374, 375, 376; and

DATE DUE

626. POLITICAL PARTIES IN REVOLUTIONARY MASSACHU-SETTS. By Stephen E. Patterson. This is the first book of recent times that develops the history of the American Revolution in Massachusetts during the 1770s. In it, Patterson explodes the myth that Massachusetts revolutionaries approached the American Revolution in a united and cohesive way. They were, the author finds, partisan in their behavior both before and during the revolution, often with an intensity that eclipsed the war itself.

320 pages   1973   cloth $12.50

637. A HISTORY OF WISCONSIN. By Robert C. Nesbit. This, the first full-length scholarly history of Wisconsin published in thirty-three years, will be of considerable value to scholars, students, and all who express a serious interest in the state's past and present. The author has utilized the resources of one of the nation's richest centers of American historical scholarship—the University of Wisconsin, Madison, and the Wisconsin State Historical Society—in bringing together this original work.

512 pages, 32 illus.   1973   cloth $12.50

607. LETTERS OF HORATIO GREENOUGH, AMERICAN SCULP-TOR. Edited by Nathalia Wright. Greenough, a sculptor, architectural theorist, and author, corresponded with some of the most prominent writers, artists, and politicians of the first half of the nineteenth century. Collected here are 241 of his letters, of which 198 are printed in their entirety for the first time. These letters, with Professor Wright's informative notes, give the student of American culture a fuller understanding of Greenough and his age.

486 pages, 10 illus.   1972   cloth $22.50

600. MERCHANT CONGRESSMAN IN THE YOUNG REPUBLIC: Samuel Smith of Maryland, 1752-1839. By Frank A. Cassell. Highly complex and stirring events marked much of the early national period in American history. Cassell goes far in illuminating the temper of those difficult times in this vivid biography of Samuel Smith, soldier, statesman, shipping magnate, Maryland congressman, and Mayor of Baltimore. Smith's views on the federal bank and the War of 1812 are revealing.

298 pages, 7 illus.   1971   cloth $15.00

587. RAILROADS AND THE GRANGER LAWS. By George H. Miller. ". . . a finely-honed account of the issues leading to the demand for government regulation of railroads . . ."—Paul W. Gates, in *Minnesota History*. ". . . [an] excellent book . . . for one there is no need to quibble with the publisher's blurb which states that this 'balanced account will be of considerable value to a broad spectrum of social scientists—historians, lawyers, economists, and political scientists.' "—*Journal of American History*

308 pages   1971   cloth $12.50

613. THE CANADIAN IDENTITY. By W. L. Morton. This new edition of Morton's classic work contains extensive revisions and a new chapter, taking into account events of the last decade. ". . . fresh and vigorous . . . it constitutes an able challenge to fresh thinking about Canadian experience which is bound to have a formative influence during the next twenty years."—*International Affairs*. ". . . valuable and exciting."—*English Historical Review*. ". . . brilliant analysis . . ."—*American Historical Review*

174 pages   2d ed. 1972   cloth $7.50; paper $2.95

20. THE ARTICLES OF CONFEDERATION: An Interpretation of the Social-Constitutional History of the American Revolution, 1774-1781. By Merrill Jensen. ". . . an excellent exposition of the complex of internal tensions within the colonies out of which the first Constitution of the United States emerged."—*Pacific Historical Review.* ". . . an admirable analysis . . . the results of a generation of study of this chapter of our history."—*The New York Times Book Review*
310 pages   1940   paper $2.50

79. REGIONALISM IN AMERICA. Edited by Merrill Jensen. Foreword by Felix Frankfurter. ". . . a useful and valuable group of fifteen essays . . . Professor Jensen is to be congratulated for making such a rich and fruitful discussion of regionalism available to the public for the first time."—*Pacific Northwest Quarterly.* "The volume offers a valuable historical insight into the development and application of regional concepts of value."—*The Professional Geographer*
442 pages   1951   paper $3.25

407. INDIAN CULTURE AND EUROPEAN TRADE GOODS: The Archaeology of the Historic Period in the Western Great Lakes Region. By George Irving Quimby. ". . . a most welcome addition to our knowledge in these areas. Armed with a broad background in North American archaeology . . . Quimby brings this knowledge to bear on the western Great Lakes region."—*American Journal of Archaeology.* ". . . a landmark in North American historical archaeology."—*American Antiquity*
232 pages, 33 figs.   1966   paper $2.95

16. THE WARS OF THE IROQUOIS: A Study in Intertribal Trade Relations. By George T. Hunt. ". . . a sober judgment on the failure of the League to function, a sane delimitation of Iroquois fictitious empire to coincide with a restricted dominion, and an able demonstration that the European trade was the major circumstance of northeastern intertribal relations, and that Iroquois history was a phenomenon of that contact."—*American Anthropologist.* ". . . classic study."—*Pennsylvania History*
218 pages, map   1940   paper $2.95

277. THE MIDDLE FIVE: Indian Schoolboys of the Omaha Tribe. By Francis La Flesche. Foreword by David A. Baerreis. "La Flesche, an Omaha and a distinguished scholar, recounted his experiences as a child in a mission school maintained by the Presbyterians in the mid-1860s . . . he presents an appealing picture of Indian youths in transit from one culture to another. It is also one of the rare descriptions from the Indian viewpoint of a mission school of this period."—*Ethnohistory*
176 pages, 4 illus., map   1963   paper $2.50

352. THE ENGLISHWOMAN IN AMERICA. By Isabella Lucy Bird. Foreword and notes by Andrew Hill Clark. ". . . originally published in 1856 and long out of print, has considerable value as a fresh, forthright account of the reactions of an intelligent young tourist to America one hundred years ago."—*The Historian.* ". . . it is a fascinating book and is here attractively reproduced."—*Journal of American History.* ". . . useful for the social history of Canada and the U.S."—*Choice*
526 pages, 2 illus., map   reprint 1966   paper $3.25